This item may be recalled before the date stamped below.
You must return it when it is recalled or you will be fined.

NORMAL LOAN

KUKAI
THE UNIVERSAL
Scenes from His Life

KUKAI
THE UNIVERSAL
Scenes from His Life

RYOTARO SHIBA

ICG Muse, Inc.
New York, Tokyo, Osaka & London

Published by ICG Muse, Inc.
420 West 42nd Street, #35B New York, N.Y. 10036

Distributed by Tuttle Shokai, Inc.
Striped House Building 2F, Roppongi 5-10-33 Minato-ku,
Tokyo 106-0032

KUKAI NO FUKEI by Ryotaro Shiba. Copyright © 1978 by Midori Fukuda.
Original Japanese edition published by Chuokoron-Shinsha. English translation
rights arranged with Midori Fukuda. through Japan Foreign-Rights Centre.

Printed in Japan.
ISBN 4-925080-47-4
First Print 2003

Cover design by Rie Ito

Jacket cover photographs:
A Pair of mandalas: one on the front is Taizō mandala, the other Kongō-Kai mandala.
(see P.306) (Credited to Tō-ji, Kyōto)

Maha-Mayuri (Kujaku-myōō or Peacock
King as Devil Destroyer) (see P.56-58)
Kamakura Period, 13th century
(Credited to Chishaku-in temple, Kyōto)

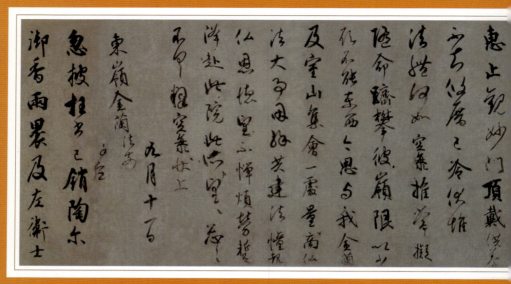

Fūshin-jō: Kūkai's letter to Saichō. (see P.264)
(Credited to Tō-ji, Kyōto)

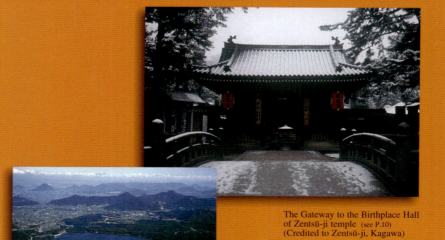

The Gateway to the Birthplace Hall
of Zentsū-ji temple (see P.10)
(Credited to Zentsū-ji, Kagawa)

Mannō-ike, overlooking a part of the
Mano Plain. (see P.9-10, P.278-279)
(Credited to Zentsū-ji, Kagawa)

Kōbō Daishi, Kūkai.
The oldest statue that exists to this day,
carved by Kōshō in 1233 to be enshrined
in Daishi-dō Hall in Tōji.
(Credited to Tōji, Kyōto)

A representative set of ritual objects Kūkai was equipped with by Huiguo. (Tang dynasty, 8th century) (Credited to Tō-ji, Kyōto)

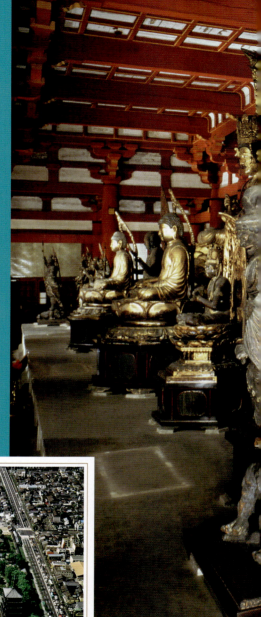

The whole precinct of Tō-ji & its neighborhood. (see P.280) (Credited to Tō-ji, Kyōto)

The sculptural images that constitute a mandala, enshrined at Lecture Hall of Tō-ji. (see P.281) (Credited to Tō-ji, Kyōto)

the Nan'en-dō hall (see P.239)
(Credited to Kōfuku-ji, Nara)

Last will of Kōbō Daishi,
dated March 15, 835.
(see P.295)

The Entrance to Kōbō Daishi's
Sanctuary on Mt. Kōya.
(Credited to Kongōbu-ji on Mt. Kōya)

Kyūkaku-jō (see P.262)
(Credited to the Nara National
Museum, Nara)

Akasagarbha (Kokuzō Bodhisattva) (see P.43, P.52)
Kamakura Period, 13th century
(Credited to Daigo-ji, Kyōto)

CONTENTS

Color Plates

Acknowledgment

Translator's Notes

ACKNOWLEDGMENT

MY greatest gratitude goes to the late Shiba Ryōtarō, the author of the original text, *KŪKAI NO FŪKEI* (空海の風景). If it had not been for the rare magnanimity with which he allowed me to render his book into English, this work would not have come into being as it does today.

I still remember very well how that two-volume story of Kūkai came into my life in 1975 when it was first published in Japan. It was also the year of special significance for those who were interested in Kūkai, as his birth in 775 A.D. had occurred exactly 1200 years before. In Zentsūji City where Kūkai was born (and where my family had lived for three generations,) there was a definitely festive mood. On his birthday (June 15th) it reached a climax in Zentsū-ji temple that marks his birthplace and I was very happy joining those who dedicated songs and dances to our honored saint.

But another event that occured in October in that same year turned out to be even more memorable for me: *KŪKAI NO FŪKEI* or the full-scale story of Kūkai, caught my eye at a local book shop and as soon as I began to read it I found myself quickly outgrowing the folklore world with which I had associated Kūkai all my life.

KŪKAI NO FŪKEI also gave me guidance when I later wrote two English-language guidebooks—*Kagawa* in 1988 and *Shikoku* in 1993. While writing about Kūkai and the Shikoku Pilgrimage, both of which were to constitute the soul of these books, I began to feel a strong desire to write more about Kūkai in English; more precisely, something about Kūkai far above the level of guidebook lore. As soon as *Shikoku* was off my hands, I wrote to Mr. Shiba about my wish to write about Kūkai in English by translating his great work *KŪKAI NO FŪKEI*.

Mr. Shiba must have been astonished at this bold solicitation made by an unknown translator. But he soon sent me a kind answer, giving me the precious opportunity to do what I really wanted. Even after his unexpected death on February 12th, 1996, his unfathomable magnanimity was carefully respected by the Shiba Ryōtarō Memorial Foundation, aptly directed by his devoted wife, Mrs. Fukuda Midori.

Another person I shall give my profound thanks is James Kirkup, an English poet and writer, who helped me in two ways. Firstly, he has kept attracting me to the world of English language since the autumn of 1967, when he gave us *An Oral Interpretation of English Poetry* at the 17th annual assembly held in Tōkyō by the National Federation for Teachers of English. As a constant reader of his writings and then a correspondent and translator of his autobiographies of childhood and youth—*The Only Child* and *Sorrows, Passions and Alarms*, I was to spend more than thirty years before I asked him in 1999 to edit the final revision of this work: *KŪKAI THE UNIVERSAL: Scenes from His Life*.

By that time the poet himself had become well acquainted with Kūkai, partly because I—"an indefatigable correspondent" as he called me in 1978 in his *Modern Japanese Poetry* published from University Queensland Press— often referred to Kūkai in explaining something of Japanese culture or my own daily life in the vicinity of his birthplace. Mr. Kirkup, who later came to live in Kyōto where Kūkai spent almost all the latter half of his life, was to have many opportunities to know more about Kūkai, including the exhibition of *Kōbō Daishi & the Art of Esoteric Buddhism* held in 1983 at Kyōto National Museum, and a theatrical presentation of *KŪKAI* in 1984 at Naka-za, Ōsaka by Zenshin-za, one of the best troupes in this country.

Even after he left Japan in 1985 to live in Europe, his interest in Kūkai continued and this made him find and read *Japanese Pilgrimage* by Oliver Statler soon after it was published in Great Britain. Some other books of history and calligraphy I found in his library he had left me before leaving also turned out to be very helpful throughout this project. In the 1990's he revisited Japan from time to time extending his travels as far as Zentsūji City, and stayed there for several months in all together with his assistant Tamaki Makoto. Naturally he often visited Zentsū-ji temple whose precincts are comfortably shaded by the same ancient camphor tress that Kūkai himself endearingly mentioned in his autobiographical work, *The Indications of the Three Teachings*.

Indeed, I could not have found a better person to edit this story of Kūkai. The patience and carefulness Mr. Kirkup showed on that occasion was certainly more than I could ever give sufficient thanks for.

Among many others to whom I wish to express my sincere thanks there are:

Yoritomi Motohiro: an active priest of Shingon religion, a distinguished scholar of Esoteric Buddhism, a former professor of the International Research Center for Japanese Studies. He kindly answered my questions, kindly introducing very useful books and dictionaries that were to guide me through the religious phase of this work. I had come to know of him in 1994 when Mr. Yoritomi, born in Sanuki, now President of Shuchi-in University in Kyōto, presided over a symposium on *The Great Saint Kūkai and His Messages to Be Rediscovered for Today and Tomorrow*, held at the Kagawa Prefectural Library as a part of its opening celebrations.

Hasuo Zenryū, who had been President of Zentsū-ji temple for thirty years (1970-1999), never failed to lead me to better understanding of Kūkai not only through his writings but also through a personal contact I was honored to enjoy. Since the route of my dog-walking intersected with that of his daily walking, I was fortunate enough to get acquainted with him late in the 1980's. By and by, I began to regard him as a walking dictionary on Kūkai and sometimes I dared to gladly tap it. But what helped me most, I now realize, was the very sight of him. It was always a revelation to me, for I was seeing in him a true disciple of Kūkai.

Zhao Jing: She came from Xi'an, China, the then curator of the Northwest Folk Art Museum in Xi'an. I met her in 1995 when she was staying in Takamatsu, the capital city of Kagawa Prefecture, as a guest of honor. The three presents she thoughtfully brought me when she heard of this project of mine proved to be a source of immense inspiration for me, as they kept me very close to my adored Chang'an. One present was a rubbing of a bird's-eye view of the ancient Qinglong-si temple—site of an important event in this story— erected upon Lo-yu-yuan Plateau. Another gift was a rubbing of a poem by Chu Tu-nan that perpetuates an evening he once spent on this same plateau. Yet another gift was an Indian ink drawing of a magnificent temple building adorning the crest of a large rock overlooking water. Mrs. Zhao said it was a part of restored Qinglong-si temple, and that she had recently painted it from memory especially for me. She did me another favor by writing out many Chinese personal and place names in English alphabetical form.

Yu Guo Feng: Consul of the Consulate General of the People's Republic of China in Ōsaka. When I approached him in 1999, he was leading a very busy life, but he spent many hours in the evenings, painstakingly reviewing all those names mentioned above and transcribing some other Chinese words in English alphabetical form. I cannot thank these two Chinese sufficiently for what they kindly did for the completion of many chapters in this book.

Fukuoka Akira: a former senior high school teacher of Japanese classics. I turned to him, when I came across wordings I found dubious or imprecise while poring over dictionaries or reference books. His ample suggestions always helped me find a solution.

Terasaka Mikiko: a former colleague of mine, a senior high school teacher of calligraphy. She kindly supplied me with pages of precious information she gathered from many books and dictionaries on calligraphy.

Last but not least, Uemura Motoko, the chief secretary of the Shiba Ryōtarō Memorial Foundation, was most helpful in introducing me to the honorable Foundation.

All these kindnesses I received from them enabled me to bring this work to completion. As for the production and publication, Mr. Tamura Tatsuya and Mr. Murata Okinori and their staff in Tuttle Shokai Inc. did their best, to my great satisfaction.

Now I feel very happy to dedicate it to the noble soul of Shiba Ryōtarō. And to the great soul of O-Daishi-san who has always been guiding us all concerned.

TAKEMOTO AKIKO
February 21st, 2003

TRANSLATOR'S NOTES

1) British spelling is adopted in translating passages from Kūkai's writings and other classical books or documents, e.g. honour, travelling, favour.

2) Personal names, Chinese and Japanese, are given in their native order with family name first.

3) Most Buddhist terms, names of Buddhist deities and titles of texts and books are given in their Japanese pronunciation, e.g. Shingon, Kannon, *Kegon-kyō*. But those which form the core of Buddhism or Esoteric Buddhism are presented in Sanskrit though lacking diacritical marks, e.g. *sunyata, homa, karma*. The following are treated as English words: Buddha bodhisattva, mandala, Mantrayana, mantra, mudra, sutra.

4) The months of the year are based on the old lunar calendar. In Japan it had been the official calendar until 1874 when the Gregorian calendar was adopted. According to the old calendar, the New Year, which occurred usually in February, was considered to be the beginning of spring which lasted three months, just like the other seasons.

5) People's ages are given in the old way of counting. In Japan until 1945 new-born babies were one year old during their first year, because the months before birth were taken into account.

6) An asterisk shows that *the* word or phrase or sentence will be explained later whether in the same chapter or in later chapters.

7) Many of the places mentioned will be found in the maps given on P.336 –P.338.

8) Since the original was written for Japanese readers, who are supposed to be equipped with fundamental knowledge of Japanese history and its background, not a little explanation had to be added here and there in several chapters and their notes.

I. THE BACKGROUND

KŪKAI was born in 774 in Sanuki Province, which faced the central provinces* with the easternmost part of the Seto Inland Sea in between. Visitors to what used to be Sanuki Province (present-day Kagawa Prefecture) will surely find their eyes drawn to conical green hills dotted on the spacious plains usually crowned with a bright broad canopy of sea-lit skies that often turn into a grand stage for ever-changing clouds. An attractive setting like this might be a fine cradle for a child dreamer.

According to his *Memoirs*,* his background went as follows:

> My father is a Saeki *uji* of Tado County in Sanuki Province. Our ancestor long ago received the land there in reward for the services he rendered in subjugating the barbarians in the east.

Obviously this was the gist of a story that had been told and retold among his family members generation after generation for centuries until it became a family legend. In ancient Japan, the word *uji* used after a family name indicated that the family was aristocratic. Certainly the head of his family, a County Administrator, was a provincial aristocrat. But the rest of his statement does not sound wholly correct, because the person who joined in "subjugating the barbarians in the east" was not of the Saeki *uji* in Sanuki Province, as many modern historians have agreed, but of the same-named family who lived in the capital, a branch of the distinguished Ōtomo clan who had been in charge of the guard of the Imperial Court and of its military affairs.

Who were "the barbarians in the east"?
Who were their subjugators?
To answer these questions will be to explain the roots of the Japanese people and the making of the Japanese polity in its nascent stage, while

revealing what caused the two unrelated families to have the same family name of Saeki; and also to speculate on who might have been Kūkai's ancestor if this statement he made about his background was not wholly correct.

"The barbarians in the east," later known as Ezo, were among the major aboriginal tribes living all over the Japanese Islands throughout Japan's Neolithic Age or the Jōmon Period (ca.12,000B.C. or earlier–ca.350B.C.).[1] Their life, largely based on hunting and gathering, began to undergo a radical change when paddy-rice-growing people not only from the Korean Peninsula but also from some other areas of the Asian continent, or even from South India, began to migrate to many parts of western Japan, thus marking the dawn of a new era called the Yayoi Period (ca.350B.C.–ca. 250A.D.),[2] in which more and more immigrants grew more and more paddy-rice on more and more land they cultivated and irrigated. As this new civilization made an eastward advance, the aborigines living in western Japan were driven farther and farther east or assimilated with paddy-rice-growing newcomers.

As is easily imagined, paddy-rice-growers had settled where water was easily obtainable, and those who were able to irrigate their rice fields better to produce more rice than others gradually grew into local powers. By the end of the Yayoi Period, there were numerous local powers controlling their own territories. When they died, they were buried in large mounds, thus introducing a new era known as the Tumulus Period (ca.250–ca.550), which is divided into three parts—early, middle, late—according to the types of mounds. When I was following the trail of Kūkai in his home province, I was told that hundreds of mounds found almost all over the northern slope of Mt. Ōasa that overlooked what used to be Tado County were of the early type, and that many of them belonged to the Saeki clan as a local power in those far-off days.

At some time in the fourth century, the whole land of Japan, except for Hokkaidō and the northeastern section of the main island that happened to be the home of "the barbarians," was united for the first time by the Yamato Regime, which was virtually a union of several local powers that developed from what later became the central provinces (Yamato, Yamashiro,

2

Kawachi, Izumi and Settsu provinces). The Yamato clan, though managing to take the leadership of the regime, was no more than a comparatively larger clan that held sway over the southern part of what was later known as Yamato Province. That was why the Yamato Regime, even after having declared its supremacy, had to allow other local powers, if only they submitted themselves to it, to go on governing their old territories in the capacity of Local Chieftains. Unlike many small powers in and around the central provinces that came to be enlisted under the new banner, some superpowers in remote provinces, such as Tsukushi, Izumo, and Kamitsukeno, refused to surrender and remained wary and defiant for a few more centuries.

As for "the barbarians in the east," the Yamato Regime sent military expeditions time and time again. Their purpose was not the acquisition of territory, but turning those aboriginal hunters into rice-growing settlers under their control. Their usual tactic, therefore, was just to send out an overwhelmingly large force so that the mere sight of it would frighten them into submission, that is to say, into agreement to settle down and cultivate rice. In fact, the basic principle upon which the Yamato Regime was founded was not anything abstract like Confucianism or Christianity, but something very practical—paddy-rice-growing. This was to mean a great deal to Japanese life thereafter; in economy, rice was to assume the function of money until 1873 when land taxes paid in rice were changed into monetary taxes; culturally it became the pivot upon which almost all the ancient festivals of this country were, and still are, observed to please the Sun-Goddess Amaterasu* as the guardian of paddy-rice-growing.

In one of such expeditions to the east, a legendary hero named Yamato Takeru, a son of the Tennō[3] Keikō, returned from a triumphant campaign, bringing with him a large number of captives, as is recorded in *Kojiki* and *Nihon Shoki*,[4] the oldest historical works Japan has ever produced. In the latter the life of the aborigines in the east is depicted as follows:

> In winter they sleep in a den, in summer in a tree.... In climbing mountains they are as swift as winged creatures, in crossing grassland as agile as beasts taking to flight.... They keep arrows

in their topknot and a sword inside their coat. Sometimes they band together to invade the borderland to carry off men and women working on rice paddies or mulberry fields.

Their nature is fierce and violent, ... and different groups are incessantly quarreling over the boundaries or robbing each other.

Their family life is promiscuous; no distinction is made between men and women, and between father and sons.

The writers of *Nihon Shoki*, who were great readers of Chinese historians, might have borrowed their image of "savages in the steppes of Central Asia" in depicting "the barbarians in the east" of Japan. But as far as this passage is concerned, their observation would not have been very far off the mark, as the aborigines in the east were certainly tough and cunning, and their way of life was poles apart from that of the paddy-rice-growing settlers in the west. Their language must have been different, too.

Now the captives were kept for the time being at the Ise Jingū shrine in Ise Province—a mausoleum dedicated to the Sun-Goddess Amaterasu and other mythological ancestors of the Yamato clan as the ancestors of the present-day Tennō and his family. But the savages having made so much noise, "crying and quarrelling day and night," they had to be moved to the foot of Mt. Mimoro in Yamato Province. But again they "howled and roared in such a terrifying manner to the constant fright of neighbouring villages" that the Tennō decreed that they should be sent somewhere outside the central provinces. The captives, therefore, "were divided into five groups and sent over to five neighbouring provinces," as is recorded in *Nihon Shoki*: "This was how the Saegi *be* came to live in the provinces of Harima, Aki, Awa, Iyo and Sanuki."

'Saegi' means 'noise-makers.' This is fairly convincing, considering that the excited speech of a strange language certainly sounds just like a noise. '*Be*' means 'guild.' The Yamato Regime had many guilds under their direct control, such as Nakatomi *be* as the guild of Court ritualists and Fubito *be* as the guild of scribes. Saegi *be* as a guild of military men was placed among them, and that was why they were regularly sent over to the capital to guard the Imperial Court. Incidentally, Sanuki had already accepted some other groups of guild people, including the Ōtomo *be* as an army division directed by Ōtomo *uji*.

The Saegi *be* brought to those five provinces were placed under the control of provincial powers called Saegi *uji*. It may be that those local powers had to change their family name to Saegi when they accepted these guild people. Written in Chinese characters[5] as 佐伯, it read Saeki, and 'Saegi' was gradually replaced by 'Saeki' which aptly happened to mean 'an aide to the chief.' On the other hand, a branch of the Ōtomo clan, whose head had traditionally been the Chief Guardian of the Court together with the head of the Ōtomo clan, also adopted the name of Saeki, as he assumed a new responsibility of controlling all of the Saeki *uji* and their Saeki *be* in those five provinces. To make matters even more confusing, the chief of each group of Saeki *be* in those provinces was also called Saeki *uji*.

Then in 453, another Saeki *uji* appeared in Sanuki. He was born an Ōtomo *uji*—Ōtomo no Wako, one of the great-great-grandsons of Ōtomo no Takehi or the very person that had "received the land there in reward for the services he rendered in subjugating the barbarians in the east." But when Wako came down to Sanuki as a Local Chieftain, his family name was no longer Ōtomo but Saeki because of the jurisdiction he had over the Saeki *be* there.

Then which Saeki *uji* could be the ancestor of Kūkai?

Obviously the last mentioned was the person Kūkai and his family had long believed to be their ancestor, and actually he might have been such, but not the remotest, if I take into consideration what I was told by local historians during my field trip there: "the early type of burial mounds found in great numbers on the northern slope of Mt. Ōasa were of the ancestors of Kūkai's family."

On the other hand, the disparity between the Sanuki Saeki and the Ōtomo including the Ōtomo Saeki in the capital will be known by their long-retained titles conferred on them by the central government: the former's was *atae*, the latter's *muraji* at first and then *sukune*. *Atae* was for Local Chieftains, *muraji* for the leaders of the clans that served the Court. Later when the title system[6] was changed (685), both the Ōtomo and the Ōtomo Saeki were granted *sukune* as had been conferred on the most distinguished of the former *muraji* holders. After the Taika Reform (645)[7] or the great reform of the Yamato Regime following the example of Sui and Tang* China's political system, Local Chieftains were replaced by Provincial Administrators sent from the central government. But the traditional power of Local Chieftains was still so strong that the ablest among them, like the Sanuki Saeki, were given priority to assume a new post of County Administrator again with the title of *atae*. Kūkai's family, therefore, had long held the title of *atae*, until in 861 (twenty-six years after his death) they presented a petition to the Court, saying that they were a branch of the Ōtomo clan, just as were the Saeki clan in the capital, and that they would be grateful if the title of *sukune* were granted to them, too.

Their request was conceded[8] with unusual readiness. Obviously it was in honour of Kūkai whose fame was still rising and spreading. But had it not been for Kūkai, they would surely have earned what they thought they deserved, for the Sanuki Saeki around Kūkai's time were producing an unusually large number of intellectuals, scholars and Buddhist priests and they were all so remarkably active in their own fields that their request would have been considered quite natural.

One might presume that the chief of the Saeki *be* sent to Sanuki could be the forefather of Kūkai. Certainly he and his offspring gradually climbed the social ladder until "on February 5 in the fifth year of the Tennō Ninken's reign (492), Saeki *be* Nakako was made a holder of the title of *miyatsuko* (a hereditary title of the leader of the guild directly engaged in Court service,)" as is recorded in *Nihon Shoki*. But it would be quite unlikely that the chief of the Saeki *be* who had lacked both knowledge and technique in carrying out paddy-rice-growing would have been appointed Local Chieftain with the title of *atae*.

Now another set of relevant questions come to mind. What was it that had made the Sanuki Saeki a producer of so many excellent brains? What could it be that had made Kūkai the greatest genius Japan has ever produced, or the one who has been unfailingly placed among the top-ranking not only in philosophy and religion but also in language, literature, art, calligraphy, sculpture, architecture, civil engineering, education, and social work? Was there anything special in the nature of his lineage or in the milieu in which he was brought up?

Considering the fact that mixed blood, fresh and rich, can be an advantage in producing excellent brains, there might have been influxes of new blood from a variety of sources: from the different lines of Saeki *uji*, from Ōtomo *uji* who had long "kept a country house on land they got in Sanuki" for the reason mentioned previously; from some other local powers in the same province, such as the Hata *uji** and the Aya *uji** who were both of the Chinese origin, and from different groups of guild people, including the Ōtomo *be*, the Saeki *be* and the Nishigori *be* (the guild of brocade-weavers) who were originally Koreans from Paekche.*

*   *   *

As for the place where Kūkai spent the first fifteen years of his life, I was not a total stranger there because, as a boy, I happened to spend a summer at a seaside village near his birthplace, present-day Zentsūji City, Kagawa Prefecture. I can still recall several scenes of that countryside, where the sun was pleasantly bright and the white clouds shone dazzlingly high above the rural landscape that still retained a tinge of antiquity. I often heard local people recount the stories of O-Daishi-san[9] (Kūkai), in many of which he was a superman magician. Those fabulous stories, I now realize, were created and spread, long after Kūkai's time, by traveling monks known as Kōya *hijiri** who went all over this country, collecting funds to maintain Kōya-san,[10] the monastic center Kūkai founded in 816 on top of Mt. Kōya in Kii Province.

Speaking of supermen, I recently had an unforgettable experience. I was talking to a social scientist who had always seemed to me the last person to lose his reason. When our topic turned to Kūkai, he confessed, to my breathless astonishment, that he, who was born and brought up in Sanuki, cannot discuss Kūkai as a human being, and that it is only when he regards him as a superman that he feels he is on the right path and finds himself talking about him. His attitude toward Kūkai was exactly what I had seen in the farmers and fishermen I met as a boy in a seaside village in Sanuki. Is Kūkai still generally considered as such? Then, would it be irreverently bold

7

of me to wish, as I do now, that I could *see* him or just get a glimpse of him with my own eyes through my literary efforts to track him down? Generally speaking, it would be unbearably uncomfortable for anyone to be made conscious of having been revered as a demi-god for over a millennium since his death. But as long as it has been happening to Kūkai, it certainly seems as natural as natural can be. How could I explain the reason? Laden with these questions, I started on a journey to his ancestral land.

From Takamatsu, the capital of Kagawa Prefecture, I rode along the national highway that runs along the Japan Railroad Yosan Line. Even before Kūkai was born, this route had already been a national thoroughfare, as is evident from the fact that it leads to the ancient sites of the state-owned Buddhist temples—Kokubun-ji and Kokubun-niji[11]—and Koku-fu (the Provincial Government Office). I left my taxi to go and see an old kiln where roofing tiles for Kokubun-ji used to be produced. Hollowed out in the rock with funnels at the farthest end, it still remained intact in a corner of the yard of a farmhouse standing on a pine-wooded hill.

Leaving the national highway at Fuchū (the ancient word meaning 'the seat of the Government Office' is still used as a place name), I rode along a prefectural road which still retained the atmosphere of the ancient thoroughfare especially when it meandered among the hills. In between wooded hills was usually seen the blue-green patch of water of a pond.

Ponds are everywhere in Sanuki, to the amazement of those who have visited there for the first time. The weather being usually very dry and rivers running very scantily, paddy-rice-growers have had to depend on reservoirs and irrigation ditches from time immemorial. Aerial photographs taken in 1960 showed no less than fifty thousand reservoirs in Sanuki. The inquisitive may ask who built *the* pond, usually to receive a set answer "Kūkai" or "O-Daishi-san," because legend says so. Most of the ponds, however, had already been there by the time Kūkai was born. This explains why Sanuki in Kūkai's time was reportedly feeding a population as large as any of the most advanced provinces in central Japan.

Now I must mention the biggest of these ponds, which is actually the biggest in Japan. It is called Mannō-ike pond, 19.7 kilometers in circumference, 21 meters at the deepest, now irrigating 4,600 hectares of paddy fields below, which exactly corresponds to the ancient plain named Mano that used to be administratively divided into the two counties of Naka and Tado with the Kanakura River in between.

To reach Mannō-ike pond one must go farther west and turn south in the vicinity of Zentsūji City where Kūkai was born. No mountain in Sanuki is higher than 1,000 meters and the gently-sloping mountains I saw around Mannō-ike pond were comparatively higher ones. The pond itself lies at an altitude of about 200 meters, its shore indented by eleven ravines. The wide stretch of water makes me agree with an ancient poet who sang:

> I shall not call this a pond, as I feel
> as if seeing a sea beyond eighty islets.

With no human habitation around, it was still and quiet—so much so that even the slightest rippling on the water made me rather nervous. The dam upon which I came to stand was an arched dam whose foundation Kūkai built long ago. Reportedly he pondered over the shape of the dam he was going to build there and reached the conclusion that an arc would best withstand the high water pressure to which it would be subjected. The dam itself has been rebuilt several times since, including the latest improvement in 1956, but always on the original foundation laid in 821, to the credit of Kūkai as a civil engineer.

Now looking out over the plain below, I could see very clearly how the paddy-rice-growing people who first arrived on that plain made up their minds to settle there, but not until they came up here and found a large amount of water kept in the eroded valley among the mountains; with its mouth appropriately open to the north, the primeval pool seemed quite ready to provide ample water for the plain below. But it was not very long before they found it was not as beneficial as they had expected, for in the rainy season in June and July, it often overflowed and destroyed their paddies and even their lives, to their immense distress. If the water were controlled by a bank built at its northern mouth, it would turn the plain below into a really fertile land, they thought. But the building of the bank and its system of irrigation ditches connected to run all over the plain would require a tremendous amount of manpower, much greater than they could possibly obtain.

Since this situation had probably been brought to the knowledge of the central government, the newly-obtained manpower of Saeki *be* may have been applied to the plain of Mano, of all places in Sanuki. Then it would have followed that the local clan that took in Saeki *be* gradually turned that natural pool into a reservoir and the plain below into irrigated land so that they could carry out such large-scale paddy-rice-farming as had already been done in eastern Sanuki under the control of the Sanuki *uji*.

The bicultural and bilingual situation those guild people had brought about in the Mano Plain might be worth considering, too. What if they had still retained some traits of their ancestral faith or customs? One is more likely to gain deeper insight into humanity in a bicultural situation than in a simple, mono-cultural situation. The priority Kūkai had attached to thought about humanity itself, not to its superficial accessories such as culture and language, might have had its source in this bicultural situation in which he had been brought up. By the same token, the old servants the child Kūkai spoke to every day or the old women he would come across on the farm were quite likely to have had a way of speaking different from his own family's. If a bilingual situation helps one acquire a keen sense of language learning, Kūkai's unusual skill in this direction would be less hard to explain.

Kūkai's birthplace is now enshrined in Gotanjō-sho or the Birthplace Hall in the inner precinct of Zentsū-ji temple[12] in Zentsūji City, which has developed around that temple. As its formal name Gogaku-zan Zentsū-ji suggests, it stands at the foot of the foremost of the five mountains (go-gaku) that rise behind it. In Kūkai's days all these mountains used to overlook a bay named Byōbu-ga-ura (Folding Screen Bay), which has also been perpetuated in another formal name of the temple—Byōbu-ga-ura Zentsū-ji. Today the bay is reclaimed into paddy lands, but the chain of mountains is still there, looking like a five-paneled screen set up around what used to be a sea. Would this natural setting have helped make the child Kūkai a precocious mountain ascetic and a habitual gazer at sea and sky, far-off islands and white sails on boats crawling across the Inland Sea?

It was in his second year (775) that Kūkai and his family and many others that gathered on the shore were treated to an extra-fine picture of a fleet of four vermilion-painted boats with a Japanese embassy on board bravely sailing for Tang China. What made the scene even more impressive to them was that the embassy was led by Saeki no Ima-Emishi, the then head of the Ōtomo Saeki in the capital with whom the Sanuki Saeki had long been identifying themselves.

Exactly the same thing happened two years later, too, for the fleet led by Ima-Emishi, unable to catch a fair wind at this side of the East China Sea, had to sail back and wait for another occasion. But when the occasion came round, Ima-Emishi, no longer strong enough to cross 'the sea of myriad miles' but unable to decline the Imperial order, pretended to be too ill to go on board. Subsequently, two vice-envoys were ordered to occupy the place of the envoy and the fleet set sail without delay. The four pretty boats, therefore, though eagerly watched by the child Kūkai and others, were not led by Ima-Emishi, as they firmly believed. The boats safely arrived in China, but on their homeward voyage, they were caught in a storm and many were lost at sea, including one of the vice-envoys. Indeed, sailing to and from China often cost people their lives, but it was supremely meritorious as well. Through such incentives of the highest quality as these casually woven into his daily life, the child Kūkai seems to have been brought up in an exceptionally favorable environment, though in a minor county in a small province.

Some people assert that Kūkai was born where Kaigan-ji now stands—a seaside temple about four kilometers north of Zentsū-ji. In former days a maternity hut used to be built on the seaside or riverside more or less far away from home, and this custom might have given rise to this legend and even to another legend that his mother's parents' home was in the vicinity of this temple. The last mentioned was practically the only legend about the whereabouts of the residence of his mother's side or the Ato *uji*. What does this mean when in Sanuki legends about Kūkai and his father's side are practically numberless?

There were the Ato *uji* in the capital, too, who were originally Chinese naturalized in Japan some time in the fourth century. According to *The Chronicle of Titled Families* compiled in 815, there were three hundred and twenty-four naturalized families living in the central provinces alone. Among them Ato *uji* with the title of *sukune* had been fairly remarkable, producing many court officials including the distinguished three: Gembō,* a brilliant official priest; Matari who had been reappointed vice-president of the university a few years before Kūkai matriculated; and Ōtari, a younger brother of Kūkai's mother, who was selected to be a tutor to Prince Iyo,* the third son of the Tennō Kammu, at some time when Kūkai was in his teens.

Kūkai's mother as a young woman might have come down to Sanuki to get married into the Saeki family. Or it might have been that the Sanuki Saeki had invited from the capital a branch of the Atos as their guest family. As is suggested by some archeological relics, the Sanuki Saeki at that time were wealthy enough to possess a Buddhist temple of their own on their premises. Then it is quite probable that they could afford to have a Confucian scholar come down from the capital to be the mentor of the head of the family, offering him and his family a fine residence to live in and the ownership of some newly-reclaimed land[13] to live on.

In the preface to *An Introduction to Literature* he later wrote, Kūkai recalls how he learned the art of writing:

> Early in my teens I studied a great deal of literature under the guidance of my maternal uncle....

Did Ōtari visit his sister's home so often? Some people assume that he had been teaching at the provincial school in Sanuki for several years before he was promoted to be a tutor to the imperial prince.

Taking all these things into consideration, the Sanuki Saeki's having produced a Kūkai is certainly far from accidental. But what was it that had arranged everything so well? Could it be a sort of providence working in his favor?

II. Boyhood

IN looking back upon his boyhood, Kūkai must have had a favorite picture in which the leafy giants of ancient camphor trees that stood around his mansion were gleaming and rustling in the sea breeze, as he mentioned in his autobiographical work, *The Indications of the Three Teachings:*

> I was born and brought up on an island neatly fringed with pearly
> seaweed. My home overlooking a bay was comfortably shaded
> by giant camphor trees....

His boyhood seems to have been an extremely happy one. It cannot be undesirable for anyone to live in extreme happiness. His talk about his own childhood, as is recorded in *The Memoirs of Our Master,*[1] may indicate the source of his happiness:

> My father and mother thought the world of me—so much so that
> they called me by the nickname of Tōto-mono (Precious Thing).

His tone is frankness itself, free from any self-conscious shyness as modern people must feel in talking about themselves. His spirit, which could be compared to a rough-hewn wooden pillar in its honest absence of any trimming, was certainly characteristic of ancient people. The word "Tōto-mono" must have reflected a brilliant belief his parents had held: that this son of theirs was a reincarnation of an Indian saint,* because before this boy was born, they had had the same dream at night in which an Indian priest who had come to stay with them presented himself in their bedroom only to disappear in the bosom of his mother.

Or could it be an example of what might be called a cult of prodigies which is an integral part of social tradition in this country? Sugawara no Michizane,[2] who lived and died several decades later than Kūkai, was typical of those awe-inspiring prodigies and eventually he was deified as Tenjin or

13

God of the Thunderbolt after his death. But beside Kūkai, even Michizane looks mediocre. Then it would be quite probable that his parents, relatives and neighbors should have sensed something extraordinary and even divine in this child with exceptional intelligence. But how could it be explained that the same kind of awe and adoration that had made his parents call him "Tōto-mono" gradually spread all over this country to be handed down generation after generation throughout the centuries even to this day? A really inexplicable phenomenon, indeed.

What was his academic background like?

Early in the eighth century the state had started two kinds of educational institutions: a provincial school in each of about sixty provinces and a university in the capital. This system that solely aimed at preparing boys of aristocratic families for the official career they would follow in the future, was a fruit of the aristocratic system Japan had adopted after the model of China, though it was to vanish by 1185 when aristocracy was replaced by military government.

The provincial school located in the same premises as the provincial government office was popularly called "Confucius Hall." In fact, there was a hall to enshrine Confucius[3] in Chinese fashion, and beside it stood a lecture hall and a dormitory. Different provinces had different numbers of students. In the case of Sanuki, there were thirty of them. The only teacher that taught Chinese classics was called "the scholar of the province:" but his status was no higher than that of a local government official of the lowest grade. Naturally he was poorly off, presenting a discouraging reality to students if they were mercenary enough to rate the merit of learning on the basis of socio-economic efficiency. But as is easily imagined, obtaining "a scholar of the province" was next to impossible in most of the provinces that remained simply backward for the most part, and it was not long before their fledgling schools were brought to a halt, even though they were being made to revive in the 780s when Kūkai reached school age of thirteen. Those admitted to this school were boys like Kūkai whose father or head of the family were county administrators.

The university in the capital was principally for scions of those who held the fifth court rank[4] or above, but sometimes for bright youngsters of those whose court ranks were eighth or above. The rank retained by the head of Kūkai's family being the sixth, Kūkai was qualified to enter it, too, also at the age of thirteen.

Another choice he could make might have been the pursuit of Buddhism. Having already taken great interest in Buddhism, as is suggested by many of the legends of his childhood, he might have wished to learn more of Buddhism and even to dedicate himself to it. His parents, who believed him to be a reincarnation of an Indian saint, would have thought it only natural when they saw him developing his interest in Buddhism. As they had a Buddhist temple of their own, the devout ones would have been quite ready to make one of their sons a Buddhist priest. But the other members of the Saeki clan who had already produced two or three bureaucrats for the central government were anxious to make another bureaucrat of this bright boy. In fact, Kūkai, though spared the cares and difficulties many historical figures usually faced in their juvenile days, might have felt under a constant strain, spurred on by the eager expectations of his own clan who, as is often the case with those in the upper middle class, were conspicuously persistent in climbing up the social ladder.

According to *The Memoirs of Our Master*, his maternal uncle, Ato no Ōtari, advised his parents when he was around twelve that they should send him to the university, saying: "If he were to take up Buddhism in the end, studying at the university will surely do him good." But this advice was not accepted at first and Kūkai was to spend a few more years at home, probably attending the provincial school, occasionally visiting the state temple Kokubun-ji in the vicinity of the school to listen to some of the learned priests he met there.

On the other hand, considering what was happening in the capital about this time—especially a series of dismal incidents that shocked the whole capital when Kūkai was twelve (785)—it might have been only natural that Kūkai and his parents should have hesitated to take Ōtari's advice at once.

The year before, the Tennō Kammu had suddenly declared his intention to abolish the Nara Capital that had flourished for seventy-four years in Yamato Province and to start a new one at Nagaoka in the neighboring province of Yamashiro. Nagaoka at that time was nothing but a hilly wilderness. But Kammu insisted that it should be cleared for the building of a new capital.

Kammu, a man of spirit and originality, might have been trying to make himself a despotic emperor like the emperor of China, as is illustrated by the fact that one day in early winter in 785, he went up to a plateau in Katano in Kawachi Province, built an altar there after the Chinese fashion, and made a sacrifice of a calf to worship the heavens, as was done by successive emperors of China. Seeing that no tennō before him or after him has ever done such a thing, it could be taken as a challenge he made against Shintō (Japan's native religion)[5] that abhorred bloodshed and death as the height of impurity.

As some historians point out, Kammu might have intended to start a new Chinese-style dynasty, with his father Tennō Kōnin as its founder, thus to make themselves independent of the old lineage of successive tennōs. The reason for this might be explained by a complicated situation he was involved in before he eventually came to the throne at the age of forty-five, though I am not going to mention it any further as it has nothing to do with Kūkai. But Kūkai's boyhood and youth were to concur with the twenty-five-year reign of Kammu, a despot of heroic temperament, who often proved himself too immature especially when he launched one project after another or discarded one capital after another, thus keeping his bureaucrats extremely busy, while disturbing the public mind and the life of the nation to no avail.

The boy Kūkai must have often heard the senior members of his family talking about the transfer of the capital:

"What on earth made his majesty abandon that beautiful capital of Nara?"

They tried to find out the answer, but without success. As was typically shown in this case, the motivations of Kammu's behavior were usually hard to explain, because they often came from his own mental urge unfathomable to others rather than from political necessity sufficiently convincing to others.

"Saeki no Ima-Emishi must be having a hard time again...."

The boy Kūkai would have noticed an intimate but respectful tone in which they were talking of Ima-Emishi, the patriarch of the Saeki clan in the capital. After graduating from the university, he had been serving many tennōs—Shōmu (reign: 724–49), Kōken (749–58), Junnin (758–64), Shōtoku (764–770), Kōnin (770–781) and Kammu (781–806). After helping with the building of the Kōga-no-miya palace in Ōmi Province for the Tennō Shōmu, he spent almost half of his life on the two major national projects in the Nara Period: the building of Tōdai-ji temple in Nara and the founding of the Giant Buddha[6] to be enshrined in the central hall of that temple.

In carrying out these difficult tasks, he proved himself not only a good technologist but also a very good overseer in controlling thousands of laborers. Deliberate idleness and mass revolts were frequently seen on construction sites. But when Ima-Emishi came out to direct them, the laborers, impressed or influenced by his personality, refrained from voicing their discontent if they had any. He had already been in his fifties when both of the projects were finally taken out of his hands. The Court, very appreciative of his many years' inimitable services, raised his rank and offered a higher post plus an additional post of provincial administrator though he was allowed to stay in the capital. At fifty-seven he was appointed envoy to Tang China, though he declined it at the last moment, as mentioned in the previous chapter.

At sixty-four he was raised to the peerage with the junior grade of the third court rank, but the old man, instead of being overjoyed with such an exceptional promotion, had frequently expressed his wish to retire from public life. Then the Tennō Kammu decided to transfer the capital to Nagaoka and ordered Ima-Emishi to be a director of the capital-building. To the old man the mere thought of the high responsibility he had to assume again must have been depressing, but he could not help obeying the order even if it was to give him a hard time again.

But an even harder time was in store for him, for a series of dismal incidents occurred involving him the following year. The first one started when the director general of the capital-building, Fujiwara no Tanetsugu, the most powerful bureaucrat at that time, was shot to death on the construction site. There was a complicated political strife in the background. Tanetsugu at that time, hard pressed by the Tennō who was still in the old capital impatiently waiting for the completion of the new capital, had been forcing men to work day and night. On one of those nights in September, when countless bonfires were making the woods and ponds in the neighborhood glow and glitter, Tanetsugu on an inspection tour was attacked in ambush. The murderer was soon found to be Ōtomo no Tsuguto, a member of the Ōtomo clan. Tsuguto, a former subordinate of Tanetsugu, had harbored a personal spite against him, which was probably taken advantage of by a mystery man who also hated Tanetsugu.

Today it is easily imaginable that the mystery man was someone of a different branch of the same Fujiwara clan,[7] for the four branches of this clan had been at constant enmity with one another. But at that time Tsuguto's confession was considered valid: that he had been ordered to do so by Ōtomo no Yakamochi, the patriarch of his own clan. It is hardly probable that Yakamochi, a famous poet who had reportedly done a great deal for the compilation of that famous anthology of poems, *A Collection of Ten Thousand Leaves*,[8] should have ordered such a thing, when Yakamochi himself had died of illness more than twenty days before. And yet the Tennō Kammu convicted Yakamochi without making further inquiries, deprived him of the rank (the junior grade of the third court rank) he had retained in his lifetime, confiscated his land property, and banished his ashes, together with his eldest son, to a remote island of Oki on the Sea of Japan.

Obviously Kammu himself had taken advantage of this incident, as Yakamochi's having once been the chief of the Crown Prince's Office led him to the idea that his crown prince Sawara, who was his younger brother, must have been an accomplice of Yakamochi. Kammu, having been waiting for an opportunity to make his eldest son Ate crown prince, arrested Sawara and confined him at Otokuni-dera temple* in Nagaoka, and simply ignoring Sawara's petition of innocence, sentenced him to banishment to Awaji Island off the coast of Naniwa (present-day Ōsaka City). Sawara refused to eat and drink in resistance—or was not allowed to do so—until he starved to death while being sent to that island.

Ima-Emishi must have been in great distress all this while, for Crown Prince Sawara was the very person who had once recommended him for the junior grade of the third court rank along with a post of state councilor. Considering all the contributions he had made to the state, this reward seems quite reasonable. But as no one from the Saeki clan had ever been promoted to such high honors, Fujiwara no Tanetsugu made an objection against it.

18

Sawara had been on bad terms with Tanetsugu. Trying to check him, Sawara might have been elevating the status of Ima-Emishi as high as possible.

Tanetsugu submitted his complaint to Kammu, who worked out a compromise solution that Ima-Emishi should retain the rank, but not the post. This infuriated Sawara, who made a direct appeal to Kammu, insisting that he should be permitted to put Tanetsugu to death. Because of this abnormal measure he proposed, Sawara was kept away from government business, to his greater indignation. Then Tanetsugu was found dead. Rumor had it that Sawara inspired someone to assassinate his enemy, and Ōtomo no Yakamochi was falsely charged, as mentioned above. Involved in this incident, many officials of the Ōtomo clan and the Ōtomo Saeki clan were punished, inevitably quickening their decline.

After the unnatural death of Sawara, the royal family was afflicted with a number of misfortunes, and all of them were imputed to the curse of the dead crown prince. Then more and more people began to raise their voices against Nagaoka Capital itself, saying that it would be ominous to make a capital of such a blood-stained place. This naturally prevented the construction work from going well, even if "more and more farmers are being pressed into service, causing great distress among them..." as is written in the imperial edict of that year. Indeed, it was a period of darkness for everyone.

Listening to the senior members of his family talking about what was happening to the Ōtomo and the Ōtomo Saeki in the capital, the twelve-year-old Kūkai would have thought about what was awaiting him in the future even if he were to make himself a bureaucrat as successful as Ima-Emishi.

At fifteen, however, he left home for the capital, never to return as a resident. The age limit for matriculation being sixteen, his parents might have had no choice but to take Ōtari's advice if they wanted to have their son enjoy the merit of studying at the university.

A journey to the capital, mostly by sea, was far from easy. Getting a lift in a government boat that came round regularly was practically the only means available, as no commercial activity had begun yet. Usually it took a dozen days from Sanuki to Naniwa-zu port as a gateway to the new capital.

Before entering the new capital still under construction, Ōtari took Kūkai to Nara. What was his reaction when he saw for the first time what used to be the imperial capital with its eastern suburbs beautifully laid out with many gorgeous buildings of large Buddhist temples? In my opinion, he just took in everything without feeling any sense of oppression, for this country boy, round-faced and rather short in stature, would not be daunted by anything, as he was to remain all his life. Walking up and down the broad thoroughfares, sometimes casting a challenging glance at one thing, sometimes proudly ignoring another, the youth must have appeared utterly imperturbable.

Ōtari must have brought him to Saeki-in temple the Ōtomo Saeki had recently built at the Sixth Block on the Fifth Street. Ima-Emishi, the head of the family, immensely serviceable in carrying out all those national enterprises, had always been generously rewarded. This made him very rich. But as he preferred living in a simple way, usually dressing himself like a Buddhist monk, he had had a great deal of savings by the time he decided to build their own temple. His brother Mamori, also in the government service, naturally did his bit. This enabled them to have a larger temple than might be expected of a non-aristocratic family. The temple itself is gone now, but the remaining plan shows how large it was.

Ima-Emishi, known for his readiness to help his clansmen, must have extended his invitation even to the Sanuki Saeki, saying: "Please feel free to visit this temple as your own." Kūkai must have taken that word literally, seeing that in later years he seems to have made it a rule to get accommodation there when he came to Nara.

Now Ōtari and Kūkai were guided by the resident priest into the main hall, with the thirty-feet-wide frontage, crowned with a thick roof of cypress bark. Behind the inner doors especially opened for them, they saw the sanctum dedicated to their guardian deities: the central image was of the Great Healer,[9] eight feet tall, made of guilt bronze, attended by a couple of followers, a Sunlight Bodhisattva[10] and a Moonlight Bodhisattva, all gleaming in the candle light. A little apart from them, stood an Eleven-faced Kannon Bodhisattva.[11] Kneeling down before them, Kūkai must have worshiped them in profound delight and reverence.

Many of the leading figures in the Court had already moved up to the new capital in Nagaoka. Ōtari was among them, for he had already been made a tutor to Prince Iyo, the third son of the Tennō Kammu. The university and some other institutions of lesser importance had not yet come up in Nagaoka and the old ones in Nara were still used. To Kūkai now the university was still a thing of the future. All he had to do now was to prepare for the entrance examination, staying with his uncle in Nagaoka.

It was a day's journey from Nara to Nagaoka. Kūkai and his uncle went on cowback, following the ancient thoroughfare that led to Yamashiro Province. The first village they passed was Saki with an unmistakable landmark in it—a stretch of blue water so spacious that its surface was always rippling. His uncle must have pointed to it, saying:

"Look! That's the Pond of Saki."

It was where the poetry-making party on the water[12] used to be held by the Tennō Shōmu only sixty years or so before, when the new capital of Nara seemed to have a long, bright future before it. Now that it was abandoned, would everything associated with it be reduced to a relic of the past? As they went on, they saw many more reminders of the past: what seemed to have been Imperial palaces[13] with their vermilion pillars were seen through the trees, and Buddhist temples, which seemed to have been busy performing the Imperial prayer for the security of the state and the good health of the tennō, were now quietly resting among the emerald green woods on the hills. Kūkai would have realized how those artifacts adorned the rural landscape, and how attractive they looked against the earthen walls that surrounded the former capital. Excited by the brilliant idea of civilization that had just dawned upon him, he might have turned to his uncle, asking:

"Does Chang'an, the capital of Tang China, look like this?"

Unfortunately Ōtari had never been there. But some of his friends who had once been there had told him a great deal about ''the largest metropolis in the world totally incomparable with Nara'' and "the liveliness of the town that far surpasses Japanese imagination." Ōtari, a real gentleman, was usually a model of moderation. But once he began to impart something to this nephew of his, he just assumed an impassioned authority as if he had taken on a different personality. It may be that he was entertaining a dream that the boy would realize a dream he himself had failed to make reality.

Ambling along on cowback, Ōtari would never have tired of talking about the charms and surprises the Chinese capital would offer them.

The road became uphill when they entered the next village named Utahime. Near the top of the pass they got off the cows, and stepped into the forest sacred to an ancient rock revered as the dwelling of the god. Before the rock, they offered a *nusa*[14] tribute to him, praying for safe arrival at heir destination, as all travelers used to do in those days.

When I recently visited there, a farmer's wife I happened to meet at the entrance to the forest said: "Since the road was paved, the forest has lost its proper darkness, and the god seems to have abandoned this old place of his. That's why we haven't had anything good lately...."

The long winding path goes down through pine woods and bamboo thickets both mixed with Japanese oaks and myricas. Then it suddenly opens to a wide stretch of plain that forms the southern part of Yamashiro Province, where the hills in the background appear a little more imposing than those I saw in Yamato Province. Those neighboring provinces, I now realize just as a boy Kūkai must have done, have fairly different pictures to offer to travelers.

When the path began to go along the Kizu River, they came to a smoky, pine-wooded village of Haji *be* or a guild of potters that produced *haji* earthenware according to the primitive technique of the Yayoi Period. Though their ware was being replaced with *sue* ceramic ware manufactured by Sue *be* or another guild of potters whose ancestors had come from Korea during the Tumulus Period that followed the Yayoi Period, the native Haji *be* still managed to live up to their guild name by meeting the demand for ritual objects or miscellaneous pots used by the commonalty. Haji *be* were also known as fanatically conservative animists. They abhorred death as the height of impurity, and did not like their village defiled by anyone, even a traveler, who had recently had death in his family. That was why Ōtari had to declare to men and women they met in the path that crossed the village:

"Fortunately, we have had no death in our family in recent years."

But seeing the villagers still staring at them with suspicion, he might have added in a rather mocking tone:

"That's too bad for you, but I am a Confucian and I can't see the point of your argument."

They entered Otokuni County in which the Nagaoka capital was now being built. With its western border thickly flanked by the mountain mass of Tamba Heights, its geography is not likely to inspire open-minded cheerfulness in the human mind. The eastern part of the county being a wet land covered with rushes and reeds, the western part slightly higher and properly dry had been judged suitable for the seat of the new capital. Unfortunately, however, it appeared much smaller than the old one, as the Katsura River bordered its eastern suburbs. But this river, together with the two other rivers it joined at Yamasaki in the southern suburbs of the capital, was to make a good waterway that went straight down to the Inland Sea by way of Naniwa-zu port. Having a seaport as an entry to the capital was an inestimable advantage that could never be enjoyed in the inland capital of Nara, as the Tennō enthusiastically pointed out in his proclamation of the transfer of the capital, even if by doing so he may have been just shutting his eyes to many disadvantages he himself may have had to admit.

The Nagaoka capital as first seen by Kūkai was far from the image of a new capital, with roads and grounds left unpaved beside many unfinished buildings. Streaks of smoke were seen rising from the tileries on the mountain sides in the west, but apparently they were incapable of producing enough tiles to cover all the roofs of those buildings. That was why a great number of old tiles, probably ripped off from the abandoned Naniwa-no-miya[15] palace in Naniwa or from some disused office buildings in Nara, were piled up on the roadsides, along with many other parts of buildings, only to be exposed to all weathers. One ox-cart after another passed by, cutting the ruts deeper and deeper until they looked like paralleled ditches.

"Look over there! That is the central office in the Court."

Ōtari must have pointed to a huge building in the north, which alone was shining with the new tiles crowning it. The central office just inside the central gate to the Court was where all the court officials, formally attired, assembled at every ceremonial event, presenting a magnificent picture of officialdom. Ōtari, burning with expectation that his nephew would join that most respected circle some day and rise even to the peerage if his fortune and talent permitted, could not help calling his attention to that palace of bureaucrats, eagerly wishing that the very sight of it might prove an inspiration as well as a good introduction for this promising young man.

III. At the Turning Point

HIS uncle Ōtari would have expected Kūkai to enter university the next year after spending a year preparing for the examination. But again he let the chance slip by. The reason is unknown. Had his interest in Buddhism been intensified as he met more and more priests in Nara which he liked to visit from time to time? No definite answer is found in any of the research materials I turned to.

Kūkai was to spend three years in all at his uncle's, probably in Nagaoka, reading Confucian classics and learning how to read and write poetry and prose. This was actually when and how Kūkai was given a sound education and such a good grounding in the art of writing as extolled in *Shoku Nihon Koki*[1]: "Kūkai as a young man could not put his brush on paper without creating a fine piece of writing."

In fact, what he learned from his uncle far surpassed the level of the preparatory course for matriculation. Highly gifted as he was, Kūkai's talent would not have bloomed so beautifully if it had not been for the fertile soil his uncle thoughtfully provided for him about this period of his life. This is especially true, seeing that Ōtari was practically the only teacher Kūkai had regularly studied under for a certain period of time. Kūkai himself was fully aware of it, as he wrote in the preface to his maiden work, *The Indications of the Three Teachings*: "I revered my teacher from the bottom of my heart and treasured up his words in the depths of my mind." Though written in the embellished rhetoric of his day, Kūkai must have really meant what he wrote, gratefully declaring to whom he owed the scholarship he had obtained. What he learned at the university seems to have left less impression on him as far as his references to it in his literary remains are concerned.

At the age of eighteen, Kūkai finally entered "the City of *Sophora japonica*." By "the City of *Sophora japonica*" he meant the university. Pretentious as it may sound, it was a jargon of the Six-Dynasties style[2] adopted by all intellectuals at that time. The university offered several courses to choose from: Chinese Classics, Literature and History, Law, Astronomy and Calendric Studies, Chinese Language, and Calligraphy. Among these the Chinese Classics Course or what might be called Administration Course which Kūkai took in deference to his uncle was the most important course of all, for the university had been founded as the nursery of high officials required by the central government. The regular teaching staff of each course consisted of one professor, two assistant professors and two or three instructors.

The students of the Chinese Classics Course were expected to read *The Book of Filial Duty and The Analects of Confucius* as required texts and two or three elective subjects from among *The Spring and Autumn Annals, The Book of Songs, The Book of Documents, The Book of Changes* and *The Book of Rites*. Each text had to be read along with its authorized commentary. Free interpretation of the set texts was out of the question, for only those who were able to repeat from memory any part of those commentaries were allowed to pass the higher civil service examination. Could this have been an attempt to standardize the thought of higher civil servants? In China this examination system lasted very long, until the end of the Qing Dynasty (1912), and that might be counted as one of the causes for a long cultural stagnation it had to suffer. Fortunately, however, at some time during the Tang era, more and more students began to turn their backs on that stuffy air of the Confucian Classics Course, preferring to take the Literature and History Course; yet many of the graduates proved themselves to be excellent bureaucrats, even creating a fortunate derivative—the golden age of literature. In Japan, too, the same thing was to happen a little later.

Students of the Chinese Classics Course usually found it very hard to get through their curriculum. But Kūkai seems to have had enough time and energy to learn some other subjects that were not required. One of them would have been spoken Chinese. Otherwise, when he was in China years later, he could not have carried on a conversation so fluently as to astonish the natives. Another subject would have been calligraphy. Even his extraordinary accomplishment in calligraphy as witnessed also in China would be more credible, if we assume that he had been paying regular visits to a master of calligraphy in his university days. The other subject would have been literature which fascinated him throughout his life.

These extracurricular lessons he took would have been a sort of remedy he prescribed for himself to relieve the pain he had to suffer when his overflowing artistic talent was unduly restrained in the narrow range of the Confucian Classics Course. The brilliant reward he would gain by going through that purgatory was "success in life," as he was often told. But what if trial after trial in that purgatory were to lead him to have doubts about "success in life" and to carry him away into the mysteries of the universe? He would no longer feel like wasting his time with the Confucian classics in the Confucian society that now seemed to him a dull pageant of faded dolls, as he persistently argued in *The Indications of the Three Teachings*. Confucianism may enable one to master how to control society as a functionary of the ruler; but it will be of no use to one who is searching for the truth of the universe. Thus Kūkai had to abandon the university to quench his thirst for knowledge and wisdom, just as a parched traveler in the desert runs to an oasis.

* * *

What would have become of him if he had taken the Literature and History Course? His creativity more or less satisfied, he might have automatically graduated from the university, soon to find himself in the government service, just as the poet official Yamanoue no Okura[3] had done several decades before. Not of noble lineage, Okura was usually left out of promotion and had to suffer depression from time to time, and not until he was over seventy did he rise to the junior grade of the fifth court rank.[4] The following poem he made on his deathbed seems to echo his suppressed cry of remorse:

> What a useless life I have lived—a man
> who did nothing to immortalize his name!

Kūkai might not have come down in history or he might have become another Okura at best if he had taken the Literature and History Course at the university.

Some people may have a question: "Doesn't one's determination to retire from the world and dedicate oneself to Buddhism come from something more serious inhabiting the depths of one's own existence?" This question reminds me of many men and women in the middle of the Heian Period (794 –1185) and after, who suddenly entrusted themselves to Buddhism when they were bereaved of their beloved ones and got tired of life. They had their heads shaven to show that they were no longer interested in this world, and hid themselves in the mountains to spend the rest of their lives there, praying only for happiness in a future existence.

Kūkai's approach to Buddhism stood poles apart from theirs, and the new Buddhism Kūkai eventually established—Shingon Esoteric Buddhism*— had nothing to do with any such stereotypical Buddhist pessimism. In fact, this sheer absence of pessimism was what differentiated Kūkai's Buddhism from the traditional Buddhism of Sakyamuni.[5] According to that new Buddhism, men and women still in the flesh are able to attain Buddhahood, or rather because they are indeed in the flesh, they are able to attain Buddhahood and able to live on in that newly-acquired blessedness. This is just one of the many evidences to show that Kūkai was not a pessimist. At least what made him run away from the university to be a Buddhist monk was not pessimism by any means. He would have laughed at such pessimists.

When a person of extraordinary talent still remains unaware of his own gift, while being left in a situation extremely unfavorable to its development, he may be forced into eccentric conduct by a sudden impulse almost independent of his own intention, or he may throw himself blindly into a field least expected even by himself, as is often reported in biographies of geniuses. But to my mind, this also was not the case with Kūkai, for what had tormented him was none other than intellectual agony, and his breaking away from the university might have been taken as a mere change of academic courses—from Chinese Classics to Philosophy—even though he had to leave the university because it failed to offer him a Philosophy Course. His intellectual agony was such that he had to relieve himself by giving utterance to it, that is, by writing his first literary work, *The Indications of the Three Teachings*, and when he reached the conclusion that Buddhism is better than Taoism[6] which is better than Confucianism, he never hesitated

28

to turn to the best of the three.

"The comparison of the three teachings" was a very popular theme of discussion among intellectuals not only in China but also in Japan, and it had often been selected as a composition theme for those who sat for the higher civil service examination. But no one in China or in Japan had ever published his thoughts about it in a form of drama as Kūkai did. Then it must have attracted great attention in intellectual circles.

As for that sumptuous style or the Six-Dynasties style which he adopted in creating that work, it seems to me to be perfectly congenial to his peculiarly cheerful disposition. His aesthetics, lying in the warmth and brightness of the world shining with cinnabar and copper, gold and silver, was totally alien to what is popularly known as *wabi* or *sabi*—a Japanese aesthetic concept of subdued beauty in rusticity or resignation which began to be appreciated in the Muromachi Period (1336–1573).

Another thing that makes this work sumptuous as well as remarkable was the large number of quotations from a variety of sources—about two hundred classics and treatises, Chinese and Japanese, that he had already digested. What enabled him to read so extensively will be found in a later chapter.

IV. Beggar Boy

THERE are many references to sexual passion in *The Indications of the Three Teachings*. The shock Kūkai felt when he was first aware of his becoming a man—when a strange tide began to flood his body—would have been greater than we modern people can possibly imagine. Judging from the vastness and flexibility of the thought he later unfolded, Kūkai as a young man could not have been a petty stoic moralist. For one thing, the desire he was born with was not mediocre, as is often the case with a man of unusual talent. For another thing, the society he lived in had never known such stoicism as was later cultivated in the warriors' class of the Edo Period (1603–1867). In fact, it was only in Nara, the former imperial capital, that there arose a notion that sexuality should be controlled by a moral code.

Students living in the university dormitory had little opportunity to meet women, but other students whose fathers were still resident in Nara must have seen much of women as they had many women servants at home. Naturally, "having a baby" was among the daily topics of their conversation, providing ample knowledge of sex for boarding students like Kūkai. There were bawdy houses to visit, too. How could Kūkai, a youth unusually curious about the inscrutability of human existence as well as the mysteries of the universe, suppress his urge to go to one of those brothels to discover the facts of life? In the permissive society he lived in, he would have been free to enjoy the company of a woman even though he had to suffer a terrible sense of disintegration as if falling into a bottomless well. But Kūkai as the thinker he later became did not take that dark side of sexual intercourse as an emblem of mutability or the vanity of life as many other Buddhist thinkers did; he just embraced both sides of it as truthful, reasoning that it can be the universal truth because both are dependent upon one another, and the converse is also true; the delicate mechanism of the secret of the universe can be found in such a union of absolute antitheses. This notion, it seems to me, can be traced back to his own personal experience he had in his youthful days.

However great a thinker he might become later, the eighteen-year-old Kūkai as observed by others around him would have been like any other boy of his time. As a student, he was by far the best in his class, as all of his teachers admitted, but they would be dishonest if they asserted that they had seen in him what he would be in the future. Generally speaking, most young men are of the same type and no one can anticipate how a certain young man will develop into something out of ordinary.

Kūkai's character, as found in later years, was by no means eccentric or offensive. He was good at reading another's mind or physiognomy to find out what the other was really thinking. He showed a good understanding of how the world works, and was able to compromise with it, too. Such a sensible attitude and companionable personality seemed quite likely to bring him at least the rank and position Saeki no Ima-Emishi had attained. A genius is often possessed by insanity or eccentricity, but as far as Kūkai was concerned, he was every inch a normal young man and free from any tendency to drop out of the world. What he said about himself in those years, therefore, was also quite unexceptional: "I worked very hard."

Though outwardly conventional, Kūkai was certainly different from other youths at least in one point: when confronted by sexual desire, troublesome yet sweet—the natural power which is life itself, he simply observed it coolly and objectively. According to his observation, one's sexual desire or libido was to be treated as something inseparable from one's entire being, and this led to the fact that one would be blamed if it hurt others; if it urged one to commit adultery and even homicide, as it sometimes does, one would be executed for it. On the other hand, Kūkai noticed another fact that sexual desire is universality itself: in whatever person it is manifested, there is no difference. It is common to all humanity. Then why should it not be treated, in a more frank manner, as something genuinely objective that can be observed by everyone? This question, that no one has yet answered effectively, was firmly planted in his mind, constantly fueling his mental torment.

He would have taken an interest in appetite, that is akin to sexual desire. The university offered a special course in medical science, and students in other courses were expected to read some books on medical science as part of their study of the Chinese classics. Their contents, largely based on Taoism, concentrated on symptomatic treatment, but at least they offered some information about the five viscera and the six entrails. Kūkai would have learned that the stomach, for instance, is another example of universality since its shape, function and position are exactly the same in everyone. If someone like the supreme god of Taoism were to come into the classroom and work magic to replace, in a moment, Kūkai's stomach with that of a classmate he was talking to, they would be carrying on their conversation as if nothing had happened. This being the case with all the other viscera and entrails, and quite probably with muscles, bones, skin, what is the use of differentiating one's own being from others'? Is it not a mere human illusion to believe in such difference? Or is it nothing but a foolish convention in human society? A petty make-believe, upon which Confucianism was founded?

Once Zilu, a disciple of Confucius, asked his master: "What is death?" Confucius typically evaded his question, saying: "I cannot yet tell what life is. How can I tell what death is?" Confucius, it seemed to Kūkai, ignored these matters essential to human existence with utmost care and deliberation as if otherwise all his teaching would cease to exist.

"What is death?"

Kūkai also asked himself that question. Only one year before he became a university student, Saeki no Ima-Emishi died. The death of the person favored by all the tennōs he served was mourned with great magnificence. But was his life a happy one? He, a model official, had been working hard till his backbone had grown painfully bent. But had he really been reconciled to his life, which was eventually rewarded with the third court rank? Probably not, seeing that the old man built a beautiful Buddhist temple, trying to entrust his soul to Buddhism; but as he was unable to tell what life was and what would become of him after his death, the Confucian remained as unsatisfied as before. This might have led Kūkai to the following question and answer:

"What is the use of Confucianism? Is it not just an ancient popular belief? If so, it would be totally incapable of unravelling the mystery of life, to say nothing of revealing the truth of the universe."

Apparently he had taken too much interest in life and death—or in Buddhism or Indian thought that deals with the workings of the universe—to remain happy and contented with the Confucian society in which he lived. He himself had been aware of this long before he ran away or kept away from the university in the year or in the year following his matriculation.

* * *

One of the characters who appear in *The Indications of the Three Teachings* is Prince Shitsuga (Leech Tusk). He is such a lascivious person that Kūkai says he will beat even Deng Tuzi, a majordomo of King Xiang in the Land of Chu of ancient China, who earned the reputation of being a great sensualist because he had as many as five children by the very ugly woman he took as his wife:

> Prince Shitsuga is so lustful that he cannot see a woman—even a most ungainly woman with dishevelled hair—without feeling desire for her.

Prince Shitsuga is also a university student. But he is always indulging himself in hunting and gambling, wine and women. In class, he is always yawning or nodding in a back seat. In a brothel, this real slave of sexual passion behaves like a monkey in rut, thus disgracing his family name as well as his own personal honor, to the immense distress of his father, Lord Tokaku (Hare Horn). In the opening scene, Lord Tokaku talks to a great Confucian scholar, Kimō (Tortoise Hair),[1] asking him to give a severe admonishment to his prodigal son Shitsuga who has already gone beyond his control.

But if sexual desire is shared by everyone, Kūkai wonders, why must Prince Shitsuga put responsibility for its manifestation upon himself alone? Kūkai would have felt even more puzzled when he found the same desire uncoiling in himself, too. What does it mean that every one of us is possessed of the same desire that, if viewed from the Confucian standpoint, has driven Prince Shitsuga out of his senses? Even Kimō, a great Confucian scholar with an awe-inspiring appearance, obviously modeled after Uncle Ōtari, cannot give any answer to these questions even though "he had completed his scholarship by thoroughly digesting the Nine Chinese Classics[2] and the Three Great Books of History[3] and by perfectly memorizing *The Memoirs of the Three Emperors*[4] and *The Eight Signs of Divination*."

Kimō shows some sympathy with the prince, admitting that very few men are able to behave like Zhan Li, a misogynist who appears in *The Chronicle of Confucius' Sayings and Doings*: "Zhan Li is an exception. Usually a man cannot help longing for a woman" and "as long as a man is a man he cannot sleep alone." Then he offers a solution: "Work hard and make yourself a good official. Then you will sooner or later be made a high-ranking official who is able to take any beauty as his wife. Even Shun, a sacred being in the Confucian world, took two daughters of Yao[5] as his wives; in fact, a high official will be able to satisfy almost all his wishes in life."

In the next scene, the prince is approached by a Taoist hermit, Kyobu (Vacuous). He talks about how one should control oneself if one wishes to live in celestial happiness while enjoying perpetual youth and longevity. He even suggests something inadmissible to the innocent youth, saying "a beautiful woman is a hatchet that will cut off a man's life," and "a man must not let sperm escape from his body."

In the final scene, there appears a young wandering monk just like the one Kūkai became himself after running away from the university. The monk calls himself Kamei Kotsuji (One who has Temporarily Named himself Beggar Boy). His miserable appearance would surely laughed at even by any regular beggar: wearing paper clothes, carrying a roll of cogongrass mat under his arm and a chair on his back, he walks in straw sandals, his left elbow dangling a cord with a wooden mendicant bowl tied at the end, the right hand holding a rosary as humble as a horse's crupper-loop; his close-cropped head looks like an inverted copper bowl; his face as pale as an earthen pot shows distinct signs of malnutrition.

"What happened? There's not a hair on your head!" Kyobu, the Taoist, exclaims at the strange appearance of the beggar boy. Not having seen a Buddhist monk before, he just takes him as an alien and goes on asking:

"Where are you from? Who are your parents? Who is your mentor?"

Beggar Boy as Kūkai's persona is curiously free from any stereotyped lamentation, sentimentalism or narcissism such as might be expected from anyone who has recently left the world behind, kicking off all the worldly honors promised him. In fact, Beggar Boy is so high-spirited that he feels like stamping his feet in time to a happy song he sings to demonstrate his jubilation, all the while giving an account of himself to the Confucian and the Taoist who are simply curious about his identity. This immense cheerfulness Kūkai displays here can be attributed to the sunny temperament he was born with, but it also comes from his own interpretation of Buddhism, which is radiantly joyful.

"Is there any sense in asking me who my parents are?" Beggar Boy, thus parrying the Taoist's question, begins to unfold a Buddhist concept of what human existence is:

"You and I, and all other human beings have no home of our own wherever we may go. It will be an illusion if we think we have one. Do you know how our souls revolve round the Six Worlds—hell, starvation, animality, carnage, humanity and heaven? We are destined to move from one world to another. There is no permanence in one particular world. So at one time I find myself in heaven, at another time in hell."

"Hō!"

Completely aghast, the Confucian and the Taoist stare at the strange boy, who, laughing loudly, goes on saying in a mischievous vein:

"You'd like to know who I am? Well, sometimes I become your wife, at other times your father or mother."

"You... my wife?"

Horrified at the strange vision presented by the boy, the Taoist and the Confucian come closer together and ask in a trembling voice:

"What kind of thought is this? Who is your mentor?"

"Sometimes a demon is my mentor, sometimes I make friends with a pagan ascetic I may regard as intolerable at other times. A bird can be my father, a beast my wife. These things are exactly what are happening to you, too. Mister Confucian, you may advocate the creed of 'Elders first' upon which to build a superficial thought system. But it is an illusion or nonsense because it is unable to exist. Time has no beginning nor ending. Since times without beginning, you and I and all others have been constantly transmigrating, as time and everything in the universe are rolling round and round the endless circuit of the Six Worlds. So you see, it doesn't make any sense to ask where I come from or who my parents are."

What Kūkai was then talking about was the basic concept of the universe in Indian thought. Or it was an oral interpretation of the everchanging world of the mandala[6] he had already grasped even before the thought system of the mandala itself had yet been introduced into Japan.

What if one should believe in this view of the universe? One will find historical time meaningless and all historical facts nonsense. The emperor will cease to be majestic, much less so his government officials who are no more than tools however high they may be placed in the hierarchy of his court. Once reduced to transmigrators, they will all lose their identities, just rambling round and round the Six Worlds along with beggars, fishes, insects, vapor, trees, minerals and so on; and all the value systems that have ever existed in human societies will vanish in a moment.

But Kūkai, who knows how to adjust himself to the level of others, just makes mention of where he comes from:

"I was born and brought up on an island neatly fringed with pearly seaweed. My home overlooking a bay is comfortably shaded by ancient camphor trees... and I have seen two dozen springs and autumns."

The last mentioned was obviously what he added in the final version he made at twenty-four.

Then Beggar Boy returns to his favorite theme on Indian thought. The Indian people were extremely strong in abstract thinking, but when they explained their thought to others, they used not only logic but also poetic dramaturgy or metaphor, just as Beggar Boy did in answering the Taoist's question: "What makes you carry so many things with you?"

"I have been traveling by long stages since I received an invitation from the Emperor Buddha. He is now in Nirvana (the Buddhist paradise). But when he was about to enter the Nirvana, he declared to his disciples who gathered around him that Maitreya should be his successor, and gave him his own seal to consolidate his declaration. Then he beckoned his ministers, such as Manjusri and Mahakasyapa, and ordered that they should go out to every corner of the world, propagating his thought while spreading the news that Maitreya, his successor, had come to the throne."

Sakyamuni was in actual existence on this earth. But Maitreya is an imaginary being. Viewed from the standpoint of Confucian realism, Maitreya's presence itself is to be regarded as nonsense. But to Kūkai living and thinking in the multi-dimentional world of Indian thought, nothing could be more real than this.

The idea of Maitreya as the future Buddha who would come down to save the world was first propounded in *The Sutra on Maitreya's Ascent to the Tusita Heaven* that appeared around 100B.C. when Mahayana Buddhism[7] came into being in India:

> 5,670,000 years after Sakya's death, Maitreya will be born on this earth to save firstly 9,600,000 people, secondly 9,400,000, lastly 9,200,000.

But 5,670,000 years are too long for anyone to wait. Then the Indian imagination of great ingenuity invented a solution: "It would be more recommendable for people to go straight to Maitreya's Land than just to go round and round the Six Worlds, waiting for Maitreya's arrival here."

Now that such a solution is presented, anyone can leave at any moment for the Tusita Heaven or Maitreya's Land so that one can bask in his blessed company there, though not in this lifetime but in the near future—after one's death—when one starts a new life in the Tusita Heaven.

As to what the Tusita Heaven is like, it is depicted as a place flooded with rotating light whose rhythmical radiance regularly reveals the beautiful vision of a forty-nine-storied palace; Maitreya, living in his own palace that stands at the center of that heaven, is always offering words of wisdom; the climate is neither cold nor hot; the inhabitants are all wise and virtuous; even babies are born both physically and mentally as developed as eight-year-olds on this earth; food and clothing are provided all their lives which will last 84,000 years without being ruined by senility; men and women are coming and going in a leisurely manner; some couples are seen shaking hands, which is how they make love.

Kūkai, who wishes to be born in that heaven, makes Beggar Boy declare:

"Viewed from any angle, this earth is not dependable at all. True the Himalayas look as high as the Milky Way, but on the last day on earth they will be burnt to ashes. True, the oceans are spacious, but they will run dry till every drop will vanish. This land, though stretching as far as the eye can reach, will melt till it merges into nothingness. So the one and only sensible way for us to take will be to travel to Maitreya's Land to find refuge there."

By "traveling to Maitreya's Land" he would have meant "living up to the truth of the universe" or "living in the metaphysical world of truth." Beggar Boy goes on:

"So as soon as I received the news dispatched by the Emperor Sakyamuni, I fitted myself out for the journey; I fed my horse, oiled my carriage, and left home for good to travel day and night. But a passage to Maitreya's Land, I soon found, is by no means easy to follow. It is very steep and multi-forked; there is no guide or sign post to be seen around. It was not long before my carriage was broken, my horse gone. That is why I am carrying all these things myself. As for food, I have to beg at people's doors, as I am doing now."

The Confucian and the Taoist, now feeling rather small before this strange boy, bow low and say in a respectful tone:

"You are a brave one, indeed, to undertake such a special journey...."

"Thank you." The beggar says calmly.

* * *

But what was it like being a beggar in the actual society in which he lived? A new political structure brought into being by the Taika Reform (645) had turned the whole land and all the people in this country into the property of the tennō, and those who were made into allotment farmers had to pay three kinds of tax: land tax, labour tax and produce tax. Throughout the Nara Period (710–784), this system was being enforced but without success, because more and more allotment farmers who could no longer bear the heavy burden of taxes chose to run away from their lands and turned themselves into amateur Buddhist practitioners,[8] leading an easy life usually in the mountains. As for food, they occasionally came down to nearby villages to beg. What if these fugitive farmers kept increasing? It would be a great threat to the political structure founded solely on the land-allotment system. Naturally the government had been eager to check this illegality, issuing frequent orders that no one should arbitrarily make oneself a Buddhist practitioner, while encouraging people to look down upon those who had gone against this rule as abominable.[9]

Beggar Boy in this drama was obviously one of those offenders. That was probably why Kūkai simply ignored where Beggar Boy stood in the actual society of Japan and just made him declare that he was on his way to the Tusita Heaven in obedience to an Imperial command. This youthful courage is admirable, but it is pathetic when viewed in a different light.

*   *   *

Ōtari, who had been unfailingly ready to help his nephew in every way possible, must have been deeply shocked and disappointed when Kūkai expressed his wish to leave the university for good and make himself such a beggar-like Buddhist monk. Naturally he tried hard to dissuade him, using all his erudition and force of persuasion, whose power was such that Kūkai had to counterattack it by writing a strong dramatic work, *The Indications Given to the Deaf and the Dumb* (one volume), whose final version was *The Indications of the Three Teachings* (three volumes). Seeing that the date given in the preface to the former was December 1, 797, when Kūkai was twenty-four, and that the age limit for taking the higher civil service examination was also twenty-four, this must have been the very final opportunity for him to make clear that he would go on pursuing Buddhism, instead of starting an official career after passing the higher civil service examination, as was eagerly expected by his uncle Ōtari and many of his clansmen and relatives.

Ōtari, on reading that work, would have been greatly dismayed to find all the admonitions and arguments he had given him so far had been turned into the speech of Kimō, the Confucian, only to be vigorously refuted by Beggar Boy, who at the end of the drama triumphantly declares the righteousness of his own choice of Buddhism. With all his efforts thus completely frustrated, Ōtari would have felt too exhausted to struggle any further. But at least he had to say, as is mentioned in the preface to *The Indications of the Three Teachings*: "Don't you think it is disloyal of you to disavow all the favours you have received from the state as a university student?" and "Once you have dropped out of this society, how could you perform your duty toward society? How could you put into practice those Confucian virtues of benevolence, righteousness, decorum, wisdom and fidelity?"

Trying to answer these questions, Kūkai puts forth some arguments, but they are more or less lacking in the high-spirited confidence that usually marks his pronouncements. Later on, when he returned to society as the supreme master of Esoteric Buddhism, he was extremely mindful of the welfare of the state, demonstrating the power of his religion in ensuring the security of the state, while launching one social initiative after the other. Naturally it was his sense of mission that drove him into such activities. But still I doubt that he was completely free from a guilty conscience at having arbitrarily rejected "the favours he had received from the state."

V. The Morning Star Flew into His Mouth

A
CCORDING to *The Indications of the Three Teachings*, which is practically the only material one can turn to in pursuing Kūkai in his youth, Kūkai at nineteen happened to meet a monk who, though unidentified, tuned out to be the first guide he met on his way to the Tusita Heaven.

Kūkai was a frequent visitor to Daian-ji, one of the largest temples in Nara, as he was able to meet there many scholar priests, including those who had once studied in Chang'an, China. Daian-ji was also where the Chinese priest Jianzhen[1] and the Indian priest Bodhisena[2] used to live. That was probably why one felt there as if one were somewhere in Chang'an or in India. What was more, Daian-ji was considered to be a small-scale reproduction of one of the palaces in the Tusita Heaven, as the temple legend goes:

> Jatavanavihara Monastery[3] in India was modelled after a palace in the Tusita Heaven; Ximing-si temple* in China is modelled after that Indian monastery; Daian-ji in this country is modelled after that Chinese temple.

This meant that entering the precinct of Daian-ji, beautifully laid out with magnificent buildings—a pair of pagodas, the main hall, the lecture hall, the dining hall, the library hall, the belfry and so on—was really like stepping into the Indian world full of brilliant symbols, as Kūkai must have been keenly aware.

Chinese civilization that set a high value on practical matters had no use for the truth of the universe or for the profound mystery of life. The Chinese who valued history, had always attached great importance to the when and the where, the who and the what. Indian civilization presented a perfect antithesis to this, for what occupied the Indian mind was a revolving mechanism of abstract thought. Instead of asking who and when, they simply asked what life was in the truth of the universe, and not until they reduced themselves to an abstract point or a universal being by discarding everything that indicated their identity such as name, race, position in their society and so on, did they begin to think about this favorite theme.

The Indian civilization Kūkai came in contact with at Daian-ji was becoming more and more attractive to him even though as a university student he was acquainted with Chinese civilization. Accommodating these antipodes in himself, what would become of his identity? Torn in two? In fact, at Cape Muroto in Shikoku, he was soon to have a most extraordinary experience, in which he felt as if he had been rent asunder.

Who could be the monk Kūkai happened to meet? Some say he was Gonzō, a great authority on the Three Treatises* who lived at Daian-ji. Others say that he was one of those scholar-ascetics, ordained or not, who divided their time between study at temples and asceticism in the mountains, just as Kūkai did in his twenties. It does not matter who he was or what he was, but to my mind, someone of the latter type seems more easily associable with Kūkai at this stage in his life.

"Friend," said the monk, "if you really have such an interest in Buddhism, let me tell you something that will be of great help to you."

What he imparted to Kūkai then was an arcane technique for memorizing whatever he read in "tens of thousands of Buddhist scriptures." That technique, though originated in India, had nothing to do with Sakyamuni's Buddhism, as it was part of Mantrayana, a new religion that had started in a climate quite different from that of Sakyamuni's Buddhism. Fragments of that new religion, which had already been introduced into Tang China, were gradually spreading to Japan. In years to come, Kūkai himself was to sail over to China to bring back the whole body of the new religion, to organize it into a newer religion framed by a perfect logic of his own invention, and to call it Shingon (Mantra) Esoteric Buddhism.

The fragment of Mantrayana Kūkai as a young man was initiated into by that monk was a sort of mnemonic called "mantra-reciting for invoking Akasagarbha,"[4] which required reciting Akasagarbha's mantra one million times in a certain place within a certain period of time. While practicing this ascetic discipline again and again, a certain stratum dormant in human consciousness would awaken and begin to produce a mystical illumination by which one would be able to memorize whatever one reads in Buddhist scriptures. Mantra is the language, not of human beings but of theoretical beings or dharmakaya Buddhas[5] as immanent intellectuals.

The bodhisattva named Akasagarbha is a symbol of all the phenomena in the universe and it will present itself before anyone who marvels at the miraculous profundity of any of those phenomena. For example, such a gracious natural function as gentle rain that helps vegetation grow is a Bodhisattva itself, and as soon as it is recognized and appreciated as such, Akasagarbha that fills the universe will readily be recognized. The essence of nature is pure and incorruptible, and when it works for the benefit of human beings, it will unfailingly provide them with a source of happiness and wisdom.

"Let us call it Akasagarbha (the great void that embraces all)," said those who started Mantrayana in India. They could not bring themselves to believe in Sakyamuni's Buddhism, because what he advocated—emancipation from earthly desires—seemed to diminish the spirit to the point of death. They preferred to take a positive view of life because all living things must go on living as they do, so long as they are alive. Now they simply chose to admire nature and marvel at every blessing and benefit they received from nature. They extolled their own life, too, since it is part of nature. Then, going a step further, they assumed that such great admirers of nature as they were should receive a special favor from nature, and that Akasagarbha as the essence of nature would be immensely generous in rewarding those who invoked it in a proper manner.

Kūkai must have felt a tremor of happiness when he learned Akasagarbha's mantra and intoned it to himself: "*Namo akasa-garbhaya, Om arika mari muri svaha*...so this is how the essence of nature expresses its essence...."

To a successful invoker, the mantra-reciting can be a magical force that enables him to communicate with the universe. Because of this mysterious function it offers, Kūkai must have perceived in it science—what might be called absolute science. A great amount of knowledge of Buddhism he acquired at the library hall of Daian-ji had given him a great pleasure. But knowledge alone could not satisfy him; there was something lacking, he thought. Then in this mantra-reciting for invoking Akasagarbha, he perceived what we call natural science that satisfies the utilitarian in humanity: if only one finds out the law of nature and learns how to control it, one will be able to receive as much benefit as one likes from nature as the source of all wisdom.

Modern people who have approached science in a way different from Kūkai's may find it easy to laugh at such notions. But which type of science can be said to be authentic, the one whose function Kūkai perceived in the fragment of Mantrayana, or the other that modern people believe they know? If Akasagarbha as the essence of nature were to be the judge, which of the two would stand the test? No human being as a mere part of nature would be qualified to answer this question.

"Find a right place," said the monk to Kūkai. In order to invoke Akasagarbha by reciting its mantra, one must first find a right place where the will of the universe is most likely to descend.

"Well, what about Mt. Katsuragi in Yamato Province?"

Kūkai, a good mountaineer, might have asked that with a tinge of impertinence. Mt. Katsuragi, opened by En no Ozunu,[6] a mountaineering ascetic who preceded Kūkai by a century or so, had been known for its readiness to provide ascetics with inspiration.

"I don't know. It's up to yourself to find out," said the monk, a real expert in such matters.

"If I find it myself...." muttered Kūkai to himself, feeling a surge of excitement rising in himself, "I might be able to transcend humanity and acquire divinity!"[7]

This excitement was to endure throughout the ensuing years of his youth, keeping him active and happy even in the midst of difficulties.

Trying to "find a right place," Kūkai climbed one mountain after another in and around the central provinces, but was unable to get any stimulating response, so he decided to try mountains in Shikoku, his native island. It was a sunny island adorned with the camphor trees he liked so much. It was never very cold even in winter, owing to the Japan Current that flows off its southern and eastern coasts. Such a mild climate may have suited his spiritual temperature. Or could this choice be just a reflection of his endearing disposition as well as of his good upbringing? In such a serious situation as Kūkai was then placed, some might have chosen to go north, seeking for the severe forms of nature as found on Mt. Tateyama in Ettchū Province or on Mt. Haguro in Dewa Province; both had already been known as mysterious abodes of divine spirits. But Kūkai was probably the last person to drag a solitary shadow in scenery so drained of color[8] as we find in winter in the north, because pathetic sensibility of that kind was quite alien to his mentality. This was especially true, considering that what he was pursuing was not Sakyamuni's Buddhism that aims at emancipation from earthly desires, but Mantrayana or what was later known as Esoteric Buddhism that takes a positive view of life exactly as it is.

On hearing where Kūkai had eventually gone, the monk would have laughed an affectionate laugh, saying: "Ha! So he has gone to Shikoku! Clever lad!"

By way of Awaji Island lying like a stepping stone to Awa, the easternmost province of Shikoku, Kūkai entered his home island through the port of Muya. As for the boat, he would have hired one from local fishermen.

Now Kūkai was traveling down Awa Province, asking the locals: "Isn't there any mountain known for its mysterious aura?" It was not long before he was informed of Mt. Ōtaki, only about 600 meters above sea level, not very far from human habitation even in those days, as it is no more than eleven kilometers west of present-day Anan City. Experienced mountain ascetics would have found it mediocre. But to Kūkai it turned out to be a memorable mountain and seeing that he liked mentioning it even in his closing years, it was probably where he succeeded for the first time in mantra-reciting for invoking Akasagarbha, thus marking the start of his career as an ascetic of Mantrayana. But something much more significant was awaiting him at Cape Muroto in the neighboring province of Tosa.

"I'd like to go to Cape Muroto in Tosa Province. Am I on the right path?"

Kūkai asked the villagers he met at the foot of Mt. Ōtaki he was leaving behind. Some must have turned pale at the mere thought of going to Cape

Muroto, and tried hard to dissuade him, repeating how dangerous it was: "It is a land of ogres, no fit place for any human being."

The chain of the Shikoku Mountains lies east and west across the island, while its W-shaped coastline in the south is silhouetted against an edge of the Pacific Ocean, with its eastern V forming Cape Muroto. The cape bears a huge, triangular cone covered with countless peaks huddling together, looking like a monstrous multi-horned roll-shell, the two sides of which drop sheer into the ocean below, to terrifying effect. Certainly it does not look like a place for any human being to live in or travel to. What was more, the interior of Shikoku Island was so mountainous that the inhabitants of even neighboring provinces like Awa and Tosa used to have no means of access to each other.

"How about going along the beach?"

But the unanimous answer he received was: "Only if you were a bird." The coast, consisting of cliffs and reefs for the most part, was constantly being pounded by huge waves of the ocean. Then the only access available would be a mountain route, but the problem was that most ravines ran east and west, preventing the southward traveler from going along the ravines. All he could do then would be to pick his way through the thick forests on the ridges, cutting off creepers with a sickle, branches with an axe, sometimes taking more than a day to go only one hundred meters or so. Drinking water must be very hard to obtain.

As for Cape Muroto itself, a scholar in the village would have described how the edge of the V-shaped highland, worn by weather and waves, formed itself into precipices hanging over the roaring ocean: "That's where the land ends. Seas and skies are all that you have before your eyes. That's why it is called Hotsu-no-Misaki or End Point."

"End Point! Where the land ends?"

Kūkai exclaimed. Wasn't it the very place he had been looking for? The youth whose poetic sentiment was always ready to soar into a metaphysical world must have taken it as an entrance to heaven.

*　　*　　*

Mt. Ōtaki overlooks many islands and complicated coastlines that include a couple of promontories at the junction of which lies a village named Tsubaki (Camellia). It is while crossing this village that southward travelers suddenly feel, even in winter, that they are entering a subtropical region.

"Isn't it fun to see such an outlandish place as this?" said my driver, Mr. Miyamoto, whose taxi I had picked up in downtown Tokushima (the capital city of Tokushima Prefecture or what used to be Awa Province) to follow the trail of Kūkai as far as Cape Muroto. Mr. Miyamoto in his sixties told me that he had had no accident since he started driving his own taxi in 1934, and that together with his pilgrim passengers he had made many a circuit of the Shikoku Pilgrimage[9] route. He still keeps a bell and a pair of straw sandals so that he can accompany his pilgrim customers to some of the local temples, as he happily does several times a month.

After passing the village, he stopped and took off his sweater. I soon found that the mountain pass we were driving along was a doorway to a land of warmer climate. For the first time I realized how the warm current that runs in the offing affects the temperature of the land. Going through the forests of camellias and camphor trees that stood along the pass, I thought about Kūkai and felt that no personality could be better compared to a warm current than Kūkai's.

By and by, my taxi ascended a foggy mountain, then rushed out onto a bay only to run up into another mountain. After following several such zigzag routes between seashore and mountain, probably just as Kūkai did, we reached Hiwasa Bay with a modest sand bank flanked by mountains and cliffs. The narrow strip of land lying between sandbank and mountains was crowded with houses, approximately one thousand in number. Even in Kūkai's days, several sedge-roofed huts would have been seen in this neighborhood, and streaks of smoke from salt-burning on the seaside. An islet that lies just at a stone's throw from the edge of the beach looked picturesque, capped with a clump of black pines with some of their branches broken off by the wind. The surf sounded very wild, but human habitation from time immemorial had given the scenery a tamed look, as Kūkai must have noticed, too, feeling every pore of his body comfortably relaxed.

"To my mind, Hiwasa was the last village O-Daishi-san had seen on his way to Cape Muroto," said Mr. Miyamoto, calling Kūkai O-Daishi-san as many local people do in Shikoku. Probably he was right, seeing that there is no temple on the pilgrimage route between Yakuō-ji (the 23rd temple on the Shikoku Pilgrimage) in Hiwasa of Awa Province and Hotsumisaki-ji (the 24th temple) on Cape Muroto in Tosa Province. Before reaching Muroto, Kūkai might have had to descend to other inlets to look for food. But the extremely sparse population in them could hardly have produced the comforts of decent human habitation.

When I visited Yakuō-ji, a mountain temple overlooking Hiwasa Bay, it happened to be a fête day especially for men and women who had reached their "critical ages": forty-two and sixty for men and nineteen and thirty-three for women. The stone steps that led to the main hall and the pagoda above were being covered with one-*yen* coins dropped by those men and women. I was told that they had brought with them as many coins as their age so that they could drop one on each step of their way, thus fulfilling their wish to drop as many evils as they had picked up in their life so far. This strange sight being endlessly unfolded before my eyes set me wondering what it is in Kūkai that has attracted so many men and women unthinkingly to indulge in such superstitious conduct, after he has been dead for nearly twelve centuries.[10] But unable to find any answer, I felt disturbed as if my own image of Kūkai—Japan's most genuine metaphysical thinker who succeeded in creating a huge system of thought of watertight perfection—were about to be intensely disfigured in the turbulent air current just crossing the wintry sky.

My map shows that it is only sixty kilometers or so from Hiwasa to Hotsu-no-Misaki (End Point) at the tip of Cape Muroto. But I think Kūkai took more than twenty days to cover that distance, as he had to hack a path with axe and sickle. Before leaving Hiwasa, he must have equipped himself with as much food (mainly dried fish) as he could carry on his back. Food was scarce in the mountains, where all he could find were nuts, small fruits and some kinds of wild grasses. This made him come down from time to time to replenish his provisions at various accessible beaches, even if it might have taken him days and nights to reach them.

A stretch of coastline beyond Mugi is fringed with small inlets that bring travelers to Yasaka Yahama (Eight-passes and Eight-beaches), as they are named by the locals. Even today these beaches are almost deserted probably owing to the forbidding view of the incessantly fluctuating dreary ocean tide. Was it on such a solitary beach that Kūkai came down to collect shellfish and seaweed?

In one of those mountains that rose along that coastline, there was a fishermen's village named Sabase (Mackerel Current).

"I had a hard time in Sabase."

Kūkai in his later years happened to tell someone about what he once experienced there, thus giving rise to a famous legend that goes as follows:

> One day Kūkai saw a fisherman coming along the path leading his horse laden with salted mackerel. As he had been feeling very hungry, Kūkai begged him for just one of his fish. But the man who took him as a good-for-nothing beggar monk just cursed him and went on his way. But before going far, his horse suddenly fell on its side and began to wriggle as if about to die. The man, realizing that this was a punishment inflicted upon him for what he had done to that traveling monk, ran back to catch up with him, apologized for his unkindness and offered him a mackerel. It was not long before he saw the horse rise to its feet and begin to walk again as if nothing had happened.

This legend may suggest that Kūkai came down to the seashore from time to time to obtain food. But what did he do when all the coastlines that came into his view consisted of sheer precipices, like the ones that stretch twenty-five kilometers between No'ne to the tip of Cape Muroto? Even today when we can drive safely along the coastal highway, the sight of endless cliffs, thunderously washed and drenched in clouds of spray, is frightening indeed, as if they were signposts to the ends of the earth. Then Kūkai, confined to the depths of the mountains for several days and nights on end, must have been suffering terrible hunger.

Another kind of torment he had to face in the mountain especially at night would have been encounters with numberless spirits: rock spirits towered over him all of a sudden; a tree spirit with burning eyes was about to seize him as he glimpsed it over his shoulder; a peak rose out of darkness and spread its black wings to soar into the sky; ravines and glens uttered incessant cries with their jaws wide open; spirits of dead men and women sprang from the ground to snatch him by the collar. To Kūkai, they were not mere fantasies but widely-acknowledged realities or members of Japanese society.

To calm down these spirits, the Japanese had developed some Shintōist rituals, but they were not very efficacious. Then in the middle of the sixth century Buddhism arrived in Japan soon to be accepted on a national scale, as it was considered to be a new procedure to take the place of the old ritualism of Shintō. Orthodox thinkers of Indian civilization would have been astonished if they had seen the fruit of their thinking being treated in Japan as if it were a sort of cure-all. Sakyamuni was so strict about this matter that he forbade his disciples to practice magical rituals even at people's request. Sakyamuni, a firm believer in the reasoning power of human beings, employed his reason in assimilating himself with the universe, thus starting a religion of freedom from illusion.

Two centuries had passed since Japan saw the advent of Buddhism[11] equipped with magnificent temples, artistic rituals and exotic deities resplendent with gold. The initial reaction the Japanese showed toward that new importation was undoubtedly utilitarian. By and by, however, their attitude changed as orthodox Buddhism was gradually introduced into Japan[12] to make them realize that Buddhism was not some kind of medicine but freedom from illusion, which could be attained only by immersing themselves in the thought system sustained by tremendous volumes of language. Thus the Japanese intellect slightly matured in the intellectual class, and the six departments of Nara Buddhism—Kegon, Hossō, Sanron, Kusha, Jōjitsu and Ritsu—began to be accommodated in the state temples[13] in Nara. They were certainly helpful to those who wanted to learn the Indian way of thinking, but of no use to those who asked for something more, saying: "So what? What comes next? Doesn't it offer any benefits?"

It was in such circumstances that Kūkai came across what he later called "primitive Mantrayana" as opposed to "genuine Mantrayana" or Esoteric Buddhism. Though primitive, it was remarkably responsive to its invokers. This fact seized Kūkai's attention, proving that Kūkai was a medium as well as a logician, however inconsistent that may sound. The medium in him must have found Confucius' view of the world too plain to be satisfying. But the Confucian culture he had acquired prevented him from becoming a mere medium and inspired him to go straight to Buddhism, that lay embedded in a vast amount of Chinese characters packed in Buddhist scriptures. In the end, the logician-medium Kūkai was to accomplish a new system of his own Mantrayana (genuine Mantrayana), and by that time all those ethnic spirits, either metaphysicized or symbolized, were to be buried deep in that new system.

But the nineteen-year-old Kūkai, wandering around the untrodden parts of Shikoku, was still an ethnic medium fighting against natural spirits, only sustained by what he believed to be the supreme deity in the universe, Akasagarbha. In fact, it was at this period of his life that he fought heroic fights against evil dragons or poisonous serpents and shut them up in caves, as recounted in some of the legends[14] about Kūkai traveling around Shikoku.

When he finally stood on the rock of Hotsu-no-Misaki, he would have felt as if he were on the threshold of heaven. All he saw around was sea and sky, and a tip of the earth—a giant rock, rust-colored and weather-beaten, meagerly planted with stunted trees. It looked like an abstract world where those basic elements of nature alone presented themselves with the utmost purity. No other place could be better than this for the one who intended to clear his mind of earthly thoughts in order to distill the law of the universe. But since the gale was so fierce,[15] as if it were going to demolish the rock-top, he had to retreat into the nearby woods to seek refuge, when he found a couple of caves at an edge of the woods.

Both of the caves were fairly deep. The left one was uninhabitable because of its leaky roof, but the right one with a dry interior seemed to make a perfect place for meditation. Seating himself comfortably at the farthest end, Kūkai must have been very happy, muttering to himself with growing confidence:

"Someone... the will of the universe... is taking care of me."

Even today one can visit that place that remains as it used to be. Its mouth, viewed from inside, looks like a window, from which all that can be seen is sea and sky[16] divided by the horizon, the rest of the world completely deleted by the thick frame of the rock. What would become of his mind if his gaze were restricted, day and night, day and night, to this simple structure of the universe? I am not going to indulge in any vain

51

imaginings about it, but I must mention here the most extraordinary experience he had in that cave—a supernatural event that made Kūkai what he was for the rest of his life. According to *The Memoirs of Our Master*, he told about it as follows:

> One morning, I was meditating in the cave at Cape Muroto, when the morning star[17] I was then gazing at flew into my mouth and I saw before my eyes a figure of Akasagarbha enveloped in his halo.

The same event is mentioned in *The Indications of the Three Teachings*, also in a serious tone. In fact, this searching experience did allow him to enter upon a new stage of his life: the Confucian actualism remaining in him completely shattered, his spirit had been sent out into an abstract world never to return, even if his body still remained in this physical world. The unusual confidence with which the Beggar Boy told the Confucian and the Taoist about his having received an invitation to the Tusita Heaven must have been traced back to this acute experience that worked upon him like radical surgery.

INTERLUDE 1. THE ORIGIN OF ESOTERIC BUDDHISM

O NLY three hours before I began to write this chapter, I was eating at a restaurant in downtown Ōsaka, when I suddenly had the notion that I should go and see a peacock, especially an Indian peacock, the sight of which might be a clue to what ancient India was like.

Soon I was on my way to the nearest zoo. Walking along the street busy with auto traffic, I tried to feel as if I were a peacock-hunter skulking around a jungle in ancient India, carrying a big net with a long handle; he would have had a stoop because his knees were thin and weak; he was not Aryan but aboriginal, maybe Dravidian or Negrito, a humble creature always cowering in his own small world of folklore.

The first peacock I saw in the zoo was what was scientifically called *Pavo muticus*. The plump bird on a swinging perch in a small cage had a busy neck repeating a triple exercise: stretching it to its full length, giving it a good wriggling and telescoping it abruptly into the body. I felt rather uneasy as if I were facing some unidentified creature.

Then I went round to see Indian peacocks (*Pavo cristatus*) kept in a different place, together with many other species of birds. The huge cage whose top was largely open to the sky was spacious enough for them to fly around even in flocks. The Indian peacocks I saw there were also sitting on a high perch. During the day they move around on their stout legs, but towards the evening they fly upon the perch to stay there quiet till the next morning. All of them sitting with back toward me, I was unable to see their lustrous neck of vivid blue peculiar to the Indian peacock, even though I was generously entertained to a gorgeous pageantry of feathery tails, disproportionately voluminous and uncannily colorful as if painted to pander to the taste of magicians.

"*Neo—*"

The loud cry of the peacock, sulky and nasal, resonant and far-reaching, was frighteningly dismal to human beings sparsely inhabiting the jungle—so much so that even peacock hunters might have turned pale. By and by, however, some native tribes, like the Dravidian, began to flatter and worship the bird so that they might share in its magical power. Roughly speaking, this was how Mantrayana was germinated in India.

The peacock is a foul feeder. To sustain its big body, it had to prey on anything that came its way, including venomous snakes and poisonous spiders, to the astonishment of the people. The bird, they thought, was equipped with supernatural power, which they revered as the core of yet another incantation.

As a matter of fact, incantations were indispensable to keep people alive. In other words, they needed innumerable incantations to cope with a wide variety of sufferings from toothache to enemy attack, to say nothing of many epidemic diseases that contaminated a large part of this subcontinent. To those living in that harsh climate, incantations were also part of nature rather than something man-made. According to their belief, the words they used in incantations were not human language, but a language immanent in nature, a kind of esoteric language, the speaker of which would be responded to by the will of nature. In those days when incantations did work, nature and people were not antagonistic to each other, and a human body itself being a microcosm, they thought they were able to fuse into the macrocosm by the medium of incantations.

Men and women die of poison, while the peacock does not mind eating poisonous creatures because it is naturally impervious to poison. This enviable ability, the people thought, might be transferred to them when they were poisoned, that is to say, they might induce the peacock's ability by invoking the bird. This was how the Peacock Incantation as a piece of primitive Mantrayana came into being. The cry of the peacock being incorporated into the words of invocation, the invoker would have sounded like the revered bird, or even more so.

Considering the fact that the Brahmans or the Aryan priestly class also had a large number of incantations of this kind, they must have been really indispensable for survival in ancient India. Only Sakyamuni would not employ them, even though some of his disciples, who were formerly

Brahmans, still made use of them when requested by people. What was it that made Sakyamuni disapprove of incantations? His doctrine? His disciples' making a living as shamans? There is good magic and evil magic; the former is for faith-healing or self-defense, the latter for evil purposes such as putting someone to death. Some say it was only the latter that Sakyamuni forbade, the former being regarded with kindly tolerance.

Sakyamuni's Buddhism did not last long in India. Even if they might live up to his teachings, the majority of people thought, all they could gain was a high level of freedom from pain that was concomitant with life. What seemed even more disappointing or discouraging to them was that attaining that level was so very difficult that very few—probably geniuses only—would be able to achieve their purpose. Naturally many preferred to take a positive view of life. Prompted by this ethos, primitive Mantrayana began to be molded around the core of incantations and made a steady progress until it was sublimated and unified by the Buddhist idea of *sunya*[1] (the idea that there can be no static existence) and eventually developed into what is called purified Mantrayana or Esoteric Buddhism.

It was around 1600 B.C. when the Aryans invaded India on horseback and conquered the aborigines. In order to rule the newly-obtained land, they initiated the caste system, placing themselves higher than the aborigines. On the other hand, their habit of thought which reduced everything to the abstract to an almost paranoiac degree made their civilization a very distinctive one. For instance, in their Sanskrit language there was no such expression as "the peacock does not mind eating poisonous creatures." Instead, they said "the peacock eats poisonous creatures by virtue of its antidotal powers."

Because of this idiosyncratic preference for abstraction, the first thing they did when they took up the Peacock Incantation kept by the aborigines was to abstract the antidotal powers of the bird. Then they pondered over what poison was and came to the conclusion that poison was one and the same whether it was of cobra or of spider or even of evils in the human mind that prevent one from achieving deliverance of one's soul. In the human mind, they thought, there were three kinds: covetousness, anger and delusion. They believed any poison, as long as it was poison, would vanish if

properly processed by the abstracted antidotal function of the abstracted
bird. Now that the antidotal function of this bird was thus sublimated into a
Buddha's function, the bird was no longer a mere bird but a sacred being or
a Buddhist deity. Grand names, such as Maha-Mayuri (Peacock King as
Devil Destroyer), were dedicated to the bird, while the Brahman ascetics
who also revered the bird tried to emulate it, using their supple bodies and
limbs, in order to expiate their sins. How long did it take before the bird was
eventually incorporated into what was later known as purified Mantrayana or
Esoteric Buddhism? One millennium? Or two? Or even three?

Not all people of ancient India were meditators. Many were engaged in
trade with the Mediterranean. This was especially true from the first century
through the sixth or seventh century in the south-western coastal areas on the
Arabian Sea. The main items for export must have been firstly slaves,
secondly diamonds, followed by gold, antimony, marble, cotton fabric,
spices, perfumes, rosin, Indian indigo, ivory and various other goods.
Sakyamuni had disapproved of the pursuit of commercial profit, for he
regarded it as covetousness or one of the three evils that vitiate the human
mind. No wonder only two hundred years after his death his religion lost its
influence in India and suffered changes in quality or was replaced by a new
religion called Mantrayana, especially in the trade ports on the south-west
coast of India. Some diamond dealers may have spoken out in public:
"Sakya's teachings will not do us any good. Rather, it only depresses us."

As is easily imagined, those trade merchants had naturally kept up
innumerable incantations to add to their happiness and prosperity.
On the other hand, the Indian people who had a preference for a grand-
scale idea of the universe began to feel it unbearable to have so many
fragments of incantation left unorganized. At some time during the sixth
century, some local philosophers, obviously prodigious though unidentified,
finally succeeded in putting all those miscellaneous pieces together into a
system according to their magnificent view of the universe. The key to their
success was their invention of Mahavairocana as the incarnation of the truth
of the universe, just as Christianity invented God and made it the core
around which to build up a system of truth. In other words, it occurred to the

Indian philosophers that such an absolute fiction alone was able to impart truth to all fruits of human thinking attracted to it. This led them to deny or transcend Sakyamuni as a human being who actually lived on the earth for a certain period of historical time. Thus purified Mantrayana started when the Indian philosophers declared: "This great system was expounded in mantra (the language of the universe) by Mahavairocana itself for the benefit of human beings."

Of all the fictions we human beings have ever invented, no other could be more perfect than Mahavairocana, which is considered to be the whole of the limitless universe while being concurrently immanent in everything that exists in the universe. Mahavairocana consists of two elements: wisdom and mercy. The philosophers who originated this religion considered the principle of the universe as limitlessly intelligent and boundlessly kind to everybody and everything that exists there. What a sharp contrast they made to Sakyamuni who just perceived in it something cruel and even demonic, considering starvation and the four sufferings everyone must suffer: birth, aging, illness and death! If compared from this point of view alone, Sakyamuni might feel outshone by Mahavairocana.

By and by, the Peacock King as a Devil Destroyer was sublimated into an incarnation of Mahavairocana, and its incantation was reckoned as one of the four greatest incantations because of its meritorious power "to get rid of fears, enemies and all kinds of calamities and difficulties if properly invoked," while the *Maha-Mayuri Sutra* was "sure to reward with peace and comfort if a good observer of the Buddhist Commandments recites it in a proper manner." Such a vast scale of ancient Indo-Aryan imagination as was typically shown in the enhancement of a mere bird is really amazing to us modern people. But even in those far-off days, Kūkai was the only person in Japan who was temperamentally capable of participating in that imaginative sphere.

At first Kūkai, perplexed with the two contrasted religions from India, must have asked to himself: "Is Mantrayana a sort of Buddhism?"

As was easily noticed, Buddhist images first introduced into Japan looked like ascetic monks in simple robes, while images of Mantrayana were dressed up in a dazzlingly gorgeous manner, because they were modeled after the men and women of the wealthiest class in India, all wearing coronet, necklace, bracelets and ankle rings, their skin usually painted flesh-color. Even a less ornate image of Akasagarbha wore a coronet, and held in the right hand a *cintamani* jewel[2] as a symbol of worldly happiness and prosperity.

In Kūkai's days Mantrayana had not yet spread very widely even in India, as is known by the fact that the Chinese Buddhist priest of great fame, Xuanzang,[3] who made a long, difficult journey to India to collect Buddhist scriptures, does not seem to have witnessed much of Mantrayana during his journey (627–645) around India. But Kūkai in Japan, comparing the two religions from India, perceived the evolution of Buddhism and came to the conclusion that Mantrayana was a great development of Sakyamuni's teaching, and this idea of his, which actually corresponded to the reality, remained unshaken throughout his life.

*　　*　　*

Let us take a look at the ritual for the invocation of the Peacock King. Firstly a portrait of Maha-Mayuri (the Peacock King) seated on a golden peacock is hung up on the wall. Then on the altar before it the necessary implements are arranged: a *karma* hand pounder* to destroy devils, a peacock tail-feather laid out in a chest for Sanskrit texts,[4] and thirty-five peacock tail-feathers placed in a bottle. There are three other altars: one for *homa*,* another for Vinayaka (a tutelary god of Buddhism to be invoked for wealth, love, childbirth and recovery from illness), and the other for the Twelve Guardians of sun, moon, heaven, earth and the eight directions of the earth. The rite of *homa* is given three times a day at the altar for *homa*, twice for Vinayaka, and once for the Twelve Guardians. In each of them, the invoker keeps reciting Maha-Mayuri's mantra, making his mudra (symbolic signs with the fingers), so that he could gradually unite himself with that deity. In Esoteric Buddhism, the invoker not only offers his worship to that deity but also introduces himself into its functions by abstracting his physical self, until he eventually succeeds in receiving from him whatever he wishes to obtain.

Kūkai took up this kind of ritual, too, not as a magician or shaman, but as an ascetic of Esoteric Buddhism, his mentality being so constructed as to appreciate such ritualism to the full. It gave him a great intellectual pleasure, as it enabled him to get acquainted with the structure and the movement of the universe, even allowing him to operate its mechanism for the benefit of human beings. Certainly performing it was something at once interesting and terrifying, but he did it with convivial relish. Skeptics and cowards would be the last to bring themselves to perform such rituals.

"The invocation for the Peacock King gives me the shivers...."

A priest I met at Chishaku-in temple[5] in Kyōto once confessed to me, referring to the frequent thrills he felt at night when his body was almost irresistibly drawn to the countless shears, razor-sharp and fatal, filling the darkness around. What was it that enabled Kūkai to absorb himself in such terrors? Something rooted in his sunny temperament?

VI. Preparation for the Great Leap

IT is unknown how Kūkai spent his twenties, excepting that at twenty-four he completed that dramatic work. Since in the persona of Beggar Boy he was to keep on with his journey to the Tusita Heaven, it is obvious that Kūkai went on seeking his way there. But how?

According to *The Memoirs of Our Master*, one day when he was twenty, Kūkai came to meet Gonzō at Daian-ji in Nara and expressed his wish to take the tonsure and receive the Ten Commandments for a Buddhist Novice. Gonzō took him to a temple under his supervision—Makino'o-san-ji* in the neighboring province of Izumi—and allowed him to fulfill his wish there. This gave him the outward appearance of a Buddhist monk, but he remained unordained all the same. In fact, it was not until "March twenty-fifth in the twenty-third year of Enryaku (804)," as is recorded in *Shoku Nihon Kōki*, that he was made an official monk. In early summer that year, the thirty-one-year-old Kūkai was going to leave Japan to study in Tang China as a government student of Buddhism. There was no delaying his ordination any longer. Then what had kept him so long an unofficial monk?

Part of the reason for this may be found in the social situation. By that time there had already been many—probably too many—official priests, and the government was trying to discourage applicants for official priesthood, making it a rule that they should have led an ascetic life at least for three years, and setting them extremely difficult examinations. There were two more hurdles that had recently been added: one was an age limit that accepted only applicants aged thirty-five or above, though this rule was valid for only three years (799–801) when Kūkai was twenty-six to twenty-eight; the other was an oral test in Chinese. Such linguistic testing had nothing to do with the ability to follow Buddha's teaching. But the government had to do something to put a spoke in their wheels when more and more smart alecs of plebeian classes were anxious to obtain official priesthood that would enable them to lead an enviable life, with food and clothing amply provided, their person honored by the state and respected by people, as long as they were successfully controlling their carnal appetites.

None of these hurdles except the age limit could be too high for Kūkai. But he, a sincere seeker for the truth of the universe, could not bring himself to be an official priest—a position that seemed to him just as vulgar as that of any government official. Gonzō understood him very well and approved his decision to remain unordained. What was more, the kind man, appointing himself as a spokesman for Kūkai, must have been using his influence lest the government should come to stand in his way. Indeed, even in this most difficult period of his life, Kūkai seems to have been spared real adversity, always protected, though not directly, by Ato no Ōtari, Professor Okada from Sanuki Province who had been the president of the university when Kūkai was there and some official from the Ōtomo Saeki and the Sanuki Saeki who would be helpful in case of need.

Another remarkable thing Gonzō did for Kūkai about this period of his life was to have appointed him a *gonji-o* or layman servant to himself. Certainly it was a modest post, but it enabled him not only to listen and learn from this great scholar regularly through their daily routine but also to have a free access to any of the temple libraries in this country if only he gave Gonzō's name as a messenger sent by him. The libraries of state temples were open only to those whose social or hierarchical positions were of considerable importance. Then this post provided by Gonzō would have been of inestimable advantage to him.

Thus Kūkai in his twenties was able to spend most of his time applying himself alternately to ascetic practice in the mountains and to intense study at temple libraries, reading not only "ten thousand volumes of Buddhist scriptures" but also all kinds of books available in Japan at that time. This sort of life he kept leading for about a decade on end may have resulted in that unusual self-confidence he was to retain for the rest of his life.

*   *   *

What was considered Buddhism in Japan at that time—Nara Buddhism offering the six departments of Kegon, Kusha, Jōjitsu, Hossō, Sanron and Ritsu—was more philosophy than faith. All of them, though built around

Buddhist thought, were actually Indian thought. But unless Kūkai had
mastered all of them, it would not have occurred that no sooner had he come
in contact with Esoteric Buddhism in Chang'an, China, than he understood it
quite perfectly. Mastering even one of these thought systems was considered
a most difficult thing to do. But Kūkai, visiting one temple library after
another, mastered them one by one all by himself probably with the sort of
diligent patience we see in a beast that cracks and chews one bone after
another with its sharp teeth. Especially his mastery of Kegon doctrine
enabled him to obtain a sort of prescription for the creation of Esoteric
Buddhism.

The same thing had happened in India, too: the *Kegon-kyō* sutra, when
taken up by theorists, proved to be a powerful catalyzer to change primitive
Mantrayana into purified Mantrayana or Esoteric Buddhism as a new
metaphysical world quite different from what had been known as Buddhism.
How many centuries did it take to go through that process? The period from
the germination of Indian thought that far predated Sakyamuni's Buddhism
to the completion of the *Kegon-kyō* sutra (c.400A.D.) is fabulously long. Then
more than a century was spent before purified Mantrayana came into being
through the catalysis of Kegon doctrine.

Now on an island far away from India, Kūkai as a young man was going
through that same process, spending only seven years or so building the
foundation from which to make the great leap to purified Mantrayana.
Unbelievable as it may sound, this was exactly what he was doing in his
twenties. His mastery of Kegon doctrine does suggest his having had the entrée
of Tōdai-ji in Nara, the headquarters of Kegon doctrine, the largest state temple
of the greatest importance. At the mere sight of its magnificent gate, some
recruits might have felt too small to have anything to do with that temple.
But Kūkai apparently took it for granted to make the most of this institute,
studying at its library or attending lectures though not qualified to do so.

What kind of thought does the *Kegon-kyō* sutra offer?

To my mind, no other sutra has ever had a greater influence upon
Chinese and Japanese thought than the *Kegon-kyō* sutra. That unique view of
the world that tells us "a particle of dust contains the whole universe" would
be traced back to this sutra. "One is all and all is one," or "absolute

antitheses are identical with each other" which forms the foundation of Nishida Kitarō's philosophy,[1] also derives from this sutra, and so does the idea earnestly advocated by Zen[2] Buddhists and martial artists of Japan: "Rest amidst motion; motion amidst rest."

According to this sutra, all things that exist in the universe fulfill each other, completely digesting each other while entertaining an infinite relationship with one another with no distinction between them in their perpetual circulation in perfect harmony; all things that exist in the universe and their motions are all expressions of Vairocana's Buddhahood. A step further, and it would become the world of Mahavairocana of Esoteric Buddhism, from whose interior one would be able to get limitless divine favors if only one could master how to communicate with it, as the Indian thinkers thought in the sixth and seventh centuries and Kūkai did around the turn of the ninth century.

But had he not been fascinated by the efficacy of primitive Mantrayana jealously kept by mountain ascetics and allotment farmers turned beggar monks, Kūkai might have satisfied himself with the world of the *Kegon-kyō* sutra. As it was, he had to go further. But how could he when he did not know which way to go? According to *The Memoirs of Our Master*, the following was how he went through that difficult period of his life:

> I had studied Buddhism both Hinayana and Mahayana, reading all sutras available, but I could not dismiss a doubt that prevented me from going on. So I prayed and prayed, day and night, for something that would guide me along. One night I had a dream: a man came to me and said that the *Mahavairocana Sutra* would be exactly the one I had been looking for. Overjoyed, I searched and searched until I found it in the basement of the east pagoda of Kume-dera temple[3] in Takechi County in the Province of Yamato.

It sounds almost legendary. But one can quite imagine what sort of agony the young man had to suffer when gripped by such a philosophic problem. Unable to find his way out, he must have been almost beside himself, looking more or less insane when crossing the precincts of Daian-ji like a blast of visible wind or sitting at table, with set eyes, unable to eat even a mouthful, or just letting his former classmates pass by as total strangers even when he met them in Nara. His consciousness drifting even in the daytime, he might have suddenly sat up at midnight only to drown his burning eyes in the dark. If someone came to him, one of these days or nights, and gave him the title of the sutra he had been looking for, he would have failed to recognize him, even though the title itself might have begun to ring in his ears from that moment on.

The *Mahavairocana Sutra* that constituted the core of Esoteric Buddhism was brought to Chang'an, China, by an Indian priest. Then it was translated into Chinese. About ten years later, it was introduced into Japan probably by Gembō,* a government student of Buddhism who returned to Japan in 735. By and by, the copies were made[4] and they were kept at large temples, as was always the case with newly-introduced scriptures. But all those copies of the *Mahavairocana Sutra*, buried deep in the piles of Buddhist literature in those temples, were simply forgotten until about seven decades later when Kūkai happened to dig one up in "the basement of the east pagoda of Kume-dera temple."

Why had they been neglected so long? Probably because the *Mahavairocana Sutra* did not belong to any of the six departments of Nara Buddhism as an authorized religion. Otherwise it would have been studied without fail by official priests as well as by applicants for official priesthood, while scholar priests who gave lectures to the tennō would undoubtedly have taken it up. In other words, the total lack of social demand had left that sutra unnoticed or neglected for such a long lapse of time. Or it may be that such a specific thought as was delivered in it was destined to wait till the advent of a genius with the specific turn of mind able to appreciate it to the full.

Kūkai's encounter with this sutra turned out to be of immense significance in the history of philosophy and religion in the East, because all lines of purified Mantrayana, except the one Kūkai established later and named Shingon Esoteric Buddhism, were soon to disappear firstly in India, then in China; the one introduced into Tibet in the eighth century had already been changed in quality.

Who could be the person who told Kūkai the whereabouts of the *Mahavairocana Sutra*? Was he one of those wandering monks who had heard of that sutra while frequenting Kume-dera? Or was he Gonzō, a scholar of extensive reading? Or Kaimyō also from Sanuki Province, a resident priest of Daian-ji, who had been in Tang China in 770s or around the time when Chinese Esoteric Buddhism was at its zenith? Anyway Kūkai jumped to his feet and ran all the way to Kume-dera. Would he not have had the look of some frantic ghost?

The acute pleasure that flooded Kūkai when he took that sutra in his hands defies the imagination. Did he spend all day reading in the pagoda, staying at night at the monks' quarters in the pine forest nearby? As for food, he might have gone begging from door to door in the village. Or he might have received a regular meal from the temple in the capacity of a messenger of "Venerable Gonzō."

He must have found himself reading that sutra with considerable ease and rapidity, because its theory, however complicated and alien to those of other sutras, was along the same lines with that of the *Kegon-kyō* sutra he had been eagerly studying for many years. Naturally what interested him most was Mahavairocana as a vigorous expansion of Vairocana in the Kegon world. Unlike Sakyamuni as a historical being, Vairocana was a super-historical, abstract existence which, representing the truth of the universe, could be regarded as the principle of the universe itself. It had been called by a number of epithets, such as Henjō, Kōmyō Henjō, Jōman and so on, all meaning "metaphysical being that gives light to all that exist in the universe." Kūkai, who intensely favored this idea of Vairocana, was anxious to know more about it, asking: "So what will come of it?" The *Kegon-kyō* sutra would not answer him. But the *Mahavairocana Sutra* gave him a satisfying answer: Mahavairocana, though essentially the same as Vairocana, was an even more vigorous, thoroughly omni-present function; it offered men and women an ability to obtain release from being mere dust in the universe, saying that they all have kept the seed of Buddhahood within them, and that by following its precepts and practices, anyone can achieve enlightenment here and now. What is more, it declares them capable of sharing in the power of any Buddhas and Bodisatvas as its sacred agents, if only they have mastered how to communicate with them.

To Kūkai Nara Buddhism was intolerably far from satisfactory because its supreme purpose was to acquire autonomous freedom from the carnal desire men and women are born with. Only a very few will be able to attain it in life; the majority must wait until they are dead and released from the body as the source of carnal desires. Death will come to everyone sooner or later. Yet can it be appreciated so much simply because it brings Nirvana (Buddhist paradise attained by extinction of individuality and desires, with release from effects of karma or fate)? Will every death bring Nirvana? The answer he got from Nara Buddhism was rather disappointing: "Not necessarily."

"What nonsense ! "

Kūkai must have been feeling indignant while reading about such ideas in all those Buddhist scriptures that were supposed to have echoed Sakyamuni's speech. Only the *Kegon-kyō* sutra, fairly detached from Sakyamuni, brought him a little relief. He pondered over the matter: not only death but life should be done justice to, since both are realities in the universe; if life was valorized as such, carnal desires as natural attributes to life would also be recognized as realities in the universe or manifestations of Vairocana itself omnipresent in the universe.

This idea of his was to be fully confirmed and celebrated when years later in Chang'an, China, he took up the *Rishu-kyō* sutra, which was to constitute the very groundwork of the thought system he himself established later. Unlike many other sutras that abound in poetic embellishments, the *Rishu-kyō* sutra discloses the very core in the opening chapter, and that with utmost frankness:

> Orgasm they share, being pure in itself,
> deserves the rank of Bodhisattva.

> Desire shooting at the target, being pure in itself,
> deserves the rank of Bodhisattva.

> Touching each other, being pure in itself,
> deserves the rank of Bodhisattva.

> Binding each other in love, being pure in itself,
> deserves the rank of Bodhisattva.

> Perfect freedom in their union, being pure in itself,
> deserves the rank of Bodhisattva.

The word "love" used in Buddhist scriptures means sexual love, and "binding each other in love" does not mean anything metaphysical but a physical union of man and woman in sexual intercourse.

In the medieval ages in Japan, some priests who put a literal interpretation on this part of this sutra decided that sexual intercourse should be the very best ascetic practice for anyone to attain Buddhahood. They formed a school—Shingon Tachikawa School—and their principle was fanatically believed in by the Tennō Godaigo (reign: 1318–1339). Naturally, that was a deviation from Kūkai's idea that nothing in the universe exists in vain: everything there, being essential in the making of the universe, is pure and, if metaphysicized, can be a truth that deserves the name of Bodhisattva. But this was not Sakyamuni's idea. His association was so stoic that monks and priests were not allowed to have even a picture of a woman in their living quarters.

No one but Kūkai, I now realize, has ever taken up sexual desire so seriously as to build it up into a metaphysical world of a great and grandiose beauty. Then, in a further effort to make it accessible to everyone, he created many works of tangible art that still send us into rapturous ecstasy.

To my mind, a thinker is born, not made: whatever thought a thinker comes to embrace or create, it is essentially rooted in his own nature, instead of coming upon him all of a sudden like a revelation or a gift from heaven.

By reading the Chinese version of the *Mahavairocana Sutra*, Kūkai was able to grasp its theory. But as for the ritualism that includes mantra-reciting and mudra-making,[5] indispensable in communicating with divine beings, he could not obtain even a rudimentary knowledge of it. Translators, probably finding it too difficult to explain, left the most part of it as it stood in Sanskrit original. Kūkai had acquired some knowledge of Sanskrit probably at Tōshōdai-ji in Nara, but this he found was of little or no use. The only solution, he thought, was to go over to China to be initiated into it by a master of Mantrayana. No other students who had ever been to China could have explained their purpose in going there so clearly as Kūkai could.

VII. SAICHŌ

THERE was another Buddhist priest who was going to China about his time. His name was Saichō. He had not yet met Kūkai nor heard of him, though they were destined to be regarded as rivals. Saichō, senior to Kūkai by seven years, had already achieved fame and high status, revered and patronized by the Tennō Kammu himself. Saichō was by no means arrogant, but so far he had had no need nor occasion to become acquainted with Kūkai who was still living in obscurity.

When young, Saichō was a mountain ascetic, too. At twenty he climbed Mt. Hiei that rose to the northeast of what was soon to be the Heian Capital—present-day Kyōto—and built a temple which later became Hiei-zan Enryaku-ji or the headquarters of the Tendai religion[1] he later started. The structure he built there would have been a hermitage. But he called it a temple and named it Hieizan-ji after that mountain; he had intended to make it a nursery for a new Buddhism he was going to launch, as is suggested by the following prayer he repeated with youthful ardor while cutting a path up that mountain with sickle and axe:

> May all the Buddhas in the highest stage of enlightenment send
> thy blessings to this mountain I have chosen for thy teachings!

Saichō had already known what official priesthood was like: being bureaucratized, priests were more officials than Buddhists; warmly protected by the state, they were no better than drones in society, whatever amount of Buddhist literature they might have memorized to satisfy their pride. As to their ability to approach or to attain Buddhahood by means of their kind of Buddhism, they themselves were quite uncertain.

"Does such Buddhism really deserve the name of religion? Is it not merely rote learning or at best scholastic pursuit?"

Saichō in his teens seems already to have been asking himself that. Certainly what they were following in the six departments of Nara

Buddhism was none other than Indian logic and epistemology. But by the time he climbed Mt. Hiei to build his own temple, Saichō had been eagerly searching for some other way that would really help him approach Buddha Sakyamuni.

*　　*　　*

Saichō was born in Ōmi Province just northeast of the Home Provinces. According to the family legend, his ancestor came from overseas during the reign of the Tennō Ōjin, who was supposedly ruling over what later became the Home Provinces from some time in the latter half of the fourth century to the beginning of the fifth century. This period corresponds to the one strongly marked by a newly-introduced iron culture that was soon to spread all over the country. This had naturally involved an influx of large numbers of people from abroad, bringing with them iron culture.

According to *Nihon Shoki*, a Chinese called Yuzuki-no-kimi arrived in Japan, "leading other Chinese from one hundred and twenty prefectures" that existed in the Korean Peninsula.[2] As naturalized Japanese, they were made into the guild people of Hata *be* directed by Hata *uji* and engaged in sericulture in the northern part of Yamashiro Province—where the Heian capital was to come into being several centuries later. The Hata clan, though they had come from Paekche on the Korean Peninsula, claimed that they were Chinese, and that descendants of Shi Huangdi, the first to declare himself Emperor of China, even though his dynasty Qin proved to be very short-lived (221 B.C.–206 B.C.).

Achi-no-omi, a legendary ancestor of Aya *uji* who formed the guilds of scribes and twill-weavers in Japan, also arrived here about the same time by way of the Korean Peninsula, "leading other Chinese from seventeen prefectures" on the Korean Peninsula. He also declared that his pedigree could be traced back to the Emperor Lingdi, the twelfth Emperor of the Later Han Dynasty (25A.D.–220A.D.).

The forefather of Saichō, who also arrived in Japan about this time, traced his descent back to the Emperor Xiandi, the last Emperor of the Later Han, as is specifically recorded in *Eigaku Yōki*, a historical record of Mount Hiei, *Sōgō Bunin*,[3] and *Genkō Shakusho*,[4] suggesting that Saichō and his family had been firmly convinced of the fact. This was something very common in those who were called "alien stock" in *The Chronicle of Titled Families*, the official directory compiled in 815 by the government. Living in Japanese society, they must have found it to their advantage to establish that they were originally Chinese closely associated with that advanced civilization, even though they might have gone too far when they identified themselves as descendants of Chinese Emperors. But as for the claim that their ancestors were Chinese, they would not have been wrong, considering the fact that Later Han China had long had jurisdiction over northern Korea.

In the case of Lelang County whose capital was Pyongyang, it was established in 108 B.C., and during the four centuries that followed, Chinese officials had been sent there from the central government. Naturally this prompted a large number of Chinese to come and settle there, allowing Chinese culture to flourish there to a great extent. Even after the Later Han was overthrown in 220 A.D., Lelang County managed to survive until 313 A.D. when it was destroyed by the native Koguryo. It was quite probable, therefore, that many Chinese had once become naturalized in Koguryo and Paekche, another region coming into prominence on the Korean Peninsula, before they finally emigrated to Japan, though some had crossed directly in Japan soon after they had witnessed the decline and fall of Lelang County.

Saichō's forefather who arrived in Japan "was granted a piece of land in Shiga and a new family name and title—Mitsu no *obito*" as is recorded in *Eigaku Yōki*. "Mitsu no *obito*" suggests that he was made the chief of Mitsu, a lakeside village near present-day Sakamoto in Shiga Prefecture. But by the time Saichō was born (767), the family had left Mitsu and moved to what was then called Furuichi near Kokubun-ji in Ōmi Province.

Another family legend concerning a person of his ancestry goes as follows:

> In the third year of the Tennō Kenzō's reign (487 A.D.)—about half a century before Buddhism was introduced into Japan—the then head of the Mitsu family surprised his neighbors by modelling a Buddhist image about three feet tall out of the clay he had dug at the edge of a rice field. What on earth could it be? When they saw him worship it with the utmost reverence, they were filled with awe.

In the same account related in *Eigaku Yōki*, that person is identified as Saichō's father, Momoe. But this is impossible because he could not have lived so long ago. Whoever he was, this story may reveal what sort of impression the family made upon their neighbors. As for Saichō's father, there was nothing strange about him. Family tradition accorded him the ability to read Chinese books, while his graceful appearance and kind-heartedness had made him popular among his neighbors. Layman as he was, he was a devout Buddhist, as is known by the fact that he once climbed Mt. Hiei, built a hermitage there and practiced asceticism as penitence. By virtue of this austerity, they say, he was able to beget Saichō. Though I do not take this very seriously, it seems quite probable that as a boy Saichō was greatly influenced by his father who was sincerely willing to dedicate this son of his to Buddhism.

The boy Saichō or Hirono (Wide Plain), as his parents named him, was twelve years old when he left home, presumably through the efforts of his father, to stay and study at Kokubun-ji in Ōmi Province. Three years later, one of the twenty priests in that temple died. To fill the vacancy the fifteen-year-old Hirono was allowed to apply for licensed priesthood. At eighteen he passed the examination and began to call himself Saichō (the Purest). Two years later, on April 6, 785, he was officially ordained at Kaidan-in at Tōdai-ji. Thus Saichō, an orderly person, proved himself to be a model of steady progress in attaining official priesthood. But only three months later, he gave up everything he had acquired: he abandoned a post he had just obtained at Kokubun-ji and climbed Mt. Hiei to lead a secluded life there. Before leaving the temple for good, however, this thoughtful person, probably afraid of being mistaken for an unofficial monk, collected all the official papers he had received so far and kept them carefully in a well-carpentered chest. Otherwise, they would not have survived to this day.

The prayer he wrote soon after he began to live on Mt. Hiei includes the following:

> The three worlds[6] revolving for ever and ever are
> all for suffering and pain, not for any comfort.
> All kinds of lives that circle and circle in woe
> are destined to gloom and grief, not to any joy.

Compared with the high-level creativity Kūkai showed in *The Indications of the Three Teachings*, this prayer seems to be a stereotype of Buddhist pessimism. But if stereotype applies best to this innocent and gentle person's work, this writing of his may reflect such a serene phase of his character. Though outshone by Kūkai in creativity, Saichō surpassed his contemporaries in intelligence with which to detect the reality of things, and once he detected it, he was able to pursue it with unusual courage and persistency.

Unlike Kūkai, Saichō was by nature a man of exoteric rationality and lucidity. Though he retired to a mountain as Kūkai did, his motive was quite different from Kūkai's. The sincere student in Saichō just wanted complete freedom from the daily routine and mundane business he had to attend to at the state temple. Now in the mountain he was able to dedicate all his time and energy to reading sutras and their commentaries and treatises in order to find answers to his questions: "We think we have Buddhism in Japan, but do we really have one when its six departments—except Kegon—are more concerned with Indian logic than sutras? Can I correct this error by building a new synthetic order, in which sutras will be placed at its center while treatises and disciplines will be accorded appropriate subsidiary status?"

As Saichō pointed out, sutras were neglected in Japan, though they had been imported in great numbers to be copied and kept in the libraries of large temples. It was commonly believed in Japan that sutras were not for studying but for reciting to invoke their mystical power.

At his hermitage on Mt. Hiei, Saichō studied many sutras, including the *Hoke-kyō*, the *Kegon-kyō* and the *Konkōmyō-kyō*.[7] He undertook the daily practice of *shikan* meditation as well. How did he become familiar with this ascetic meditation peculiar to the Tiantai religion, one of thirteen Buddhist religions in China? Had his former master Gyōhyō of Kokubun-ji happened to be initiated into it by his Chinese master Jianzhen and passed it on to him? Or did he acquire it from his reading and teach himself, exercising a great deal of imagination? The last-mentioned seems to give a more appropriate picture of Saichō about this time.

It was not very long before he came upon a sutra that was to drive all the doubts out of his mind. This naturally set him thinking over the validity of making that sutra—the *Hoke-kyō*—the very core of the new religion he was going to establish. The *Hoke-kyō* had long since been imported into Japan and the Prince-Regent Shōtoku, who made a commentary on this sutra, *HokkeGisho*, had extolled it, saying: "It is the king of sutras." If so, Saichō's appreciation of it may not sound so impressive. But probably no other person in Japan could have read it with greater understanding than he. What enabled him to do so was his knowledge of the *Kegon-kyō*.

Then while reading *A Commentary on the Daijō Kishin-ron*,[8] he came across a remarkable statement: "The Tiantai sect established on Mt. Tiantai in China is founded upon the *Hoke-kyō* sutra." Saichō must have been excited to find that his own idea had already been realized on Mt. Tiantai in China.

The *Hoke-kyō* sutra was completed some time in the first century in northwestern India. The authors, though unidentified and having lived in different ages, were all gifted poets who were able to command brilliant rhetoric. No other sutra was more successful in grasping the essence of Sakyamuni. It had transcended Hinayana principles Saichō was doubtful about, too. What had been handed down as Sakyamuni's own words was preserved as its base, but it was organized by the principle of *sunya* as the sole truth with which to grasp the whole universe. *Sanya* is zero, in which everything is included, as was already proclaimed in the *Hannya-gyō* sutra. This idea of zero, when adopted in the *Hoke-kyō* sutra, becomes something magnificent: zero is the universe itself; it is at once the maximum and the minimum; all the phenomena in the world, packed in zero, are precisely connected and combined with each other; the minimum includes the maximum, and vice versa, thus creating the great unity of the universe.

What is more, the *Hoke-kyō* sutra never indulges in philosophy even when it explains its structure, but pertinently admires Buddha in resplendently beautiful rhetoric that never fails to make listeners or readers sense the truth of its world. The many allegories and episodes cleverly woven into it are also helpful in inducting them into its mythological world.

Saichō wanted to know more about the Tiantai principle founded upon this sutra, but he soon found it was impossible to do so in Japan. A Chinese priest, Jianzhen, who had arrived in Japan about thirty years before, had brought with him several books along these lines, but all he could get from them was just a glimpse of a huge system. In order to master its entirety, he thought, he would have to go to China. The principle itself, established by a Chinese philosopher-monk Zhiyi (538–597), had already been on the wane with the advent of Zen and Mantrayana. Saichō in Japan never knew such a religious climate in China. But even if he had been informed of what was happening to the Tiantai religion in China, he would not have changed his mind, because he firmly believed that: if the Tiantai principle was introduced into Japan, they would eventually have the first religion deserving of the name.

Saichō was by no means worldly-wise. But somehow or other, he was fortunate enough to acquire one patron after another who came to minister to his needs. This was especially true in the first half of his career that concurred with the reign of the Tennō Kammu (reign: 781–805). Unlike all the other tennōs before him, Kammu tried to model himself after the Chinese Emperors, administering personnel himself, and making basic decisions in politics. He also criticized and defied Nara Buddhism, whose interference with politics was such that he found it more and more unbearable. In the fourth year of his reign he left Nara for good and began to build a new capital in Nagaoka even though he had to abandon it before it was completed. But this was to make him discover Saichō on Mt. Hiei.

Before deciding on the seat for the new capital, a detailed survey was made in the Yamashiro Basin. The report on that survey presented to Kammu included a comment as follows:

> This place is ideally located,[9] with each of the four directions properly provided with an auspicious feature. The only thing that worries us is a high mountain that rises to the northeast. The northeastern corner being the Demon's Entrance, that mountain should be treated with utmost care if the new capital is to be inaugurated here.

This was how Kammu, no longer the Confucian rationalist he used to be but a firm believer in the Way of *Yin* and *Yang*,[10] always in fear and trembling at "the revengeful ghost of the former Crown Prince Sawara," turned his eyes to "a high mountain that rises to the northeast," which happened to be Mt. Hiei where Saichō had been living for seven years. Could it be only by chance? The Chief Councilor of the State who presented the report above was Fujiwara Hokke no Oguromaro. According to a legend that came into being later, Saichō's mother came from the Fujiwara Hokke, and her younger sister was the wife of Oguromaro himself. It seems totally improbable that the two families, so different in social background as Saichō's and Oguromaro's, should have been related by marriage, but they might have struck up some kind of intimacy.

Saichō's former mentor Gyōhyō of Kokubun-ji in Ōmi Province, an influential prelate with ample connections in the Court circle, might have been supporting Saichō, the best disciple he had ever had, saying: "A young priest named Saichō, though living on Mt. Hiei now, is sure to emerge as a new leader of Buddhism."

Gyōhyō came of the Hata clan that was then in the limelight, as they had dedicated their own land when the site of the new capital was decided upon. Because of this unusual generosity, some were led to the assumption that the Hata clan themselves had conducted a political campaign to remove the capital to their own land. Gyōhyō had a very good network to make use of for Saichō who was also of "alien stock."

Oguromaro, during his surveying trip, may have climbed "a high mountain" and met Saichō at his hermitage. Naturally Saichō would have talked about what he was doing there and about the new religion he was going to start some day. Kammu was still struggling to break with the old Buddhism in Nara. How could Oguromaro remain indifferent when he was listening to the young priest of graceful personality proclaim his noble aspiration with such ardor?

Later on, Kammu himself also climbed that mountain, guided by Oguromaro, and visited Saichō at his hermitage and listened to him when he unfolded what he thought about the new Buddhism he was going to introduce from China. Thus Saichō won the monarch's favor, which was to be intensified as the years went by. Saichō's foreign background also might have worked to his advantage. Kammu, whose mother Takano no Niigasa was of a family that still retained some native traditions of Paekche in the Korean Peninsula, felt a special affinity with those of "alien stock."

In 794 the capital was transferred from Nagaoka to the Yamashiro Basin, and the years that followed saw the construction of the new capital making steady progress. In 796 the Tennō's administrative office was completed. The following year turned out to be quite memorable for Saichō: his hermitage or Hieizan-ji on Mt. Hiei was made a state temple to be sustained by national tax, while Saichō himself was appointed one of the ten Buddhist priests to serve at the Imperial chapel,[11] though usually he was allowed to stay and study at his own place on Mt. Hiei. Naturally for Saichō this was a very great step forward to the realization of his dream of going to China in order to introduce his cherished principle into Japan.

By that time Oguromaro had been dead. Then another Court official of great importance came to offer his help. Wake no Hiroyo was his name. Seeing that Saichō was the least likely person to ingratiate himself with the influential ones of the time, his sheer helplessness itself might have had some effect upon them, his monomaniacal eagerness to pursue his selfless dream inspiring them to extend their helping hand toward him.

Wake no Hiroyo was a son of Wake no Kiyomaro known for his courage with which he successfully checked the ambitious advance of Dōkyō (?–772), the leader of Nara Buddhism, who went so far as to make his way to the throne. Kiyomaro, still a young military officer of the fifth court rank, was sent to Usa Hachiman-gū shrine[12] in northern Kyūshū to consult the oracle about this matter. The pronouncement he brought back from the oracle: "The man of injustice shall be got rid of" infuriated Dōkyō, who at once exiled Kiyomaro to southern Kyūshū. But when Dōkyō's patron, the female Tennō Shōtoku, died in the following year, Dōkyō was sent away to Yakushi-ji in Shimotsuke Province and Kiyomaro was called back. With the advent of Kammu's reign, Kiyomaro was promoted to a high position. In building the Heian capital, he was appointed director for the construction of the Imperial palace. Though he was to die soon after Saichō became one of the ten Buddhist priests to serve at the Imperial chapel, he must have been feeling a profound sympathy toward Saichō who stood alone against Nara Buddhism.

Now his son, Wake no Hiroyo, approached Saichō with the intention to carry out what his deceased father Kiyomaro would have done for Saichō. He visited Saichō at Hieizan-ji and listened to him, leaning what Tiantai religion was like. The truth it offered, with which to grasp the universe, the world and humanity, seemed to him all the more interesting because he had never heard of such a doctrine. If this principle was introduced into Japan and flourished, Hiroyo thought, it would be a severe blow to the old Buddhism in Nara, to the profound gratification of his father's soul. It would also be in line with Kammu's policy. No wonder Hiroyo was prompt in promising Saichō help when he expressed his wish to go over to China to obtain a complete library of the Tiantai principle.

Hiroyo, seeing that this project was too big to handle casually, decided to do some spadework for it. Otherwise, the following would not have taken place: in November, 801, a public lecture on "the three principal scriptures on the Tiantai principle"[13] was given by Saichō at Takaosan-ji on Mt. Takao, a temple owned by the Wake clan. That event turned out to be very political as well as religious, for the lecture was honored by an Imperial message of appreciation as soon as it was over. Obviously Hiroyo, who organized that event, had fully explained to the Tennō what the lecture was about and what it was for. What made the event even more political was that about a dozen elders of Nara Buddhism, much older and much more experienced in priesthood than Saichō, were summoned to be the audience of the lecture, and that by an Imperial command, to their great embarrassment. But even greater embarrassment was still in store for them: when the lecture was over and the royal celebration of it was announced, Hiroyo came to Zengi, their representative, and requested: "His Majesty would be pleased to know what you thought about the lecture. Would you please take the trouble of collecting your opinions or comments?"

Now that the Tennō's appraisal had been issued, all that they could say in the memorial was:

> Through the lecture on those scriptures, we were able to lean how skillfully the Tiantai principle summarizes all that Sakyamuni preached in his lifetime, thus manifesting his spirit to perfection. The immense profundity of that principle was something we have never known before. Our pleasure of having been acquainted with it was such that we dare to present this paper to His Majesty to express our heartfelt gratitude.

Never had they been humiliated so severely. But they were smiling politely, suppressing their anger. Years later, it was to erupt, taking a form of revengeful attacks against Saichō. Some of the dark clouds that overshadowed the latter half of his career had thus risen on Mt. Takao on one of the happiest occasions of his life.

*   *   *

Kūkai, especially alert to this sort of information, must have heard that Saichō had made a brilliant debut at Takaosan-ji. Priests in Nara who told Kūkai about it were all exasperated at what they took as Saichō's arrogance. Kūkai, well acquainted with them, was naturally in sympathy with them, but that was not all that he felt. To Kūkai, still remaining a mere wandering monk, though burning with ambition to bring about a drastic change in Buddhism in Japan, Saichō's having been so fortunate as to make his first public appearance in all the glory of the Tennō's favor would have been a severe shock. It may be uncharitable of me to call that feeling jealousy. But considering the unusual amount of emotion he was born with, the ill feeling that gnawed his heart then would have been more than he could express.

What made Saichō even more intolerable to Kūkai was the Tiantai principle he had taken up. Kūkai had read Buddhist scriptures even more extensively than Saichō. What was more, his ability to judge scriptures on a comparative principle was such that no Buddhist priest or scholar who preceded him or followed him has ever surpassed him, as is confirmed by his work of established fame, *The Ten Stages of the Development of Human Mind*. Quite probably Kūkai then had already been able to tell what Tiantai principle was and where it stood in China, a faded principle that had outlived its popularity. In later years, Kūkai was to attack it severely: being exoteric, it would easily be understood by reading the literature concerned; it may explain the structure of the universe, but it falls short of being a proper religion because it fails to give satisfying answers to the natural questions people will ask: "So what will come of it? What should we do?" Because of this fatal weakness he saw in the Tiantai principle, Kūkai must have already discarded it as of lesser importance, even before he heard of Saichō.

Nightly lying under a straw mat, Kūkai might have groaned and glared in a fit of fury: "By making use of the Tennō's favor, is he going to impose such an imitation upon the State?"

INTERLUDE 2. THE ENVOYS TO CHINA

O UR understanding of the Japanese in those days would be very incomplete if their great aspiration towards universality were not taken into account: a universality which would unite them with the rest of the world. To the Japanese, Buddhism was universality itself, as it allowed them to transcend social classes, nationalities and even races.

According to *The Chronicles of the Sui Dynasty*, the Japanese envoy who came to Sui China in 607 gave as the reason why he was there:

> "We have heard that the Bodhisattva Emperor of China thinks highly of Buddhism. That is why the Ruler of Japan has sent his envoy here to worship him."

In other words, what the Tennō of Japan intended was not to offer his vassal homage to the Chinese Emperor but to adore the Bodhisattva Emperor who, unlike the Emperors of preceding dynasties[1] who had oppressed Buddhism, made himself a patron of Buddhism. Thus by positing the credo that they should live up to the universality of Buddhism, the Tennō—bravely rising above earthly conventions, even if only on a rhetorical level—implied that even the ruler of such a small country as Japan could establish an equal relationship with the Emperor of China.

Japan had sent two more envoys to the same dynasty, and fifteen to the ensuing Tang Dynasty though two of them had had to turn back halfway owing to unfavorable weather. The voyage to China was extremely dangerous, partly because their navigating expertise was still very primitive, and partly because the boats they built were not strong enough to sail across the East China Sea. In fact, their shipbuilding techniques remained on the same level as those learned from the Paekche long before it perished in 660.

Incidentally, Arabian navigator-merchants who had already brought the Mediterranean Sea under their control were coming up along the coast of southern China, expanding a riotously flamboyant world of adventure and money-making. Their advanced knowledge of astronomy and oceanography, which had long since enabled them to cross the Indian Ocean, soon made them discover the seasonal wind that swept over the East China Sea, helping them sail even farther up along the Chinese coast.

As far as shipbuilding was concerned, the Chinese were superior to the Arabs. Thus the two peoples, helping each other, were creating high-level technology, which spread quite rapidly as far as the Korean Peninsula, but not to the Japanese islands. That was why a lot of grumbling was heard from among Japanese who had to cross the sea to reach China: "Our boat is not dependable at all. I'd rather take the Silla boat."

Some were fortunate enough to have their wish fulfilled on their return voyage. The northern route the Silla boats took along the coast of the Korean Peninsula was safer than the southern routes.[2] Naturally the Japanese used to take the safer route, too. But they had had to give it up since Japan-Silla relations became strained in 660 when Silla-Tang allies defeated Paekche to whom Japan had sent reinforcements.

The Four Boats, as the fleet for the Japanese embassy to China was generally called, were newly built for each crossing. These boats, flat-bottomed like a washbowl, could not plow through waves as the Chinese or Arabian boats could on a keel fixed to the sharp-edged bottom. Japanese boats had sails, too, but if the wind shifted, the masts were flattened and many oarsmen had to be called upon to pull the oars, usually to no effect. The masts in Chinese boats were firmly fixed into the framework of the boats, but those of Japanese boats, just set between the deck's boards, were so constructed as to sway and rattle even at the slightest wind. In brief, the whole thing was a mere assembly of planks and poles, which could hardly stand the violence of a stormy sea.

The Four Boats usually accommodated three hundred to five hundred people, including a large number of oarsmen. The mortal fear of those who had to cross "the three thousand *ri*[3] of waters" in such primitive boats was so great that all but a few exceptions—like Buddhist monks eagerly seeking the truth—regarded that voyage as their last journey. No wonder some pretended to be too ill to set out on the journey, and others just ran away though they knew they would be exiled to remote islands when caught.

VIII. THE BOATS TURNED BACK AND SET SAIL AGAIN

KŪKAI, thirty years of age, had recently come to the conclusion that he had to go to China to complete his knowledge of Esoteric Buddhism. But how could he get to China when the Four Boats—with Saichō in one of them—had already left their home port, Naniwa-zu. About a quarter century had passed since the last embassy had been sent to China. How many years would it be before the next[1] was dispatched?

But it was not long before the boats were back at Naniwa-zu, for on the sixth day of their voyage, when they were still crossing the Inland Sea, they were caught in a tempest. The damage it inflicted upon the boats was such that they had to turn back. That was in midsummer, 803.

Kūkai could hardly have believed his ears when he heard the news at some temple or other in Nara. From this moment on, his movements and feelings seem to become less difficult for me to imagine: he would have jumped to his feet and begun to think about what steps he should take to obtain a passport to China. Their departure, he heard, would be postponed till about the same time next year.

Obviously the first thing he should do was to be granted official priesthood. So far he had simply ignored this. Why? Probably because he was unable to remain indifferent to what was happening within himself: whatever he was doing, wherever he went, he was persistently assailed by sexual desire, which must have been stronger by far than that in the majority of people, as is often the case with great thinkers; the monomaniacal continence they impose upon themselves is likely to help them form a habit of mind that is drawn only to the essence of things. As a mountain ascetic, Kūkai also would have mortified his flesh to a great extent, only to find it of no avail.

But at long last he came to find a solution when a new world was revealed to him while reading the *Mahavairocana Sutra* in "the East Pagoda of Kume-dera." It was a world where sexual appetite was wholly approved of, though a means of sublimating it was openly and deliberately proposed. The world he discovered then, trembling with a strange sensation within himself, might be taken, if viewed in a certain light and from a certain angle, as a world of sexual appetite philosophized into thought—more precisely, a world where even what remains unphilosophized is also fully accepted as part of the real existence of the universe. This may explain why Kūkai, living so long ago, still seems to retain the warmth and vital fragrance of human physicality.

For Kūkai as a vigorous young man, therefore, it was impossible to confine himself in a monastic dormitory, obediently observing the code of continence as all the official priests were expected to do. Sometimes, when he had "an ecstasy," as the *Rishu-kyō* rapturously extolled it, he must have fancied himself living as a layman medium all his life. But by the time he decided to go to China after reading the *Mahavairocana Sutra*, he must have gained confidence in his ability to become an official monk, not because he felt confident he could keep his flesh under control, but because he had succeeded in transcending the level of continence by building up a new world—a new type of Mantrayana which he named Purified Mantrayana.

This thought system of his own making, however, needed to be authorized in China; that was, he had to meet someone in China who would initiate him into the orthodoxy of purified Mantrayana from India. Otherwise the system of thought he created would never be approved of by the Japanese government, and if he made himself an official monk, he would be forced into the dull life led by all the other official priests in Japan: transferred from one state temple to another, they were just following the daily routine of sutra-reciting for the benefit of the state, only looking forward to being promoted. If this was all that they could receive in return for a continence that was no better than voluntary semi-suicide, no life on this earth could be so joyless. In those days when priesthood was considered to be a shield against evils, official priests supported by the state were a sort of human sacrifice it could offer to preserve the state from calamities and to relieve the Imperial family of the trials of birth, illness, aging and death. How could Kūkai have consented to throw himself into such a miserable situation?

But if his system of thought were to be finalized and authorized in China and so recognized as such in Japan, he would be able to live in a different world of his own even if he were an official priest. Before arriving at this point, he had lived through his twenties, and when he finally made up his mind to go to China to carry out his plan, the Four Boats had already departed. But they soon returned as if they had done so just to take him on board. This will also be counted as one of the many strokes of good fortune that illuminated the course of his life.

Among the many who could help him obtain a licensed priesthood in such a hurry, the most instrumental would have been Gonzō of Daian-ji, for his profound scholarship and virtuous character had attracted a large number of supporters and friends not only in the Ecclesiastical Office but also in government and Court circles. On hearing of Kūkai's wish to go to China in order to perfect the principle he had finally made up for himself, Gonzō must have been delighted to use his influence for him, and it was not very long before Kūkai was formally ordained and the official report was submitted to the government.

But it was by no means easy to have an unknown priest join the embassy to China. Gonzō and other spokesmen for Kūkai went to those in authority and eagerly explained what sort of person Kūkai was, what he had been doing so far, and how he needed to go to China "to prosecute his studies on the *Mahavairocana Sutra*." But even to the professionals in the Ecclesiastical Office very little was known of the *Mahavairocana Sutra*.

"Is it not some useless nonsense?"

Some must have expressed their doubts, referring to Saichō: "Saichō is going to China to bring back the Tiantai religion, a new system molded around the core of the *Hoke-kyō* sutra. Naturally he has to purchase many scriptures, so Kūkai may ask him for the *Mahavairocana Sutra* and any other sutras he needs."

Then Gonzō had to explain to them what Purified Mantrayana was—a newer Buddhist religion from India.

His uncle Ōtari also did as much as he could, visiting many acquaintances he had made as a tutor to the royal prince, and to Prince Iyo himself. The Ōtomo Saeki, who had been appreciating the budding genius in

Kūkai, also would have gained many sympathizers for him when they said: "He is one of us. When a university student, he often came to see us. Yes, the old man (Ima-Emishi) had also predicted what he would become in the future."

At long last Kūkai was permitted to go to China as a government student who was to "stay and study Buddhism there for twenty years." This ought to have meant that all the living expenses needed in that interval would be supplied by the government. As it was, all he received from the government was forty *hiki*[2] of coarse silk, eighty *tan*[2] of cotton cloth and one hundred bundles of cotton. Converted into gold and silver, they would not amount to much; they would only help make small presents or tips to those who took care of him at offices or temples he visited or stayed at in China. The envoy and the vice-envoy were amply supplied with gold—two hundred *ryō*[3] and one hundred and fifty *ryō* each. But the rest of the embassy had to raise the necessary funds for themselves.

In the case of Saichō, whose visit to China had been approved of by the Tennō Kammu himself, and whose status was not a government student but an introducer of a new religion who would soon return with the envoy after the purchase of the library concerned and whatever else was needed, all his expenses had been amply provided for both officially and personally. The gold and silver presented by the Tennō and his Crown Prince alone must have amounted to several hundred *ryō*. Naturally all the powers in the Court followed their examples. What was more, Saichō was allowed to have his own suite that consisted of an interpreter, copiests, and students who were to stay and study on Mt. Tiantai for twenty years.

Kūkai also intended to introduce a new religion into Japan. But his, unlike Saichō's, had not yet been acknowledged in Japan, and this handicapped him a great deal. But after all Kūkai was able to do no less than Saichō did. The Kūkai who appears in hundreds of folktales and legends is often depicted as a superman who wrought miracles and wonders. Indeed, he looks like one, considering the fact that he had obtained so much money from so many subscribers in such a short period of time before starting for China. He must have fully employed his preacher's gift in making a speech whose purport would have been: "The Buddhism we have had so far was not satisfying enough, but now I have found a truthful Buddhism that will answer all our needs. Fortunately, it has already arrived in Chang'an, and if you kindly help me bring it from Chang'an, you will soon find that you have done greater good than dedicating a temple to old Buddhism."

Again the Ōtomo Saeki did their best, while Gonzō was tireless in witnessing to Kūkai's authenticity, thus bringing him many supporters. His uncle Ōtari would have succeeded in making Prince Iyo, the then Lord Chamberlain of the Household, his greatest patron. Naturally the Sanuki Saeki did their best for him, too. Other local powers on the same island would also have done their bit. Considering the high agricultural productivity in Shikoku at that time, what they contributed must have been considerable. In the years to come, Kūkai was to set up dozens of Buddhist temples[4] on that island probably in return for the kindnesses he had once received from them.

As it turned out, the very spirit of self-reliance Kūkai showed on that occasion was to keep him independent of the state and the Court through the rest of his life. Usually he placed himself on a par with the state and the Court, and sometimes elevated himself even higher. Certainly this would be the expression of his overflowing self-confidence in the belief that he had mastered the truth of the universe beside which even the sovereign of the state was as good as nothing; but I suspect that he had made an unspoken demand upon the state: "I owe you nothing in having acquired this system of mine. So if you want to share its benefits with me, you should become my disciple and bow down before me."

The envoy to Tang China was Fujiwara no Kadonomaro, the eldest son of Fujiwara no Oguromaro who had directed the survey of the Yamashiro Basin with the result that his report for it had drawn Kammu's attention to Mt. Hiei and eventually to Saichō who had been there for years. On his first visit to Saichō at his hermitage, Oguromaro would have accompanied Kadonomaro who was also on the Council of State. Now Saichō, a Buddhist mentor to the Tennō and a future reformer of Japan's Buddhism, was going to China. Naturally Kadonomaro, the envoy, was well aware of the great mission Saichō had taken upon himself, but he had hardly known of Kūkai who had only recently come to join them. This may have led to the moody, rather casual manner with which he had received Kūkai when he paid him a formal visit, accompanied by his uncle Ōtari and someone from the Ōtomo Saeki.

"Um.... So you are Kūkai...." he muttered. Then he might have voiced his permanent preoccupation: "I hope we shall be able to return home safely."

His gloominess would have largely been attributed to his conviction that he would never be able to see his home again—the very same conviction that had tormented all the envoys before him. In March the year before, the Tennō had held a farewell banquet for the embassy, at the height of which the Tennō beckoned Kadonomaro forward and, after giving him a cup of *sake* (rice wine), sang a poem of his own making:

> This cup is not just for ordinary farewell,
>   but for our sincere prayer
>   for thy safe return
>   to us all.

Listening to these words with a profound bow, Kadonomaro could not restrain his tears, which "fell to the floor like so many raindrops," and "all those present were moved to tears, too," as is recorded in *Nihon-kiryaku*.[5]

*   *   *

On May 14, 804, the Four Boats were about to set sail from the port of Naniwa-zu. The port, an arm of the sea running deep into the land, was provided with many good anchorages. On top of the pine-wooded plateau that overlooked the bay, stood a Reception Hall for foreign visitors. The bay, though drained in later ages to make part of downtown Ōsaka, used to be dotted with white sandbanks or what were called *yaso-shima* (eighty islets) round which boats sailed in and out.

Around the ship-builders' huts below the Reception Hall, men could be seen putting the finishing touches to the wooden boats mainly by caulking the joints with dried seaweed. As all of the woodwork was jointed, joints were easily widened when hit by strong lateral waves, but caulked with the seaweeds like this, it was hoped the weeds would swell and stop the gaps, thus preventing leakage of water. The Arabs had already been using asphalt to caulk the joints, but the Japanese had never known even how to use iron nails to fix them together.

Such being the case, a safe voyage seemed to be the last thing they could manage. Then all that they could do was to pray and pray for divine protection, domesticating the boats by treating them as human beings, offering them names such as Haya-dori (Swift Bird) and Saeki (Aide for the Chief) along with the junior grade of the fifth court rank, as could be seen by the brocade cap placed on the prow of each boat.

Kūkai arrived at the port when the boats were about to cast off. A large amount of baggage he had brought with him was carried into the hold of the boat by a dozen porters he had hired. He would have to hire porters again and again in China, too. The boat Kūkai took was the leading boat with the envoy Fujiwara no Kadonomaro on board.

Kadonomaro had changed his name to Kanō, so that it might sound more refined and Chinese, as was done by many Japanese going to China. Saichō, who was to take the second boat with the vice-envoy, had been waiting for the delayed departure at Dazai-fu in Tsukushi in northern Kyūshū. Dazai-fu, the administrative headquarters of the governor general of the eleven provinces in the Kyūshū district, was where the Japanese embassy made it a rule to come and stay for a while on their way to and from China. It was also practically the main entrance to Japan for those coming from overseas.

When the envoy decided to return to the home port the year before, they had been off northeastern Kyūshū, and Saichō had been allowed to land in Kyūshū and stay at Dazai-fu when he expressed his wish to do so. As would be expected from any Buddhist priest in Saichō's place, he spent most of his time at local temples, praying for a successful voyage when they sailed the next year. The Buddha he was eagerly invoking then was the Great Healer, four images of whom he had carved himself soon after he arrived in Dazai-fu. But Saichō, not being a shaman by nature, could not have been a great invoker. The Tiantai principle he was pursuing also had very little to offer in this direction, as Saichō himself had noticed. He wanted to arrange it to his satisfaction one day when he built up his own religion—the Tendai religion. As far as praying or invocation was concerned, no other religion could excel the Mantrayana, benefiting from a superior system with profound methods for operating the universe. To Kūkai, confident in his ability in this direction, Saichō's amateurism might have seemed laughably like playing to the gallery.

The Four Boats were now smoothly sailing across the Inland Sea. When his boat was passing off Tado County in Sanuki Province, Kūkai would have been leaning over the port bulwark, gazing upon the far-off beach. His parents must have come out to the beach to wave to the boat their son was sailing on. The last time he had come home, his mother had sighed over "the twenty years" she would have to wait before seeing him again, for government students were all expected to stay in China for twenty years; Kūkai would be over fifty next time he was home, and his parents might no longer be alive.

"Don't worry, Mother," Kūkai must have turned to his mother, saying in a tone with a tinge of impudence in it: "It won't take me so long, you know."

Though he dared not explain himself any further, he had often said to himself that twenty years would be twenty times more than he really needed. He knew he had already mastered almost all of that system and all that he had to do in China was to receive a finishing touch from a proper master who had been initiated into the orthodoxy of purified Mantrayana from India; if everything went well, it might all be done in a single day. In fact, the ultimate initiation was certainly performed in a single day and his stay in Chang'an turned out to be only fourteen months, as he had anticipated.

It was illegal for a government student to return home before the term expired. But this might have been part of his premeditated plan. This shortened stay did enable him to spend all the funds he had collected for his "twenty year's stay and study" in order to acquire the whole system of purified Mantrayana. Though not so bold as to disclose this prospect even to his mother, he might have dropped a hint the last time he saw her, probably because he was not completely free from that Confucian moral: "One should not make a long journey while one's parents are alive."

The Four Boats sailed slowly westward, stopping here and there. Leaving the Seto Inland Sea behind, they passed the Kammon Channel and sailed on the rolling sea of the Hibiki Sea, then across the very dark waters of the Genkai Sea, until they reached Hakata Bay. At its farthest point was an anchorage called Nanotsu.

Saichō would have come to the beach of Nanotsu to meet the envoy and the vice-envoy. There were many local dignitaries, too, including the Under-Secretary of Dazai-fu, the Governor of Chikuzen Province, the superior of Kanzeon-ji temple, each accompanied by his own attendants. It was a dazzlingly sunny day and the hot air was shimmering over the beach.

The envoy, after taking the salute from each of them, stepped over to Saichō and showed him great courtesy as if he were his own mentor.

"So this is Saichō...."

Kūkai, though from a distance, must have observed Saichō intently, as if wanting to see right through him. His build was smaller than he had imagined. The slim figure surmounted by a large head looked like a mallet planted in the sand. It was impossible to study his facial expression, but there was no sign of obsequiousness about him. This was something Kūkai had least expected of Saichō, who he believed was very wise in the ways of the world. Kūkai might have felt a need to revise his image of Saichō.

"To the one who has succeeded in joining the truth that extends itself all over the universe," Kūkai often pondered with youthful ardor, "earthly power will be looked down upon as something no better than dust."

It was unfailingly from this viewpoint that he judged others as well as himself. What was his revised opinion of Saichō like?

"So you see," someone came up to Kūkai and whispered to his ear, "that is Saichō, one of the ten Buddhist priests to serve the Imperial chapel."

The voice betrayed the bitterness of his character, which had made his reception in the Court circle a rather dismal affair. He was a young man named Tachibana no Hayanari, a student of Confucianism who was to further his studies in China. During the voyage so far, Kūkai had remained silent and aloof as if he were still alone in a mountain forest. Hayanari was the only person who came up to him to talk, occasionally challenging him in argument. Beside Confucius, he seemed to have read the Legalists,[6] Laozi[7] and Zhuangzi,[8] even though he had found not one attractive enough to give it his full devotion. That was probably why he was inconsistent in his opinions: when he wanted to attack the academic bigotry of the university, he would cite Han Feizi, a Legalist, and when the fancy took him, he would just switch to Zhuangzi, declaring that all but Zhuangzi were imposters. Usually Kūkai enjoyed debating as a sort of pastime, but in the boat he might have preferred not to take up such an aimless argument for fear of getting seasick. But Hayanari could not help hanging around Kūkai. So far he had been proud that no one was more intelligent than he, as was acknowledged by others, too. But the erudition and strong memory he found in this strange Buddhist monk he met in the boat for the first time were undoubtedly much more than a match for him. Hayanari must have been amazed at the extent of Kūkai's reading that had extended even to pornographic writings.

"What was it made you a Buddhist monk?" Hayanari asked. "With that scholarship of yours, you'll surely be appointed to be a tutor to a royal prince. Don't you think so?"

Kūkai smiled but said nothing, which drove Hayanari to ask a more pointed question.

"Don't you want a woman?"

"Of course, I do," Kūkai pronounced this time. "That's why I've chosen Buddhism."

Hayanari, when he came up to Kūkai to attract his attention to Saichō, must have given his own impression of Saichō:

"I suppose he is a proper bore."

This derogatory comment he made about Saichō was partly intended as a tribute to Kūkai. But Kūkai would not accept it and replied, not hiding the contempt he felt for Hayanari: "Do you think so? I don't...."

To Kūkai now, his only reservation about Saichō concerned his infatuation with the Tiantai principle. What was the use in taking up a principle that showed only a mild interest in the essential vitality of human beings? It was simply unbelievable to Kūkai how a clever person like Saichō who had gained prestige in the Court circle should be so stupid as to make that erroneous choice. He could not have acted as despicably as Hayanari had in making insinuations about Saichō. Kūkai would have liked to say just to drive away this busy body always buzzing around him like an annoying fly: "At least he made himself a Buddhist monk and this fact alone proves that he is better than you, a Confucian."

In fact, what is the use of learning so much Confucianism? Is it not after all a man-made code for a human society? Is it not foolish to embrace it only to feed one's self-conceit? Kūkai went on saying to himself in growing excitement: "What if Saichō speaks to me? I'll be quite ready to have a long, serious talk with him so that I may release him from his rigid misconceptions and help him face the truth in a more honest frame of mind and make him realize, before arriving in China, what an imperfect system he has been captivated by. As a fellow thinker with a similar aim in view, I shall be qualified to do so. Anyway, that's our business, not Hayanari's."

Soon a long train of people was to follow the straight thoroughfare leading to Dazai-fu. The first view of Dazai-fu was of a huge earthwork lying across the field ahead. Was it a Japanese version of the magnificent ramparts[9] that surrounded castle cities of China? Or as its epithet Mizuki (Water Castle) suggested, did it conceal a sort of defensive device that could be used to flood the neighborhood in case foreign invaders landed in Hakata Bay?

At the stately gate standing at the end of the thoroughfare, the Chief Secretary and his attendants were waiting for the arrival of the embassy. Their splendid display was in the Chinese rather than in the native Japanese style, as was Dazai-fu itself, a virtual outpost of Japan's diplomacy and foreign trade, constantly receiving visitors from overseas. Popularly called Tō no Mikado (the Court in the Remote Province), Dazai-fu was certainly a replica of the Court in the Heian capital, its city neatly checkered with twenty-four streets running north and south, and twenty-two east and west.

While staying there for several days, Kūkai spent many hours walking around the city, visiting Kanzeon-ji temple and the school and the hospital[10] there, making acquaintances who were to come to his aid in one way or another when he returned from China two years later.

There is no evidence, however, that Kūkai and Saichō came in contact with each other. Naturally they would have exchanged bows when they passed each other in the guest house where they were staying or in the street. Saichō would have known who Kūkai was, but probably that was all he knew about him. Considering what happened later, Saichō was ignorant of Kūkai's reason for going to China, conceivably not because Kūkai kept it to himself, but because Saichō did not interest himself in Kūkai to the extent of trying to enter into contact with him personally.

As for Kūkai's purpose in going to China, the envoy Kanō must have received formal notice of it. But his knowledge of Buddhism—especially of purified Mantrayana or Esoteric Buddhism—was so limited that it probably never occurred to him that he should introduce Kūkai to Saichō. Or he may have done so, but in a very casual manner. Even so, Saichō would have reacted promptly if he had taken any interest in Esoteric Buddhism. As it was, Saichō, totally ignorant of Esoteric Buddhism, was hardly any the wiser about it when he himself took it up in Yuezhou, China. In fact, not until he returned home and was forced to embrace it by the Tennō did he begin to realize its importance. Saichō's indifference to Kūkai at Dazai-fu must have been disappointing and displeasing to Kūkai. Did this fortify his impression that Saichō was arrogant?

The Four Boats were again at sea. Slowly sailing along the northern coasts of Kyūshū, they were heading for the Gotō Islands or the Five Islands that lie furthest west of Japanese territory. The mere sight of the Islands may have caused them unusual strain and exhaustion. Some may have been driven mad, as is recorded in the annals of voyages to and from China. As the islands were fringed with numberless islets and reefs with swift tides surging all round them, it was a real adventure to sail as far as Tanoura port on the northern tip of the westernmost island. It was where they obtained the final supplies of food and water and made the final repairs to the boats while waiting for a fair wind.

In fact, a fair wind was a practical impossibility in summertime when the wind usually blows from China to Japan. If only they had waited till fall when it begins to blow from Japan to China, they would doubtless have been sailing before the wind. But unaware of this simple fact, many an embassy to China set sail in midsummer,[11] with the result that they were often wrecked.

On July 6, 804, they had a fair wind or what they considered as such, and the Four Boats left Tanoura. Later Kūkai recalled that moment and wrote:

93

Led by Kanō, we ventured out to sea, forgetting our own
interests, only prompted by a sense of duty....

But the fair wind lasted only a single day. On the night of the following
day, the head wind began to rock the boats. The sea was dark; the clouds
were low. Waves pounded the clouds; wind set the sea boiling. It was not
long before "torrents of rain tore the sails, and axe-blows of wind broke the
rudders," as Kūkai wrote in the preface to *The List of the Items Introduced
from China*. It was impossible to know what was happening to the other
boats. As the envoy reported, "We kept our torch burning on high, but no
response came from the third and the fourth boats." The second boat alone
was responding, but only for a while.

IX. DRIFTING ON WATER AND ON SHORE

THE first boat was left to make its way alone. All night long it struggled on against the violent wind. The day dawned on a clear sky, but the boat was still at the mercy of high seas. If everything went well, it would take ten days or so to cover the shortest distance—800 kilometers—from Tanoura to the mouth of the Yangzi River.

The ten days passed. But there was no landfall. The boat was just drifting at the mercy of the waves with no firm direction. Twenty days passed but things remained the same. There must have been signs of panic in the cabin. But quite probably nobody asked what seems to us today a very natural question: "Is the boat really keeping on the right course?"

The ocean-going peoples in the Western world had already adopted astronavigation that enabled them to establish their position at sea. But what the Japanese used for the same purpose was Chinese-style astrology: when night fell, the professionals—masters of the Way of *Yin* and *Yang* and *Urabe** diviners—would stand at the bow with certain implements and consulted the stars in order to seek help for their fortune-telling. Naturally sunrise and sunset helped them keep a sense of direction, but these phenomena were useless in bad weather or at night.

The daily rations for each was 1.8 liters of sun-dried steamed rice, which was harder than uncooked rice. On land it could be softened in hot water. But in the boat where making fire was virtually banned, it had to be soaked in unboiled water that was also rationed at 1.8 liters a day. No food could have been more insipid than this. But after a lapse of twenty days or so, they must have been put on shorter rations. On the other hand, with more and more people suffering from dysentery or depression, the cabin would have been turning into a sort of inferno.

What was Kūkai doing all this while? Priests on the boat were expected to be engaged in sutra-chanting day and night in order to call upon divine protection. Then did Kūkai join them? Or was he sitting quietly in an obscure corner, as if he had turned into a stone monument? A dozen years before, when he had had a strange experience in Cape Muroto—when the morning star flew into his mouth—he was awakened to the meaning of his existence on this earth, and from that moment on, he had been feeling, even at casual moments in daily life, that his life was directly controlled by the will of the universe. Now at the heart of this dangerous situation, he must have felt it even more keenly. Even when the boat creaked and squealed as if about to break in two, he must have remained cool and calm, his faith firmly centered on the notion: "The will of the universe is going to allow me to master Esoteric Buddhism. Whatever befalls us—howling winds, towering waves, groaning timbers, illness—they all have their source in universal providence. The depth of providence is unfathomable. But it will be explained by Esoteric Buddhism—by none other than Esoteric Buddhism, already in existence in Chang'an, China. Now I am on my way there to obtain it, and since my existence is responsive to the will of the universe, I shall never drown. This boat, even though damaged severely, will surely reach the coast of China simply because it carries me on board. There can be no doubt about it."

In the eyes of Kūkai, all the others on the boat would have appeared helplessly stupid because of their inability to see this plain fact that they would never fail to arrive in China as long as they were in the same boat with him.

Looking back through the history of this country, it may safely be said that Kūkai was the only person who, while able to reach elevated levels as a thinker, was able to enter the interior of the universe as a religionist. Shinran* and Dōgen* who also distinguished themselves in history were more thinkers than religionists, their thinking having made them too transparent to be the religionists they thought they were. In other words, they had already deprived themselves of archaic mysticism, whereas Kūkai's mind seems to be archaic mysticism itself, which he typically attempted to expand in order to cover the whole universe, and that by means of dynamic logic of his own invention.

Kūkai was seated in a corner of the cabin. But was he really there? He, a thinker and religionist, would have been lost in the depth of the universe.

Wearing a dark ocher robe over his head, he might have remained there immovable, except for his eyes dramatically glaring from within the hanging folds of the robe.

But when I think of his other persona that made him a man of the world, I may have to draw another picture of the one who was amazingly skillful in manipulating human society—so much so that some tend to look upon him with suspicion. Then Kūkai in the boat may have taken advantage of this opportunity to clarify what he was and where he stood in Japanese society.

People in perpetual fear were eagerly turning to *Ura-be* diviners, masters of the Way of *Yin* and *Yang*, and Buddhist priests, but none could be of any service to them, as Kūkai complained to Hayanari. The divination practiced by petty officials called *Ura-be* was based on the "tortoise-shell-burning" that was prevalent on the steppes of Manchuria and North China. When it arrived in Japan by way of the Korean Peninsula, the Tsushima and the Iki Islands, it managed to find its way into the Court where it eventually found a home in the Department of the Shintō Religion.

"Without any scripture or theory, it's nothing but an ancient custom," said Kūkai to Hayanari, who must have repeated or amplified Kūkai's speech in addressing his congregations.

The Way of *Yin* and *Yang* that had made itself a kind of pseudo-science by adopting minor elements of Taoism, could not have appealed to Kūkai. Hayanari, a Confucian who defied the supernatural, was also quite ready to deride the masters of the Way of *Yin* and *Yang* for their professed ability to communicate with the supernatural.

What annoyed Kūkai even more was the Buddhist priests, even though he himself was bundled into the same category. What had they been doing so far? Cramming their heads with prescribed knowledge merely to pass the examination to obtain official priesthood? Yet totally unaware of what they were, they just took it for granted that the sutra-chanting they were performing would appeal to the will of the universe. Was not this the height of make-believe? Hayanari, who could not help making himself a spokesman of Kūkai, would have denounced them, too, hotly arguing against the worthlessness of what they mistakenly believed to be Buddhism.

Hayanari was a most difficult person to live with, for he never tired of finding fault with anyone or anything he saw around him, as if he had been born with an inexhaustible stock of hostility against the world. To him, the national authorities and bureaucratic aristocracy, as illustrated by the envoy Fujiwara, mediocre in talent but high-ranked because of his birth, were simply repulsive. He disliked every other person in the boat—from high officials to technicians including medical men, the captain of the boat and the ship-carpenters: the former, though unfailingly high and mighty on land, were now being condescending enough to flatter the latter who were far from competent however busy they might appear.

The only person who was spared Hayanari's attacks was Kūkai, who had made himself totally alien to any other person in the boat because of the ideas he held: he had not only looked down upon Confucianism but also openly defied what was known as Buddhism in Japan, even though it had been valued by successive tennōs—so much so that some called themselves "a servant of the Three Treasures (the Buddha, his speech and his followers)." Before he came to know Kūkai, Hayanari had sometimes regretted his having been born as a misfit in this society. But seeing Kūkai who had to live in terrible solitude because of his ideas totally dissimilar to any other's, he could not help feeling he was more fortunate than Kūkai.

"Beside him," Hayanari must have muttered in a sigh of relief, "I am still a normal one."

This secret relief and a strange sympathy for him had made Hayanari an ardent admirer of Kūkai. But his admiration, expressed through his deep-rooted frustration, could not help taking the form of abuse against all the others:

"We are no better than trash. So it wouldn't matter a bit even if we were lost at sea. But Kūkai is an exception, and divine protection will surely keep him safe. This means, you see, we too shall be safely brought over to China simply because we are in the same boat with him."

*   *   *

In the end, they were at sea for thirty-four days, as the envoy Fujiwara wrote in the report he presented to the Tennō: "Wandering between life and death, we had been subjected to high seas for thirty-four days." Chinese writing, largely affected by a rhythmic flow of words, sometimes fails to express exact details. It would have been factually impossible for them to have been tossed about on the high seas for so many days on end. Certainly the first tempest that lasted several days blew them far off their expected course. But for the rest of the voyage they were just sailing this way and that in a variety of weathers until they arrived off Fuzhou (present-day Fujian Province) where no Japanese embassy had ever been seen before.

Days earlier, they would have been able to anticipate landfall by the yellowish tinge they saw in the sea water. Then they finally came in sight of a few islands, but none of them showed any sign of human habitation. On August 10, they saw in the distance a reddish coast dominated by mountains. Coming nearer, they saw more reefs and uninhabited islands and islets. The sun was scorchingly hot. Everything seemed strange and forbidding. But they had to find some bay in order to land. The one they put their boat into was "on the southern edge of Chi'an Town of Changxi Prefecture in the Province of Fuzhou," as they discovered later. That used to be the land of Min-Yue tribe, a branch of Yue tribe. But by that date in the Tang era, this mountainous, semitropical region had already been Sinonized and controlled by the Provincial Governor of Fuzhou, even though the natives were ready to rise at any moment if the central government relaxed its grip upon them. In fact, about a century later, when the Tang Dynasty fell (907), a semi-independent state named Min was to come into being though only for a while.

At long last, all on board could leave the boat and stand on the sand. Now the envoy's interpreters and secretaries had to come in contact with the local authority. To their dismay, however, few inhabitants were seen around a small number of houses that stood on the rare plots of land at the foot of a huge mountain mass. The scanty beaches were solitary, too, only sparsely dotted with fishing boats. The fishermen they met spoke a language totally incomprehensible even to the interpreters. By using gestures they managed to have one of them take them to someone who could read and write, from whom they were told where they were and where they should go next: a local station to check the entrance of pirates or smugglers. They followed his directions only to be directed there to the next stage: Chi'an Town, seat of the local military forces, where they met the Commander who was also administrating the town. But all he could do for them was to suggest their going to the office of Changxi Prefecture. The Prefectural Magistrate they met there, however, could do nothing but advise them to go over to the Provincial Government Office in Fuzhou, the capital of the Province of Fuzhou. He advised them to go by sea, because crossing a couple of huge mountain masses was practically impossible, especially when they had a large amount of cargo to carry. Another information he gave when they were leaving made them even more uneasy: "I'm afraid you may not be able to meet the Provincial Governor there. The former Governor has recently left his post owing to illness, and the new one has not arrived yet." The Provincial Governor of Fuzhou was practically the Provincial Governor General as he was supervising the administration of several other neighboring provinces that later became present-day Fujian Province.

The Japanese set to sea again. They sailed down along the coast as far as the mouth of the Minjiang River. Then a few days' upstream voyage along the river brought them to the port of Fuzhou, the provincial capital surrounded by magnificent ramparts built at the beginning of the Tang era. The origins of the city itself dated back to about 200B.C. when the king of Min-Yue tribe built his castle there.

At the foot of the bank they anchored the boat. But only the negotiators could leave the boat, since the Chinese law prohibited aliens from landing on Chinese territory until they had obtained official permission from the Provincial Government Office.

"We are the Japanese embassy on our way to Chang'an," said the negotiators to the reception clerk at that office. But the dismal appearance they presented led him to doubt their statement and to decide that they were nothing but smugglers. In fact, there might have been some cases in which trade merchants from overseas, trying to make direct trade with local merchants without paying customs as they should, disguised themselves as a custom-free embassy from a tributary of Tang China or as unfortunates who had happened to be driven there by a storm at sea.

By that time the new Provincial Governor General Yan Jimei had arrived. But he, the superpower in this remote region, was the last person to take any trouble to meet the suspicious or the unidentified. Soon all the Japanese were being treated as criminals; a Chinese official and his men came to the boat and drove all of them out on to the river beach, shouting: "Do not carry anything with you!" Then after a thorough inspection, the boat was shut up.

"I am the envoy representing the Japanese government."

The envoy Kanō vigorously proclaimed his identity through his interpreter, but the Chinese official would not accept it, saying: "If you are really the one you claim you are, why not show the royal message you have carried with you or the paper with the state seal stamped on it?"

To his vexation, the poor envoy could not produce either of them; as for the royal message to the Chinese Emperor, no envoy to Tang China had ever carried one, according to the established custom of the Japanese government that wished to keep Japan as independent as possible (see Note 3 for I), whereas Tang China expected all other countries that had anything to do with her to act as her tributaries. In other words, by not presenting such a paper, Japan evaded the opportunity to admit it was a tributary of China even though in fact that was what she was. As for the seal-stamped papers, the envoy had carelessly put them in charge of his archivist who had taken the second boat.

By that time the envoy had again and again had his negotiators carry a letter in his own writing to the Provincial Governor General Yan Jimei. But Yan Jimei simply ignored it, as is described in *The Memoirs of Our Master*:

> The Governor General opened the petition, but giving a glance at
> it, he just put it aside. The same thing happened again and again.

The realism with which this entry was written needs some consideration. The fact that all the appeals the envoy made were simply rejected by the Governor does suggest that his style was bad. It might have been that the more the envoy wrote, the more the Governor became convinced of the validity of the report he had received from the reception clerk: "They are smugglers, though they assert they are an embassy from Japan." At home, Fujiwara no Kadonomaro was considered to be among the most intelligent and the most proficient in writing and speaking in Chinese, and that was why he was chosen to be the envoy to China. Not until he was thrown into this difficult situation in China had he ever realized that he was not equal to that honorable post. Probably Kūkai was coolly observing what was happening.

Being a good writer in Chinese himself, he might have been feeling rather sympathetic toward Yan Jimei who had been forced to read such unreadable stuff again and again. He would have been able to imagine what Yan Jimei would have done with it, and this might have led him to describe the scene as vividly as if he had seen it himself on the spot, when he came to talk about it to his disciples in later years. In reading *The Memoirs of Our Master* compiled by his disciples who did worship him, some entries like this should be taken with a grain of salt. But it would allow us to see a very forceful personality in him, if this entry had been based on a speech he might have made: "The envoy presented his appeal again and again, but all the Provincial Governor did was to glance at it in disdain."

X. His Writing Saved the Difficult Situations

THE envoy Kanō had done everything he could. What more could he do now? October temperatures in this subtropical region were still quite high. But it was a real ordeal to be left on the wet sand day and night in all weathers. How many days did this miserable situation last? Different entries in the different versions of *The Memoirs of Our Master* suggest varying numbers of days from five or so to twenty days.

The envoy was at his wits' end, when one day someone, probably Hayanari, who must have been taking bitter delight in seeing the envoy forced into such a plight owing to his own incompetence, came up to him and offered a solution:

"We know very well you have done everything you could. But it doesn't seem to have improved the situation. I wonder what will become of us if we are left here any longer. We'll all surely fall ill and die.... If I may give you some practical advice, I should say that you might just as well commission someone to write for you. The Chinese think highly of literature. However often you might send a petition to the Governor, it would be of no use if not written in proper style. Fortunately, we have an excellent writer among us. I mean Kūkai. He will surely prove himself to be equal to that task."

"Kūkai? That priest?"

The envoy, who had been sitting on a mat spread on a barely dry spot on the sand, rose to his feet and looked over the people lying or squatting on the beach. When he saw the small figure of Kūkai in the distance, he slowly walked down to him and spoke to him with the utmost politeness, as was required by a Confucian code: anyone, not excepting the emperor, who asks any other person to write for him must treat him as his mentor:

"I am afraid I cannot tell what to do now to save this situation. But I have just heard that you are a master of composition. I should be very, very grateful to you if you would kindly accept my wish and write for me a petition to the Governor."

At this moment Kūkai, who had remained obscure so long, just shoved the curtain aside and presented himself on to the stage of Japanese history. It would not have been very long before he was led to a dry spot on the beach; then came a wooden box to be used as a desk, upon which a brush, an inkstone containing ink, and paper were neatly placed. The tall grasses surrounding that spot must have looked like a folding screen placed for him round this outdoor study. People were seen, but not heard. Kūkai's writing does imply the rapidity with which it was composed. In fact, he is reported to have been a fast writer, as he would have been in composing this petition, the draft of which still remains in his literary collection *Shōryō-shū*[1] edited by Shinzei, one of the best disciples he had in later years.

The petition, which is kept under the title of *A Letter to the Governor General of Fuzhou, Written on Behalf of the Envoy*, is certainly among the most impressive of all the literary writings he produced in his lifetime. The contemporary style he adopted is excessively ornate, but in the case of this petition it just helps make his logic brilliantly clear and powerfully persuasive, while his rhetoric, transcending the level of mere embellishment, never fails to strike sympathetic chords in the reader's heart, as it sounds like a piece of music composed by the writer's voice. It opens:

> Kanō presents this letter to Your Excellency,
>
> Lofty mountains, though mute, are so attractive to beasts and birds that they endeavour to reach them even from afar with indefatigable eagerness. Deep water, though silent, inspires fishes and dragons to steer their way to it with unremitting zeal. Likewise, even savages beyond the Borders, enticed by the virtuous illumination upheld by the Chinese Emperor, are simply intent on reaching His Land in defiance of all the dangers they must encounter on their way.

By offering, first of all, the sincerest tribute to the great glory of Chinese civilization, Kūkai must have been trying to fill the Governor General with comfortable pride and pleasure, so that it might open up a channel to his very heart, upon which the destiny of the ten dozen people on the wet sand depended. As to how the Japanese came to know the greatness of the Chinese Emperor, he explains:

> We Japanese on our islands, having always regarded the climate
> of China as unfailingly exemplary, have long been convinced that
> she has been governed by a saintly ruler.

This passage is based on a Confucian notion: where there is a saintly
ruler, there is exemplary climate (as a blessing from heaven). This certainly
adds to the dignity of his speech, instead of sounding merely diplomatic. He
goes on:

> The sovereign of Japan, therefore, does wish, as all of his
> predecessors did, that the virtue of the Chinese Emperor would
> kindly be imparted to him, too....

Then he refers to their voyage to China, describing what terrors they had
to face and how they finally found themselves in this part of the Chinese
territory, attributing that great good fortune not to their own ability but solely
to the extended virtue of the Tang Emperor.

But Kūkai, not quite certain whether or not Japan, a solitary island
country on the eastern sea, has come to the knowledge of the Governor
General of such a remote region of China, has to explain how different they
were from all those minority tribes:

> The tributary delegations of the Seven Western Tribes and the
> Eight Northern Tribes are not granted an audience by the
> Emperor; the former are only allowed to crawl on knees as far as
> the balcony, the latter only to proceed to the main gate before
> making a long, profound bow with forehead to the ground.
> Whereas the Japanese envoy was graciously allowed to occupy
> the seat for the principal guest when he expressed his wish to do
> so.

This had actually happened about half a century before (753), at the
Imperial Court of Tang China, when the Emperor was going to receive New
Year's congratulations from visiting envoys: the Emperor was seated in the
center, facing south, his guests seated on both sides, with the envoy and the
vice envoy from Silla on the first pair of seats on the eastern side, and those
from Japan on the second pair of seats on the western side. Ōtomo no

Furumaro, the vice-envoy from Japan, on seeing who were on the principal seats on the opposite side, raised his voice against the wrong order of precedence and was allowed to change seats with those from Silla.

The Japanese, who considered what Furumaro did on that occasion to be really admirable, were fond of talking about it until it began to sound almost like a legend. In the eyes of the Chinese receptionists, there was little or no difference between Silla and Japan, both being beneficiaries of Chinese civilization; Silla more saturated with it might have been placed higher. But Furumaro would not admit this, and pointed out the fact that Japan had been politically independent of China from the very beginning even if less influenced by it than Silla, and that Silla, beside being a vassal state of China, had been tributary to Japan, too.

Kūkai now, thus trying to make it clear where Japan stood in the international society of the Tang Court, goes on writing:

> How could we be compared with those insignificant savage tribes?

His intention was not to assert Japan's superiority to others; but his fear that the Governor General might be ignorant of Japan had made him take a bold stance and use such a grandiose tone in his writing. In fact, Japan at that time had rarely come to the knowledge of the Chinese in general, as the Japanese were made keenly aware wherever they were in China.

Now Kūkai had to give a good reason why the Japanese envoy had failed to prove his identity by producing a tennō's message addressed to the Chinese Emperor or a state-sealed paper when he was requested to do so. As mentioned before, Japan had made it a rule not to send a tennō's message to the Chinese Emperor, just to keep her politically independent of China or at least to demonstrate her wish to be so. As for the state-sealed papers, the envoy had foolishly entrusted every one of them to his archivist who took the second boat. But the envoy (through Kūkai), instead of admitting his own fault, argued his case by expatiating upon the origins of such means of identification:

> Bamboo tallies or copper seals as identity tokens came into being
> in a society where precaution against wiles and tricks was

necessary. Conversely, such things are unnecessary where people are good and honest, as in Japan. I am happy to say that Japan has always been on good terms with China and when we made presents to her, no state-sealed paper has accompanied them, yet no trouble ensued because our envoy, one of the closest confidants of the sovereign, had never been wicked or dishonest. That is why this tradition of ours has been maintained even to this day.

Such forced logic may sound like sophistry. But among the educated Chinese such sophistry was appreciated as a sort of wit, as Kūkai must have fully taken into account.

Then he had to prove his statement that the Japanese are good and honest. He refers to a passage from a Chinese book, *Writings of Prince Huainan*: "To the east of China, there is a land where people are good and honest and well-mannered. For that very reason, it is called the Land of the Wise."

When this book was introduced into Japan in the previous century, those who read this passage simply believed that the land mentioned here must be Japan because no other land existed "to the east of China." They happily quoted this here and there until it became common knowledge among intellectuals in Japan. Liu An, the editor of *Writings of Prince Huainan*, died in 122B.C. during the reign of Emperor Wudi in the Han Dynasty. Japan at that time, just entering the transition period between the Stone Age and the Bronze Age, could not have possibly been "the Land of the Wise." Probably the literary men who took part in producing *Writings of Prince Huainan* were deeply imbued with Taoism and their Taoist imagination might have created such an impossible land. Nevertheless the Japanese who had recently awakened to civilization through contact with China never failed to quote this statement in explaining what their country was like, just as Kūkai did on this occasion.

Those from "the Land of the Wise," Kūkai complains, are now being treated as undesirables, their cargoes examined, their boat shut up, simply because they carried no identity tokens with them. But he never forgets to show a good understanding of where the other party stands:

... But I know the action you took does conform to the law and is in accord with reason, setting an example of what a government official should be.

Then comes the closing paragraph, in which he makes an appeal, eagerly invoking the Governor's grace:

... we are now in great distress, abandoned here on wet sand. Our wretched appearance may belie what we really are. But if you would be so merciful as to extend your hand toward us in the cause of humanity, showing mercy to those from afar and rendering kindness to immediate neighbors, the gracious Tang Court will surely attract an even greater number of peoples who will flow in like so many streams that join to form a greater river.

On reading this petition, the Governor General smiled. He at once issued an order that the boat be opened so that the Japanese could enter it and that a messenger be dispatched to the Imperial Court in Chang'an to inquire what could be done for them. The prompt action he took then indicates his astonishment: "Could this really be written by one of those aliens abandoned to grief on that wet sand? Even the Emperor's secretaries would not be able to make a better job of it...." Great emphasis on literature had constituted a main part of Chinese tradition. Literature as they regarded it was the base of civilization, the foundation of politics, a grand enterprise to be carried out through the whole course of its history. Considering that the Governor General himself had also had his literary ability examined again and again before he attained his present post, the level of his literary judgment must have been fairly high, and this would also have contributed to the extent of his astonishment.

I wonder what it was that had kept Kūkai from offering a helping hand to the envoy until he was asked to do so. His modesty? Considering the behavior pattern he showed in his lifetime, he does not seem to have been a man who showed the sort of modesty appreciated by the sophisticated of later ages. In the years to come, he was to show some modesty on certain occasions, but in fact it seems to me to have been a part of his premeditated plan.

As is known by many of the episodes recalled from his lifetime, Kūkai had a genius for playing a distinguished part in any dramatic situation he came across in his actual life. To my mind, this was among the most remarkable gifts he was born with. Let us recall how in that dramatic work of *The Indications of the Three Teachings*, the real stage-conscious Kūkai acted as a beggar boy who displayed a critical spirit in comparing the three teachings' ability to enhance the level of human mind. Then the same sense of stage-management and dramaturgy must have started to work again while he was observing what was happening on the wet sand of the Minjiang River: Kanō, the envoy, whose talent does not fit him for his post, is confronted by the Governor General who represents the immovable authority of Chinese bureaucracy, thus putting all of his compatriots in mortal danger; then someone like Hayanari comes up to the envoy and presents him with "a knight" who is to bring about a miraculous change in their situation. In other words, the dramatist Kūkai, by just making use of what was being unfolded before his eyes, succeeded in making his first public appearance in such a dramatic and impressive way. Had it not been for this inborn, superlative talent, the image he left in history might not have been so overwhelmingly great as we see to be today.

Now the Japanese were able to return to the boat. The Governor General Yan Jimei, expressing his sympathy for Kanō, cordially requested him to wait for a while until he received a directive from the Imperial Court in Chang'an. Food, water, and some other necessities were generously provided, while thirteen houses were built in haste so that they could live in comfort. Minor officials and seamen must have regarded this change as a miracle or a divine wonder. In fact, from that time on, Kūkai was to be enveloped in a lingering aura of mystery created by his devotees or admirers, and it could rightly be said that the ten dozen people saved by Kūkai on that occasion did assume some historical significance as the first witnesses of the miracles Kūkai wrought.

Thirty-nine days had passed before the messenger returned from Chang'an with an Imperial order that the Japanese embassy should be treated as national guests. Thus the embassy was to receive even greater hospitality. At the banquets frequently held by Yan Jimei, Kūkai already known as the one who wrote for the envoy would have been discussed a great deal, even if his lowly status had kept him in the background. The Japanese envoy receprocated with a banquet every time he was honored with one. Naturally poetry and prose were exchanged on such occasions. The great reputation Kūkai was then building up just defies my imagination.

There was a literary circle in Fuzhou, too. Its membership, mainly consisting of government officials, included local intellectuals and wealthy merchants. As was always the case with such a literary circle in China, they met regularly to emulate each other in poetry-making and to talk about what was happening in the literary circles of Chang'an. It was not long before Kūkai was invited to such a meeting on the recommendation of Yan Jimei. Every time Kūkai improvised a poem, they held their breath in admiration. Some may have exclaimed: "No poet in Chang'an can beat you...."

To them it was simply unbelievable that the young Japanese, who spoke a totally different language at home in a remote island country that still remained backward in literature and that, to the best of their knowledge, had not yet produced any literary talent, was able to speak current Chinese fluently[2] and then to compose poems, and that in superb Chinese. Could humanity sometimes take on the aspect of divinity? Sometimes they must have felt uneasy as if they were in the company of a superman or demigod.

One of the officials Kūkai met in China—in Fuzhou or Chang'an or on their way to Chang'an—was Ma Zong. According to *The Old Tang History*, Ma Zong was accomplished in literature and this made him keep in touch with the literary circle in Chang'an, even while he was occupying a variety of posts, including provincial governor of Qianzhou, governor general of Annan (where he did much to Confucianize present-day North Vietnam), commander-in-chief of Huaixi, and finance minister in the central government. It is unknown at what stage of his career he was when he met Kūkai. But his admiration for him, as is expressed in the following poem,[3] would have been acknowledged by anyone who came to know Kūkai:

> What made you come from afar? I believe
> it was not to show off the talent you had
> astonished us with. Let us hope that you
> may go on pursuing profound truths; for I
> know even here in China you are a rarity.

Toward the end of November when the mountains of Fuzhou began to be touched with autumnal tints, the magnificent procession of the Imperial Messenger of Inquiry entered the capital of Fuzhou, the sight of which is reported to have moved all the overjoyed Japanese to tears.

Not all of the Japanese were allowed to go over to Chang'an. As a rule, only the envoy and his suite with one or two government students were invited. The rest would soon leave Fuzhou for Mingzhou to wait there for the embassy on their way home. The one authorized to choose the members was not the envoy but the Governor General. When it was announced in due time, Kūkai was staggered to find that he was not on the list but was ordered to stay in Fuzhou. What on earth, Kūkai wondered, had made the Governor General take such an unexpected decision?

"I'm afraid he is going to make you his Chen Lin," said Hayanari.

Chen Lin, a man of literature, was especially proficient in writing appeals or public letters. It was about the time when Cao Cao, who was later to found a kingdom that developed into the Land of Wei (220–265), was still fighting against his rival Yuan Shao. At one time Yuan Shao ordered his secretary Chen Lin to write an appeal against Cao Cao. The appeal he wrote, beginning with Cao Cao's background, placing the focus especially on his step-grandfather who had been a eunuch infamous for his wickedness, was a great help in making all its readers hate Cao Cao. But after all Yuan Shao was defeated, and Chen Lin had to surrender to Cao Cao, too. But Cao Cao, instead of putting Chen Lin to death, just appointed him his own secretary. This proved to be a very wise decision, for Cao Cao, a distinguished poet himself, immensely enjoyed Chen Lin's writings, saying: "Whenever I get a headache, I read Chen Lin. The effect is miraculous."

High officials in Tang China were all men of letters, and Yan Jimei was no exception. This meant he was subjected to constant rivalry. But if he were to have a Chen Lin with him, it would surely help him retain his high position in the official world, as Hayanari imagined.

"Oh, no!"

Kūkai groaned. He regretted the ovation he had received, if it was only to visit this misfortune upon himself. What could he do now to escape the cruel claws of Yan Jimei? He took up his brush and wrote to him again:

A Japanese Buddhist monk Kūkai cordially submits this letter.

So far I have lived in obscurity, usually wandering around cloud-capped mountains, sustaining myself only on vegetables, lying in snow[4] with an elbow for my pillow. My speech and conduct, therefore, do not deserve any consideration. But because of a vacancy that happened to occur before our voyage,[5] I was allowed by the Japanese government to come and stay in Chang'an for twenty years to study a new doctrine of Buddhism.

He goes on writing, as formality requires, about how hard he has to study, his talent not being equal to the heavy responsibility he assumes. Then he comes to the point:

I have just found that I am not allowed to go to Chang'an. I know that you have a good reason for making this decision, but if I were to stay here in Fuzhou, how could I carry out the very task I am expected to do in Chang'an?

Then, changing his tone and topic, he begins to admire Yan Jimei in the wording that sounds too sugary for modern tastes:

Your excellency, we have observed that with your great virtue appreciated by the Emperor, your benevolence has reached far and wide: young and old are united in admiration of that virtue, filling the streets with happy voices; men and women arm in arm praise your merits in concert, flooding all ears with immense pleasure. Appointed by the Emperor himself, you are steadily mending the ways of the outer world with wonderful skill, while persuing the truth of the inner world with great integrity. Now let me remind you that I have been sent to China to master the way to attain that very truth so that I might propagate it in my country someday in the future. I shall be immensely grateful if you would kindly reconsider your decision and allow me to go and study in Chang'an.

After all Kūkai was allowed to go to Chang'an. Hayanari must have been wild with joy. By that time the envoy had been quite ready to leave for Chang'an with his suite of twenty officials and two students. All the expenses required for their journey to and from Chang'an were to be paid by the central government of Tang China. In Confucian China, the distinction between principal and subordinate was clarified by the code of propriety: when peoples beyond her borders sent their missions to show their admiration to her, as they often did, China as prime host had to show them a great hospitality; if they presented some tribute to her, she had to return several times the worth of what she had received, besides paying for everything they needed while traveling across her territory, led by the official guide sent by the government, central or provincial. The total expenditure for such hospitality amounted to so much that the national treasury was often hard pressed.

The envoy was offered a horse with a saddle thickly embedded with pieces of gold, silver, lapis lazuli, crystal, coral, agate and giant clam. The rest of his party were also allowed to go on horseback. In the early morning of November 3, 804, they left Fuzhou in a procession under a starry sky through the trailing smoke from torch lights held on high at regular intervals.

XI. Travel to Chang'an

THERE was a long journey ahead of them—2,700 kilometers. They were in a hurry as they intended to attend the New Year celebration at the Tang Court. Each day, as the envoy reported later, they set out under the stars and traveled on and on until they stopped to sleep under the stars. No record remains of which route they took. But according to *The Daishi's Travel to Chang'an* by Kuwabara Jitsuzō, who published it in 1921 in the form of a lecture, the route to Chang'an had already been established by Kūkai's time and even when the author himself followed Kūkai's trail in the 1900s it had not changed much.

Their first destination was Hangzhou. Kanō's party would have taken at least seventeen days or so. Moving up north, they were having cooler weather every day. To cross the piled-up mountain masses that crowned the mountainous province of Fuzhou, they first followed the path that went along the Minjiang River. Once it rained, the path was washed away, putting the hoofed animals in great difficulty. The horse-drawn carts were often overturned, preventing the party from going on. On rainy days native travelers usually stopped and waited till the rain stopped. But Japanese travelers in China were generally too impatient or in too much of a hurry to stop and wait. To the resentment of local coolies they had hired, Kanō's party was no exception.

"*Wo*[1]—what a mad lot!" The coolies may have whispered among themselves, complaining of the march they were forced to make as if they were heading for a battle front. The word Jipang[2] had not yet come to the knowledge of common people in China. They called the Japanese *Wo* and Japan *Wo-guo*.

From Hangzhou they went by water—along rivers and canals. Since most rivers in China flow from west to east, canals were dug north and south to connect rivers. Travelers northward, therefore, had to go up or down the rivers and sail up the canals until they reached their destination—Yangzhou or Luoyang or Chang'an. On seeing the canal, Hayanari must have shouted, noisily banging on the side of his boat: "Look, this is the emblem of the Great Tang!"

Indeed, this magnificent art of civil engineering, which was credited to Yangdi, the second Emperor of the Sui Dynasty (581–619), was certainly a pleasant surprise to the Japanese. But the very same canals had led the dynasty to an unexpectedly early fall: when they were completed after years of tremendous labor by millions of people, the Emperor began to enjoy sailing in a dragon boat between Yangzhou and Luoyang, accompanied by many Court ladies, indulging himself in "mountains of meat and lakes of wine," as the Chinese expression goes. Needless to say, it was not for such sumptuous excursions that the Emperor had carried out all that unprecedented construction work. As his dynasty had risen in the dry lands of North China, he felt the need to strengthen his influence over the fertile land south of the Yangzi River by waterways, collecting local rice as a tax in kind. The canals, thus brought into being by the short-lived Sui Dynasty, were to be of immense value to the ensuing Tang Dynasty. In its fledgling stage, the Tang Court was very small-scale in everything, its government officials numbering no more than six hundred and fifty, but in twenty years it was to increase to more than thirteen thousand. To feed that great consumer capital, the canals soon proved to be her life line.

Several days' sailing brought them to Yangzhou, whose wealth and prosperity had made it so attractive that Chinese poets all harbored the dream of spending their last years there. Hayanari must have given voice to his longing to stop there, even for a short while: "We simply must visit Yangzhou." But the boats had to sail on and all that they saw wistfully through the sallows and willows beginning to shed leaves on the banks would have been a distant view of it dignified by brick pagodas, tiled roofs of what seemed to be wealthy merchants' villas, and part of the darkened walls that surrounded the city.

"Yang comes first, Yi second. Do you know what that means?" Hayanari might have asked Kūkai, intending to test his knowledge of such secular matters. He was referring to the standards of commercial prosperity in China, as Kūkai, an extensive reader, could easily have answered. Yangzhou was where rice and all the other commodities produced south of the Yangzi River were collected to be shipped to the north. Yi or Yizhou, the capital of Yizhou Province, was a common way of referring to Chengdu or the capital of present-day Sichuan Province.

The life of local people, as seen from the boats sailing along the canal, was terrifyingly squalid. They defecated into the canal. As the water moved very slowly, the excrement remained stuck there, sometimes with bodies of dead cats and dogs. The very same water was used for cooking. Some Japanese must have been feeling as if their lifelong adoration for "the Great Tang" was on the wane. In Japan, a mountainous country that abounds in streams and springs, people had naturally developed the custom of washing everything. This was the origin of many religious practices.[3] Like the native Chinese, many Korean residents from Silla did not mind squalor, nor did Arabian and Iranian settlers who had come from dry land. Only the Japanese as temporary visitors felt concern about what they saw.

Ennin, a Japanese priest of the Tendai religion, who came to Tang China thirty-four years later than Kūkai, also passed Yangzhou on his way to and from Chang'an. According to his journal, *The Pilgrimage around Tang China in Search of the Truth,*[4] which has won a world-wide fame for its detailed description of what he saw and the people he met, his party had a very hard time in the boats, "many suffering from dysentery... and diarrhea...."

In Kūkai's party, many were also afflicted with the same ailments, and must have been experiencing the acute misery of being invalids in a foreign land. At night Ennin's party usually slept in the anchored boat and sometimes at a government residence in some town or other. But Kūkai's party rarely left the boats as they were usually on the move even at night. The sail-boats were manned by rowers. But when wind was not favorable, buffalos were hired. With ropes tied round them, the animals moved slowly along the banks, hauling the boats across the early winter landscape divided by the broad belt of water.

From Bianzhou they proceeded by land. Horses were available at the way-stations. Instead of going on horseback, many took a horse-drawn carriage only to endanger themselves. On unsprung wheels, it rumbled on along the deep-rutted road. Overhead was a sheet of flax stretched between the four solid corner poles, against which one might bump one's head at any moment, risking concussion of the brain. Falling into a doze would have been fatal. Coccyx, backbone, inwards constantly shaken up and down, they were unable to eat or drink. Probably Kūkai was the only person in the party to have maintained his usual poise. Having been a mountain ascetic throughout his twenties, frequently exposing himself to all weathers at all seasons, he must have made himself almost impervious to any such physical strain.

"Look, Baima-si temple!" Someone said, pointing to a temple seen in a small valley below. The carriage stopped. All the passengers got off and squatted down, trying to take what little rest they could, appreciating terra firma. Probably no one but Kūkai was strong enough to pay a visit to that ancient temple. Built in 67 A.D. by the Emperor Mingdi of the Later Han, it was considered the first Buddhist temple built in China. The first batch of Chinese versions of Buddhist scriptures is reported to have been produced here with the help of some Indian priests invited from India. Kūkai would have made a round of its spacious compound, occasionally casting his gaze upon the thirteen-storied clay pagoda. Meanwhile his coach might have left without him. If so, none of his companions would have cared, for they all knew he was sure to catch up with them sooner or later. Indeed, he was robust, his movements as sprightly as if his body was moved by some special internal mechanism. Those who had once seen in him a ministering angel were now seeing an indefatigable athlete, thus becoming even more convinced that, despite his childlike, round-cheeked face, he was no common mortal.

A short ride eastward brought them to Luoyang, the ancient capital that had been supplying ample materials for books of history and literature. The Japanese on their way to a government residence there for an overnight stay must have been beside themselves with joy, as all the things they had once read of in books were now on display one after another—the massive walls that guarded that castle city, the gate wide open as if especially for them, the Luoshui River spanned by Tianjin-qiao bridge as the hub of the city's throbbing life.

Walking around the city, Hayanari, a historian, must have been happily telling Kūkai about the dynasties Luoyang had seen. Luoyang, dating back to the eighth centuryB.C. when King Cheng of Zhou established his capital here, was possibly the oldest city still standing in the world. Situated in the basin, it was shielded by the surrounding hills; rivers were also helpful, the Luoshui crossing it, another flowing in the east, the other in the west, enabling it to import commodities from all directions. Since a better place could hardly be found, it had been the seat of many other dynasties: the Later Han (25A.D.–220A.D.), the Wei (220–265), the Western Jin (280–316), the Northern Wei (494–534) and the Sui (581–619); and now the Tang Dynasty had made it their second capital.

"Luoyang is the kitchen of Chang'an," Kūkai might have observed. Though intensely speculative as a philosopher, he was a born economist who was able to detect where the energy of human activities had its source. Naturally this ability was to help him greatly in later years, when he came to engage in his own projects. In fact, the rice needed by Chang'an was first collected in Luoyang. Then it was carried by a newly-built canal as far as Shanzhou, though at the perilous gorge of Sanmenxia a mountain route had to be taken.

In fact, Chang'an often went hungry when a long spell of rain or the ensuing flood disrupted waterborne mobility. This caused the price of rice in Chang'an to soar and that in Luoyang to drop, thus encouraging shrewd business activity, and eventually helping to make the Chinese a business-minded people. When rice in Chang'an began to run short, the Emperor himself came down to Luoyang together with his family, ladies and retainers who were also accompanied by their own families, retainers and servants; these brought their own families with them, until the moving population swelled to tens of thousands. No wonder the price of rice in Chang'an soon returned to normal levels.

The party resumed its hurried journey. Before them they had the most difficult peak to overcome, known for the ancient checking station—Hangu-guan—placed at the top. Even the approach to the foot of the mountain proved to be a two days' ordeal. A dark ocher path meandering among the mountains, deeply rutted in the wildest way imaginable, could no longer be called a path but a torture rack for travelers. From time to time, carriages were overturned, throwing passengers and baggage to the ground. Kūkai, a good walker, must have chosen to go on foot. Pedestrians were looked down upon in China, and coolies might have taken him to be an eccentric.

The ascent to the checking station was even harder. As the path was no wider than the axle of the carriage, it was impossible for two carriages to pass each other; one or other of them had to turn back, or coolies from both sides came out to widen the path by digging at the cliffs with hoes. The work took half a day, but it could all be undone in a single rainfall. The higher they went, the rockier the mountain became. Hoes would not work any more. Then they had to send forerunners, who cried warnings to other carriages not to come down till theirs had reached the top.

There were two checking stations bearing the same name. The new one built at the beginning of the Han era was what Kūkai's party was heading for. The old one, 150 kilometers west of the new one, had witnessed many scenes of historical interest as the Japanese travelers must have fondly recalled. Laozi, deeply depressed at the decline of Zhou in whose service he had worked, is said to have passed this station[5] on his way to somewhere in the west. Mengchang-jun, the then minister of administration in the Land of Qi, known for his generosity which was so great as to keep thousands dependent upon him, was once running away from the Land of Qin, closely followed by assassins sent by the king there. When he came to this station, he found, to his horror, that the barrier was closed as it was around midnight. Then an idea dawned upon him: one of his dependents that happened to be with him then was good at mimicking a crowing cock. Mengchang-jun asked him to perform his speciality. No sooner had he begun to crow than all the cocks kept at the station began to crow. The barrier-keeper woke up and opened the barrier, thinking it was already dawn, thus unintentionally rescuing the brave one who was to become one of "the four distinguished lords"[6] of the Warring States Period (403 B.C.–221 B.C.)

It took four days to get over the mountain—two days' ascent to the new station and two days' descent to Tong-guan station at its foot. Then three days' journey along the level road brought them to the hot-spring resort on the wooded hill named Mt. Lishan. It was a fashionable outpost of Chang'an with its sophisticated elegance reflected in its scenery. As everyone knew, it was a seat for the Huaqing-gong palace built by the Great Emperor Taizong at the beginning of the Tang era.

"Look! Mt. Lishan!" Hayanari shouted. It must have been touching to see the youth, usually too stubborn to get along with others, his head popping out of the dusty carriage, now smiling all over his face in genuine happiness. The romance of the Emperor Xuanzong (reign: 712–756) and his favorite consort Yang Guifei (719–756) had turned this spa into a place of poetic interest. Toward the end of his fifties, the Emperor Xuanzong, whose custom was to leave Chang'an in October and spend all the winter at this resort, was to meet here a young beauty of the Yang family. It was in the early spring of 742 that the following scene occurred:

> In early spring when cold was still lingering, she was invited by the Emperor to take a bath at the Huaqing-chi hot spring—her lustrous flesh having been cleansed by the softest water, she appeared bewitchingly defenseless in the arms of her maids.

These famous lines had not yet come into being, but even before Bai Letian[7] put them in his immortal epic, *A Song of Everlasting Sorrow*, it was widely known how she had been invited by the Emperor to bathe at the Huaqing-chi hot spring, and even such intimate details of her bathing scene were being talked about a great deal. Kūkai knew very well what had made Hayanari so excited, as he himself was probably feeling as if he were seeing her enchanting figure shimmering behind the trees on the hills. He must have sounded sympathetic when he nodded to Hayanari, saying: "Yes. That's Mt. Lishan...."

Chang'an was flanked by a couple of rivers: the Weishui and the Bashui, both joining in its northeastern suburbs, thus forming a sort of outer moat for it. The Bashui was spanned by the Ba-qiao bridge, more than two hundred meters long, a feat that had never been equaled in Japan. About four kilometers' ride after the bridge brought them to an uphill road named Changlepo, about five kilometers long, sparsely fringed with tea houses where travelers—especially embassies from abroad—would take a rest and put on fresh clothes so that they would look respectable in the Imperial

Castle of Chang'an. It was already December 21.

The then Emperor Dezong was now on his deathbed after about a quarter of a century's reign. But on being informed of the Japanese embassy approaching, he issued an order to send his receptionist to Changlepo Station. It was not long before he appeared, leading as many caparisoned horses as the members of the embassy so that they could enter the castle in a procession of proper grandeur.

The most welcome news they received from him then was about those in the second boat who had already arrived there: they had been at sea for as many as fifty-four days before managing to arrive on September 1 at Ningbo in Mingzhou; but having had no such troubles as those in the first boat did, they could arrive in Chang'an earlier—on November 15. No news being more welcome than this, a surge of excitement carried them away for a while even though they soon had to find that the vice-envoy, Ishikawa no Michimasu, had died of illness in Mingzhou. As for the other boats, there was no telling what had happened to them. Not until the envoy was back in Japan did he learn that those in the third boat were safe, though the boat itself was broken to pieces when cast on a solitary island in the South Seas. As for those in the fourth boat, nothing was ever heard of them.

*   *   *

Chang'an, consisting of two wards of one hundred and ten blocks each, was the largest metropolis the world had ever seen. When viewed from a distance, a long stretch of the eastern rampart looked like a somber line drawn along the horizon. A closer look showed three gates notched in it. Those from abroad were all expected to enter by the central gate— Chunming-men gate—that stood at the end of the uphill road of Changlepo.

The first thing they saw inside the gate was not working-class life as seen in the downtown area, but a quiet neighborhood with a civic center and a fashionable quarter arranged side by side. Occasional passers-by seen on the street, therefore, were usually noblemen or government officials. The block on the right hand side was no longer a block but a palace—the Xingqing-gong palace. A large number of tiled roofs of special grandeur were seen above the long walls with a number of two-storied gates in them. It had long been a detached palace in which Imperial princes resided until the Emperor Xuanzong himself came to settle there, and even attended to government affairs there. This naturally led to a great deal of improvement being made in the old palace, when the whole place was gradually transformed into a real wonder of architecture. This mania of the Emperor's quickly infected ministers and wealthy merchants, who spared no expense to make their residences rival all others in beauty. This trend, which extended from the closing period of Xuanzong's reign in 750s to the beginning of the present Emperor Dezong's (reign: 779–805), had been deplored by sensible people who called those extravagant luxuries "wooden monsters," probably sensing in them a foreboding of the decline of the dynasty. But by the time Kūkai came to stay in Chang'an, the beautification fever had subsided and its brilliant monuments stood shining everywhere, demonstrating how beautiful a metropolis could be at the apex of her maturity. All that Kūkai could do then was to appreciate it to his heart's content.

XII. SPRING IN CHANG'AN

HOW can we describe that miracle in the history of our planet, the prosperity of Chang'an? Kūkai could now become a part of her life. By saturating himself in her urban culture that was universality itself, he was finally able to realize what civilization and what humanity meant. At home in the remote uncivilized island country of Japan, he may have had only an abstract notion of them. Had he not gone through this melting pot of Chang'an, he would have grown into a different sort of person with a different type of sensibility, instead of becoming one of the very few Japanese who have attained a universality far beyond the limitations of nation or race.

Kuwabara Jitsuzō, a Japanese scholar of Oriental history mentioned in the previous chapter, was the first who made the effort to find out what Chang'an—the very place where the East and the West intersected—used to look like. Then another Japanese, Ishida Mikinosuke, the author of *Spring in Chang'an* first published in 1941 and gradually expanded in later years, finally succeeded in enabling us to *see* what sort of life they were leading in Chng'an and what kinds of culture from other lands were thriving there. As there was no particular record along these lines, Ishida had to start from scratch, collecting relevant items of information not only from authorized histories such as *The Old Tang History* and *The New Chronicles of the Tang Dynasty*, but also from literary sources like *The Complete Prose Works of the Tang* and *The Complete Poetry of the Tang*. Then he put them together carefully until at last the daily life of that ancient metropolis was truly presented in his epoch-making work. The following poem, *Spring in Chang'an*, written by Wei Zhuang (836–910) was appropriately quoted by Ishida on the first page of his book of the same name:

Chang'an in February is
enveloped in fragrant dust,
while the six broad thoroughfares keep ringing
with the musical clatter of hooves and carriages.

Maidens at every upper window look like so many
flowers rivalling the crimson blossoms flourishing
their tens of thousands of branches just outside.

From a pleasant chatter behind a rattan blind,
I just catch a question: "Who could ever be
so bold as to appropriate spring in Chang'an?"

From earliest times,
the quintessence of spring in Chang'an
has been embodied in the maidens
in those elegant chambers.

But lo!
What could we do now
when they are all being carried away
on fleet steeds or in smart carriages
driven by those who have been to
the Apricot Garden?[1]

When the Japanese embassy arrived in Chang'an, it was not yet the season of "fragrant dust."[2] But the thoroughfares were certainly throbbing with the jingling rhythms of traffic, with brightly-colored and high-spirited activities, and the kaleidoscopic patterns of passers-by. The last mentioned would have been what interested them most. Even Kūkai must have found his eyes drawn to a red-haired, blue-eyed man in a sheepskin coat leisurely walking away in leather boots.

"Iranian ...." Hayanari might have suppressed an excited shout at the sight of him.

Foreign guests were supposed to stay at guest quarters accommodating over one hundred people. Two different types of accommodation were available there: those from Arabia or Iran could sleep in beds and keep their shoes on indoors, and those from Silla or Japan could sit or lie on the floor, exactly as they did at home. But the place to which Kanō's party was then being guided was a government residence in Xuanyang-fang block, probably because the guest quarters were all already occupied, as an entry in *The Old Tang History* informs us: "In December, the envoys from Tibet, Nanzhao and Japan paid a visit to the Imperial Court to offer their tributes." The Tang Court had placed Tibet above Japan. Nanzhao, a rising nation in present-day Yunnan Province, had probably sent a larger embassy than Japan's.

The New Year arrived. But the Emperor Dezong was dying, and this kept the whole capital rather subdued. On January 23 he died. Five days later the funeral was held, and the Japanese embassy members were seen among the mourners who gathered around Chengtian-men or the inner central gate. On the same day the Crown Prince ascended the throne, but the capital in mourning was quieter than usual. Naturally the national guests also refrained from walking around the town, as is reported by the envoy: "Keeping to our residence, we mourned for the late Emperor day in and day out."

January moved into February. The envoy must have been expressing his wish to the clerk in charge: "We must start as soon as possible." We may think that he should have stayed longer and enjoyed sightseeing in and around Chang'an, but if he wanted to observe the rules of propriety, he had to leave there as soon as he had finished his business, as his party had occupied the government residence, keeping the large personnel in charge fairly busy. When we consider all the dangers and difficulties he faced on his way to and from China, being an envoy was no sinecure. This was especially true in the case of Kanō who happened to be in Chang'an in deep mourning and could not indulge even in a glimpse of her "gay quarters."

In due time his wish was granted and they were allowed to leave on February 10. Many reciprocal souvenir gifts were delivered to him along with an Imperial message that included the following entries: "We wished you could stay here longer but since you insisted on going so soon, we shall allow you to leave.... since national mourning kept you unusually busy, you should take your time over your return journey....we hope you may accept our gifts ... and our invitation to the farewell banquet," and " ...on your return you shall inform them of our national mourning."

On the day of their departure Kūkai and Hayanari were seen among those who came to see them off at the end of Ba-qiao bridge, where they broke off sprigs of the willows[3] on the bank to present to the departing, with wishes for their safe return. Kanō and other Japanese were weeping since they knew this might be the last sight of one another. Considering Kūkai's character, he was probably the only Japanese who remained dry-eyed. In this respect, he would have been more Chinese than the Japanese who used to be easily moved to tears.

The envoy, receiving the willow sprigs from Kūkai, may have gratefully replied: "I cannot thank you too much for the great help you have given me both in Fuzhou and here in Chang'an."

In Chang'an, Envoy Fujiwara had to communicate with the envoys from other countries, and again he had to ask Kūkai for help. Even today we can read what he wrote for the envoy—a farewell letter addressed to Yuan Yu, a royal prince and envoy from Bohai[4]—as its draft was later included in *Shōryō-shū* as the complete collection of his literary writings. Recently I read it and his typical style left upon me the impression that I was beholding a most gorgeous butterfly which, with its furry trunk lightly pressed by the tip of my small finger, leisurely flutters its wide wings, scattering its powdery scales.

"Back home, I shall make a full report of all you have done for me," the envoy added, thus expressing his wish to return the kindnesses he had received. But to Kūkai this would have sounded unbearably patronizing, suddenly reminding him of the repugnant vulgarity of the Court circle.

About twenty days later Envoy Fujiwara and his party reached Yuezhou, where they took their leave of the Imperial Guide, Wang Guowen. Then guided by a local official, they came to the port of Mingzhou to board the boats that had been awaiting them. On May 18 they set sail and in less than twenty days they arrived at Tsushima Island off the northern coast of Kyūshū.

*   *   *

Kūkai and Hayanari were simply happy, riding side by side in the fresh air of early spring. So far they had been confined in the official world of

Japan, always speaking Japanese, rigidly bound by their official status. What was the use of living in Chang'an? But from this moment on, they were able to live on their own and in their own places, Kūkai in Ximing-si temple in Yankang-fang block, Hayanari in the university dormitory.

Kūkai must have felt a surge of pleasure flooding his heart. The dry weed on the roadsides had already been thickly dotted with young shoots of the leek family, which they saw were now spreading all over the fields and hills, scenting the air all round them. All the people of Chang'an—men and women from all walks of life—could hardly wait for spring to arrive. Even as early as mid-January when temperatures often dropped below zero, there were some who went to seek the first sign of spring in fields and hills. As it was already February 10, Kūkai and Hayanari must have seen many on horseback or in carriages passing by. A boy on a white horse, as depicted by Li Bai (701–762) in his *Playboy Song*, might have been coming down a hill soon to present himself in a narrow lane* in downtown Chang'an:

> A playboy from Wuling comes riding
> down the lane east of Golden Market,
> his white horse with a silver saddle
> gently walking in the spring breeze.
> Where can he be going, after having
> trodden upon so many fallen flowers?
> Behold! How he smiles as he enters
> a tavern attended by a Persian girl!

During the Tang era, Wuling,[5] the suburban area north of the Weishui River, was not only known as the residential area for wealthy families but also closely associated with playboys whose unmistakable characteristics was a Chinese version of chivalrous dandyism. Golden Market meant the West Market Place, near which lay the Yankang-fang block where Kūkai was soon to move.

Sometimes young women were seen on horseback, too. Horse-riding had been a fashionable sport here since it was introduced by Persian girls. As anything that comes into fashion is intended to enhance sexual appeal, the women and girls of Chang'an were eager to adopt Western-style outfits and manners—so much so that they were often frowned upon by conservative elders. Kūkai and Hayanari must have doubted their eyes when they saw girls wearing white silk blouses and flaring crimson skirts, hair piled up under a hat, with booted legs, boldly riding around the fields.

"Do you not regret being a Buddhist monk?" Hayanari may have teased his friend when they saw an amazing beauty passing by. Some of the girls they saw would have been Caucasians from Central Asia.

To the Tang Dynasty known for its internationalism, racial discrimination was unthinkable, partly because the founder of the dynasty was of mixed blood, and partly because the successive Emperors of the same dynasty had been looked up to by peoples around its borders as their *Tengri Khan* (Heaven's Emperor). Many foreigners, therefore, had been promoted to high official posts, while the educated Chinese were quite ready to appreciate foreign cultures. This naturally had the effect of attracting more and more non-Chinese to come and live in Chang'an. About one percent of the whole population of one million were non-Chinese. Especially those from Central Asia, whose appearance and culture were totally different from those of native Chinese, were to give the most distinctive features to the urban culture of this metropolis, as is illustrated in the following scene depicted by the poet Li He (791–817):

> On a moonlit night, there appears
> on the veranda of a lofty palace
> a boy curly-haired and green-eyed.
> Seated with his knee drawn up high,
> he begins to blow a reed producing
> a melody as if from heaven, making
> a beauty in the garden below weep
> bitterly for the sight of their home.

Such exoticism would have been an inexhaustible source of inspiration for local poets. Their music was also irresistible to Chinese ears, and it was eagerly sought after or even learned by many until it became a familiar sound in Chang'an. Kūkai could not have been impervious to such pleasant influences. It is difficult to assess what part they played in the building of his thought. But at least they would have helped him grasp what the real world was like and of what it consisted.

On returning to the the government residence, Kūkai collected his things and came to say goodbye to the clerk in charge, who had already called several men to help him move. With his baggage heaped on a cart, they were soon on their way to Ximing-si temple along a wide, busy street. Lining various streets, elm trees, pagoda trees (*Sophora japonica*) and willows, now trembling in a chilly wind, would soon be in bud again. The Chinese, who were the first to carry out city planning, are said to have lined their streets with trees as early as the Spring and Autumn Period (770B.C.–403B.C.). In the boulevards of Chang'an, ancient pagoda trees were especially impressive, their huge, leafy canopies adding a generous elegance to the palaces, mansions, stores and residences that stood among them.

Chang'an was divided into two parts—the East Ward and the West Ward—by the central thoroughfare running north and south. The East Ward with fifty-five blocks in it contained mainly residential districts for aristocrats or high-ranking officials; the West Ward also with fifty-five blocks was hardly more than a conglomeration of bars, stores, shops and houses for the common people. The Xuanyang-fang block in which Kūkai had been staying so far was in the East Ward, and that block alone had as many as twenty-one graceful mansions in it. It was also where the Yang family that produced Yang Guifei used to live. Kūkai, slowly moving into the hustle and bustle of plebeian life in the West Ward, must have been all agog at the different things he encountered in the various blocks he passed by.

The grandeur of Ximing-si temple spread widely over the southwestern corner of the Yankang-fang block was something beyond what Kūkai had ever imagined. In fact, it was the largest Buddhist temple in Tang China, built to the design of Xuanzang, a great Buddhist priest popularly known as the author of *The Memoirs of the Central Asia and India*.[6] Xuanzang, who had made the taxing journey to and from India to bring back the manuscripts of six hundred and fifty-seven Sanskrit texts besides many Buddha-images and some of Sakyamuni's relics (645), was deeply revered by his contemporaries high and low, until he became almost a mystical figure. But he himself was simply absorbed in his own project of producing Chinese versions of these scriptures. Then unexpectedly he was ordered by the Emperor Gaozong (reign: 649–683)* to build a temple that was later to be known as Ximing-si temple.

To Xuanzang, already near the end of his life, this command must have been something of a trial, for his translation project was still far from finished. Nevertheless, he accepted it. In making a plan for the temple, he had an image of a temple modeled after the Maitreya's Palace in the Tusita Heaven. The inspiration for this concept came from what he had seen in Central India—Jetavanavihara—which he was told was modeled after the innermost temple of the Tusita Heaven. Then pondering over the poetic lines he read in many Buddhist scriptures, he drew a plan, arranging the whole thing in Chinese fashion. He who had been trying to bring Buddhism closer to the Chinese through his literary efforts was now seeking to achieve the same purpose by means of architecture. The result proved to be magnificent in conception and structurally impeccable. Fortunately, the Tang Dynasty was still resourceful enough to allow him to fully materialize this noble project. Thus Ximing-si temple, built by the right person at the right time in history, has never been surpassed in scale by any other Buddhist temples ever built on earth.

To Xuanzang, however, it was far from satisfying, for the innermost temple of the Tusita Heaven consisted of thirty-six temples on that scale, according to the scriptures he had read. But to Kūkai who used to be a frequent visitor to Daian-ji in Nara that had been modeled after Ximing-si temple in Chang'an, being able to live in this temple must alone have seemed as gratifying as being allowed to take a further step toward the Tusita Heaven according to another specially premeditated divine arrangement.

Looking up at the towering gate, he might have felt as if he were entering a castle city. In fact, it was a miniature city with allegedly four thousand buildings in it, surrounded by long walls densely lined with pagoda trees. A considerable number of buildings were appropriated for toilets, laundry and other living facilities for bathing, dining, robe-making and medicine-processing, perfectly furnished and conveniently placed along the clear streams made to encircle the precinct. There were a couple of hospitals, too.

On entering the gate, he had his eyes drawn to a three-storied building of unusual dimensions. Going farther on, he saw many more huge buildings, including a five-storied auditorium, a seven-storied pagoda and the massive stonework foundation for the belfry.

Guided by a priest in charge, he was soon brought to a hall, at the entrance to which he saw a corridor running right to the other end, lined with double-leafed hinged doors. He was shown into a room, which was almost a cube in shape with a wooden floor, yellow ocher walls and a window facing south. This was supposed to be his own quarters during his twenty-year stay in Chang'an. Some of his predecessors stayed much longer; one for thirty-eight years, another for twenty-five years, and Yōchō, who had occupied this very room just before Kūkai, had spent thirty years before he left Chang'an that very morning with the embassy. When he went to see them off that morning, Kūkai would have talked to Yōchō, who had made himself a master of Three Treatises and Buddhist music, especially the vocalism of Buddhist scripture. On his return he was to be appointed chief priest of Bonshaku-ji, a state temple newly built in Ōmi Province.

The following episode in his closing years suggests a close friendship he had struck up with Kūkai: Yōchō had recently been made privy to the Tennō's idea that he should take a post at the Ecclesiastical Office. As it meant that he had to engage in something more secular than religious, he wished to decline the offer and asked Kūkai to make a draft of his answer to the Court. This reveals the fact that even the master of Three Treatises who had studied in Chang'an as long as thirty years had to rely on Kūkai when he needed a really convincing piece of writing[7] that would enable him to have his own way. The copy still remains in *Shōryō-shū*. As was expected, Yōchō's wish was fully understood by the Court. Then it happened that the Court also turned to Kūkai for their answer to Yōchō, whose copy also remains in *Shōryō-shū*. This sounds like a joke. But this may reveal the sort of magnanimity with which Kūkai was able to do quite calmly what might be frowned upon by us modern people who tend to be rather rigid in such matters.

"Priest Yōchō was always sitting there, reading scriptures."

The Chinese priest who knew Yōchō for years must have pointed to a spot that shone less brightly. But Kūkai would not have turned himself into another Yōchō. His passion for literature and his strong curiosity about what was happening around him were sure to keep him from being desk-bound. Then what was his daily life like? In the preface to his *List of the Items Introduced from China*, he wrote:

... I had been visiting one temple after another, intending to find
out my right master under whom to study.

This may sound quite plausible. But I do not think that was exactly what
he was doing then, for in Chang'an anyone who took an interest in Esoteric
Buddhism could easily tell who was "the right master" for him to study
under: Huiguo in Qinglong-si temple was the only person in Chang'an who
had been initiated into the authorized heritage of Esoteric Buddhism. Then
the first thing he should do after settling at Ximing-si temple would be to go
to meet Huiguo at Qinglong-si temple. But somehow or other, he did not do
so until June. Then what was he doing all this while? We may imagine he
had been happily walking around the town of Chang'an, his multiple talents
allowing him to become well-adapted—probably over-adapted—to the
civilization of Chang'an as an emblem of universality.

In fact, he could not enter a brush maker's shop without learning how to
tell good calligraphy brushes from not-so-good ones and how to make good
ones with the secret skills of a master. Likewise, he learned how to make
Indian ink sticks, too, according to the family legend of Kobai-en Ink Stick
Maker that still exists in Nara City, the capital of Nara Prefecture.
Apparently, his eagerness to learn anything new made him stop at every
construction site of banks, bridges, houses as well as temple buildings. On
the other hand, his literary talent was soon to make him a regular guest at
many poetry-making parties regularly held by high-ranking officials in
Chang'an.

One of the places he enjoyed visiting was the West Market Place in the
vicinity of the Yankang-fang block he lived in. It was interesting to see how
a caravan that had been traveling all the way from the lands unknown to him
removed the bundles from the camels' backs. Another attraction was an
open-air show of Persian girls' dancing. Dressed in silk gauze, their bodies
became pink when they danced, energetically whirling round and round on
tiptoe. In fact, it was called a whirl dance. Sometimes whirling girls, as the
people called these danseuses, jumped incredibly high as if capture the
clouds. Bai Letian depicts a dancing girl as follows:

> Whirling girl,
> whirling girl,
> thy heart
> beats to the strumming of the strings,
> thy hands respond to the drumbeat.
> Like a whirling snowflake or
> a dry mugwort[8] before wind.
> thou dost spin left,
> spin right,
> never showing
> any
> sign
> of
> f
> a
> t
> i
> g
> u
> e

Yuan Zhen describes the intensity of their movement:

> The whirling wind that rises from her frantic dance
> goes crashing against the sky that falls in pieces.

Li Duan remarks upon their appearance:

> Their skin gleams like pearl,
> their noses look like cones.

Kūkai in the crowd would have been standing on tiptoe, watching a dancing girl in a brief skirt flaring around her waist like a crimson halo. Kūkai as we know him is believed to have been a strict observer of the code of chastity. But this does not mean that he had only a mild interest in women. On the contrary, very few could have been more attracted to the opposite sex than he. Considering the distinct, flowery unctuousness explicit in his literary style or the special interest he took in the *Rishu-kyō* that declares: "Binding each other in love, being pure in itself, deserves the rank

133

of Bodhisattva," he could not have been a dry stick of a saint. Certainly he kept away from women all his life, but he kept devoting even greater energies to sublimating his urge, believing that the act of sublimation would be the surest way to "attain Buddhahood here and now." Then Kūkai among the onlookers of dancing girls, must have been intensely busy trying to abstract his visual pleasure in her into ecstatic purity.

Hayanari often visited Kūkai at his quarters in Ximing-si temple just to talk about what he had seen or experienced in the town. Naturally they were often seen walking together. Sometimes Hayanari would have taken Kūkai to "a narrow lane," happily repeating a local saying in Chinese: "Do not talk of Chang'an until you see her narrow lanes."

All the blocks in the capital were divided by thoroughfares about eighty-meters wide, and those especially of the West Ward were connected to numberless narrow lanes fringed with brothels and bars that in the evenings were vibrant with songs, strings and coquettish voices. Many people, high and low, strolled about. As the metropolis always accommodated four thousand foreign guests, including envoys and their suits, rubbing sleeves with them in narrow lanes would have been one of the pleasures of being in Chang'an. Those who came up to Chang'an to sit for the higher civil service examinations annually numbered one thousand, and sometimes more than two thousand. Naturally they also enjoyed the life of the narrow lanes. Some of the applicants for the examinations were non-Chinese from beyond the borders. In the previous era of the Six Dynasties (220–581), the Emperors favored native Chinese of noble birth. But in the present Tang Dynasty the Emperor made it a rule to take the best brains regardless of their race. His duty, he thought, was to give kindness and security to all the peoples in the world, and that without any distinction between Chinese and non-Chinese. This broad-minded principle of universality established by the Tan Emperors could not have been lost on Kūkai, seeing that he himself, in establishing his own thought system in years to come, adopted the very same principle, taking human beings simply as human beings, regardless of their race, nationality, customs, class, rank and sex.

Gallants and dandies might be called the flowers of the narrow lanes.

Contemporary poets in Chang'an were so fond of writing about them that "*playboy Song*" was becoming a new brand of fashionable poetry. The one made by Cui Guofu perpetuates a scene he caught sight of at a gay quarter named Zhangtai:

> A dandy riding down Zhangtai
> drops a coral-whip to see his
> white horse wayward. He just
> snaps off a twig of a wayside
> willow to improvise a new one,
> incidentally winning the heart
> of a barmaid in the spring sun.

Many bars in the narrow lanes were tended by Caucasian girls from beyond the western borders, as Li Bai wrote: "... how he smiles as he enters a bar tended by a Persian girl." Was it a sort of exoticism shared by local poets that the picture of a Chang'an playboy would be incomplete without a blue-eyed girl beside him? Catching a glimpse of such bar girls, Kūkai must have been surprised to find how much they resembled Esoteric Buddhist images modeled after the wealthy and fashionable of India.

The following poem by Li Bai might have been what happened to Kūkai and Hayanari:

> Those lingering around Qingqi-men gate[9]
> will be beckoned to by a Persian girl who
> just comes up and takes them in by her
> warm hands to get them drunk
> beside her
> golden cask.

What if such a girl beckoned Kūkai and tried to pull him in by the sleeve? He might have calmly allowed himself to touch her by the warm hand. As his constant passion was to turn everything into thought, he might have taken that precious experience as further significant material in composing his ideas, or as something that added to his knowledge of what the pleasure of being in the rank of Bodhisattva was like, as is proclaimed in the *Rishu-kyō*: "Touching is pure in itself and it deserves the rank of

Bodhisattva." But he would not have gone so far as to be led into her bar, as Hayanari did, who was quite at liberty to enter any bar and even to see the day dawn with a girl in his arms. On his way home, he must have come round to pay a visit to Kūkai and recounted the whole story, as he knew his friend would surely enjoy being provided with anything new to him as long as it added to his knowledge of what this world was made of. While explaining what the interior of the bar looked like, Hayanari might have recited the following poem by Jia Zhi:

> Wearing makeup, she stands behind the counter,
> facing the hanging willow in the lane.
> Unrefined wine of golden colour
> relaxes her guests, while
> pipes and songs keep them
> too happy to leave.
> This is how she
> makes those Chang'an
> dandies drink themselves to death.

Repeating the closing lines with relish, Hayanari would have laughed noisily as if he were one of those happy-go-lucky drunkards. Fed up with this clamorous merriment, Kūkai might have tried to steer him back by citing a sobering poem that ends with the following advice—humorously impossible advice that Li Qi offered to his younger friend leaving for Chang'an to prepare himself for the higher civil service examination:

> Never feast your eye on gay quarters,
> Otherwise, you will soon be wasting
> your time, and thus lose your chance.

But to Kūkai's mind, Li Qi was far from admirable. He passed the examination and became a government official but found himself a misfit. Soon he left office and returned home. His career so far was more or less similar to Kūkai's. But unlike Kūkai, Li Qi took to Taoism and eagerly tried herb medicines so that he might enjoy eternal youth and longevity, as some legendary Taoist hermits are said to have achieved. Kūkai could not help laughing at such an easy-going attitude in Taoists who, in their effort to attain truth, just turned to medicines, not to their thought and ascetic practices required by their thought. After all, the courage he showed in releasing himself from the world was just a gesture, not an action from sincere thought or principle, as was often the case with a failed Confucian. Why could he not be so brave as to go exploring into the universe, Kūkai might have wondered?

XIII. A Variety of Thoughts on the Universe

KŪKAI saw many temples dedicated to religions whose interpretations of the universe were different from those of Buddhism or Esoteric Buddhism. Those temples were easily recognizable by their exotic appearance. Kūkai would have naturally taken an interest in them and tried to find out what kinds of thought their disciplines offered.

One of the religions was Zoroastrianism. The Zoroastrian temple consisted of a hall and a small gate, both built of large white bricks. In Luoyang Kūkai must have seen one or two temples of this type. In Chang'an he saw many more, especially around the Yankang-fang block in which he lived. On festive days a large number of Iranians, male and female, gathered together to enjoy a variety of entertainments shown around the gate—conjuring tricks, acrobatics and dances to exhilaratingly rhythmical music.

Kūkai must have been a familiar figure among the spectators. They called themselves Iranian; but many other peoples, including Chinese, called them Persian and their temples Persian temples. As there were a great many Zoroastrians in Chang'an, the Chinese government had opened a new government office to control them, mainly to deal with matters concerning their residence. Kūkai must have entered one or two of their temples. The Chang'ans and the Japanese under Chang'an influence, not having considered Buddhism as closed or exclusive, generally maintained a liberal attitude toward other religions, vaguely presuming that they must belong to different branches of Buddhism. Kūkai in a Zoroastrian temple, therefore, would not have been experiencing any of the tension one might feel on encountering some unknown religion.

There were flames burning on the altar. Kūkai would immediately have thought of *homa*—a fire service in Esoteric Buddhism, the whole system of which had not yet been revealed to him. There was no *homa* in Sakyamuni's Buddhism. Sakyamuni rejected things of this kind as heretical. But Kūkai had taken a keen interest in *homa* because it was adopted by Esoteric

Buddhists even though it was discarded by Sakyamuni. *Homa* had come from Brahmanism as the native religion of India. Brahmans, who worshiped heaven, used fire in holding services dedicated to heaven. Fire, they thought, was the only medium through which heaven was able to assimilate food: offerings thrown into fire would burn producing smoke that rose to heaven; when heaven had accepted such tributes, it would be happy and return happiness to those who had made offerings. Esoteric Buddhists who appeared several centuries after Sakyamuni passed away adopted this idea and seized every opportunity to please heaven by performing such fire services.

In India the notion of *homa* remained at that level for a long time. But by the time it was handed down to Kūkai by way of China, fire had come to be interpreted as truth, with wood chips representing evil passions; the former was the medium for destroying the latter. Kūkai developed this even further when he invented a trinity in which the *homa* officiant, the flaring fire before him, and the image of the deity he is going to invoke enthroned beyond the fire are one and the same; this would enable the officiant to attain Buddhahood when his three actions—physical, verbal and spiritual—were fused with those of the deity. But this form of sublimation belongs to his later achievements. To the Kūkai who had just begun to explore Chang'an, the fire in a Zoroastrian temple was just another thing to excite his curiosity.

"Does this fire have anything to do with *homa* in Esoteric Buddhism?" Kūkai may have asked a Persian priest he met there. The Zoroastrian priest was not expected to be a stoic, as Buddhist priests were. Probably he was accompanied by his wife who, quite imaginably, would be wearing a very light silk dress on her voluptuous body, jewels glittering on her ears, breast and arms, and a long sash tied loosely around her waist, as was often depicted in Chinese poetry. Even if his passion was stirred by her, Kūkai would not have considered it to be shameful.

According to his thought, this physical world is all composed of incentives to passions or illusions that disturb the mind, but these incentives should not be rejected because they could be a springboard to Buddhahood one might attain here and now; then what one had to do as an ascetic postulant for Esoteric Buddhism was to master how to transform whatever incentives one might encounter in daily life into that springboard leading in a flash to purification or sublimation.

In later years his further study of the *Mahavairocana Sutra* led him to call this instantaneous purification "internal" *homa* as distinct from "external" *homa* actually produced with fire. Kūkai at that Zoroastrian temple, however, had probably attained this level of thought, and he would not have felt ashamed of the passion he felt at the sight of that enchanting woman as long as he was able to treat it as a precious means towards self-purification.

Naturally it was with proper pride that the Persian priest talked about his religion founded by Zoroaster, who lived and died more than a millennium before. Kūkai, a comparative philosopher by preference as well as by nature, would have been mentally very busy, making comparisons or reservations while listening to the following exposition:

> The two elements that compose the universe are good and evil. Ahura Mazda, good and light, creates everything good, while Angra-mainyu, evil and dark, produces everything evil. They are in conflict, trying to destroy each other. This is what the universe is. Ahura Mazda, the good god in heaven, leads his own army; Angra-mainyu, the evil god in hell, leads his own army, too.

This image of the good god in heaven as a leader of a host of angels and holy spirits resembles that of the God in the Christianity of the Nestorian school which had also arrived in Chang'an. Like Christianity, Zoroastrianism prepares the Last Judgement at the end of this world that is predicted to last 12,000 years. At the Last Judgement, the dead who have been good in this life will come to life again to enjoy life in eternal bliss.

"What do you mean by good?" Kūkai asked, feeling it hard to suppress a smile at Zoroastrians simple enough to draw a sharp line between good and evil, ignoring the plain fact that it is totally impossible to do so.

"Everything that comes from the good god is good," answered the priest, repeating the simplistic logic he had presented before.

Some details may have made Kūkai feel he was being entertained with a fairy tale. In Buddhism, immortality is denied, but in Zoroastrianism all of its absolute elements, including the human soul, are immortal. When one dies, one's soul stays with one's body for three days. Then it is blown by wind as far as the tribunal, where the three judges will weigh on the scales everything one did during one's lifetime and decide whether one's soul was good or bad. If judged good, it will be allowed to pass a solid bridge that leads to heaven; if judged bad, it will be pushed on to a narrow, frail bridge that is sure to send it down into a deep gulf below, which is hell. The one who is found neither good nor bad will be sent to the purgatory that exists between heaven and hell to stay there until the Day of Resurrection. The first half of this story does resemble a Buddhist folktale I heard in my childhood, while the latter part has something in common with Christianity. It may be that some Japanese Buddhist priest brought this story back to Japan. But that priest could not have been Kūkai, for he was always eager to make his thought as clear as crystal.

As for the reason why fire was worshiped, the priest explained: "Fire is the son of Ahura Mazda, the good god. Worshiping fire, therefore, is revering the good god and the light as his essence; likewise, bathing in the light will increase one's ability to achieve the purification of one's own soul." The metaphysical thinker in Kūkai would have found this simplistic rationale rather unsatisfying.

*   *   *

Iran had been Islamic for a century and a half since the Sasan Dynasty that had adopted Zoroastrianism as its state religion was destroyed in 651 by the Islamic Arabs. Central Asia too had been converted to Islam, since 711 when Samarkand was occupied by the Islamic Empire. This meant that most of the Iranians or the Central Asians who had recently arrived in China were Muslims and naturally they had their own places of worship, even though they were not yet formally recognized by the Chinese government. Could Kūkai, the soul of serendipity, have visited one or two of those places to see how the Muslims worship their god Allah and learned about the Koran upon which this religion was based under the influence of Judaism and Christianity ?

*   *   *

Uighurs were often seen in the West City. Many of them were trading merchants. The Uighurs, originally a horse-riding people on the steppe, used occasionally to invade the Mongolian Plateau, thus posing a threat to the agrarian population of China. By and by, however, they learned the virtues of commerce, found east-west trade very lucrative, and came to engage in trade, some living in Chang'an as merchants, others leading their caravans to and from the Market Places in Chang'an.

The Uighurs were originally an ancient Turkish race of Mongol descent. But about the time they were discovering the benefits of commerce, there was a great deal of racial mixture with Soghds of Iranian origin, thus producing more and more men and women who looked rather like Iranians. In the meantime, the Uighurs discarded their old shamanistic religion and began to adopt a new religion called Manichaeism.

Many Manichaeist temples were also seen in and around the block Kūkai lived in. These temples, surrounded by Uighurian shops, stores and dwelling houses, had naturally become a center of the Uighurian life, directed by three kinds of leaders: the bishop who controlled all the temples, supervisors to take care of each temple, and priests as direct instructors of the people. Manichaeism developed in Iran. Mani (ca.215–276), the founder of this religion, had been well-informed of various religions and philosophies, including Christianity and Buddhism, before he created Manichaeism by making momentous revisions of Zoroastrianism that had already become Iran's state religion. As was expected, because it was prohibited in Iran, Manichaeists had to leave their homeland to find refuge among other peoples like the Uighurs.

The Manichaeist churches had adopted a calendar with seven days in the week. On Sundays many Uighurs, male and female, were seen to go to their churches. The priests had a day off on Monday. On the altar of their church no fire was burning; no idol was seen, either. The most characteristic aspect of Manichaeism was its stoicism that prohibited meat-eating, drinking, homicide and adultery. Kūkai would have visited one or two of their churches and eagerly listened to the priest, who, unlike the Zoroastrian priest, was forbidden to marry. The universe as they viewed it was also made of two elements: light and darkness; the father of light is the good god, the king of darkness the devil. Instead of fighting incessantly as in Zoroastrianism, the two elements are well-balanced and remain at peace until some time in the future when the balance is upset and fighting starts. In Zoroastrianism the good god will finally win to turn this world into a place of goodness and beauty, whereas Manichaeism does not embrace such optimism but proclaims that the fighting will last for ever and ever....

To Kūkai who had already known, by learning the *Kegon-kyō* sutra and the *Mahavairocana Sutra*, that the universe is being operated by a truth that transcends good and evil, the doctrine he learned at a Manichaeist church would have sounded like yet another fairy tale.

* * *

Another different type of religion Kūkai came to know in Chang'an was Christianity or what was called Jingjiao (Brilliant Religion) in Tang China. Its church, a white-towered building with green-tiled roofs, had generally been considered a symbol of exoticism of Chang'an, so Kūkai may have had a more favorable image of this religion.

Christianity, more precisely, the Nestorian school of Christianity, had already been in China for one hundred and seventy years, and was to vanish in 845 when it was involved in the anti-Buddhist movement encouraged by the Emperor Wuzong of the same Tang Dynasty.

The doctrine set forth by Nestorius (?–ca.451), a pontiff of Constantinople, had originated from his genuine concept of God: Jesus, the son of God, can be identified with God; but Jesus, who was conceived by the virgin Mary, was not a divine being but a human being; it was not until he left the flesh of Mary that he began to take on divinity. As this naturally led to the idea that Mary, a mere human being, need not be worshiped, Nestrius was declared a heretic (431), deprived of his pontificate and banished. He went eastward accompanied by his followers, spreading their religion to Iran, Sogdiana and East Turkestan until 635 when their descendants several generations later reached China.

The leader of this mission was an Iranian priest named Arapon (probably Abraham). The Emperor Taizong, after listening to Arapon and his companions who came to meet him at his Court, permitted them to make Chinese versions of their scriptures to propagate their religion all over his land. The next Emperor Gaozong worshiped him, too, and appointed him to be Great Master of the Achievement of National Tranquility. Then after a brief decline, the religion gained power again under the protection of the sixth Emperor Xuanzong, who issued a special command that the Christian church, which until then had been mistakenly called Bosi-si (Persian Temple), should thereafter be called Daqin-si (Roman Temple), lest it should be confused with the Zoroastrian temple which had also been generally called the Persian Temple by the Chang'ans. It was favored by the seventh, eighth and ninth Emperors, too. In 781, during the reign of the last-mentioned, the Emperor Dezong who died soon after the Japanese embassy arrived in Chang'an, a monument was set up in the precincts of the Roman Temple in Yining-fang block to celebrate the great popularity Jingjiao or Brilliant Religion had won in China. The epitaph, written in two languages —Syriac and Chinese—recounts the creation of Heaven and Earth, the original sin committed by man and woman created by God, the birth of Christ as the son of God; then comes an explanation of how this religion was brought to Chang'an, referring to Alapon, the Emperor Taizong, and what was later called Daqin-si or the Roman Temple built by his order in Yining-fang block. Twenty-one priests were also ordained by his order (implying that they were all treated as official priests maintained by the Chinese government). At the end, there are two names: Idzdubzid from Balkh in Tukhāra, who dedicated the monument, and Jingjing, a Christian priest, an Iranian who composed the epitaph.

If Jingjing lived to a great age, Kūkai may have seen him somewhere in the precincts of the Roman Temple.

Later, probably during the Emperor Wuzong's oppression of Buddhism and other religions that lasted from 842 to 845, that monument was buried deep in the earth to remain there for almost eight hundred years. In 1625, when the whole of the prosperous splendor of Chang'an had long since turned to farmland, a local farmer unearthed the monument, which created a great sensation especially among the Jesuit missionaries who had come to stay in Ming China. But when reported to Europe, it was looked upon with suspicion, many asserting that it must be a fake by the Jesuit missionaries themselves, as it seemed quite improbable that Christianity should have arrived in China so many centuries before. By and by, however, one circumstantial evidence after another began to be found to prove its authenticity. Then around 1890s a Japanese scholar of Buddhism, Takakusu Junjirō, came across the very name of "Jingjing, a priest of Daqin-si temple" while reading *The List of Buddhist Scriptures: Newly Provided in the Era of Zhenyuan*. Takakusu announced this discovery through a French magazine devoted to Oriental studies, thus providing a great step toward the conclusion that the monument was authentic.

Incidentally, Kūkai in Chang'an must have read the same *List*, and when he found that most of the newly-translated scriptures were of Esoteric Buddhism, he must have confirmed the validity of his belief that Esoteric Buddhism was a recent development of Buddhism in India.

Chag'an as was witnessed by Kūkai could be compared to a base for a world exposition of thoughts—probably the most gorgeous one the world has ever seen, though I could hardly imagine what tremendous stimuli it had given to Kūkai, a born thinker of vigorous imagination.

XIV. The Two Indian Masters and Abbot Huiguo

"THEN you should visit Abbot Huiguo of Qinglong-si temple."

Kūkai must have received this unanimous advice from many locals who had found out his reason for coming to Chang'an. They were right, for Huiguo was the only person in China who had been initiated into the legitimate heritage of Esoteric Buddhism, and as he had so far baptized three Emperors, he was known to all who had taken any interest in Buddhism. But Kūkai would not follow the advice, for the time being at least. Why? This sort of procrastination that occurred occasionally in his life may be attributed partly to the peculiar sense of timeliness he was born with. What if he had gone to meet Huiguo as soon as he arrived in Chang'an?

The receptionist at the entrance would have asked what his business was, and might have refused to accede to his wish to meet Huiguo. Or even if he had been allowed to meet him through the good offices of some influential person, the abbot himself, not knowing what sort of person he was and what level his religious and scholastic achievements had attained, might have failed to treat him as he had wished. Huiguo had a large following. This meant that a new pupil had to wait for several years—living in the temple and learning from some senior pupils—before he was allowed to go and listen to his master.

Naturally Kūkai would have liked to go to meet Huiguo as soon as possible. But he was not going to do so until the time came when he would be immediately recognized, accepted and initiated into the whole system of his religion. Ecclesiastically such a leap was unthinkable. But to Kūkai, it was not a leap nor a fantasy, but a sort of maneuver he would have naturally followed, when we consider the behavior pattern he showed on several momentous occasions in his life.

Another reason for his delay in going to meet Huiguo would have been that he had to make preparations for it, learning Sanskrit under two Indian priests—Prajna and Munisri.[1] The following episode he read in *The List of Buddhist Scriptures: Newly Provided in the Era of Zhenyuan*, mentioned in the previous chapter, must have attracted Kūkai's attention, since it concerned one of his respected masters:

> The great Indian priest Prajna was once ordered by the Emperor Dezong to make a Chinese version of the *Roku-Haramita-kyō* sutra.[2] Prajna had already been known as a great master of Buddhism before he left for China of his own choice. In 782 when he arrived in Chang'an, he looked like a beggar because of the hardship he had had to suffer on the way. But the Emperor Dezong accepted him and treated him cordially.
>
> Now Prajna was dismayed when he saw the text he was ordered to translate into Chinese was written in Iranian instead of his own language, Sanskrit. Prajna went to Yuanzhao (the editor of the *List* mentioned above, who lived in Ximing-si temple) for advice and received the suggestion that he should turn to some Christian priest of the Roman Temple. The Christian priest to whom Prajna went to ask for help was Jingjing who had composed the epitaph on the monument set up in the precincts of the Roman Temple, as mentioned before. Soon the two priests were seen working together, even though neither of them seemed suited to that project: Prajna was mono-lingual in Sanskrit, Jingjing, bilingual in Iranian and Chinese, but no Buddhist. At first Jingjing made a rough draft of the Chinese version, which Prajna brought to someone (probably Yuanzhao), who read it and pointed out the Christian bias in the interpretation of the text. Prajna, coming back to Jingjing, complained about his errors. But Jingjing would not accept the change, as he believed he was right. Finally their disagreement led them to agree to ask the Emperor Dezong to give judgement. The two came to the Emperor and each gave his own version of the quarrel.
>
> The Emperor pondered over the matter for a while and then said: "You have different teachings to preach: the Messiah's and Sakya's. Nevertheless you worked together on the same text,

despite your complete divergence of opinion. Naturally you have failed to produce a proper rendition. The solution is for each of you to make his own version."

They did as they were told. In the case of Prajna, he did much to find out the original text in Sanskrit, but after obtaining it, he was able to work happily until he had completed it with the help of another Indian priest, Munisri, who had arrived in Chang'an earlier than he.

As he wrote in *The Summary of the Transmission of the Legitimate Heritage of Esoteric Buddhism*, Kūkai regularly visited Liquan-si temple to learn Sanskrit from these Indian priests, Prajna and Munisri. The latter, who was to die in June the following year, was probably too weak to spend much time with Kūkai. The former, though already over seventy, seems to have enjoyed tutoring Kūkai, and Kūkai himself must have taken it as a great good luck to be able to learn from him the very language that had produced the thought that had become his own. In India Prajna belonged to the Brahmanic caste. Probably he had a classical appearance with curly hair, a big nose, wide-winged eyebrows, deep-set eyes that gleamed like a shady pond in the mountains. Once Kūkai asked him what part of India he had come from, and the answer he received then is recorded in the preface to *The List of the Items Introduced from China*:

> Plajna was born in Kashmir. As a child he joined the Buddhist order and spent his youth at Nalanda Monastery.* After studying at various places in India, he decided to make the journey to China to propagate his religion.

Prajna expressed his wish to visit Japan, too. But he knew, to his regret, that he would not be able to do so: "Seeing that I have never had either boat or opportunity to cross the sea to reach Japan, it seems as if I were not destined to do so. That is why," he went on saying, pointing at the piles of scriptures he had placed on the desk, "when you return home some day, I should like you to take back all these sutras in my own translation."
This was how Kūkai was charged by the translator himself with these precious scriptures: a new rendition of the *Kegon-kyō* sutra (forty volumes),

the *Roku-Haramita-kyō* sutra (ten volumes), the *Shugokaishu Darani-kyō* sutra (ten volumes) and the *Zōtō Emmei Kudoku-kyō* sutra (one volume). Strictly speaking, Prajna had completed them in collaboration with Munisri.

Indian priests at that time maintained the same kind of ardent belief in the universality of their own religion that has always been held by Christian missionaries, who would go anywhere on earth to spread God's word. On the other hand, Tang China which was aspiring towards universality from the very beginning (618), easily directed Indian priests' missionary zeal to its capital of Chang'an, until 845 when the flow was suddenly checked by the Emperor Wuzong. So the fortunate contact Kūkai had happened to make with Prajna and Munisri at that time would never have failed to inspire him, just as a magnetic substance, when brought into a magnetic field, never fails to become magnetized. This may explain why Kūkai remains the only Japanese whose thought, easily transcending the insularity of sectarianism, parochialism, regionalism, nationalism and racism, still holds true for any human being on earth.

Kūkai was said to have learned Siddham from a Chinese priest Tanzhen who lived in Qinglong-si temple, but as was recently made clear, Tanzhen had died by the time Kūkai arrived in Chang'an. But it was quite possible that there were several priests who had made themselves authorities on Siddham under Tanzhen, and Kūkai must have come to one or the other of them to learn this Indian science of linguistics. Siddham originally meant the phonetic syllabary of Sanskrit. But Siddham as Kūkai learned it must have included Sanskrit phonetics as a whole. The Sanskrit language, comprising a well-developed linguistic philosophy as well as the grammar with its long history, had made itself a vast civilizing force. Since each element in the phonetic syllabary was intended to be expressive of something in the making and movement of the universe, Sanskrit was considered a sacred language only to be used in dealing with matters of the metaphysical world (Brahman).

But is it really possible for any human brain to master such a vast language as Sanskrit in five months or so before he came to meet Huiguo at Qinglong-si temple? As some scholars assert, he might have already had a good grounding in it in Japan—during that mysterious period in his twenties, under some Indian priests he met in Nara.

Meanwhile, spring had blossomed into the peony season. People in Chang'an, high and low, were extremely fond of the gorgeous peony blooms. Reportedly some high-ranking officials and wealthy merchants were eager to pay immense sums for a single peony plant. When the season came round, all the gardens, including the most celebrated ones of Daci'en-si temple in Jinchang-fang block and Ximing-si temple where Kūkai had taken residence, were open to the public that never tired of adoring the ravishing flowers.

Kūkai, who was occasionally swept away by the peony craze, must have realized the truth expressed in the poet Bai Juyi's lines:

> The flowers open and fall, open and fall,
> to send all Chang'an crazy for twenty days.

*   *   *

Abbot Huiguo was the first Chinese to accede to the two different systems of Esoteric Buddhism: one is the spiritual principle based on the *Vajrasekhara Sutra*, the other is the physical principle based on the *Mahavairocana Sutra*. The former was introduced into China in 720 by an Indian priest Vajrabodhi (671–741) who came from Southern India, the latter in 716 by another Indian priest Subhakarasimha (637–735) from Central India. Both of them, kindly treated by the Emperor Xuanzong, were soon to be made his resident mentors.

Vajrabodhi was succeeded by Amoghavajra (705–774). He was not Chinese, either, but the great contribution he made to the Tang Dynasty is extolled in the epitaph on the memorial stone that is still preserved at the Shaanxi History Museum in Xi'an. Obviously Kūkai had seen the stone and studied the epitaph, seeing that what he wrote about him in *The Transmission of the Legitimate Heritage of Esoteric Buddhism* mainly comes from this source. As to where Amoghavajra came from, opinions differ: Kūkai says it was South India, while others mention North India or even some other lands beyond the western border of the Chinese territory. It was from Amoghavajra that Huiguo absorbed the Esoteric Buddhism based on the *Vajrasekhara Sutra*.

Huiguo was born in 746, a son of the Ma family in the suburbs of Chang'an. As a boy he left home to live in a Buddhist temple in Chang'an, studying under one of Amoghavajra's disciples. At seventeen he met Amoghavajra, who, finding the boy Huiguo unusually intelligent, adopted him as his own disciple. At nineteen he received the *abhiseka** baptism from his master. At twenty, after receiving the precepts that the Buddhist monk should follow, he inherited the whole system of Esoteric Buddhism his master had acquired. About this time he was initiated into another system of Esoteric Buddhism—the physical principle based on the *Mahavairocana Sutra*. As for the initiator, some mention Amoghavajra, while others name Xuanchao (Hyonch'o in Korean), a priest from Silla, a disciple of Subhakarasimha. Whoever he might have been, Huiguo's having been entrusted with the two different systems of Esoteric Buddhism was to make him an outstanding figure in the history of Esoteric Buddhism in China. But was he really able to propagate it successfully as he was expected to?

In China, different religions from different lands had been benevolently protected by successive Tang Emperors. In fact, Buddhism from India had been treated even more sympathetically than others, as is known by the fact that all the Buddhist scriptures introduced into China were translated into Chinese. No other administrative body that has ever existed on earth could have carried out such a large-scale translation project as Tang China did: there was a specific establishment called the Sutra Translation Institute,where they worked systematically in many groups, in which one recited a Sanskrit text, sentence by sentence, another put it into Chinese, the third edited it, the fourth checked it, comparing it with the original. Doubts or controversial points were discussed by hundreds of specialists and authorities who were invited to the Institute. A great many volumes of Esoteric Buddhist scriptures were also translated in this way, directed by Indian priests such as Subhakarasimuha, Vajrabodhi and Amoghavajra, and by the time Kūkai arrived in Chang'an this translation project had almost been completed.

As far as such things were concerned, Esoteric Buddhism seemed to have been successfully transplanted to China. Unfortunately, however, what the Emperor and the Chinese in general expected of Esoteric Buddhism was not the thought it upheld, but the incantation practice it offered as a sort of supplement. The whole purpose of Esoteric Buddhism is to allow its followers to attain Buddhahood here and now—a peculiar dynamism that can never be expected from any other Buddhist religions in which the likelihood of attaining Buddhahood during one's lifetime is an infinitesimally small possibility. But this astonishing fruit of human thought offered only by Esoteric Buddhism did not appeal to the Chinese Court, while incantation practice was in constant demand, and kept all those Indian priests busy to that end. In fact, Vajrabodhi, who is said to have ordered every meal from heaven, was famous for the faith cure he successfully practiced on a dead princess, who was actually brought back to life, though only for a while.

The commonest request made by the Court was intercession for rainfall. One episode tells us that the Emperor Xuanzong invited Subhakarasimha and ordered him to invoke rainfall. But the Indian priest rejected his request, saying: "This is not the right time. Should I obey you now, I shall surely invite a terrible storm." But the Emperor insisted on his doing as he was told. Subhakarasimha, though very reluctant, got his follower to bring a bowl, filled it with water, and stirred it with a knife, chanting a *dharani* (a longer type of *mantra*) for rainfall, when a dragon jumped down before their eyes, the sky turned very dark, lightning flared, the rain began to fall in cataracts, flooding all the rivers around Chang'an, inflicting considerable damage even to the interior of the castle capital, to the astonishment and remorse of the Emperor.

What the Emperor Xuanzong saw in Amoghavajra was also a great practitioner of mystical incantation rather than the great thinker he really was. Amoghavajra, never sparing himself to please him, went so far as to compete with Taoist practitioners to defeat them. Nevertheless Xuanzong favored Taoism, and so did the succeeding Emperors. For one thing, it was a reaction against Zetian Wuhou's* overprotection for Buddhism in the previous era. For another thing, Taoists invented a legend that the Imperial Family of Tang China could be traced back to Laozi who was considered to be the founder of Taoism, because both had the same family name—Li.

On the other hand, Taoism as the indigenous religion of China was no longer a primitive religion to make people's wishes heard or to divine their fortunes, but a religious composite or synthesis embracing the philosophy of Laozi and Zhuangzi, and when Buddhism began to arrive in China in the first century, Taoism unfailingly appropriated Buddhist theories, especially those concerning the making of the universe. Buddhists were not very happy about it, but they knew that Buddhism had owed a great deal to Taoism, too, before it adapted itself to the climate of China and struck root in the new soil. For instance, in translating Sanskrit texts into Chinese, many words conveying metaphysical ideas had to be coined, but probably as many words were loaned from the philosophical terms of Taoism or the thought of Laozi and Zhuangzi. Thus the terminological analogy between Buddhism and Taoism led to a general impression that the two teachings were analogous to each other, which naturally made the Chinese prefer Taoism. The chief representative of this general preference for Taoism was the Emperor Xuanzong, who, having been temperamentally attracted to supernatural beings, went so far as to appoint Taoists to one government post after another for the first time in the long history of China. The next Emperor Suzong also appointed one of them as prime minister.

Confronted by the growing power of Taoists at Court, all those Indian masters of Esoteric Buddhism could not help resorting to minor elements such as incantations, faith cure, or even something like Iranian sleight-of-hand just to keep in touch with the Court. Indeed, Esoteric Buddhism in China might have been called an unlucky seed dropped on an infertile soil.

Amoghavajra died at seventy in 774. The then Emperor Daizong put his Court into three-day mourning to express condolence to their revered one. Indeed, the Tang Court never failed to show such cordiality toward Amoghavajra, but this was largely because of the inimitable ability he showed as a practitioner of mystical invocation. Now that he was gone, none of his disciples was able to preserve the brilliant and attractive image of their religion as their master had. No wonder Esoteric Buddhism in Chang'an began to wither as if deprived of life-giving sunshine.

This does not mean Amoghavajra had no disciples to succeed him in his religion. In fact, he had initiated the best six of his disciples into the system he had kept alive. They were Huilang, reportedly the best of the six, Huichao (Hyech'o), a theorist from Silla, Hanguang from Jinge-si temple on Mt.Wutai, Yuanjiao and Juechao from Baoshou-si temple on the same mountain, and Huiguo, the youngest of them all, who was later to meet Kūkai. They were all excellent scholars and devout ascetics. But in ability to perform mystical invocation, none could emulate their master.

Naturally, they did their best in this line all the same. For example, one moonlit night in 778, four years after his master's death, Huiguo, thirty-three of age, gave a prayer on top of Guan'yintai Hill (Kannon Bodhisattva Hill) and succeeded in invoking a clear image of a Kannon Bodhisattva on the full moon to the heart-felt pleasure of the men and women who had gathered around him. At another time, he invoked rainfall, too. But generally speaking, his performance did not have the virtuosity of his master's, which often made the over-joyed Emperor leave his seat to kneel down before him. Nevertheless, the Tang Court treated Huiguo cordially, granting him Dongta-yuan temple[3] when he was thirty-one, thus enabling him to start a place for *abhiseka* baptism there. In the ensuing year, the title of the Mentor of the State was conferred upon him even though he was still very young for such a great honor.

Two decades had passed, and Huiguo became the only person in Chang'an to have succeeded to Amoghavajra's system. Huilang and the others had died one after another; Huichao from Silla had returned home. Huiguo's following was by no means small. Several had already earned distinction: among them were Yiming, Yiman, Yicheng, Yiheng, Yiyi, Yizheng, Yicao, Yiyun, Yuantong, Yilun, Bianhong from Java and Huiri (Hyeil) from Silla.

But Esoteric Buddhism as a religious power in the Court had long since fallen far behind Taoism. Huiguo, quiet and disinterested by nature, had failed to make his activities properly impressive and spectacular. That naturally constituted a drawback for Esoteric Buddhism that was originally so devised as to be presented in a brilliant manner with even a theatrical effect, lacking which people could not help feeling it had declined. It would have been quite probable, therefore, that Huiguo and his religion had already ceased to be attractive to talented youths with intellectual powers.

"Abbot Huiguo has long been ill. I am afraid he might not recover."

Kūkai must have heard people talk about it in whispers. Several priests in Ximing-si temple with whom Kūkai made friends must have informed him of what had been happening in Qinglong-si temple: Huiguo at fifty-seven, realizing that he would not get well again, called his seven best disciples to his bedside and gave them his final instructions, so that they could carry on his religion even after his death; among the seven were Yiming whose priesthood was the longest of all, and Weishang who was to strike up a friendship with Kūkai through literature. But Huiguo's illness did not take a serious turn for a few more years.

Since the end of the previous year when the Japanese embassy had arrived in Chang'an, Huiguo must have often heard of "a Japanese student priest of Esoteric Buddhism, who is unusually intelligent." In fact, it did not take long before his literary talent was known to cultivated gentlemen in Chang'an. The sensation he had created in Fuzhou might have already been reported to the capital. If not, a Chinese custom of exchanging poems at every banquet, official or private, must have allowed Kūkai to have ample opportunities to display his talent. Gentlemen in Chang'an were unusually responsive to poetic talent, and once they found an excellent one, they simply could not keep it to themselves. Kūkai is said to be best in prose, second best in poetry. But his poems must have been remarkable enough to attract more and more Chinese gentlemen who eagerly wished to exchange poems with him. This alone kept him very busy, as Shinzei wrote in the preface to *Shōryō-shū*: "In Chang'an his exchanges of poems were such that even a large wicker basket overflowed with drafts of poems he made for others and poem-sheets he received from them." Among those who made friends with Kūkai about this time was a government dignitary named Zhu Qiancheng, who referred to Kūkai in a poem he made:

In literature he leads learned Chinese.

Then how could Huiguo remain ignorant of Kūkai as a new literary wonder now in the limelight? Quite imaginably, Huiguo was being kept informed of how Kūkai was astonishing the priests of Ximing-si temple with his profound knowledge and understanding of Buddhism and Esoteric

Buddhism. The more he knew about Kūkai, the more anxious he became to meet him, probably just as Kūkai had expected.

But according to the preface to *The List of the Items Introduced from China*, his encounter with Huiguo is related as follows:

> ... I had been visiting one temple after another, intending to find out the right master under whom to study, when one day I happened to meet Abbot Huiguo at Qinglong-si temple.

Such a chance meeting would surely provide an attractive highlight in his story. But it does not really sound likely that the one who came over to Chang'an to acquire the legitimate systems of Esoteric Buddhism should meet the supreme authority on them only by accident. This deviation from fact does seem to reveal, contrary to his own intention, his calculating manipulation of human psychology.

*   *   *

One day in June 805, Kūkai finally went to meet Huiguo, accompanied by five or six priests of Ximing-si temple, including Zhiming and Tansheng. All of them, personally acquainted with Huiguo, must have been happy and proud to help their worthy friend enter upon a new stage of his life.

Qinglong-si temple in Xinchang-fang block was in the East Ward. But even in that quiet half of the capital, there was a large amusement center around Daci'en-si temple and a small one around Qinglong-si temple that stood on a hill. Then Kūkai and his friends must have been working their way through a jostling crowd in a noisy street lined with show-booths and bars before they reached the foot of the hill.

What happened at Qinglong-si temple is described by Kūkai in the preface to *The List of the Items Introduced from China*:

> On seeing me, the master Huiguo broke into a broad smile and said in happy excitement: "I have been anxiously waiting for you for a long time. Now you are here! You are here! Dahao! Dahao! (It's really good! It's really good!)"

We can almost see the old man overjoyed even to a pathetic extent at Kūkai's arrival. "Dahao! Dahao!" Kūkai recorded as he heard it, probably a colloquialism at that time, makes us almost hear him crying out his joy. Huiguo goes on saying:

> "My days are numbered. (He was to die at the end of the same year.) But so far I have had no one to succeed me in the systems of my religion. Now that you have come, you shall be made my successor by receiving all the *abhiseka* baptisms without delay."

Huiguo, smiling all over, made this outright declaration on the spur of the moment, presumably without making any inquiry about Kūkai or giving him any test or examination. This was indeed a total departure from the usual practice. But everything was to be carried out exactly as Huiguo had decided.

XV. THE EIGHTH PATRIARCH OF ESOTERIC BUDDHISM

AS Kūkai had no master of Esoteric Buddhism to study under in Japan, he had to teach himself the hard way. As it turned out, however, he had done it so perfectly that when he came to Huiguo, the Chinese master had nothing new to teach him, except some secrets to be transmitted by word of mouth and some prescribed gestures and actions required in the performance of specific rituals. As for the thought itself, Huiguo had only to confirm what Kūkai had mastered on his own.

At Huiguo's request, Kūkai came to stay with him at Qinglong-si temple. Very soon a series of *abhiseka* baptismal ceremonies took place in quick succession: the first on June 13 and the second in early July were for initiation into the two different systems of Esoteric Buddhism; the last one on August 10 was for the conferment of the status of the great *acarya* (master) to succeed Huiguo and become the eighth patriarch of Esoteric Buddhism. Thus Kūkai, who had just arrived as a recruit, was made not only the head of Huiguo's following but also the legitimate successor to his mantle.

As can be well imagined, there were strong objections at first to this unprecedented decision Huiguo had made. Zhenhe, a dignitary of Yutang-si temple, came to meet Huiguo and expressed his displeasure at what he was doing for Kūkai. As his own master was Shunxiao,* a co-disciple of Huiguo under Amoghavajra, he had developed a sort of friendship with Huiguo, which entitled him to address him freely about anything he liked. That was probably why the unhappy disciples of Huiguo rushed to Zhenhe to tell him what was happening at their temple. Zhenhe, greatly surprised, promised them to come and talk to their "crazy master."

"That priest from Japan has not yet become your disciple, has he? Then how would you have decided to make him your successor even before you have taught him anything?" Zhenhe asked Huiguo sharply, accusing him of an aberrant decision. Huiguo listened but remained silent, occasionally shaking his head slowly, until at last Zhenhe flung out in a rage. But the following morning, Zhenhe was to change his opinion: he came to meet Huiguo again and withdrew all his objections proffered the day before. Then, to their astonishment, he went round Huiguo's disciples, earnestly persuading them that Huiguo was right when he made that decision, while he himself, by trying to put a spoke in his wheel, had shown himself to be terribly in error, and that they should never again question what their master was doing for Kūkai.

What made Zhenhe change his mind so completely was a dream he had had the night before, in which he was beaten away and trampled to pieces by the Four Guardians of Buddhism.[1] Zhenhe came to meet Kūkai, too. After making three profound bows to him as if he were in the presence of a Buddha, he confessed his own wrong and begged forgiveness for it. The utmost courtesy he showed to Kūkai on that occasion testifies how terrified he was of the divine wrath of the Four Guardians and how deeply he was impressed by the fact that Kūkai was so possessed of such divinity as to be guarded so firmly by those heavenly beings. Because Kūkai was not a liar, I believe all this was what had actually happened. But seeing that this episode is recorded in *The Memoirs of Our Master*, Kūkai in later years must have been recounting all those happenings to his disciples, incidentally revealing a tendency to self-glorification[2] rather than a proper humility.

* * *

What Kūkai was learning from Huiguo was the symbolism that composes a large part of this religion: the symbolic meanings charging each of the Sanskrit characters, *mudra* (symbolic gestures made by fingers or fists), *samaya* (objects or seals possessed by deities) and *mantra* (speech of *dharmakaya**). Huiguo transmitted all of them by word of mouth or by active demonstration. Even Kūkai was unable to master them all in such a short period of time, so he wrote down what he learned in a notebook, which is now known as *The Record of the Treasured Secrets*. It is unknown whether he made the notes in his master's presence or later in his own room.

On the other hand, he was reading a great deal, as we learn from *The Memoirs of Our Master*:

> All this while, I had been reading more than two hundred volumes of sutras including the *Mahavairocana Sutra* and the *Vajrasekhara Sutra*, and newly translated treatises on various sutras, always comparing the Chinese version with its Sanskrit original.

He must have been too occupied to eat and drink and sleep regularly.

Kūkai, the first Japanese to learn Sanskrit, must have mastered it before he came to meet Huiguo. Otherwise, when everything was over, Huiguo would not have said: "Now you have received all that I have retained both in Chinese and in Sanskrit. It is as if all the water I have kept in my bottle has been poured into yours to the very last drop."

Later Kūkai recalled this comment his master had once made, and told it to his disciples, as was recorded in *The Summary of the Transmission of the Legitimate Heritage of Esoteric Buddhism*. In the same book, one can read Kūkai's own opinion about this matter: "In reading sutras, one must not fail to study the Sanskrit original as well. Reading sutras only in Chinese is no better than reading them in *kana*.³"

These entries do reflect the fact that Esoteric Buddhism in China was being retained by Huiguo and many other Chinese priests who were still in the habit of thinking in Sanskrit. Then it would have been quite natural that Kūkai should have perfected his Sanskrit under the Indian masters, Prajna and Munisri, before he went to meet Huiguo.

In India, *abhiseka* or sprinkling water on the head of a crown prince used to be the highlight of a coronation ceremony. In Buddhism, too, a Bodhisattva is supposed to receive *abhiseka* baptism when he or she is raised to Buddhahood after finishing the training stage of Bodhisattvahood. In Esoteric Buddhism, there are a variety of *abhiseka* baptisms: the commonest is for novices desiring to be received into Esoteric Buddhism; the most solemn is for the conferment of the status of *acarya* (master), in which "water of Five Wisdoms⁴" is poured over the head of the receiver.

Prior to the initial baptism, there was a rite called Flower Casting, in which one had to cast a flower on a mandala diagram spread on the altar to see which image of Buddha or Bodhisattva one's flower would fall upon, thus making the choice of one's lifelong guardian deity. Huiguo's flower fell on the Bodhisattva named *Dharama-cakra-pravartana* which means "the Buddha's preaching that is likened to a wheel crushing all illusions." His master and baptizer Amoghavajra is said to have been pleased with it.

On June 13, the first *abhiseka* baptism for Kūkai took place. The hall in Qinglong-si temple had been decorated with utmost magnificence and formality, incense smoke permeating the whole place, one hundred kinds of food offerings arranged on the altars, hundreds of guest priests seated in orderly array. Then Kūkai was seen to proceed to the mandala to the choir's chorus of a Sanskrit hymn. The flower Kūkai cast fell on the central image of Mahavairocana. His master and baptizer Huiguo shouted in wonder and exaltation:

"Mysterious! Mysterious!"

Huiguo must have been reminded of his own master Amoghavajra whose flower was also said to have fallen on the image of Mahavairocana, which made his master and baptizer Vajrabodhi declare in joy: "Amoghavajra will surely make this religion grow and flourish."

Exactly the same thing happened in the second baptism Kūkai received in July. As there was no Flower Casting at the final baptism in August, Huiguo who regarded these double signs as very significant conferred upon him the Esoteric Buddhist name of *Henjō Kongō* 遍照金剛, one of the appellations held by Mahavairocana himself, meaning "the Universal Adamantine Illuminator." It may seem the height of audacity to name a human being after Mahavairocana as an embodiment of the truth of the universe. But it is by no means as extravagant as one might think, because the one who receives the final baptism is supposed to participate in revealing and demonstrating the truth of the universe exactly as Mahavairocana does.

Even to this day, a variety of *abhiseka* baptisms are given to Kūkai's followers. Flower Casting occurs, too. One who is going to cast a flower (now a sprig of the Chinese aniseed tree[5]) has one's face masked, holds the sprig between the upright middle fingers of the joined hands, and then is guided to the mandala spread on the altar. Then one stretches one's arms and, instead of casting the sprig, just drops it. Whichever image it may fall on, one's guide will pick it up and place it exactly on the central image of Mahavairocana so that one may be favored by Mahavairocana just as Kūkai was. What a sad imaginative lapse or miserable retrogression to small-minded formality! Formerly, a meritorious soul was able to identify himself, as Kūkai did, with the truth of the universe. But not now. No one can tell when this new tradition started.

I had long wondered what the *abhiseka* baptisms Kūkai received at Qinglong-si temple were like. The only answer was the one I once received from Sakai Eishin, a priest of Chishakn-in temple in Kyōto: "There is no knowing, because it is kept under the seal of secrecy." Recently I asked the same question of the same person only to receive the same answer. A quarter century had passed and he was now residing at Fudō-ji temple in Toyonaka, Ōsaka. But I found impressive the same answer given in the same tone as if it testified to his unchanging faith.

*   *   *

When the final baptism was over on August 10, Kūkai, now the eighth patriarch of Esoteric Buddhism, held a banquet to express his gratitude not only to the hundreds of priests who had attended the three special events held in his honor but also to those who had assisted him in various ways during the ceremonies. It cost a great deal of money to host five hundred guests in all. But when in Chang'an, he had to do as the Chang'ans do. It proved to be a very grand affair, greatly ennobled by the presence of dignitaries, including those from Daxingshan-si temple where Amoghavajra used to reside.

By the same token, Kūkai had to make a present to his master Huiguo, even if he could not afford anything expensive, as he wrote in a note he sent along with the presents:

> I wished I could make a proper return for all those kindnesses you have shown me. But after all I could not afford even a single rare item of any value. I shall be very grateful if only you will

kindly accept these lowly things: a humble surplice and a small
zappō incense burner.

The surplice must have been of flax. *Zappō* is something like cloisonné
ware, so the incense burner must have been a pretty, glittering object, made
of colorfully-glazed silver. Though not very expensive, they would have
made endearing presents that reflected his original, lowly status of a student
priest from abroad. But there was another package containing five hundred
kan-mon[6] of coins that he sent to Huiguo on the same occasion. It was a
tremendous sum of money. What could it be for? For making up what
Huiguo spent on those ceremonies? Or for the purchase of the ritual
implements the legitimate successor to that religion had to possess? But
seeing that the complete set of twenty ritual implements were of specialized
workmanship produced by first-class craftsmen chosen by Huiguo, including
Yang Zhongxin who was working regularly for the Imperial Court, five
hundred *kan-mon* of coins could not possibly have covered the expenditure.

Among other things Huiguo had equipped Kūkai with were five kinds of
huge mandala scrolls and also five kinds of large scrolls of portrature of
successive patriarchs of Esoteric Buddhism. All of them had to be newly
painted by more than ten artists—also first-class, like Li Zhen in the service
of the Imperial Family—who were all invited by Huiguo to his own temple
to do the work.

As for the sutras and treatises Kūkai was to bring home, there were one
hundred and forty-two sets of two hundred and forty-seven volumes, all of
which were newly translated, and therefore not yet known in Japan. Among
them, the latest translations by Amoghavajra—one hundred and eighteen
sets of one hundred and fifty volumes, still kept by Huiguo at his own
temple, not yet being entered in the official list because no extra copies of
them had been made yet—had to be copied by more than twenty transcribers
hired by Huiguo.

How could Kūkai manage to pay for all the expenditure incurred for
them? Did Huiguo defray all the costs? It seems quite unlikely. Buddhist
temples in Chang'an were subjected to very strict financial management;
some of them were even notorious for their avarice. Huiguo, known for his
indifference to money, was a rare case, as is expressed in the epitaph Kūkai

later wrote for his deceased master:

> His four cardinal behaviors (walking, standing, sitting and reclining) were perfect in their effortlessness; his three actions (physical, verbal and metaphysical) were always spontaneous but unfailingly correct.... Unlike others, he never put aside whatever he received, for he spent it on bringing a large mandala into being, on another occasion on repairing his monastery.

Obviously Huiguo spent a large sum to make Kūkai his successor, but as the president of a national institute, he would not have gone so far as to do damage to its assets. This meant that Kūkai had to make up all the deficit for himself. With no patrons to turn to, money worries must have been weighing upon his mind. But somehow or other—probably by making the best use of the funds he had brought with him—he managed to settle all the bills, and no trouble ensued.

The following items were what Huiguo handed over to Kūkai as a token of the newly inaugurated patriarch: Eighty samples of Sakyamuni's ashes; a three-paneled stand made of sandalwood, upon which the images of the Buddha, a host of bodhisattvas and guardians of Buddhism are carved in relief; a large mandala diagram, drawn on a sheet of white cloth, with four hundred and forty-seven deities depicted on it; a *vajra-dahatu* mandala diagram, drawn on a sheet of white cloth, with one hundred and twenty *samaya* (objects or seals that represent deities) are depicted; a *vajra* pounder decorated with gold, silver, pearl, coral and amber; a pair of bronze gilt bowls; a bench made of ivory; a white trumpet shell.

Originally they were brought over to China by the Indian priest Vajrabodhi. Then they were handed down to Amoghavajra, to Huiguo, and now to Kūkai. This meant that all those treasured objects would be no more in China if Kūkai returned home with them. This fact alone shows how unusual Huiguo's decision was. No wonder many were strongly against it, though only temporarily.

Lastly Huiguo offered Kūkai five more articles among his personal possessions, intending that they would serve as mementos of him, or subsidiary tokens of the succession.

When he had finished everything he had to do, the old man literally became a shadow of himself and died four months later. According to the preface to *The List of the Items Introduced from China*, Huiguo said to Kūkai when the final baptism was over: "My life on this earth is coming to an end; it will not be long before I breathe my last.... I was always afraid that I might not live to see you receive everything. But now I can see you perfectly equipped with everything—doctrines, scriptures, secrets, images, and implements."

His pleasant sigh of relief can almost be heard between the lines. The old man went on to say: "Now that you have done everything you intended to do here, you should return home as soon as possible and present to the State what you have received here, so that you can propagate the teaching and bring happiness to the people over there."

Huiguo must have meant what he said. But the thoughtful person might have meant more than he said, observing that Kūkai, having spent all his funds, could not afford to stay there any longer.

XVI. Leaving Chang'an

THEN it so happened that a special envoy from Japan arrived in Chang'an on a mission to congratulate the new Emperor Shunzong on his accession to the throne. The envoy, Takashina no *mahito* Tōnari, must have been astonished to find that Shunzong was no more. Shunzong had reigned only several months before he abdicated in favor of Xianzong and died soon after that. The congratulatory presents the Japanese Court had prepared for Shunzong would naturally have been passed on to Xianzong.

Kūkai and Hayanari went to meet the envoy in a courtesy call at the guest quarters where he was staying. The purpose of their visit was also to ask him to accompany them home on his return journey, for when government students returned home, they had to apply to the Tang Emperor for permission through the envoy of their own country.

Instead of expressing their personal requests abruptly, Kūkai would have begun by making it clear that they had already done all they were expected to do in Chang'an, that it would be impossible for them to learn any more even if they were to stay here any longer, and that it would also be more beneficial to the State, if they returned home and offered it the benefits of their achievements.

Then Kūkai would have asked when the next envoy would be sent here, revealing their wish that they might take advantage of his return journey. But the envoy would not be able to tell when, as it was always decided upon by what might be called a passing fancy of the tennō. Since 630 when the first envoy was sent to Tang China, sixteen envoys had been sent at very irregular intervals; sometimes in two successive years, but at other times there were twenty years or more in between.

The envoy would have naturally expressed an opinion more and more Court people at home were beginning to support: that the sending of the envoy to China should be discontinued. He may have added his own view that there would be no more envoys sent to China—the worst scenario that must have made homesick Hayanari nearly scream in despair.

Certainly there were several reasons for abolishing this practice. Firstly, the dangers they had to face on their way to and from China were becoming more and more unacceptable, even though such fears had been totally ignored in the previous era when the introduction of Chinese culture and civilization was unanimously considered indispensable. Secondly, Japan had already learned a great deal from China, thus having achieved her original aim to a satisfying degree. Thirdly, Japan's first batch of intellectuals was beginning to entertain a narrow-minded patriotism, saying: "Certainly our embassies had done much towards the importation of Chinese culture and civilization. But what do you think about the way the Tang Court treats us, as if we were one of those vassal countries? How could we bear such humiliation?" Such a sense of distinction was also what Japan had acquired through studying Chinese classics, that drew a sharp line between native Chinese and those non-Chinese living outside Chinese territory. Fourthly, as the commercial trade was becoming more and more active at Chinese seaports south of the Yangzi River, more and more Chinese trade merchants were finding Japan a very good market, while the Japanese saw the advantages of purchasing from them all things Chinese, including Chinese classics and Buddhist scriptures.

Lastly, the national treasury had virtually gone bankrupt after being pressed hard by one project after another launched by the Tennō Kammu. Recently one State Councilor Fujiwara no Otsugi had hotly argued this matter and concluded: "Achieving the stabilization of national life is an urgent necessity. Let this take precedence over all else: namely, that there should be no more military expeditions[1] and no more construction of state buildings." Even Kammu had to agree with him. But he was to die the next year, leaving the State on the verge of exhaustion. Then how could anyone think of sending another envoy to China? In fact, it was thirty years before another envoy—actually the last envoy—was sent to China. By that time (838), Kūkai had been dead for three years. If their wish to return home with the envoy Takashina had been rejected, Kūkai and Hayanari would never have been able to see their home again.

If the envoy had been a stickler for regulations, as many government officials were, he would have said: "Isn't it very selfish of you? Don't you know the rule? I have never heard of a student returning home so soon for his own convenience. Even if the Tang Emperor should have allowed you to do so, what do you think our Court will say? So you had better wait till I return home and find some opportunity to present your request to them." As it happened, the envoy did his utmost to help them. What made him do so? Was it natural kindness? Kūkai's skill in persuasion? Or the probability that there would be no more envoys to China?

The envoy Takashina, though by no means influential in government circles, was of royal descent, as is recorded in *Shoku Nihon-gi*: "On the fourth year of Hōki (774) Prince Yasuyado (a grandson of Prince Takechi, a son of the Tennō Temmu), was demoted to subject status, receiving the family name and title—Takashina no *mahito*." Probably well-educated and refined in demeanor, he must have been considered well fitted to make the congratulatory mission to China.

Since their request was granted by the envoy Takashina, Kūkai and Hayanari had to write their petitions to the Tang Emperor. In his petition, Kūkai wrote how fortunate he had been to be able to come over to China; how he had studied under the Indian priests, Prajna and Munisri; how he had met the Chinese priest Huiguo who had readily allowed him to accede to the whole of the two systems of Esoteric Buddhism he had preserved; since his duties as a government student had been perfectly fulfilled, he would be very grateful if he were allowed to return home with the envoy Takashina, so that he could spend the rest of his life carrying out his religious mission at home, instead of staying on in Chang'an to no purpose, just waiting for the expiration of his twenty-year term. The draft of this petition still remains in the *Shōryō-shū*.

What Kūkai wrote about his returning home so soon in the preface to *The List of the Items Introduced from China* runs as follows:

> I am fully aware that the crime I have committed by returning
> home so soon is inexpungible even by the death penalty.

It seems that returning home prior to the expiration of the term was considered high treason against the Japanese Court. The envoy Takashina must have needed considerable courage in complying with their unusual request.

The case of Hayanari was even harder to handle. Though not equal to Kūkai, he was obviously among the most brilliant students Japan had ever sent to China. That was why he soon won the nickname "Ju,[2] the talented" from the Chinese intellectuals who came to know him through exchanging literature and calligraphy. But as a student of Confucianism, he was hopeless. He had been preparing for the entrance examination to the university since his arrival in Chang'an. But his inability to speak Chinese had prevented him from entering the university. Meanwhile, he had spent all the money he had brought with him from Japan.

"Shall I make a draft?" Kūkai may have offered such help. Or Hayanari at his wits' end may have asked him for help. The youth depicted by Kūkai in the petition was indeed a shiftless one:

> Unable to conquer the mountains and waters lying between the two tongues, I have not yet matriculated,.... Before being allowed to enter the woods of *Sophora japonica* (the university), what little funds I have brought with me have melted away.... though the grant I have gratefully received from your government has kept me alive.

Then he went on writing about how useless it would be for such a destitute person as he, who could not possibly afford to buy either books or presents for his tutors, to go on staying in Chang'an as long as nineteen more years:

> I feel as if I were no better than a mole cricket[3] crawling about in the gutter. Indeed, it is a national loss for Tang China, too, to go on keeping such a useless person as I am.

Kūkai may have gone too far when he compared his poor friend to such a lowly creature as a mole cricket. But he had to. Otherwise, the Emperor might not grant his petition. Poor Hayanari would have agreed with Kūkai.

In the due time, the Japanese envoy, who had presented these petitions along with his own memorial to the Tang Court, was allowed to have an audience with the Emperor Xianzong. It is uncertain whether or not he was accompanied by Kūkai and Hayanari. According to *The Memoirs of Our Master*, the Emperor not only agreed with their choice to return home, saying "It stands to reason," but also presented a rosary to Kūkai with the statement: "We had intended that this priest should stay here and become our mentor. But now that he has to go home, he shall have this rosary as a memento of us." The envoy gratefully received the rosary for Kūkai—a rosary of crystal beads and nuts of *bodhi-druma* or Buddha's tree.

By that time the Emperor must have heard about Kūkai having created both the text and calligraphy of the epitaph dedicated to the late great master Huiguo, who had long been among the mentors to the Tang Emperors. It was not improbable, therefore, that the Emperor had already read the whole of the epitaph on the monument.

Huiguo had passed away on December 15, 805, at Qinglong-si temple. In his dying hour, he cleansed himself with hot scented water, made the *mudra* or manual sign of Mahavairocana, lay calmly on his right side, and breathed his last at the age of sixty. On January 16, the following year, the funeral service was held at his own temple, Dongta-yuan, in Qinglong-si temple. On the following day, his coffin was borne along to the burial place in Mengcun Village in the eastern suburbs of the capital, followed by a long train of mourners numbering more than one thousand. It was then and there that the monument was erected.

It was not necessarily because Kūkai was heir to Huiguo's religion that he had been chosen to create both text and calligraphy for that epitaph. For such a distinguished person as Huiguo, both text and calligraphy were usually entrusted to personages or professionals of first-class importance. This fact alone indicates how Kūkai had been held in high esteem in Chang'an. The draft remains in the *Shōryō-shū*. But the monument, a fairly large stone with one thousand and eight hundred characters carved on it, has disappeared, for the neighborhood has long since turned into farmland.

*   *   *

The following story about an event that is considered to have occurred on this occasion or about this time has given rise to a famous legend of "Priest

Five Brushes," as is recorded in *The Honourable Life of Kōya Daishi* and *Tales of Times Now Past*:

> Long ago, in one of the rooms near the Emperor's living room, there was a calligraphy done by Wang Xizhi* upon a couple of white walls, each about two metres wide. But as the years went on, one of the walls had crumbled away and was repainted white. On that blank wall, Kūkai was requested to create his own calligraphy.

In fact, it was quite improbable that a mural work done by Wang Xizhi (321–379), a high-ranking official and calligrapher living in the era of the Eastern Jin (317–420) whose capital was Jiankang (present-day Nanjing), should have existed at the Imperial Palace of the Tang Dynasty in Chang'an. But the story goes on:

> Kūkai came into the room, dipped five brushes in Indian ink, took two in both hands, one in the mouth, the other two between his toes, and did a five-line calligraphy at one stroke. Then he found one character missing. Instead of putting in that character, he put all the remaining ink into a bowl, held it up and poured the contents all over the unfinished work, to create a huge character of 樹 (arbor) perfectly done in one vigorous sweep. The Emperor, struck with wonder, conferred upon him a title of "Priest Five-Brushes."

As for what "Five-Brushes (Go-Hitsu 五筆)" means, there are various opinions. Some think that it meant "the five rules in calligraphy" advocated by a Chinese calligrapher, Han Fangming, who had some influence upon Kūkai. Others recall the fact that the Tennō Saga, who came to admire Kūkai's calligraphy very much, specifically called his handwriting Go-Hitsu (Honourable Handwriting 御筆) and its homonym, they assumed, was the origin of that fabulous story.

Whatever "Go-Hitsu" means, it seems quite certain that Kūkai in Chang'an had acquired that name, as is known from the following episode recorded in the *Gyōreki-shō*, the journal of Enchin,[4] a nephew of Kūkai or a son of Kūkai's niece, who came to stay and study in China nearly fifty years after Kūkai did:

One day I came across a Chinese priest named Huiguan, who, finding I was Japanese, asked: "Is Priest Five-Brushes faring well?" Judging that he meant Kūkai, I answered: "The priest you kindly mention is no more." The Chinese priest, beating his breast in great grief, exclaimed: "What a pity to have lost such an unprecedented talent!"

*　　*　　*

Kūkai had returned to Ximing-si temple to spend his remaining time in Chang'an. He must have been unusually busy continuing to take lessons in Siddham and Sanskrit, collecting and copying Buddhist scriptures and Chinese classical books, and learning how to make things Chinese, including medicines, dyestuffs and processed foods. He acquired such knowledge directly from their makers with whom he made friends while exploring the town.

He never neglected social life, either. When invited by high officials, writers and artists, he made it a rule to accept the invitation and then to invite them in return. This rarely left him alone, especially when more and more of his admirers vied in having him in their literary gatherings, to which he took Hayanari from time to time, as is known by some poems presented to them as a pair. Had it not been for Kūkai, Hayanari would have remained obscure instead of being known as "Ju, the talented" in the fashionable society in Chang'an.

The news that Kūkai was going home deeply shocked those who had been appreciating his company. Trying to express their reluctance to part from him, they presented him with farewell poems or letters, calligraphic works from the ancient past, books of literature, or rubbings from monuments. Many of these presented by Zhu Qiancheng, Zhu Shaoduan,Tan Qing, Hong Jian and Zheng Shenfu still remain, testifying to the warm friendship he had struck up with those high-ranking intellectuals during his fourteen-month stay in Chang'an. Nor could any other Japanese who had been in China be compared with Kūkai in this respect.

In mid-March, 806, Kūkai and Hayanari were seen among the Japanese embassy delegation leaving Chang'an on horseback by Chunming-men gate. While crossing the fields radiant with peach and damson blossom, they would have seen the mist of late spring languidly hovering over the Bashui River. Looking back at the castle capital of Chang'an, Kūkai must have been feeling as if he were being torn in two. As a private person, he would have been reluctant to leave there. Seen from any angle, he was much more suited to live in Chang'an than in his own country where everything was still helplessly limited and provincial. Had he been relieved of the status of government student and his self-imposed mission to propagate his religion at home, he might have chosen to stay in Chang'an all his life, just like many of the talented in Tang China who just remained true to their preference for Chang'an: those who were transferred to provincial offices poured into poetry their regret at having to part with her, those staying away from her for many years expressed their undying longing for her, while those who were fortunate enough to go on staying there never tired of extolling her beauty. It was improbable, therefore, that Kūkai should have felt no emotions about departing from her for good—at least the artist in Kūkai, who had been keenly aware that only in Chang'an would he be able to fulfill himself, and where his exuberant taste and brilliant creativity were fully appreciated by the like-minded.

Kūkai wrote nothing about such personal feelings. But the following story found in *Record of Things Heard, Past and Present* may reveal something of the sorrow or regret that occasionally crossed his heart:

> The Tennō Saga, who had found in Kūkai a very intimate friend, often invited him and enjoyed talking about calligraphy. On one such occasion, Saga was showing his collection of calligraphic works, ancient and contemporary, when he took up a scroll he treasured most of all, saying:
>
> "Look. This was done by a Chinese though I cannot tell who he was. To my mind, very few could possibly attain this level however hard they might try. That is why I value this more than any other."
>
> Kūkai was listening while Saga went on pouring out his admiration, and it was not until he was asked for his own opinion that he disclosed the authorship of that work, saying:
>
> "Well, I think I must have done it myself."

Certainly he had done it himself while he was in Chang'an, but it was typical of Kūkai's self-possession to keep quiet about it till the last moment, consequently putting proud Saga to shame.

> At first, Saga was incredulous and insisted that it was done by a Chinese, saying in a tone of sharp reprimand: "I can hardly believe you. How could you explain the vast difference between this writing and yours? Frankly, this is much better than yours."
>
> Kūkai told him to expose a corner of the scroll and see what he would find there. The Tennō did as he was told and saw there, to his astonishment, a dated note which said that it was "done by Priest Kūkai at Qinglong-si temple."
>
> Now the Tennō could not help believing Kūkai but still with reservations because of a great difference between his writing then and now.
>
> "... Certainly it is yours," said Saga. "But could you explain what has changed your writing so much? To be more frank, I should like to know what has made you suffer such a sad decline."
>
> "One's handwriting changes according to where one creates it," answered Kūkai. "In a large country like China, one's handwriting may gain the sort of dash as is shown on that scroll. But in a small country like Japan, it suffers decline...."
>
> The Tennō, deeply ashamed, never again entered into this sort of argument with Kūkai.

Beside Kūkai, fearless and calm, Saga must have been feeling very insignificant not only because of his poor connoisseurship but also because of the lowly status he had displayed as the king of a small country. This episode, probably a true story, may express his unspoken regret that his genius, best suited to a large country, had to be confined to a small one.

Meanwhile, they came to the other end of Ba-qiao bridge. That was where well-wishers plucked sprigs off willow trees on the bank and offered them to each of the departing as a farewell token. Kūkai received a great many sprigs from all those sending him off, clergy and laity alike. Though he was feeling it hard to suppress his overflowing emotion, he would have controlled himself as his newly-obtained status required him to, keeping his back straight, and with dry eyes, looking calm and graceful in the spring breeze that kept fluttering his sleeves. He had nothing much to say, for he had already delivered all his thoughts in the poems he had presented to them. The following poem he dedicated to Yicao, one of the best friends he had made at Qinglong-si temple, may reveal what sort of friendship they had been enjoying:

> Embracing the same principle under the same master, we have
> been enjoying the profound pleasure of meeting one another.
> But now, in accordance with *sunyata* the white fog must leave
> for peaks afar, never to return. Let me promise you, my friend,
> I shall often visit you, *not* in my dreams, *but* in my thoughts.

XVII. RETURN TO JAPAN BY WAY OF YUEZHOU

ORTY days' journey brought the embassy to Yuezhou, present-day Shaoxing famed for its local wine. The castle capital near Hangzhou Bay was surrounded by wide stretches of rice paddies divided only by waters of small canals, with Mt. Guiji rising to the south. The view of the mountain would have reminded travelers of that famous rivalry[1] between the kings of Yue and Wu in ancient China. Yuezhou on the canals was enlivened by commercial activities, and the effects of its prosperity had extended even to Buddhist temples which attracted a large number of renowned priests from all over the country. The envoy Takashina and his party were to stay there for five months.

Kūkai, who wished to collect many more books while staying there, wrote a letter to the Governor, asking for financial help: "... in Chang'an I spent all my funds... here I cannot afford to hire any copyist...." Collecting books at that time usually meant hiring copyists. He also mentions what sort of books he wanted to collect: "... not only Buddhist scriptures but also books of literature, astronomy, medicine, art and any other fields, as long as they add to the happiness and welfare of people." Most of the books he had obtained in Chang'an had been on Esoteric Buddhism. In Yuezhou he intended to acquire a variety of books to meet the needs of various fields of human life. What kind of answer the Governor gave is unknown. But the great generosity he showed on that occasion is apparent, when we see that what Kūkai obtained in Chang'an was three hundred odd volumes, while the number he entered in *The List of the Items Introduced from China* was four hundred and sixty one volumes, proving that about one hundred and fifty volumes were added in Yuezhou. As works of literature and calligraphy and stone rubbings were left out of the *List*, the total must have amounted to an even greater number.

Among the many renowned Buddhist priests who had come to live in the noted temples in Yuezhou, there was an Esoteric Buddhist priest named Shunxiao. As he was one of the ten Buddhist priests serving at the Imperial chapel, it was quite likely that he was the most prominent in the Buddhist society of Yuezhou. According to *The Memoirs*, Shunxiao and Huiguo were fellow disciples of Amoghavajra, though another source reports that Shunxiao, a disciple of Subhakarasimha, reached master's rank under Yilin (Uirim in Korean) from Silla. Whichever may be true, it is quite probable that Shunxiao was well acquainted with Huiguo. In *The Memoirs*, there is an entry that enables us to imagine a scene in which Huiguo and Shunxiao were talking to each other in the presence of Kūkai.

Kūkai in Yuezhou would naturally have visited Shunxiao at Longxing-si temple where he was residing. It was then that Kūkai heard of "a Japanese priest named Saichō" who had visited there the year before to be initiated into Esoteric Buddhism by Shunxiao himself. Did this mean that by now Saichō in Japan had already been propagating Esoteric Buddhism? Kūkai must have received quite a shock. He would no longer have the honor of being the first to introduce Esoteric Buddhism into Japan.

* * *

About two years before, when his boat arrived in Mingzhou, Saichō went straight to Mt. Tiantai in Taizhou and when he finished acquiring the whole system of the Tiantai religion, his plan was to return to Mingzhou whence he would sail back to Japan. Unable to speak Chinese, he never thought of exchanging literature with local intellectuals, as Kūkai did. Saichō was not necessarily lacking in literary talent; but his prose style was more suited for expounding logic than for producing literature in the baroque style which was then in fashion. As a poet, he was not always brilliant. As a neighbor, he was not sociable, either.

When he arrived back in Mingzhou on March 25, 805, he found that he had to wait more than forty days before his boat set sail. It was just intolerable for him to have to spend so many days doing nothing in particular. Then he discovered that Yuezhou was "a stronghold of Buddhism." Yuezhou, he was told, was "quite a distance" away—about one hundred and twenty kilometers. But as long as he could collect more Buddhist scriptures, he did not mind extending his trip there. The first person Saichō met in Yuezhou was the Governor, who, according to his request, issued a formal letter of introduction presenting him as "the high priest dispatched by the Japanese government, whose specific mission is to introduce Chinese Buddhism into Japan under the sponsorship of the Tang Court."

After reading this letter, Shunxiao at Longxing-si temple thought it his duty to pass on his Esoteric Buddhism to this high priest from Japan. Therefore, Saichō was offered what amounted to a windfall by Shunxiao. Shunxiao, unlike Huiguo, was not an heir to the legitimate heritage of Esoteric Buddhism, while Saichō, a student of the Tiantai religion, had never intended or prepared to learn Esoteric Buddhism. But Saichō, eager to obtain anything he could, thankfully accepted the offer. With his ample funds, he was easily able to copy one hundred and fifteen volumes of one hundred and two sets of scriptures. But the number of ritual objects he was equipped with was only seven, when the complete set as Kūkai brought back consisted of twenty. This did reflect the limited nature of the Esoteric Buddhism Shunxiao had acquired, but Saichō remained ignorant of this until years later.

For Kūkai, the only consolation was that the Esoteric Buddhism Saichō brought home was just a portion of the whole body of that religion. But even in China such a small amount passed as Esoteric Buddhism. Then what if Saichō had returned home earlier and introduced it as such? Would it not be too late, even if Kūkai, a late comer, might assert the authenticity and legitimacy of what he had brought back? This might be so especially when Saichō was revered and favored by the Tennō Kammu himself, while Kūkai had long been nobody—practically an illegal monk—until only a few years before, when he was reluctantly permitted to go and study in China. Kūkai, by nature fairly combative, might have regarded this as a sort of religious persecution inflicted upon him.

While in Yuezhou, Kūkai is said to have encountered a great scholar of the Kegon doctrine, Shenxiu, to master its arcana under him. Though this was just another intellectual digression he made in China, it was soon to be of some use on the occasion of his being approached by the elders of the old Buddhism in Nara when it was severely attacked by Saichō.

* * *

In late August, 806, the envoy Takashina and his party set out on the return voyage. Which route they took is unknown. Neither is it known how long it lasted or what happened at sea, as all documents concerned are lost. Only *The Honourable Life of Kōya Daishi* contains a brief description of the voyage: "... at sea the boat was frequently at the mercy of the waves," though it is not known whether this was reality or rhetoric. But the following entry was obviously factual: "In the boat everyone began to talk about the demise of the Tennō Kammu.... Daishi (Kūkai) went to the seamen and tried in vain to find out the source of the news and further information. But he sensed it was true."

Certainly it was true: the Tennō Kammu, aged seventy, had died on March 17 that year. Before leaving Mingzhou (present-day Ningbo), Japanese seamen might have heard of it from some Chinese seamen who had recently been in Japan. The swiftness with which the news on the other side of the East China Sea came spreading to this side does testify the fact that the sea had already been traversed with considerable frequency by Chinese trading merchants.

Kammu's death would have made Kūkai look back upon his life with a certain emotion: Kammu had ascended the throne when Kūkai was nine, and the following twenty-five years of his reign, unusually eventful, had coincided with Kūkai's boyhood and youth, in which he had always been made conscious of his presence mainly through what was happening to Saeki no Ima-Emishi and Ato no Ōtari.

On the other hand, the politician in Kūkai may have had a foreboding of what would become of Saichō without Kammu as his greatest patron. In fact, Kammu's death was gradually to work to Saichō's disadvantage.

There is no way of finding out exactly when Kūkai returned home, as all the documents available only make vague references to it. So I should suggest that one day in autumn, 806, they landed at Nanotsu, and came to the reception hall in Dazai-fu to stay there for a while as they had done on their way to China. Hayanari, who had been terribly homesick, may have

179

been tearful when he stepped on the shore of Nanotsu, expressing his wish to be home in the capital very soon. But since Japan's official practices at that time were carried out in a Chinese fashion, their arrival back had to be first reported to the Court by the express messenger sent from Dazai-fu, and not until the official order was brought to them could they tell when they would leave for the capital.

While waiting for that order, Kūkai must have been compiling *The List of the Items Introduced from China* so that he could present it to the Court as soon as he was back in the capital. As it turned out, however, the *List* had to be entrusted to the envoy Takashina, because Kūkai was not allowed to go back to the capital with the envoy.

In the preface to the *List*, dated October 22, 806, probably the same day as the envoy, his suite and Hayanari departed for the capital, Kūkai had described his having returned home so soon as "the crime inexpungible even by the death penalty." But he went on writing with proper pride: "Nevertheless, I am delighted to the bottom of my heart that I have at least been able to bring back this golden principle before my life expires."

In fact, he could not have been too proud, for what he was going to offer to this country was something of a value greater than any other it had received. To make this fact clearly known, he gave a good explanation of the essence of Esoteric Buddhism which was totally incomparable in value with any of the exoteric religions Japan had ever known. Lastly he stated how it had been transmitted, mentioning Amoghavajra, Huiguo and himself, thus making clear the meritorious significance of his having been made the legitimate heir to that religion. Only the dull-witted could have remained unmoved when reading these passages.

* * *

Some officials at Dazai-fu would have asked Kūkai wonderingly, when they discovered the purpose of his visit to Chang'an:

"You mean... you have brought back Esoteric Buddhism? Have you not heard of Saichō? He is creating a sensation as its proponent. Everyone in the capital is talking about the *abhiseka* baptism he performed on the authorities of Nara Buddhism by Imperial order."

It was probably from these officials in this outpost of the central government, who were sometimes better informed of what was happening in the capital than those who were living there, that Kūkai learned what Saichō had been doing all this time in the capital: Saichō, after returning home the previous year, had prepared his own *List of the Items Introduced from Yuezhou* and presented it to the Court.

To Saichō's dismay, what attracted Kammu's attention most was not the system of Tiantai religion for whose importation he had been sent over to China, but the Esoteric Buddhism he had happened to acquire in Yuezhou. When he had left Japan a few years before, none but Kūkai and his supporters had been interested in Esoteric Buddhism. But now the tide had changed. Why? Probably the key was in something like a stone rubbing Kammu found among the things Chinese delivered to him by the hand of the envoy Kanō—a rubbing of the epitaph created by the Emperor Xuanzong himself[2] for his esteemed master of Esoteric Buddhism, Yixing,[3] who died in 727. Another heroic master of Esoteric Buddhism, Amoghavajra, had already been known in Japan as the savior of the Tang Dynasty once brought to the brink of ruin because of Xuanzong's infatuation with his favorite consort Yang Guifei. Kammu's attention was then being partially drawn to Esoteric Buddhism which still remained unknown to Japan, when he found in *The List of the Items Introduced from Yuezhou* presented by Saichō a large number of Esoteric Buddhist scriptures, and discovered that Saichō himself had been initiated into that very religion.

The hasty order Kammu then gave to Wake no Hiroyo reveals how enthusiastic he was in taking up that new religion: "We have had no Esoteric Buddhism so far. But Saichō who knew what we really needed brought back that new teaching. Indeed, he deserves to be called the Mentor to the State. Now you shall help Saichō administer the *abhiseka* baptism upon some selected priests of profound knowledge and high virtue."

It was soon decided that Takaosan-ji temple owned by the Wake clan should be the place for that baptism and a specific altar for it should be built there. Then Kammu ordered Ono no Minemori, a newly-appointed chief secretary for that occasion: "Regardless of expense, everything shall be prepared perfectly." As it turned out, Saichō's knowledge of *abhiseka* baptism was so limited that what he requested did not amount to much; but more than twenty artists were invited to paint a single portrait of Mahavairocana and a single large mandala scroll, while many embroiderers were summoned to work on more than fifty banners.

On September 1, 805, eight priests of "profound knowledge and high virtue," including Gonzō, Kūkai's mentor, were invited or rather dragged out of their old seat of Nara Buddhism to be baptized by Saichō at Takaosan-ji on Mt. Takao in the suburbs of the capital. They must have been very reluctant to go there, but they could not disobey the Imperial order.

Then on September 16, Kammu himself was baptized by Saichō. This meant that Saichō was now recognized as the supreme master of Esoteric Buddhism in Japan. On January 3, the following year, Saichō presented a petition to the Court, requesting that his Tendai religion should be allowed to have a certain number of students to be ordained annually,[4] in the same way as the six branches of Nara Buddhism. On January 26, when this petition was granted and he was allowed to have two students ordained annually, his religion was officially recognized, even though those who practiced Nara Buddhism were not very happy about it.

Then Saichō submitted another petition, expressing his wish to start two courses at his own institute—the Tendai Course and the Esoteric Buddhism Course—so that he could have priests of two different specialties on Mount Hiei. Was he trying to keep up with the times when he thus placed the Esoteric Buddhism he had just happened to acquire in Yuezhou on an equal footing with his long-cherished Tiantai or Tendai religion? Kammu was ready to grant this petition, too, thus making Saichō's Esoteric Buddhism an officially-recognized religion, with Saichō himself as its supreme authority. To confirm this, Kammu went so far as to order the Department of Civil Administration to issue a certificate for it. But this proved to be the last favor he granted Saichō, as he passed away on March 17 in the same year.

It is hard to guess what had made Saichō start the Esoteric Buddhism Course at his own institute. Had he consulted his own conscience, he might have felt more or less guilty of opportunism. Probably he could not help being involved in Kammu's eagerness to expand Esoteric Buddhism in Japan, and as long as everything went well with him, he was naturally very happy, even though his satisfaction was largely the result of ignorance.

Another information center in this neighborhood was Kanzeon-ji temple, whose stately appearance had made it a sort of figure-head in demonstrating Japan's national power to foreign visitors, who usually entered this country by way of Hakata Bay. This was also one of the three temples in Japan, together with Tōdai-ji in Nara and Yakushi-ji in Shimotsuke Province in the east, where the state examinations for priestly ordination were conducted. Naturally Kanzeon-ji, which had a large number of scholar priests coming and going to and from Nara temples, was kept very up-to-date.

When Kūkai visited that temple, he must have found that they were very nervous about Saichō's Esoteric Buddhism then growing with unusual vigor and rapidity, threatening to provoke a drastic change in the Buddhist climate in Kyōto (the Heian capital) and Nara. Naturally, they would have expressed their resentment against Saichō, whose propagation of his Tendai religion had usually taken the form of assaulting their old Buddhism.

Kūkai must have told them about what he had brought back or the legitimate heritage of Esoteric Buddhism—about its history, its doctrine and its ritualism. In introducing his own religion, Kūkai, unlike Saichō, never denounced the old Buddhism they had held. In fact, he seems to have always —throughout his life—felt a certain sympathy or debt of gratitude to old Buddhism represented by the Kegon doctrine; by mastering this doctrine or by going through the realm of Vairocana Buddha in its base at Tōdai-ji, Kūkai was able to fathom the depths of the realm of Mahavairocana Buddha all by himself even before he went over to China.

On the other hand, some priests in Nara had already been aware of the shortcomings of their Buddhism, even before it was pointed out by Saichō. Regretful about their oncoming decline, they were soon to turn to Kūkai for help, as they saw in him someone pitted against Saichō. Already in Tsukushi, while listening intently to his theories, the priests of Kanzeon-ji may have been seeing their protector in Kūkai.

What was the reason for Kūkai having been left alone in Tsukushi? Probably the Court was embarrassed at the advent of another introducer of Esoteric Buddhism, and they had to have the matter investigated by the specialists at the Ecclesiastical Office in Nara. They must have been overwhelmed by the gorgeousness of the items Kūkai had brought back and by the significance of his having been ordained as the legitimate heir to Amoghavajra's line of Esoteric Buddhism, while what Saichō had brought home from Yuezhou would have been found limited and provincial.

According to *The Chronological Record of Kōbō Daishi's Career*, Kanzeon-ji received a letter from the Court by way of Dazai-fu. The letter, dated April 29, 807, was virtually the official response to the *List* Kūkai presented to the Court the year before by the hand of the envoy Takashina:

> ... Priest Kūkai travelled far and wide, and absorbed the great principle. Obviously he left home empty-handed but returned home fully equipped. His achievements are really meritorious and praiseworthy. For the time being, he shall have a good rest at Kanzeon-ji, receiving proper attention as a guest priest, until he is formally summoned.

If this letter was an authentic one, we see that the Court offered a great compliment to Kūkai especially when they quoted probably from *Zhuangzi*:[5] "he left home empty-handed but returned home fully equipped." But this rhetoric seems to me too grandiose to be used in an official letter. Could it be a forgery produced in a later age?

Another reason we can think of for his having stayed in Tsukushi for nearly a year is that he himself chose to do so probably with official permission obtained through the effort of Gonzō, a powerful personage at the Ecclesiastical Office in Nara. In fact, Kūkai needed a quiet place where he could give undivided attention to putting in order the tremendous number of materials he had brought back, and thus begin organizing what he had learned so far, so that he might establish his own system.

Or it may have been that he wanted to stay away from the capital until the right time arrived. What if Kūkai, still unknown in this country, had presented himself in the capital too soon? The majority would have ignored him or even cast a cold eye upon him. Or Saichō and his followers might have stood in his way or set a trap for him. Saichō was the last person to do such a dirty thing, but Kūkai, disgusted with unpleasant hearsay about what he had been doing in the capital, might as well have imagined him as such a crafty person.

Kūkai himself would not have minded being left in Tsukushi, for he was quite sure that his *List* would sooner or later be fully acknowledged. The envoy Takashina would report to the Court how highly his talent and scholarship were esteemed by the Tang Emperor as well as by celebrities he met in Chang'an and other places in China. Hayanari would never tire of talking about his respected friend to everyone he met. It would not be very long before the Court began to feel very impatient to have him back in the capital, especially when all those items he had entered in the *List* were still being retained by him.

There are some legends concerning Kūkai about this time. One of them says that he built a temple while he was staying in Hakata and named it Tōchōmitsu-ji, as is recorded in *The Sequel of the Topography of Chikuzen Province*,[6] though there is no knowing whether the temple so named really existed or not. Another legend declares that he was making a thanks-giving pilgrimage around the Shintō shrines[7] in Kyūshū and Sanyō-dō. He may have done so, but it could not have been the sole reason why he had been away from the capital for nearly a year.

Among several things he is supposed to have done while in Tsukushi, only one thing is certain. On February 11, 807, Kūkai gave a memorial service for the deceased mother of a Tanaka who was then the vice-secretary of Dazai-fu. According to the prayer Kūkai dedicated on that occasion, he not only painted images of thirteen different Bodhisattvas of Esoteric Buddhism but also helped Mr. Tanaka copy the *Hoke-kyō* sutra and the *Hannya-shin-gyō* sutra[8] before he performed the service—obviously Japan's first Esoteric-Buddhist-style memorial service. Was he trying to return the kindnesses he had received from Tanaka when he was alone and helpless, as if totally abandoned in that remote province?

XVIII. Two Years on Mt. Makino'o

IN autumn, 807, Kūkai left Tsukushi. Probably in the summer of the same year, he had received an Imperial order, as is recorded in *The Honourable Life of Kōya Daishi*: "You shall come up to the capital to spread the sacred teaching you have brought back...." The date is unknown, as the paper itself has been lost. Taking his status into consideration, he had at long last left Tsukushi because he had received the Imperial command, or some other official order. But when he got off his boat at Naniwa-zu, the entry port to the capital, he began to walk south toward Izumi Province, instead of heading for the capital in the north. Probably he had obtained another order, just before leaving Tsukushi, that he should live in Makino'o-san-ji on Mt. Makino'o in Izumi Province.

Makino'o-san-ji was where Kūkai in his twentieth year received from Gonzō the Ten Commandments for a Buddhist Novice. As the temple was still under the supervision of Gonzō, it was quite possible that Gonzō had chosen this temple as a place for Kūkai's temporary residence when Kūkai confided in him that though he had just received the order to go back to the capital, he would prefer to stay away from the capital until some time later, because he needed more time to study all those texts and papers he had brought back, and thus to build up his own religion into an unassailable system. Nara Buddhists, represented by Gonzō, had naturally been impatient to have Kūkai come back to the capital and help them check Saichō's advance. But Gonzō, who deeply sympathized with Kūkai's wish, again approached the Court and obtained for him official permission to live in Makino'o-san-ji on Mt. Makino'o.

When he had settled in at Makino'o-san-ji, Kūkai unpacked the parcel of scriptures he had carried all that way. As for the other scriptures and objects he had brought back from China, he had sent them all to the Court before he left Tsukushi. Now Kūkai was about to perform his most important lifework—the creation of a new system of his own Esoteric Buddhism, independent of either Amoghavajra's or Huiguo's, on the hypothesis that the two systems of Esoteric Buddhism—the Realm of the Indestructibles of spiritual principle and the Womb-store of physical principle (see Note 6 for IV)—are virtually one.

The two different currents of purified Mantrayana were introduced into China by two Indian priests—Subhakarasimha and Vajrabodhi. Subhakarasimha (637–735), the former king of Magadha in Central India, was initiated into Esoteric Buddhism by Dharma-gupta of Nalanda Monastery. To carry out his master's order to introduce it into China, he traveled by land and arrived in Chang'an in 716. He was already eighty then, but he lived to a greater age, producing a Chinese version of the *Mahavairocana Sutra* and many other sutras he had brought with him.

Vajrabodhi (669–741) came from South India. After studying at Nalanda Monastery, he traveled all over India as a Buddhist ascetic. At thirty-one, he met Nagabodhi and studied under him for seven years until he was initiated into his Esoteric Buddhism. Then he received a divine message on Mt. Potalaka that he should propagate his religion in China. Unlike Subhakarasimha, he took a sea route to China and arrived in Chang'an in 720. He also spent the rest of his life in Chang'an, translating many sutras he had carried with him, including the *Vajrasekhara Sutra*.

Vajrabodhi was succeeded by Amoghavajra (705–774), his best disciple and co-translator. After his master's death, Amoghavajra fulfilled his dying wish by making a voyage to Ceylon (present-day Sri Lanka) and South India in order to obtain a large number of original texts of sutras, including the vast volumes of original texts of the *Mahavairocana Sutra* and the *Vajrasekhara Sutra*. These two sutras had already been translated into Chinese, but Vajrabodhi, who knew these translations were of selected chapters from the original texts, wanted Amoghavajra to go to Ceylon and South India to study the original texts under some great masters like his own master, Nagabodhi.

Meanwhile, the two different channels of Esoteric Buddhism remained unrelated to each other, even though both were being transmitted to many priests. In China none but Yixing, mentioned in the previous chapter, had ever acquired both of them. Then Huiguo was also initiated into both of them. Naturally Huiguo often mentioned with proper pride that he had acquired "both currents of Esoteric Buddhism." But how did he succeed in allowing the two contrasted principles—spiritual and physical—to coexist in himself when their severe internal contradictions must have threatened to destroy his identity? When somehow or other he overcame the difficulties, he came to the conclusion: "They are compatible because they are virtually one." But he could not expound this proposition logically, because it derived from his intuition rather than his intellect.

"I hope you will be able to demonstrate this proposition," Huiguo may have told Kūkai while giving him oral instruction. Honest Huiguo may even have confessed: "To tell the truth, it was too much for me. I knew I had to. But I had grown too old before I could attempt anything."

Thus the idea of compatibility or oneness of the two channels, though proposed by Huiguo, had to be presented by Kūkai by composing a precise logical explanation. In other words, the intuition that in Huiguo had remained unformed had to be refined and crystallized into one solid system. Was it this tremendous project weighing upon his mind that made Kūkai choose to stay in remote retreats for nearly three years before he finally presented himself in the capital?

* * *

Makino'o-san-ji where Kūkai stayed for two years had allegedly been started by En no Ozunu, a legendary mountain ascetic who lived and died in the eighth century. He is said to have conquered peak after peak with bird-like agility and inaugurated a sanctuary wherever he felt strong communion with the deity of the place. All the places he declared sacred had a certain geographical feature in common—a small valley surrounded by forested peaks that rose like so many petals of a huge lotus flower. Kūkai, originally a mountain ascetic, shared Ozunu's tastes. That was probably why many temples in Japan have a legend that *the* temple was inaugurated by En no Ozunu and was restored by Kūkai. According to the temple legend of Makino'o-san-ji, its locale is depicted as follows: "It is surrounded by eight thickly-forested peaks, with forty-eight waterfalls and thirty-six caves in them."

Though constantly engaged in intellectual thought, Kūkai was by no means desk-bound, for he was able to think best while walking—not sauntering along beaten tracks, but making his way through the untrodden parts of the mountains, climbing up grassy cliffs, or striding across rocky dales. One of these wanderings once brought him to Mt. Kōge, whose air he found so sweet and so refreshing that he came back years later and built a hermitage there, naming it Kōki-ji (香気寺: Fragrance Temple), which seems to testify to his delicate sensibility. Even today the leafy paths that run around that mountain, wet and dark even in the daytime, abound in aromatic plants, and in their seasons they keep the whole mountain fragrant. Kōki-ji is still there, though the characters of the temple name are changed into Kōki-ji (高貴寺: Highly Honoured Temple), a secluded seminary for the Shingon Ritsu sect[1] known for its strictness in observing the precepts and the rules of discipline (*ritsu*), which naturally tends to keep the laity away.

The following poem was composed by Kūkai at his hermitage there.[2]

> Sitting alone in a hermitage within a hushed wood,
> I see the day dawn and hear the Buddha's voice in
> a bird's singing. A bird sings just as a man thinks.
> Voice, mind, clouds, water are all being unveiled.

Several years ago I visited Kōki-ji and found that its distinct dignity had kept it more like the hermitage Kūkai had mentioned in this poem than a temple such as the word invokes in us today. It partook of a grove of academe, too, as I was told is still found in India. Now I recall a young traveling monk I met there. It was in the 1960s when all the universities in Japan were being agitated by the students' movement. I was not sure whether or not that ethos had something to do with a change the monk had made in the course of his life: after leaving law school in his university without taking a degree, he made himself a Buddhist monk, probably several years before we met; first he went up to Kōya-san or the monastic center Kūkai established on Mt. Kōya in Kii Province (present-day Wakayama Prefecture), and learned Shingon doctrine or the thought system of Esoteric Buddhism Kūkai created and named Shingon religion; then he set out on a journey to further his thought and study, including the annual pilgrimage he made around Shikoku.

Taking advantage of having met such an earnest pursuer of Kūkai and his religion, I asked him a few questions about Kūkai. I still recall the pleasant intellectuality with which he gave his answers to my questions. The only question I still remember was: "Esoteric Buddhism before Kūkai still remained for the most part on the folklore level. But once it was taken up by Kūkai, it was refined, purified and crystallized into a grand system of perfect logic, to the great credit of Kūkai. But has this feat of his intellect not deprived his future followers of any chance to make some contribution toward the development of the Shingon doctrine?"

The point of my question will become clearer when we think of what happened to the followers of Saichō, who had been kept too busy with outstanding business matters to sit and study all those scriptures he himself had brought home from China. Ennin and Enchin were able to do much for the development of the Tendai religion when the former established Esoteric Buddhism and the latter made it flourish. Some others who pored over different sutras Saichō had left on Mt. Hiei were even able to start new Buddhist religions, which are now known as Kamakura Buddhism:[3] Sōtō-shū by Dōgen, Jōdo-shū by Hōnen, Jōdo-shin-shū by Shinran, and Nichiren-shū by Nichiren.

The young monk, who had been listening to me in a guest room open to the breeze from the cryptomeria forests, turned a smiling face to me and said: "I do not think so. Kakuban did something."

Kakuban (1095–1143), once the chief abbot who presided over the head temple on Mount Kōya, tried to adopt Jōdo pietism,[4] which seemed to be quite antagonistic to the supreme tenet of Esoteric Buddhism: the attaining to Buddhahood in this very existence. Kakuban, who was forced to leave Mount Kōya partly for this and partly for other reasons, came to settle in Negoro in the same province where he founded his own religion and called it Shingi (newly-interpreted) Shingon Religion. Certainly he did something, but he seems to have been the only person who tried to improve on the logic Kūkai had constructed.

Interlude 3. The Three Imperial Princes

KŪKAI, a son of a mere provincial nobility, ought to have been quite unaffected by any of the political disturbances that had been disrupting the central government in the capital. As it happened, he had been involved in one soon after he returned to Japan, when his uncle Ato no Ōtari became a political refugee, as he wrote to tell Kūkai, probably when he was still staying in Tsukushi.

What made Ōtari a political refugee was an affair in which the Imperial Prince Iyo he had been serving as tutor until recently was forced to kill himself on a false charge of high treason. As his mother, Yoshiko, had been from the influential Fujiwara (Nanke), Prince Iyo, the third son of Kammu, had always enjoyed appropriate power. During the reign of Kammu, he became the Lord Chamberlain of the Household. The wealth he gathered from a large number of manors he possessed had enabled him to live in a stately mansion, which was often visited by his father Kammu—a sure sign of being in enviable favor.

In March, 806, Kammu died and his eldest son, the Crown Prince Ate, came to the throne and became the Tennō Heizei. The two brothers, though born of different mothers, were by no means on bad terms with each other, as was seen by the fact that Iyo was appointed by the new Tennō to be Chief Secretary in the Department of the Central Affairs, with the additional post of Governor General of Dazai-fu. As attendance at the latter was excused, he was able to remain in the capital as before. When everything was going well for him in this manner, who could have imagined the cruel fate that lay in store for him?

The tragedy can be traced back to one of the many family quarrels of the Fujiwara clan—something totally irrelevant to Prince Iyo himself. It occurred in October, 807, the second year of Heizei's reign, when Fujiwara (Nanke) no Otomo, informed Fujiwara (Hokke) no Uchimaro, the then

Minister of the Right, that Fujiwara (Shikke) no Munenari was trying to provoke Prince Iyo to rise against the Tennō Heizei. Munenari, when caught and examined, pleaded that it was not he himself but Prince Iyo who had suggested the plot. We do not know the whole truth of the matter, though some assert fairly reasonably that it was part of a plot Fujiwara (Shikke) no Nakanari was then fomenting. Prince Iyo and his mother were sent to Kawara-dera temple in Takechi County in Yamato Province to be confined there without food and drink until on a cold day in November they were forced to commit suicide by poison.

Kūkai in Tsukushi must have been shocked by the news. He had once had an audience with Prince Iyo when he visited him with his uncle, probably soon after he came up to the capital or about the time he matriculated the university. Then later, when he was collecting donations for his study in China, he must have visited him again to ask for his patronage. Now that the Prince, his greatest patron, had been forced to kill himself as "a traitor," it would have been safer for him to keep away from the capital, as his supporters in Nara had probably warned him.

Many of the attendants and servants of the Prince Iyo and his mother were reduced to wandering or even to beggary. Ato no Ōtari was no exception even if he was no longer tutor to Prince Iyo. As he had no other person to turn to, he went to meet Kūkai at Makino'o-san-ji. When he heard the whole story from him, Kūkai seems to have said without a moment's hesitation: "Don't worry, Uncle. Stay here with me as long as you like."

"Don't you mind protecting a man who might be wanted as a political offender?" Ōtari asked, amazed at the readiness with which Kūkai decided to take him.

"Not at all," said Kūkai calmly, as is easily imagined when we learn of the firm attitude he maintained when he came to face the sovereign or state power in the years to come.

From this day on, Ōtari was always to be seen beside Kūkai as his layman secretary until he died in 830 at the great age of eighty-seven. In order to adjust himself to his new occupation, he dressed in a priestly robe, his head shaven, and called himself by the priestlike name Eishin, though he remained a layman who had an ordinary family life as before. This life style he adopted then was to become a new tradition of his family and it lasted even to the

Meiji era (1868–1912), as the head of the Ato family, from generation to generation, served as layman secretary-general of Tō-ji, the first state-owned Esoteric Buddhist seminary that Kūkai started in 823 in Kyōto. Even today the Ato family are living in the vicinity of Tō-ji, which fact alone may testify to the thoroughness with which Kūkai protected them.

By the way, Kūkai was to extend a helping hand to the person who, after Ōtari, had become tutor to Prince Iyo—Kiyomura no Toyonari (see Note 7 for XII).

Ōtari, thirty years senior to Kūkai, was sixty-five or so when he came to live with Kūkai at Makino'o-san-ji. His good knowledge of the workings of the Court turned out to be of inestimable help to Kūkai in the years to come, as we can realize by the fact that whatever official action he might take, it was unfailingly to the point as well as very timely.

While living together at Makino'o-san-ji, they would have had an occasional chat with each other, Kūkai incidentally chaffing Ōtari about the irrelevant kindness he had once offered him: "When I was going to be a Buddhist monk, you put the biggest obstacles in my path, didn't you?"

"Yes, I did. But not out of ill will, you know."

Honest Ōtari might have hotly excused himself to the point of counterattacking his nephew by referring to Mr. Turtle Hair or the poor Turtle that was tuned on its back again and again by the Beggar Boy.

Certainly Kūkai did not follow the course Ōtari had expected him to, as he had sensed that it would take him nowhere. He was right. Seeing what had happened to this poor old man would be enough to convince anyone of how unavailing it would be for a man not belonging to the Fujiwara clan to follow an official career. To Kūkai's mind, the Court was nothing but a fake, like the State itself, as he might have frankly stated.

Kūkai had now laid down a principle that could be applied to all human beings. In Chang'an, he had seen that human beings were of many different races and cultures. But Buddhism and Esoteric Buddhism had transcended all those differences. Now, as a cosmopolitan, he did not care in the least whatever part of the world he might live in or whichever race he might belong to. This naturally led him to think little of the monarch of Japan, to say nothing of the small political unit he called his Court.

This may explain why Kūkai looks so special among all the historical figures Japan has ever produced. He was the only Japanese who had grown into a universal man, instead of remaining just a member of Japanese society. So far Japan has produced many thinkers, Buddhist and non-Buddhist. Logically speaking, if one really masters Buddhism as a universal thought, one will inevitably become universality itself both physically and spiritually and will be accepted as such at any place in the world and at any time in history. But somehow or other Japan has rarely produced such an individual of the cosmopolitan type. I am not sure whether this is a result of the thinking habits of the Japanese living in a Japanese environment.

This fact may be better illustrated by thinkers of later ages: Yamaga Sokō,[1] Motoori Norinaga,[2] and Hirata Atsutane.[3] They were persons of note in Japan, but not in any other land on earth. Saigō Takamori,[4] Uchimura Kanzō,[5] Yoshino Sakuzō,[6] also bound by the limited conditions of Japanese society in their own times, could not take the bold leap forward to become men of universal significance, nor had they even dreamt of doing so. Whereas Kūkai alone succeeded in making himself a being of universal significance—a very rare case indeed.

Naturally it is very hard to create a unique universal person—a person who will be accepted at any place in the world and at any time in history, for if one wishes to become such a person, one will have to begin by totally rejecting, inwardly at least, all the authorities of one's own land. In Kūkai's case, he seems to have intended to make use of the Tennō as a tool to serve his missionary purpose,[7] though he was careful enough to hide that intention under the cover of proper allegiance.

Ōtari would have naturally told Kūkai about "many disgusting things" he had seen in the Court of the Tennō Heizei, too. The old man would not have spoken well of him, partly because he had been involved in the tragedy of Prince Iyo, and partly because his moral sense had always felt outraged by the scandalous liaison the Tennō had formed with a woman named Kusuko even before he came to the throne.

Kusuko was a daughter of Fujiwara (Shikke) no Tanetsugu who had been assassinated on the construction site of the Nagaoka Capital. She had already had three boys and two girls by her husband, Fujiwara (Shikke) no

Tadanushi. When one of the girls became consort to the Crown Prince Ate, as Heizei was called at that time, Kusuko approached the prince ten years or so younger than herself, and cast such a spell over him that their liaison soon came to the knowledge of everyone in the Court.

They were contrasted in character: the Crown Prince was rather weak and timid, and easily suffered from nervous disorders; Kusuko, energetic and fearless, had embarked on another affair with the Chief Secretary of the Crown Prince's Office, Fujiwara (Hokke) no Kadonomaro, who was to be the envoy to China when Kūkai went there—probably to keep him out of the way of her secret rendezvous with the Prince. The Tennō Kammu abhorred this, saying: "It is against the rules of liaison." He tried to keep Kusuko away from the Crown Prince by sending the Chief Secretary of the Crown Prince's Office to the remote province of Tsukushi as Deputy Governor General of Dazai-fu, and putting in his place Kusuko's husband Tadanushi so that he could officially keep an eye on his wife, to the entertainment of outsiders. But this move was effective only for a while, for when Kammu died and the Crown Prince became Tennō, Kusuko was again seen in his palace, for her husband had been sent away to Dazai-fu as Vice Governor General. Kūkai must have met him at Dazai-fu while he was in Tsukushi for nearly a year. To Kūkai, more or less acquainted with the two men closely connected with Kusuko, Ōtari's story must have sounded quite authentic.

According to Ōtari, Kusuko's purpose in approaching Heizei was not just to pursue sexual pleasure, but to establish her power in the Court, obviously prompted by her elder brother Nakanari, who wished to restore their influence that had waned since their father Tanetsugu was assassinated at the construction site of Nagaoka capital. It was not long before Kusuko made herself as powerful as she had wished, as is recorded in *Nihon Kōki*: "Cleverly seeking opportunities for love and flirtation, she got more and more into favor with the Tennō until every request of hers was granted by him," and "She had all the officials at her beck and call, sometimes browbeating them, sometimes laying them under obligations. This turned the whole Court into a very unwholesome place." On the other hand, Kusuko's brother Nakanari took advantage of this situation to make himself more and more important at Court.

But in April, 809, things became completely changed when Heizei in the fourth year of his reign suddenly declared his abdication without even consulting with Kusuko. Heizei had long been prejudiced against his brother Crown Prince Kamino, the second son of Kammu. But in an agonizing attack of neurosis that had kept him from sleeping and eating properly for a considerable period of time, he just felt it impossible to stay on the throne any longer, however unusual it might be to leave it at the age of thirty-five. Crown Prince Kamino naturally tried to persuade him to reconsider. But Heizei would not listen, though he was soon to regret what he had done, and to try to regain what he had thrown away.

*   *   *

When we look back at what had been happening in Court about this time, Kūkai's having kept away from the capital seems to have had an element of political expedience as well. On the other hand, it is quite imaginable that Kūkai, who was staying at Makino'o-san-ji, often visited Nara, probably to meet Gonzō. Kūkai, alert to political matters, could not have been unaware that he would inevitably become involved in the serious politics of the religious world if, by meeting Gonzō, he was to strengthen his ties with Nara Buddhism. When Saichō returned to Japan and was highly honored as the introducer of the new religions of Tiantai and Esoteric Buddhism, Nara Buddhism was suddenly reduced to "old Buddhism." Naturally the elders of Nara Buddhism were anxious to turn to Kūkai whose system of Esoteric Buddhism, as they had found from reading his *List*, far surpassed Saichō's.

According to the temple legend of Kume-dera, Kūkai appeared one day at that temple:

> On November 8, 807, Priest Kūkai paid a visit to this temple with his followers of saints and high priests. When he was going to give a lecture at the pagoda on *A Commentary on the Mahavairocana Sutra*, there arrived the guardian gods of Buddhism, leading over ten thousand heavenly soldiers, and they all listened to him while guarding the place.

It was quite probable that Kūkai gave a private lecture on Esoteric Buddhism somewhere on his way to Nara—probably at a private temple closely associated with him like Kume-dera. The elders of Nara Buddhism, anxious to know whether or not Kūkai's Esoteric Buddhism would turn against theirs, just as Saichō's "new Buddhism" did, must have been very pleased when they learned that Kūkai's Esoteric Buddhism was so comprehensive that it could fully embrace all six branches of Nara Buddhism. They also found that the Kegon religion housed in Tōdai-ji had already come closest to the Truth of Mahavairocana, as he later pronounced in *The Ten Stages of the Development of Human Mind.*

One of the questions they asked after the lecture would have been: "What do you think about Saichō's Esoteric Buddhism?" Kūkai, who must have already worked through a copy of *The List of the Items Introduced from Yuezhou* Saichō had presented to the Court, could easily tell what sort of Esoteric Buddhism he had brought home. He would have liked to denounce it completely, but all he actually said would have been: "There are some fragments in it, too."

Already in the lecture he had told them that Esoteric Buddhism was not a mere conglomeration of small fragments of incantation but a large-scale synthetic system of thought and ritualism. Those who had had a good understanding of him would have sensed an acute denial in this crisp answer he had made in measured terms.

*　*　*

After all, in April, 809, the Prince Kamino came to the throne and became the Tennō Saga, thus bringing about an end to the abnormal climate at Court. In July of the same year, Kūkai on Mt. Makino'o received an official summons to the capital. Ōtari, who saw this as a sign of innovation taking place at Court, must have broken into a broad smile, saying: "It's good timing for you. The time has come...."

XIX. THOSE WHO SOUGHT HIS HELP

THE temple in which Kūkai had been invited to live was Takaosan-ji. The choice of the temple had been made by the elders of the Ecclesiastical Office in Nara. They were determined to find a good place for Kūkai, who they were hoping would surely hold Saichō in check. As there were no temples available in and around the capital area,[1] what they eventually decided upon was Takaosan-ji on Mt. Takao that rose to the northwest of the capital, appropriately facing Mt. Hiei or Saichō's stronghold that flanked the northeastern corner of the capital.

There must also have been a political motivation in the choice, when we remember that Takaosan-ji belonged to the Wake clan, who had gained considerable power, and had created a general impression that they would be the last to rival the Fujiwaras in politics. The dying wish of Wake no Kiyomaro, the virtual patriarch of that family, was for it to possess a library of its own, and this ambition was fulfilled when his eldest son Hiroyo collected thousands of books, housed them in his own residence and named it Kōbun-in. It became the first private school in this country, though it was only for the younger members of the Wake family. Kiyomaro, who had once been obliged to play a dangerous role in the settling of a dispute at Court, was thus possibly trying to instruct his descendants in the pursuit of a safer course in life—by making a career not in politics but in particular-fields of learning or technology. This far-sighted plan was to work fairly well especially in the Hiroyo's lineage, that produced many distinguished figures in the field of medicine.

To have Kūkai associated with such a non-political power as the Wake clan, the elders of Nara Buddhism thought, would be the surest way to keep him safe, especially when the four branches of the Fujiwaras were at constant strife with one another, and no one could tell which would be the winner.

But problems arose: firstly, the Wakes had long been supporting Saichō since Kiyomaro, the then director of the construction of the Imperial Palace, had eagerly recommended Kammu to make Saichō one of the ten Buddhist priests serving at the Imperial chapel. Secondly, their family temple Takaosan-ji had already been closely connected with Saichō through the two memorable events he had been associated with so far: in 801 he had given a series of lectures on the three major scriptures of the Tendai religion, thus making a brilliant debut with Kammu's support, and in 805 he administered Japan's first *abhiseka* baptism in the name of Kammu. Thirdly, he was still paying regular visits there as if he considered himself a part-time resident priest. What would Saichō say if that very temple were to be transferred to Kūkai?

The representatives of the Ecclesiastical Office in Nara went to the capital to meet Wake no Matsuna, the then head of the family, and expressed their wish to have Kūkai reside at their temple on Mt. Takao. Then Matsuna went to meet Saichō on Mt. Hiei and told him about this newly-proposed plan, which Saichō was quite ready to accept. In fact, he was simply happy to have Kūkai living so close. By that time Saichō, who had already read a copy of the *List* Kūkai had presented to the Court, had come to regard Kūkai as his fellow worker in the propagation of the new Buddhism in this country. Wake no Matsuna, who was thus to help both Saichō and Kūkai in their fledging stages, is eulogized for "the meritorious contribution he made in building the foundations for both Tendai and Shingon religions," as is recorded in *Shoku Nihon Kōki.*

Kūkai must have been aware of all these efforts to find the proper place for him to reside, but he remained as detached as ever, and when Takaosan-ji on Mt. Takao was decided upon, he just moved there in compliance with the official order he had received.

Of all the mountains that surrounded the capital, the highest was Mt. Atago that rose to the west, a mountain mass commanding many mountains standing around its base. One of them was Mt. Takao with its free-standing ridge that fell to the deep ravines of the Kiyotaki River. The ravines covered with maple trees must have exhibited contrasted beauties in spring and in fall, as they do now. But probably not until *A Collection of Waka Ancient and Contemporary,*[2] the first anthology of *waka* poems compiled by Imperial command, appeared about a century later (905), did "the autumnal tints of Mt. Takao" begin to be recognized as a beautiful typical landscape feature in Japan.

Today we can take the Shūzan Highway to reach it. But in Kūkai's days a narrow path must have led to a ridge way that led down to a spot where the Kiyotaki was spanned by a single log. One had to cross over it to reach the foot of Mt. Takao, the whole of which was the precinct of Takaosan-ji.

The date of Kūkai's arrival at Takaosan-ji is not recorded. But a letter from Saichō, dated August 24, 809, proves that Kūkai had already arrived there by that date. Whether or not Saichō and Kūkai had met each other or exchanged letters before is not known. As long as the research materials on both sides are concerned, this letter carried by Kyōchin, a disciple of Saichō, seems to mark their first contact with each other. The young monk, approaching Kūkai's residence through the leafy tunnel of maple trees in midsummer, would have made a fine subject for a picture scroll. But none of his biographical picture scrolls have ever depicted that scene.

The copy of the letter, which remains with the papers preserved at Ninna-ji[3] in Kyōto, begins as follows:

> Let me present this letter to you in request for the loan of the following titles.

There are no lengthy compliments of the season such as are required in the epistolary style of this country. Probably the custom had not yet come into being, and such seasonal greetings may have been delivered orally by the messenger. The twelve titles he gave read like this:

> *How to Invoke the Mahavairocana Sutra* (one volume), *How to Invoke Mahavairocana by Performing Incantations* (one volume), *How to Perform Venerations for the Mahavairocana Sutra* (one volume), *How to Invoke Acalaceta*[4] (one volume), *How to Write Siddham* (one volume), *Sanskrit & Siddham* (one volume), *How to Read Siddham* (one volume), *The Mudras Made by the One Hundred and Eight Dharmakayas in the Realm of the Indestructibles* (one volume), *The Divination Sutra* (three volumes), *The Collection of Amoghavajra's Writings* (three volumes), *The Legitimate Heritage of Esoteric Buddhism & The Six Historical Aspects of Esoteric Buddhism* (one volume), *The Kegon-kyō sutra* (forty volumes).

These titles were obviously what he had selected from a copy of the *List* Kūkai had presented to the Court years before. A surprising fact about these twelve titles is that most of them were Esoteric Buddhist scriptures or commentaries and the rest were Sanskrit textbooks. To me this seems to reveal a dramatic contrast between Kūkai and Saichō: Kūkai had already mastered both Esoteric Buddhism and Sanskrit, while Saichō was ignorant of both. In fact, it was out of sheer ignorance that Saichō had once allowed himself to be appointed by Kammu as *acarya* or master of the highest rank in Esoteric Buddhism, and had administered *abhiseka* baptism to Kammu as well as to the prelates from Nara, and started the Esoteric Buddhism Course at his own institute on Mt. Hiei. Saichō, therefore, must now have been feeling greatly ashamed of what he had done so far. But the honest man bravely took the shame upon himself and decided to learn the whole system of Esoteric Buddhism from the very beginning by copying and studying those scriptures he would borrow from Kūkai.

In Kūkai's view, however, this action of Saichō's was far from admirable; for in Esoteric Buddhism, studying scriptures on one's own was not considered to be the correct method to become acquainted with it, as the only recommendable method was to follow an apprenticeship under a master. Was Saichō ignorant even of this fundamental rule? Or did he simply ignore it to suit his own convenience? If so, Saichō's attitude must have annoyed Kūkai, even though it was not until years later that he finally disclosed his displeasure in one of his letters to Saichō.

In surmising Kūkai's reaction to Saichō's approach, we should take into consideration the fact that Kūkai was still working hard trying to create his own theoretical system. All the other Buddhist religions in Japan had already been given final form in China. That is, they were equipped with their own complete theoretical systems as well as with a complete apparatus of scriptures, commentaries and treatises on criticism. Therefore, there had been neither need nor desire to add anything new.

In the case of the Tiantai religion which Saichō brought back, it was brought to completion when a Chinese priest Zhiyi (538–597) wrote and published *The Five Periods and Eight Kinds of the Buddha's Teachings*. More concretely, Zhiyi arranged all the Buddhist scriptures, and evaluated their contents according to the various stages of Sakyamuni's life, thus proving and expounding the superiority of his religion that was founded on the *Hoke-kyō* sutra.

In the case of Esoteric Buddhism, that appeared in the final stage of the development of Buddhism, it still remained, frankly speaking, a crude conglomeration of incantations and rituals, because its thought had not yet been organized into any theoretical system presentable in book form. Now, as had been expected by his late master Huiguo, Kūkai was to be the one person to carry out that final task. But how?

Firstly, he surveyed all the Buddhist principles known so far and reorganized them into his new religion. Then he intended to reinforce it with new rationales of his own invention so that it might not only stand firm against any attack or challenge from other religions but also impose its authority upon them.

The first rationale he needed to invent was to enable one to recognize and approach Esoteric Buddhism whichever Buddhist religion one might belong to—the theory known as "how to recognize it horizontally and vertically." The second rationale was to allow everyone to fulfill the ultimate aim of Esoteric Buddhism: "the attaining of Buddhahood in this very existence." The third rationale was intended to compare his Esoteric Buddhism with all the other exoteric Buddhist religions. It was to make clear that exoteric religions deal with the truth that can be externally apprehended, whereas esoteric religion will provide practices and theories that enable one to penetrate the truth of the universe and move along with it, thus identifying oneself with the universe itself—something that only a supreme Buddhist religion subsuming all other Buddhist religions can offer.

All these cumulative labors Kūkai was then taking upon himself in carrying out this project, though unknown to others, must have affected his impression of the Saichō he was beginning to know. Did he regard Saichō as someone easygoing enough to accept Zhiyi unquestioningly? If so, he may have been saying to himself: "Once he has been spared a great deal of intellectual work by Zhiyi, he is now trying to reach for Esoteric Buddhism, and that in the wrong method of scripture-copying, never mind its running counter to the first and foremost rule in learning Esoteric Buddhism...."

Saichō's having asked for the loan of Sanskrit textbooks must have reminded Kūkai of a striking difference between China and Japan in the attitudes they adopted in accepting Buddhism: in China, where they had government-managed translation institutes as permanent establishments, many priests were naturally versed in Sanskrit and Siddham; in Japan they just turned to Chinese translations only, thus creating an absurd situation in which even Saichō, who had been assumed to be the supreme master of Esoteric Buddhism as the latest brand of Buddhism, could neither read nor write even the first elements of the Sanskrit language.

Yet another thing that attracted Kūkai's attention must have been the modesty Saichō showed at the end of his letter: "Your humble servant, Saichō." This was probably the last thing Kūkai had expected from Saichō, a man of audacity as he had imagined from what he had done so far. In Japan, it was not until ages later that a superior or a senior humbled himself in this manner according to an established custom in letter-writing. Kūkai may have given this signature a questioning look, wondering if he should revise his image of Saichō. In fact, Saichō was very modest by nature, and even to his own disciples, he was the last person to put up a bold front. Toward Kūkai, therefore, Saichō would have been quite ready to kneel down, begging for help, and calling himself "your humble servant." In nearly thirty remaining letters Saichō wrote to Kūkai during the seven years that followed, Saichō showed even greater humility with: "Your disciple, Saichō," "A follower of your Buddhism, Saichō," and "your eternal disciple, Saichō."

In the end, Saichō never came to serve Kūkai as a disciple. But considering his sincere personality, I think this sort of self-definition came from the bottom of his heart, especially when he needed Kūkai's help to make his Esoteric Buddhism Course on Mt. Hiei credible and worthy of the name. But if this urgent necessity on Saichō's side was detected by Kūkai, Saichō's humility may have been easily taken as utilitarianism in disguise. Otherwise, Kūkai's cold rejection of Saichō, which was to occur years later, would appear unnaturally abrupt.

Kūkai's answer to this letter from Saichō is lost. But if not lost, it would not have made another high point of this part of this chapter, for all those

titles Saichō wanted to borrow from Kūkai were still being kept at Court, as
Kūkai would have written to Saichō, probably suggesting to him at the end
of the letter or orally to the messenger that he should go to the Court and ask
the clerk in charge to let him have what he wanted.

But it was not long before Kūkai had all that he had sent to the Court
returned to him, as is known by the letter he sent in 821 to the then Minister
of the Right, Fujiwara no Fuyutsugu:

> ... In the first year of Kōnin (810) the Tennō (Saga)... returned all
> these scriptures, images and mandalas I had presented to the
> Court... and allowed me to propagate my religion[5]....

* * *

Those who heard of Kūkai's having settled at Takaosan-ji came to meet
him. Some were from his home in Sanuki, others from Nara. The Wake clan,
who had recently become his patrons, were frequently seen there. There
were many noblemen and scholars, too, eager to learn anything new in the
political or cultural climate in China.

It was also about this time that Shinga, Kūkai's younger brother who was
to be the second patriarch of Shingon religion, came to stay with him.
According to the *Sandai Jitsuroku* (*The Annals of the Three Tennōs*: see
Note 1 for III), Shinga was nine when he left home and came to the capital
to start his apprenticeship to Shingon religion under his elder brother Kūkai.
As the two brothers were widely apart in age—nine and thirty-six—they
may have had different mothers.

The Tennō Saga was privately approaching Kūkai, too, as he had been
filled with admiration for Kūkai ever since he had heard of his literary and
calligraphic feats that had amazed the Chinese. According to *The
Honourable Life of Kōya Daishi*, on October 4, 809, Saga sent a messenger
to Kūkai and asked him to make some calligraphy of any lines or phrases he
selected from *New Anecdotes of Social Talks* on a couple of six-paneled
screens brought over to him for that purpose. *New Anecdotes of Social Talks*,
a three-volume collection of anecdotes about heroic souls that lived and died

during the four hundred years from later Ham (25A.D.–220A.D.) to Eastern Jin (317A.D.–420A.D.), had been widely read in Japan not only because it was very interesting but also because its writing was considered a model of Six-Dynasties style. Kūkai who wrote best in that style would have read it again and again until he was able to recite from memory any of its paragraphs.

Kūkai must have found this approach from Saga fairly agreeable, especially after he had been virtually neglected by the former Tennō Heizei. But he might have felt rather disappointed to see that the person whom Saga sent to him was not an Imperial messenger but one of the hundreds of servants he had at the palace. Kūkai at that time had not yet become one of the high-ranked priests, so Saga's treatment of Kūkai was not wrong at all. To Kūkai, however, who had regarded himself as the Emperor of the spiritual world since he received the final *abhiseka* baptism that had made him the highest incarnation of the principle of the universe, this treatment may have been rather displeasing. But the modesty he showed in the memorial he presented to Saga on that occasion was so perfect that Saga might have felt as if he could almost see him bowing to him at his feet. Such was the strange power of the Six-Dynasties style, whose secret of good writing was not to write what one was really thinking or feeling.

Those from Nara had never forgotten what Kūkai once said about the Kegon doctrine upon which Tōdai-ji temple was founded: "A step further, and it could reach the level of Esoteric Buddhism." No wonder they all wished to have Kūkai come and help them out of difficulties, saying: "We beg of you to accept the post of president of Tōdai-ji; it will surely be the salvation of our Nara Buddhism."

In Japan, where everything new has always come from overseas, "the new kicks out the old" has been a formula that explains the cultural transitions of this country. The old Buddhism in Nara now being challenged by Saichō was about to suffer the disgrace of being replaced by the new Buddhism. What would become of them if their old Buddhism were discarded? They would be deprived of official financial support as well as of the honor of being the state religion.

Kūkai, extremely busy in establishing his own religion while receiving one disciple after another, would have liked to decline this invitation from Tōdai-ji. But the negotiator, probably Gonzō, insisted on his extending a helping hand "just to form a connection with Tōdai-ji and give it a touch of Esoteric Buddhism."

Unable to be unkind to those who had always been kind to him, Kūkai could not help accepting their offer. According to *The Annals of the Presidents of Tōdai-ji*, "in the first year of Kōnin (810), Kūkai took the office of president and held it for four years." There are no details of the date. Presumably he undertook the responsibility of the post without taking up residence.

Here I laid down my pen and rang up Shimizu Kōshō, an elder of Tōdai-ji. "Any traces of what O-Daishi-san left at Tōdai-ji?"

He repeated my question, calling Kūkai by his popular appellation of "O-Daishi-san."

"Yes." I said. "The daily chanting of the *Rishu-kyō* sutra remains the only trace, I suppose?"

"No, there are several traces, I think," said Mr. Shimizu, and after thinking for a while, he said: "One of them is *shido-kegyō*."

Shido-kegyō is the four kinds of asceticism which Kūkai started in order to train his own disciples, and even today only those who have successfully gone through them are supposed to be qualified to receive the final *abhiseka* baptism. The ascetic practices of *shido-kegyō*, therefore, are indispensable for any regular priest of Shingon Esoteric Buddhism. But here at Tōdai-ji, students of the Kegon religion are all expected to go through them, and that in the elementary course, spending ten dozen days, exactly as prescribed by Kūkai himself long ago.

"Another trace that O-Daishi-san left here can be seen in *O-mizutori*,[6] though it is something rather formal," said Mr. Shimizu. "One of the four leaders of this event is called *Shushi* (Master of Incantations)."

"*Shushi*" must be a title Kūkai invented in order to give this ancient ceremony a touch of Esoteric Buddhism, as Mr. Shimizn agreed.

The following legend I found in *The Collected Records of Daishi's Deeds* seems to reflect what a great upheaval the old Buddhism had to suffer and how great was the political significance of their having Kūkai on their side:

Once there were a number of hornets in Tōdai-ji. They were much feared, as they had stung priests to death. But the fierce creatures suddenly went out of sight when Daishi took office as president there. What a great relief to everyone! No wonder everyone praised Daishi for the great power he had acquired in Tang China!

INTERLUDE 4. THE KUSUKO AFFAIR

MOST of the visitors to Takaosan-ji talked of the troubles the former Tennō Heizei was then making. After renouncing his royal status in April, 809, he changed his residence as many as five times[1] before he finally arrived in Nara on December 4 of the same year. The former capital was no longer what it used to be. But it was still the only place that was comparable to the present capital. That was why Heizei, even before he left the capital, had decided to have a new palace of his own there and ordered Nakanari, Kusuko's brother, to build it for them, obviously with the intention of making Nara his own capital.

Naturally the Tennō Saga was not very happy about this. But this gentle-natured person, at least in appearance, agreed or pretended to agree to Heizei's decision and ordered that the tributary rice from the central provinces and some other provinces should cover its expense, and that about two thousand carpenters and plasterers should be assembled from the central provinces and sent to Nara to work on the palace. But it had not yet been finished by the time Heizei and Kusuko reached there. So they had to reside for the time being in an empty mansion in the neighborhood.

Despite the desperate eagerness with which he abdicated the throne, Heizei now was anxious to regain his lost power, and it was not long before he became so bold as to issue his own edicts, in which he criticized Saga's new regime and ordered that it should be replaced by the one he himself had started, thus initiating a short but uneasy period with two tennōs in the same country. What had changed Heizei's mind so radically? Probably he was urged on by Kusuko, whose undying wish was to make herself the Tennō's first consort.

"Kusuko is a Japanese version of the Empress Wu (Zetian Wuhou, Emperor Shengshen)," Ōtari may have grumbled to Kūkai, for it was customary for Japanese intellectuals at that time—and even in later ages—to cite someone from Chinese history when they wanted to illustrate a specific type of humanity. Certainly Ōtari's observation was not irrelevant as long as their eagerness to obtain more and more power was concerned; but the Empress Wu's success was beyond comparison with Kusuko's:

> Wu (624–705), when young, used to be in the harem of Taizong, the second Emperor of the Tang Dynasty. When he died in 649,Wu made herself a nun at Gan'ye-si temple, according to the established custom that was observed by the ladies who had once won the Emperor's favour. But the new Emperor Gaozong, a son of Taizong, having found his ideal woman in Wu—voluptuous and sensual, brilliantly active and theatrical—soon took Wu to his own harem. This was an outrageous affront to Chinese morals, even though very common among the Huns in the north.
>
> Wu's origin was obscure, and this may explain the unusual relentlessness with which she carried out her enterprise. At first her status in Gaozong's harem was insignificant. But she steadily ascended the ladder eliminating her rivals by hatching all imaginable kinds of plots, while forming one alliance after another with the powerful men at Court, until after eighteen years she became the Emperor's first consort. Still not satisfied, she carried out more plots and murders to get rid of all her opponents. When Gaozong's epilepsy became serious, Wu never missed any opportunity to take his place and conduct all the state affairs herself. Past fifty years of age, she had lost her former beauty, but the power she had gained amply made up for it. When Gaozong died at fifty-five, she had enthroned and dethroned one emperor after another by using various tricks, while killing hundreds of antagonists, before she finally reached the throne. The fifteen years that followed saw many changes: the name of the country was changed to Zhou; official titles and place names were changed; the calendar was reformed; new Chinese characters were created. When she was over eighty and began to show signs of senility, she finally agreed to give the country its former name Tang. Not long after that she died, putting an end to an abnormal situation for the Tang Dynasty.

On September 6, 810, Heizei issued a decree: "The Imperial Capital shall be transferred to Nara." Saga, still pretending to obey him, appointed three inspectors to supervise the construction of "the Imperial Capital" and sent them to Nara. One of them, Sakanoue no Tamuramaro, was the ex-commander-in-chief who, during the reign of Kammu, had already won a nationwide fame and popularity through the unusual leadership he showed in subjugating the Ezo in the east. What if war broke out between Heizei and Saga? Saga would at once be able to appoint Tamuramaro as commander-in-chief. The magnetic force of Tamuramaro would surely attract all his old military officers and troops to Saga's side. The promptness with which Saga had won over Tamuramaro to his cause fully proves his acute sense of politics and strategy.

On September 10, Saga sent his express messengers to the three provinces of Ise, Ōmi and Mino to mobilize as many militiamen as possible. These militiamen had traditionally been known as the right-hand weapon of any ambitious person intent on winning control of the central power. In fact, Heizei also was soon to try to enroll them on his side—but in vain.

Saga sent a messenger to Nara, too, in order to recall high officials who had been serving Heizei. Even Nakanari, Kusuko's brother, came back, though it is unknown what sort of inducement had been offered him. Saga clapped him into prison at once, and he was executed several days later.

On the same day Saga issued an edict that Kusuko, the Mistress of the Robes with the senior grade of the third court rank, should be deprived of her court rank and office. On receiving that edict probably on the afternoon of the same day, Heizei and Kusuko must have acknowledged it as Saga's proclamation of war against them.

What made Saga act so promptly? The series of swift actions he undertook on that occasion are almost unbelievable, considering that he was usually an easy-going person, exemplary as the graceful host of his own artistic salon. His eyes were always drawn to lady after lady in his harem; he was always having love affairs and was to be father to more than fifty children. After all, he who was among the most accomplished in literature, music, chess, calligraphy and painting, was to be best remembered as the founder of the Court culture that flourished for nearly four hundred years till the end of the Heian Period (1185).

Heizei was no less cultured than Saga. Ever since they were young, their father Kammu, very eager to assimilate Chinese culture, had chosen the greatest scholars and artists of the time as their tutors. Naturally they grew up to be well-educated and cultivated, the younger showing more interest in art, the elder in politics. In fact Heizei's enthusiasm for politics was such that on succeeding to the throne he tried to carry out a political reform by unifying many of the political systems and by introducing the new post of Provincial Governor General who would keep an eye on provincial governors. Unfortunately, however, this reform turned out to be a failure, because his bureaucrats were far from willing to carry it out. This may have affected his delicate nerves, while aggravating his frustration even to the point of apathy.

Unlike Heizei, Saga would not take the initiative in politics but allowed his bureaucrats to take on active responsibilities as much as possible. Saga's promptness in that crisis, therefore, may be attributed to Fujiwara no Fuyutsugu and Kose no Notari—the two excellent strategists he had appointed as captains of the new office he had started under his direct control:[2] the Bureau of Archives. In fact, Fuyutsugu, a born strategist, was to remain unbeaten throughout his life, and his lineage (Fujiwara Hokke) was to retain its power even to the end of the Edo Period (1867).[3]

Soon Heizei and Kusuko were seen fleeing from Nara, intending to rally their militiamen in the eastern provinces. They were traveling in the same palanquin, attended by their retinue of noblemen and officials walking in procession. But no sooner had they left the former capital area than many of their men-at-arms began to run away. Probably they had known what was going to happen through their own channels of information quite unknown to the Court. When the diminishing procession approached the first village on their way, they were horrified to find that a host of militia-men Saga had sent there were ready to bar the route.

Heizei did not dare to break through this enemy force, nor did his palanquin carriers and his retinue, and even Kusuko had to agree to turn back. But when they returned, it was to see their temporary palace besieged by the enemy forces. When they managed to enter, they found themselves imprisoned. Then someone came to Heizei and told that he would be spared if only he took the tonsure and entered the priesthood. Heizei chose to accept that proposal.[4] Kusuko, left alone, powerless and helpless, was soon forced to kill herself by poison.

Three days later, Saga issued a statement proclaiming the end of the war or what was later known as the Kusuko Affair. According to the official interpretation of that affair, as Saga made clear in that statement, the guilt was not Heizei's but the fault of his close associates, Kusuko and her brother Nakanari. Now that they were gone, no others were found deserving of either imprisonment or capital punishment. The only thing that might be called punishment was the consignment of several high officials to lower positions. Thus by considerably scaling down that affair, Saga and his advisors were trying to avoid inviting any further reaction or disturbance. They took the right step, for their fears were never realized.

XX. HIS NEWLY-ACQUIRED SELF-IDENTITY

KŪKAI'S view of the Kusuko affair was quite different from Saga's. Considering the deliberate action he took soon after the affair was over, Kūkai may have seen it as a Japanese version of An Lushan's revolt that started in 755, when the then Emperor Xuanzong, already over seventy, was in the last stage of his forty-five-year reign. He had long been known as a wise ruler, but during the last ten years or so his infatuation with his favorite consort, Yang Guifei, had made him neglect politics.

An Lushan,[1] a non-Chinese commander-in-chief, who had been entrusted with three of the military detachments to guard a borderland area of the Tang Empire, seemed at first inoffensive, especially when he was ingratiating himself with Xuanzong and Yang Guifei. But he had to rise up and rebel when challenged by Yang Guozhong, a relative of Yang Guifei, who had been unjustifiably promoted a member of the Emperor's brain trust. When Luoyang fell at the end of the same year, An Lushan founded his own dynasty there, named it the Great Yan, and declared himself Emperor. But the resistance in the northern and southern parts of the empire was such that An was contemplating retreat, when because of Yang Guozhong's miscalculation he had the good fortune to advance and capture Chang'an. Xuanzong and Yang Guifei fled from the capital together with their relatives and attendants. They were going to find a refuge in the land of Shu (present-day Sichuan Province). But soon they were confronted by their own soldiers who fiercely demanded the execution of all the Yangs, including Yang Guifei. Hard pressed by those angry men, Xuanzong had to see even his beloved executed.

Certainly, this romance of Xuanzong and Yang Guifei, especially its tragic denouement, resembles the love affair of Heizei and Kusuko. But in the former, the genuine love the old Emperor had devoted to the young beauty was undeniable, and this human helplessness in love inspired Bai

Juyi to create that famous epic, *A Song of Everlasting Sorrow*. But the distinct meanness of the latter affair, sadly motivated by the senior woman's vanity, has never moved anyone to poetry. Again Kūkai must have been aware of the pettiness of his own country even in the sphere of love affairs.

As Kūkai knew very well, Amoghavajra was intensely active in dealing with An Lushan's revolt. On hearing that An's army was approaching Chang'an, he rushed back to his own temple, Daxingshan-si, built a special altar there and performed at it all the incantations with power to bring down their enemy. Xuanzong's warriors, who had been fighting hard against the high-spirited enemy force, could not help admiring Amoghavajra, especially when An Lushan, soon after he occupied Chang'an (756), was afflicted with an eye disease and then with a malignant carbuncle, and becoming more and more brutal in his conduct, as was seen in his plot to oust his own eldest son Qingxu in order to make another son, born of his favorite consort, his crown prince. Qingxu, feeling very uneasy, anticipated his father's move by killing him (757). By that time the Tang force had finally gathered strength, and Xuanzong's son, Suzong, had acceded to the throne. Then Qingxu himself was put to death (758) by one of his generals, Shi Siming, who was also to be killed by his own son (761). Those phenomena of self-destruction on the enemy's side were all gratefully attributed to Amoghavajra by his admirers, and Xuanzong's successors—Suzong and Daizong—showed even greater devotion and gratitude to Amoghavajra by allowing him to have his own temple in the Court so that he could perform all kinds of prayer rituals there to bring peace and security to the State, and posthumously by offering him dukedom—an exceptional reward to be given to a Buddhist priest.

Amoghavajra, who had thus made himself and his religion indispensable to the Tang Court, established another tenet of Esoteric Buddhism: the peace and security of the state for the welfare of the people—metaphysically speaking, the induction of Mahavairocana's Land upon earth. He created this transference himself by developing some passages of the *Daijō Mitsugon-kyō* sutra[2] he was then translating into Chinese, as some historians in later ages pointed out.

Amoghavajra, the successor to Vajrabodhi's line of Esoteric Buddhism, was naturally a great figure in the first tenet of Esoteric Buddhism: the attaining of Buddhahood in this very existence. But while living among the Chinese who, unlike the Indian people, overemphasized their polity, he began to feel dissatisfied with the personal bliss he could enjoy in the attaining of Buddhahood. Then he thought of extending that bliss to the country or the society he lived in, especially when it was in great difficulties.

*   *   *

Now Kūkai decided to do for Japan what Amoghavajra had done for the Tang Empire. The memorial he then presented to Saga includes the following:

> Priest Kūkai implores your Majesty to allow him to perform at Takaosan-ji a series of prayer rituals for protecting this country from all kinds of difficulties.

In order to demonstrate how important this enterprise was, Kūkai gives the example of China, where the rituals were performed at the Changsheng-dian palace, one of the most important buildings owned by the Emperor. As for "a series of prayer rituals," he writes:

> Among the doctrines I have learned in China, there is one that will invoke the virtues of such sutras as *Ninnō-gyō*, *Shugo-kokkaishu-kyō* and *Butsumo-myōō-kyō*, which were all compiled from the speeches Buddhas had made especially for kings.

As to the effect of those invocations, he says:

> It will eradicate the seven evils,[3] keep all seasons normal, defend the state against enemies, protect families from misfortunes, and relieve people of anxieties. Indeed, this is among the most exquisite merits of Esoteric Buddhism. Though I have had no opportunity to practice that doctrine so far, it will afford me great pleasure if I am allowed to perform it at Takaosan-ji, at the head of my disciples, beginning on the first of the coming month, and abiding there for years till the virtues of invocations are realized. It is my wish that no one interrupt me all this while....

The Tennō Saga, moved by this meritorious enterprise proposed by Kūkai, sent him a gift of one hundred bundles of cotton to cover the immediate expenses. Saga, a good poet, also expressed his heartfelt thanks in a poem and sent it to him. In a poem Kūkai wrote in response to Saga's, he mentioned the "six years" he would need to spend on the project. Saga must have been even more impressed by his whole-heartedness.

In the following year, however, Saga ordered that Kūkai should be the president of Otokuni-dera temple in the southern suburbs of the capital. Thus Kūkai's declaration that he would not leave Takaosan-ji for "six years" had to be renounced in a year. Strangely, Kūkai does not seem to have suffered much remorse. The reason may be that both Kūkai and Saga had a tacit understanding that what was expressed in Chinese writing was generally meaningful only on a literary level and not necessarily in actual daily life. In this connection, it was not until the aristocratic Heian Period, deeply imbued with the literary tradition of China was over (1185) and a new era had dawned in Kamakura that pledges or promises began to be taken literally and seriously.

* * *

What was it that made Kūkai imitate Amoghavajra? Part of the answer may be found in the legend that Kūkai was a reincarnation of Amoghavajra, which has been believed by his disciples at all periods, for Kūkai himself believed it and told it to his disciples. To Kūkai as a logician, transmigration, which constitutes a basic element of Indian thought, was the domain of science, not of religion. *Jinnō-shōtō-ki*, a historical treatise completed in 1339 by Kitabatake Chikafusa, a central figure of the Southern Court,[4] also includes the following:

> Kōbō (Kūkai) is said to have been conceived when his mother had a dream in which an Indian priest came to stay with them. In due time Kōbō was born on June 15th in the fifth year of Hōki (774). Exactly on the same date—June 15th in the ninth year of Dali of Tang China (774)—Amoghavajra died in China.

By the time this book was written, the Shingon Esoteric Buddhism Kūkai had started in Japan had come to full maturity, and this legend may have come to the knowledge of anyone who was interested in Kūkai and his religion.

In fact, his birthday had long been celebrated on June 15 both in Tō-ji, the headquarter temple of his religion in Kyōto and in Zentsū-ji, his birthplace. On the other hand, it is undeniable that Amoghavajra died of illness on that date, as is recorded in his standard biography, *The Life of Tripitaka Amoghavajra*, written by Zhao Qian, one of his laymen disciples. Kūkai in Changan must have read this book with passionate interest along with *The Collection of Amoghavajra's Writings*.

Though Amoghavajra was eager to demonstrate the amazing effectiveness of his own religion in protecting the Tang Empire from difficulties, his true self was far from being nationalistic, and he had remained resolutely universal ever since he had successfully transformed himself into an embodiment of Mahavairocana as the symbol of the truth of the universe. One appears normal when one is scrupulous about or rebellious against the common sense of the society one lives in. What if one simply transcends it? One will look like a mysterious being, just as Amoghavajra must have done.

If Amoghavajra had been a native Chinese, he would not have been able to make himself so conspicuous, as was clearly seen in the case of Huiguo. When he succeeded Amoghavajra, Huiguo was also made an embodiment of Mahavairocana. But owing to his own common sense that kept asserting itself, he appeared as normal as before. Conversely, Amoghavajra's transcendency or universality was easily achieved and maintained because he was an alien in Chang'an, completely free from all the communal bonds of Chinese society.

Looking back upon Kūkai's life, there is little or no trace of his having followed Huiguo's example, whereas many of his achievements are curiously analogous to Amoghavajra's, as if he had been imitating Amoghavajra more or less deliberately. But as was well illustrated by the case of Huiguo, being a universal man in one's own country is next to impossible. And if Kūkai succeeded in becoming one, as he actually did, he must have regarded himself as someone from a different land, probably even before he returned to Japan. If so, when he landed in Tsukushi, his feelings would have been very mixed—the pleasure of seeing his beloved native land again, and a sense of alienation, as if he was someone from afar, which must have been the metaphysical world of the *Mahavairocana Sutra* or Mahavairocana's Land as advocated by Amoghavajra. The sense of alienation he had felt then would become self-recognition as an outcome of the realization that he who already embodied Mahavairocana could no longer be like other people on earth. In order to keep alive this newly-acquired self-identity, Kūkai may have been identifying himself with Amoghavajra as a National Preceptor.

XXI. At Otokuni-dera Temple

IN November, 811, Kūkai left Takaosan-ji and moved to Otokuni-dera in Otokuni County, where the Tennō Kammu had once built the short-lived Nagaoka Capital. Otokuni-dera, founded about two hundred years before, was one of the oldest state temples in Japan.

According to the official order Kūkai received, the reason given for his transfer was that "Takaosan-ji is inconvenient." Kūkai had never complained of Takaosan-ji being an inconvenient place to live in. He had even declared, in a poem he sent to Saga in the previous year, that he would never leave that temple for "six years." Saga must have consulted his own convenience. Certainly, Saga, having found in Kūkai an ideal friend who immensely satisfied his cultural tastes as well as his intellect, was anxiously seeking out Kūkai's company.

On June 27, 811, about four months before he was ordered to move to Otokuni-dera, Kūkai, in complying with his request, presented Saga with his calligraphic transcription of four volumes of *The Writings of Liu Xiyi*, one volume of *The Poetical Works of Wang Changling* and three volumes of *The Six-line Poems on Distinguished Characters in the Zhenyuan Era*. According to the note Kūkai sent to Saga on that occasion, he made an additional present: a volume of *hihaku* handwriting, more pictorial than calligraphic, which is considered to have been invented by Cai Yong, a Chinese calligrapher in the Later Han (25–220). In Japan it had rarely been seen before Kūkai took it up and occasionally demonstrated it in this way, to the astonishment of his contemporaries who looked upon it as a sort of modernism. Kūkai was soon to create his own style of *hihaku* with birds and beasts incorporated into characters. It is unknown whether or not the *hihaku* work he presented to Saga on that occasion had already attained such a level as is seen in *Jū Nyoze*,[1] but we can well imagine how enthusiastic Saga was when he saw it for the first time.

This was how the friendship between Saga and Kūkai had developed. More precisely, Saga could not do without Kūkai for two reasons: firstly to gratify his tastes in art and literature and secondly to have his country spared calamities and difficulties through the power of his prayers. In other words, he had been drawn naturally to Kūkai.

In *The Collection of Legends Concerning Treasures Kept at Tō-ji*, there is an entry: " The Tennō Saga, while being challenged by the ex-Tennō Heizei, had a confidential talk with Daishi (Kūkai)." Seen in a certain light, the scene depicted here may appear grim. Considering that their relationship had been rapidly growing closer about that time, this legend certainly conveys a mood, though not a fact. In years to come, the two were often seen in the same room, happily talking about poetry and calligraphy. But I doubt if their relationship at that time when Saga was "challenged by the ex-Tennō Heizei" had ripened to such an extent that they would "have confidential talk" about such a serious political matter.

Certainly Kūkai was willing to emulate Amoghavajra, but he must have been careful not to make himself another Gembō, a notorious Buddhist priest who had come from the Atos or Kūkai's mother's side, and who was brought to ruin by over-committing himself in politics. His uncle Ōtari must have warned Kūkai when he found it impossible to dissuade him from becoming a Buddhist monk: "At least, do not follow in Gembō's steps..."

In fact, there were many analogies between Kūkai and Gembō (?–746). They were both unrivaled in intellect among their contemporaries. Both went to Tang China as students of Buddhism. Both won great popularity among gentlemen in Chang'an because of their unusual talents. Both were personally invited to his palace by the Emperor. Gembō, who had been in Chang'an for eighteen years (717–735), had even more opportunities to demonstrate his gifts. The Emperor Xuanzong, so much impressed by his unusual talent, conferred on him not only the third court rank that was usually granted only to his Imperial princes but also a purple robe as a token of his special favor. The last-mentioned, when reported in Japan, impressed the Tennō Shōmu so much that he decided to adopt that practice at his Court, too, and Gembō was the first to be granted a purple robe.

It was Gembō's idea, adopted and realized in 741 by the same Tennō, that each province should have a state monastery and a state nunnery— Kokubun-ji and Kokubun-niji. Since more than five thousand volumes of Buddhist scriptures and commentaries he had brought back were deeply appreciated by the Court, the high rank of *Sōjō*[2] was immediately conferred upon him, and he was promoted to be the head of the ten Buddhist priests serving at the Imperial chapel.

But Gembō was not very happy. Thoroughly imbued with Tang culture, he found everything he saw and everyone he met in Japan ridiculous, which he never tried to hide, and so soon lost his popularity. But he never minded as long as he stood high in the Tennō's favor, which he took as a matter of course and made use of to a great extent. Stalking around the Court with a haughty air, he lost no time in changing Japanese customs into Chinese ones. Presumably he frequented even the Tennō's harem and was believed to have committed adultery with the Tennō's first consort, as was written in *Dai Nihon-shi*,[3] though some say that its editors were led to that conclusion through their misreading of a certain entry in *Shoku Nihon-gi* (see Note 1 for III). Whether it was true or not, he had been notorious enough to make such a story accepted as probable.

Gembō gained even greater power by joining forces with Tachibana no Moroe, a great grandfather of Hayanari. He became most powerful at Court when the Fujiwaras were in a temporary decline because of an epidemic which had killed all of the four sons who had founded the four branches of the Fujiwaras. But in 745 when Fujiwara no Nakamaro came to the fore, Gembō was banished to Tsukushi, where he died or was assassinated in the following year. Perhaps it was when Kūkai returned home unexpectedly early, that the elders of Nara Buddhism, keenly conscious of Kūkai's resemblances to Gembō, thought it better to keep Kūkai away from the capital for the time being, lest he should become involved in Court strife, though not so fatally as Gembō had.

Their apprehension, however, would have been unnecessary, for unlike Gembō whose great ambition was to turn the Japanese Court into the magnificent version he had known in Tang China, Kūkai's undeviating wish was to establish a Buddhist kingdom of his own completely transcending any state on earth. Naturally it needed tremendous resources. Kūkai, a self-reliant person, made it a rule to help himself first, but he knew very well, as Amoghavajra did, that winning the heart of the monarch would be a must if he really wanted to gain his aim. And he had already been making himself successful in this direction, too.

*   *   *

Otokuni-dera, to which Kūkai was now ordered to move, was associated with a sinister incident that occurred in the fall of 785, as mentioned in Chapter II. Kūkai must have recalled what he heard when he was eleven: the then Crown Prince Sawara, a younger brother of the Tennō Kammu, was sent to Otokuni-dera temple to be imprisoned following a questionable accusation on the orders of Kammu, who had been waiting for an opportunity to make his own son Prince Ate his crown prince. Sawara then refused to eat or drink—or was not allowed to do so—for ten days. Then he was released to be exiled to Awaji Island, only to die on his way there. As the revengeful ghost of Sawara was supposed to curse his household, Kammu had to remain uneasy for the rest of his life, especially when his Crown Prince Ate who was to be the Tennō Heizei was afflicted with a nervous disease.

This incident in which the Ōtomos and the Ōtomo Saekis were implicated caused the former to suffer swift decline and the latter to follow the same fate though not as swiftly. Even to the Sanuki Saekis who had already had a few members in official circles, it proved to be a considerable blow, though I would not say, as some do fairly reasonably, that that incident eventually led the boy Kūkai to be skeptical about following a bureaucratic career as was expected of him.

Kūkai now would not have minded "the curse of the Crown Prince Sawara." But Saga minded it, as his father Kammu had done. It may well have been then that Saga, who intended to appease the Crown Prince's furies,[4] asked Kūkai to move to that temple to restore its former serenity and respectability, which he would have readily accepted as part of his effort to keep the state safe and secure.

Otokuni-dera is still there, even though the housing development of recent years has almost drowned the temple and a small thicket behind it, which was once a large, beautiful wood named Myōjō-no (Evening Star Woods). The temple ground, now reduced to a moderate size, is modestly laid out. It is impossible, therefore, to imagine what it was like in Kūkai's days. In fact, the ancient temple had already become dilapidated by the time Kūkai arrived there. In the letter he wrote to the Ecclesiastical Office in Nara, it was depicted as follows: "... the temple has long been left unattended, several leaks on the roofs impairing the holy images, fallen fences letting in trespassers and beasts...."

But in the garden there was a large number of *kōji* citrus trees whose luxuriant foliage was then brightly dotted with golden fruit, small but fairly palatable. Kūkai had the fruits picked and packed and had them sent to Saga. This sort of conduct may prove that their friendship had already ripened to a considerable degree of intimacy. Kūkai did the same thing when the season came round the next year, as is known by the note he wrote on that occasion: "We are now in the *kōji* season again. Here are one thousand of the golden fruits for you. I hope you may enjoy one thousand autumn seasons, blessed with golden health."

This may sound too fulsome for a modest gift of fruits. But this was by no means so, because such a compliment was an important part of Chinese culture and deeply appreciated by educated Japanese who knew that the Emperor Xuanzong's birthday was called the One Thousand Autumn Day.

On the same day—October 29, 812—he wrote another letter to Saga, a letter of resignation from Otokuni-dera. In fact, he left the temple on the same day. Now that he had fulfilled his duty there, he had to return to Takaosan-ji to carry out his own projects, as he must already have notified the Ecclesiastical Office in Nara.

*   *   *

Another thing that must be mentioned in this chapter was his having met Saichō for the first time, if we are to go by the records. It happened to be only two days before Kūkai left Otokuni-dera when Saichō came to meet him and stayed with him for the night. Whether Kūkai had expected it or not is unknown. Probably not.

Saichō had been in Nara since September in order to attend a series of lectures on the *Yuima-gyō* sutra annually given at Kōfuku-ji temple[5] in Nara. When it was over, he walked north, traveled up the Kizu River, crossed the

Otokuni Plain and the Katsura River, and went on to Otokuni-dera. When his arrival was announced, Kūkai, junior to Saichō in priesthood as well as in age, would have come out to greet him and invite him inside.

What was their meeting like? In a letter Saichō sent to someone, he wrote:

> On the twenty-seventh last month, I stayed overnight at Otokuni-dera and was honoured to meet *Acarya* Kūkai. He was so kind as to instruct me, giving me some advice, and showing several images and mandalas that represent the two lines of Esoteric Buddhism.

What was their conversation like? Judging from Kūkai's writing or what was recorded by his disciples in *The Memoirs of Our Master*, literature seems to have been richly woven into his daily life. So Kūkai would have liked to talk about the most exciting experiences they had had in their lives: the dangerous voyages to and from China, what they came across while traveling around the Continent or sojourning there, exchanging their observations and feelings about them. But Saichō, who had rarely allowed himself to go beyond the framework of Buddhism, may have come to the point as soon as possible, saying: "My Esoteric Buddhism is far from perfect. Would you kindly help me make it perfect?"

Obviously the sincere attitude he showed on that occasion came from the high moral sense he was born with. But viewed from a different standpoint, he was forced to adopt such an attitude: he had already been permitted to have his own students at the Esoteric Buddhism Course he had started on Mount Hiei, but what would he do when it was widely known that his Esoteric Buddhism was far from perfect? No wonder he thought he would have given anything to Kūkai if he would kindly extend him a helping hand. We can easily imagine, therefore, how pleased Saichō was when Kūkai at Otokuni-dera "was so kind as to instruct me, giving me some advice." Naturally Saichō never forgot to ask Kūkai to give him *abhiseka* baptism.

"*Abhiseka* baptism for you?" Kūkai must have asked in surprise. Six years before, Saichō had baptized the Tennō Kammu, some of his Court officials and the elders from Nara. Now the baptizer himself was begging him to baptize him. Greatly pleased, Kūkai may have said, smiling at the person who he thought was going to make himself his disciple: "I'll be pleased to, though not here but at Takaosan-ji, because I am leaving here very soon."

Saichō then must have asked innocently: "What should I do in preparation for that?"

"Preparation?" Kūkai may have sounded sarcastic when he asked: "What did you do when you did it yourself, may I ask?"

Saichō would have innocently told him about it, even describing everything in detail. Kūkai would have been listening to him with the utmost patience, suppressing the anger he could not help feeling when he thought of the great humiliation even Gonzō, his dearest mentor, had to suffer when he was forced to come up to Takaosan-ji to receive from Saichō *abhiseka* baptism, which was virtually a farce though authorized in the Tennō's name. But not until Saichō gave a full explanation of it did Kūkai make any comment, which I think would have been short but sharp enough to sting Saichō: "Frankly speaking, it does not sound like *abhiseka* baptism as I know it."

Then he would have told him what it really meant and how it should be given or received.

It was also on that occasion that Kūkai said to Saichō something that came to sound rather strange or incomprehensible in the years that followed:

"I shall soon be forty; it will not be long before my days are over. No longer should I like to move around. So if you wish, you shall be initiated into my religion as my successor."

Understandably Saichō was astonished at this unusual readiness with which Kūkai offered him what his heart desired. Naturally he took it very seriously and became even more eager to acquire it. But what made Kūkai say such a serious thing so casually? Imaginably Kūkai in his thirty-ninth year was keenly aware of his aging, though he was a junior to Saichō by seven years and was to live to be sixty-two while Saichō who was to die at fifty-six had only nine years before him. Then what matters here will be how they were thinking about their own aging rather than how many years they had before them. Saichō left no writing about his own aging, while Kūkai who was naturally fond of pondering over such matters, wrote a poem on what he thought about his fortieth year: *A Poem upon the Turning Point of Human Life.** In its preamble, he wrote:

> According to the sacred teaching,[6] human life used to be incalculably long in the earliest times; then it became gradually less long until it was fixed at eighty years at the most. Then the age of forty might be regarded as the turning point of human life. Now, on reaching that very point, I should like to express my feelings about it.

So it may have been that while he was talking to Saichō, a sort of obsession about his aging happened to arise in him and gave expression to the idea that had just entered his mind. At least at that moment, Kūkai must have meant what he said though it did not turn out to be a true prediction.

XXII. THEIR EXPECTATIONS TURNED OUT TO BE UNFULFILLED

A S soon as Kūkai had returned to Takaosan-ji, Saichō came to stay at Hoku-in or what used to be his own residential quarters on Mt. Takao, and prepared himself for *abhiseka* baptism. The first thing he did was to collect food supplies. The one to be baptized was expected to pay the costs of baptism, as Kūkai himself had done in Chang'an. Kūkai, after explaining to Saichō what *abhiseka* baptism meant, must have advised him not to call upon the state for help, as he had done before, but to pay it all himself. Saichō, who possessed little or no private means, had to raise a fund for the ceremony, asking the wealthy and the powerful to contribute to it. Fortunately three laymen, including Wake no Matsuna, came to receive baptism at the same time, and this was to spare him three fourths of the expenditure.

On November 15, 812, the four received baptism into the Realm of the Indestructibles. Then Saichō spent another month preparing for baptism into the Womb-store; he collected food supplies again and had some ritual implements newly made by craftsmen. But this time, to his great relief, as many as one hundred and ninety people came to join him and thus shared in the expenditure.

On December 14, all of them gathered at Takaosan-ji. The baptism held there must have been a magnificent one like the one Kūkai himself had received at Qinglong-si temple in Chang'an. According to the list of names written down by Kūkai himself, which still remains at Takaosan-ji, forty-five of the baptized were young boys. Does this mean that Saichō was on a par with those children?

There are three levels of *abhiseka* baptism: the initial level for anyone who wishes to form a connection with this religion; the higher level for ascetics to be initiated into only a certain number of mysteries; the highest level is for the conferment of the degree of master of Esoteric Buddhism.

Saichō, who intended to be a real master¹ of Esoteric Buddhism, would have naturally expected to receive the highest level of baptism. But seeing that there were so many children among the baptized, the baptism must have been at the initial level, or the higher level at best, probably to his great disappointment.

I suppose that was why Saichō remained at Takaosan-ji even after the baptism was over, eagerly expecting that Kūkai would call him for the highest level of baptism at any moment. But as he did not see any sign of it, he became very impatient and came to meet Kūkai and asked: "How many months will there be before I am allowed to receive the ultimate baptism?"

Saichō, who had probably heard how soon Kūkai was allowed to succeed Huiguo as the Eighth Patriarch of Esoteric Buddhism, would have presumed that it would take him several months or so before he was allowed to receive the final baptism. Kūkai's answer, therefore, left him incredulous: "It will take three years."

Kūkai may have thought Saichō presumptuous in thinking he would be able to become a master of Esoteric Buddhism so quickly and so easily. True, in the case of Kūkai, it took only two months or so, but it was because Huiguo acknowledged the fact that what Kūkai had taught himself the hard way in Japan, spending more than a decade of his thirty-two-year life to do so, exactly corresponded to the legitimate lines of Esoteric Buddhism. Huiguo had one thousand disciples in his life, but only two postulants— Kūkai and Yiming who died even before or soon after Huiguo died—were allowed to succeed to both systems, and only six to either of the two systems. Then how could Saichō hope to accede to the both systems so soon? Kūkai ought to have made this point clear, but he failed to do so, and just mentioned the "three years" he would have to spend before becoming a master.

"Three years!" Saichō must have exclaimed in frank dismay. "I thought I could get it in a single season (three months). But if I have to spend so many years, I think I must leave here now and come back sometime later when I find the time to devote to it."

In fact, Saichō was busy; he had to attend to his own religion first of all, and he could not possibly afford to spend as long as three years on the new religion he never thought of converting to. All he wanted was to be a master of Esoteric Buddhism in order to lend authority to the Esoteric Buddhism Course he had launched on Mt. Hiei. Kūkai might have shown some understanding of his position and given him the final baptism even if it was only for form's sake was what Saichō was thinking—something Kūkai must have already perceived.

Certainly he had told Saichō at Otokuni-dera: "You shall be initiated into my religion as my successor," expecting him to become his disciple. As it was, Saichō interpreted the words in his own way and expected that Kūkai would do him a favor by offering him a special short-term course in Esoteric Buddhism, so that he could "get it in a single season." This very phrase that betrayed Saichō's lack of seriousness toward Esoteric Buddhism must have been exasperatingly humiliating to Kūkai. To him what mattered most in judging others was not the mere good-naturedness one might casually show in daily life. He demanded whole-heartedness in devotion to his own religion, which he believed encompassed the truth of the universe.

"I have offered him the best position available. But he does not want it...." Kūkai must have muttered to himself, looking upon Saichō with growing disappointment and displeasure.

Unable to find out any solution, Saichō thought of an expedient: he would send several of his best disciples to Kūkai and let them learn Esoteric Buddhism in his stead. When this arrangement was suggested to Kūkai, he agreed, as he had no reason to object to it. Saichō, greatly pleased, chose Enchō, Taihan and a few others, and sent them to Kūkai at Takaosan-ji. At that point, Kūkai ought to have made it clear that Saichō might not have them again at Mount Hiei if they really mastered Esoteric Buddhism. The ultimate aim of Esoteric Buddhism is not merely to grasp it with the intellect but to transform oneself into the very principle of the universe. Then how could the one who had mastered such arcana abandon the harmonious union he had made with the principle of the universe? Kūkai ought to have informed Saichō of this possibility. But again he failed to do so, probably because of the unspoken resentment he had been feeling on the presumption that what Saichō was seeking was not Esoteric Buddhism itself, but someone able to teach and examine the students in his Esoteric Buddhism Course.

When viewed from Kūkai's standpoint, Saichō's first error was his reliance on book-reading. No wonder Saichō thought it the only method available, if we consider the fact that the Japanese had learned Buddhism and Confucianism almost exclusively by reading books on the subject. Saichō, who was then studying the Tiantai religion by poring over the scriptures he had brought back, naturally adopted the same method in learning Esoteric Buddhism, even though it may have run counter to the unbreakable rule in the making of a master of Esoteric Buddhism: that teaching must be transmitted directly from master to disciple;[2] in other words one must go through the apprenticeship under one's master.

Since this religion came into being in India, this rule has never been challenged. Even in Tibet and in Mongolia, where Esoteric Buddhism itself underwent a considerable change, this tradition remains unchanged and actually became intensified when it developed another tradition in which disciples, even after they acquire mastership, identify their master with the principle itself and worship him for the rest of their lives.

Kūkai had not given Saichō a detailed account of this significant rule, partly because it was something to be kept secret, and partly because he felt rather diffident toward Saichō who was senior to himself. Or he might have thought that a wise man would find it by himself; conversely, if he was not wise enough to find it by himself, then he would not be qualified to become a master of this religion. In the end, this was to be a sort of silent denial Kūkai made against Saichō. He appeared to Kūkai a double dealer who, while holding on to the highest seat in his own religion, was doing his utmost to drag in another religion so as to make his own business prosper.

Soon after he left Takaosan-ji, Saichō sent a messenger to Kūkai to ask for the loan of books, as he was to do again and again for about a year. The following is one of the letters Saichō sent to Kūkai:

> ... Never have I forgot, even while eating or sleeping, to carry out my mission to uphold the cause of Buddhism, even if I have as yet done nothing worth mentioning. For the time being, I intend to copy diligently these books I have selected from your *List*. When I finish copying them all, I should like to pay a visit to you and attend your lecture. It is only for convenience sake that I

copy these books in my place. If I were to stay at your place, I should lose a great deal of time and energy simply in carrying my food up there. That is why I have had no choice but to stay and study here. I sincerely beg of you, my great master, not to suspect me of any improper intention such as underhandedly teaching myself through the copying of these books simply for my own self-aggrandizement.

Thus Kūkai, suppressing his growing anger, was to lend him his books for about a year.

XXIII. How to Approach the Truth of the Universe

TAIHAN was one of the disciples Saichō sent to Kūkai to learn Esoteric Buddhism in place of himself. Before coming up to Takaosan-ji, he had been living at his own temple in Takashima Village in Ōmi Province. His background is unknown, though he is considered to have come from Ōmi Province as Saichō did. Judging from the entry in the nominal list of the official priests of Tō-ji (issued in 837): "Taihan: aged sixty; thirty-seven years in priesthood," Taihan who was born in 777 was three years junior to Kūkai, and ten years junior to Saichō.

When young, Taihan was in Nara, residing at Gangō-ji adjacent to Daian-ji that Kūkai often visited in his twenties. Before he went to China, Saichō was also a frequent visitor to Daian-ji. Quite probably Saichō's first meeting with Taihan occurred either at Gangō-ji or Daian-ji. Considering that Taihan had already become an official priest, their initial relationship was not that of master and disciple, but merely of senior and junior. Young as he was, Taihan had already made himself a good scholar of Buddhism with a lofty aim in life. Then it is quite probable that Saichō was attracted to Taihan.

Taihan, too, was not satisfied with the status quo of old Buddhism in Japan, and must have readily become sympathetic to Saichō when he unfolded his cherished ideas of the sort of religion they should seek after, referring to his own discovery of the Tiantai religion on Mt. Tiantai in China. Saichō's having already been made one of the ten Buddhist priests to serve at the Imperial chapel would also have attracted Taihan. Thus their admiration and respect for each other may have become an affection similar to love between man and woman, as was not uncommon among Buddhist monks. Even if so, it would not detract from Saichō's state of grace.

Eventually, Saichō went to China and brought back the Tiantai religion, thus fulfilling Taihan's great expectations. In January, 810, Taihan, who was the first to learn the Tiantai doctrine from Saichō—more precisely, not directly from Saichō but by studying books brought back by Saichō—was made the head teacher in Saichō's institution on Mt. Hiei. Because Saichō's duty in China was not to learn the Tiantai religion itself but just to bring back its whole system in the form of a library, it was not until he returned home and settled down on Mt. Hiei that he began to learn it through book-reading. While he was reading, Taihan was reading, too; thus while teaching themselves, they taught their students. This was how the Tendai principle of Japan was established on Mt. Hiei, taking at least six or seven years. Strictly speaking, therefore, Taihan was not a disciple of Saichō but a fellow student and fellow teacher of the Tendai principle.

Unlike Saichō, who had been kept busy trying to make his religion an authorized one, Taihan had more time to sit and read, and this may have led him to harbor a complaint: "Saichō has made himself the first patriarch of the Tendai religion in Japan simply because he brought back these books. That is all...."

On August 1, 811, there was a series of lectures on the *Hoke-kyō*, the most important annual event held on Mt. Hiei. Taihan, who ought to have played an important role in it, was not seen there, as he had returned to his own temple in Takashima Village. When requested by Saichō to come back, he sent a letter of resignation. It is unknown what made him behave so abnormally. But Saichō remained kind to him, and showed him a supreme kindness when on May 8 in the following year he published his will in which he offered Taihan two important posts. One was the presidency of the Tendai religion headquarters on Mt. Hiei; the other was as chief of the archives there. This naturally meant that Saichō had appointed Taihan his successor. But Taihan, instead of being pleased with it, wrote to Saichō, disclosing his wish to leave Mount Hiei for good.

Saichō, "painfully astonished by the reading of this letter," wrote to Taihan on the same day, urging him to change his mind. As for the reason why he wished to leave Mount Hiei, Taihan wrote: "I am always offending the Buddhist commandments, thus disgracing the purity of my fellow priests." Could it be true? Probably it was a rhetorical exaggeration common to literature at that time. But this may allow us to imagine a certain situation: Taihan thought of himself as equal to Saichō, above all others on Mount

Hiei. What if this pride of his occasionally came to assert itself? It would make him very unpopular among his colleagues.

On the other hand, Saichō had probably ceased to be attractive enough to persuade him to stay with him any longer. Taihan was probably a very difficult person to please. Even the promised post of the second patriarch of the Tendai religion had not held any appeal. This may testify to his indifference to power. Or was he sulking, indifferent now to all Saichō might offer him? Taihan himself would have naturally been aware of this change of feelings toward Saichō, and yet he would not mend his ways. Then could it be a case of love inevitably cooling down?

But Saichō innocently asked in his letter to Taihan: "What was it made you abandon our most intimate friendship, and leave me alone so suddenly?" Then he kindly advised him not to take whatever others might say too seriously.

Several months later, Saichō came to meet Kūkai at Otokuni-dera. As soon as his wish to be baptized by Kūkai was accepted, Saichō sent a messenger to Taihan, inviting him to come and join him for the first baptism to be given on November 15 at Takaosan-ji. Taihan declined, and did not change his mind even when he was invited again two days later. But Saichō would not give up and invited Taihan to the second baptism that was to occur on December 14. This time Taihan accepted the invitation and presented himself at Takaosan-ji to be baptized with Saichō and many others.

Taihan, who was seeing Kūkai for the first time, must have gazed long upon "the person everyone is talking about." What impression he received from him or what he thought about him is unknown. But the action he took after the baptismal ceremony was over may have some significance: Taihan chose to stay on at Takaosan-ji, instead of returning to his own temple or to Mt. Hiei with many other disciples of Saichō.

On December 23, nine days after the second baptism was over, Saichō wrote to Taihan at Takaosan-ji, reminding him of "our duty to establish the Tendai religion and hand it down to posterity," sincerely wishing that he would live up to his expectations. On January 18, 813, Saichō, unable to spend "three years" in learning Esoteric Buddhism himself, sent Kūkai his best disciples including Taihan and Enchō. But strictly speaking, Taihan had already been there. And yet Saichō asked Kūkai "to let Taihan also stay with you," thus formally accepting Taihan's arbitrary act in staying with Kūkai. Some may take this as Saichō's good-naturedness, others may see his great pertinacity, yet others may sense a bitter grief in his heart.

Saichō wrote to the office of Takaosan-ji, too, expressing his wish to provide Taihan with two things: one was a cabinet once presented to Saichō by a member of the Wake clan and still remaining at Hoku-in or his former residential quarters; the other was a new study he would like to build for Taihan somewhere on Mt. Takao at the expense of his own institute. In this way, Saichō was trying not only to retain Taihan's attention but also to make it clear to Kūkai and his office that Taihan, even if he was staying at Takaosan-ji, was the successor to Saichō's religion and his position. But these requests of Saichō's were to be ignored by Kūkai. Or Taihan himself ignored them, and Kūkai was just observing how things would turn out, probably with what was analogous to the ill will a thinker is likely to harbor against his rival.

Meanwhile, Saichō on Mt. Hiei was busy copying one scripture after another. When he finished a batch, he had someone take it back to Kūkai. Then a new batch, after being collected and packed by Taihan or Enchō, was carried up to Mt. Hiei. Kūkai was not very happy to see his religion being treated in such a mistaken way.

In learning Esoteric Buddhism, acquiring knowledge through book-reading is considered to be of secondary importance. The supreme element in Esoteric Buddhism is breathing in accordance to the breathing of the universe. Then the first thing one should do in learning it is to bring oneself to a master who is actually breathing with the universe. Only by devoting oneself to the prescribed discipline under the guidance of that master, will one have access to the universe named Buddha. The essence and true intention of that Buddha are revealed in what Kūkai called three mysteries: the body, the speech and the mind of Buddha, which are regarded as mysteries because they are not fully known to man. Since the three mysteries of the universe are working incessantly in eternity, ascetics also must continually exercise their own three mysteries by doing three things at the same time: making *mudra* (magical signs with the fingers), uttering a *mantra* (the language of the universe), and contemplating the deity they are invoking, until their own three mysteries are in communion with those of the universe; that is, they finally attain Buddhahood and begin to breathe with the universe. How could Saichō attain such heights by book-reading or scripture-copying which is actually abhorred by Esoteric Buddhists as an infernal deviation? How did Saichō dare to skip this essential process to enlightenment?

Saichō, a sagacious man, would have been aware of his departure from the right course in approaching Esoteric Buddhism. But all he wanted was to obtain knowledge of it. He had already attained the Tendai principle that also invites one to attain Buddhahood. It was called *shikan* contemplation, which enables one to purify oneself until one sees into the intrinsic nature of things in the phenomenal world. Saichō now was trying hard to assemble around this Tendai principle three other elements: *zen*, *ritsu* and Esoteric Buddhism, so that he might start on Mount Hiei a new type of Mahayanist Buddhism—something that had never been heard of either in India or in China. For Saichō, who had placed Esoteric Buddhism on the same level with *zen* and *ritsu*, it would have been only natural to approach it by book-reading. In other words, Saichō, a bold spirit, despite his outwardly gentle mien, had turned to Kūkai not to attain Buddhahood by Esoteric Buddhist method but to accomplish his own project. Viewed from the standpoint of Kūkai, such an exploitation of Esoteric Buddhism would have been an insult not only to Esoteric Buddhism but also to himself. Thus Saichō was becoming more and more insufferable to Kūkai.

Kūkai was far from intolerant toward the old Buddhism in Nara, though it was as exoteric as Saichō's Tendai religion. When requested by Tōdai-ji, the politician in Kūkai was quite ready to 'veneer' its Kegon doctrine with his Esoteric Buddhism. But when approached by Saichō, the thinker in Kūkai re-asserted himself. How could this be explained? To many people, including some scholars of Esoteric Buddhism of later ages, this intolerance Kūkai showed toward Saichō has been looked upon as regrettable. If dramatized, Saichō would be presented as a "goody" and Kakai as a "baddy." But if one reads his *Ten Stages of the Development of Human Mind*, one will clearly see that his attitude toward Saichō was undeviatingly consistent with the logic he unfolded in that work, in which he compared all the religions or teachings then known in the eastern world and graded them according to their potential in enhancing the human mind. He placed his Shingon Esoteric Buddhism in the highest grade, followed by Kegon, Tendai, Sanron, Hossō, Engaku,[1] Shōmon,[2] Taoism, and Confucianism.

Kūkai did something for Tōdai-ji because the Kegon religion it held had already come closest to his Esoteric Buddhism. As for the other religions, he just left them as they were. Then why was it that when he first met Saichō at Otokuni-dera, he almost repeated what his own master Huiguo had said to him at their first meeting at Qinglong-si temple: "I am coming to the end of my life, but I have had no successor to my religion so far. Now that you have come, you shall be my successor." ? Probably what Kūkai detected in Saichō then was a distinct gift for making himself a master of Esoteric Buddhism though it needed to be perfected by going through the prescribed disciplines under the guidance of a master. As it turned out, Saichō just returned to his own religion, soon after he received the *abhiseka* baptisms.

On April 13, 813, Saichō presented Kūkai with a *hiki* of silk in wishing him the compliments of the approaching summer season. A large number of books he borrowed on that occasion included even those on the Tiantai religion—*A Commentary on the Hoke-kyō Sutra* composed by Zhiyi, *A Commentary on the Hoke-kyō Sutra* by Zhanran and *The List of Buddhist Scriptures: Newly Provided in the Era of Zhenyuan*. Saichō himself possessed these titles, but he wanted to compare his with Kūkai's. In the letter he sent to Kūkai on this occasion, there is an entry: "... the month is approaching when I am expecting to receive the *abhiseka* baptism (probably higher-level baptism), as you kindly allowed me to last year." It is unknown what Kūkai's answer about this matter was, as the letter itself was lost probably in 1571 when Mount Hiei was attacked by Oda Nobunaga[3] and many papers and documents were burnt to ashes. As it was, Saichō never again went to Takaosan-ji for the reason to be mentioned in the following chapter.

Saichō's greatest concern about that time might have been more for Taihan than for anything else. By that time anyone could see quite clearly that Taihan had no idea of returning to Saichō. Obviously Taihan was fascinated by Kūkai and his religion. Then what could it be that made Taihan dislike Saichō and his religion so intensely? If Taihan preferred Esoteric Buddhism so much, he would be able to devote himself to it at the Esoteric Buddhism Course on Mt. Hiei. Was it not why he had been sent to Kūkai? But something emotional had prevented him from behaving as he was expected to by Saichō. This made Saichō highly emotional, too—emotional enough to ask him to return a book he had placed in his custody: *Shikan Guketsu*, an indispensable book for the Tendai religion: "To you this book will no longer be of any use. To me and to my religion, this is of the profoundest import." Such irony, which might better be left unspoken, is rarely found in his style which was usually serene, reflecting his personality. Probably Saichō was annoyed rather than angry. A sure sign of deep attachment. But to Taihan, who was no longer interested in Saichō, such devotion must have been simply embarrassing.

That letter ends with the signature: "Saichō, a poor old man, discarded by the one he had regarded as his comrade in pursuing the noble purpose." This may reveal the fact that even such a brave man as Saichō who had determined to launch a great new religious venture could at the same time be a mere sentimentalist.

* * *

Kūkai at that time was having his reputation raised higher by building the Nan'en-do hall in the precinct of Kōfuku-ji in Nara. How that hall came into being is told as follows:

> One day, Fujiwara Hokke no Uchimaro, who used to be the Minister of the Right about the time Kūkai returned from China, went to Takaosan-ji to meet Kūkai.
>
> "To my regret," said the old gentleman who was known for his unerring judgement and wise discretion, "we are on the decline. We now have only three or four seats at Court. I wonder if you could help us retrieve our fortunes through the mysterious efficacy of your religion?"
>
> "Well," said Kūkai, "let me recommend you to worship Fukū-kenjaku-kannon Bodhisattva.⁴"

Sakyamuni would be surprised if he were told that this was also a branch of the Buddhism he started. But since its germination in India, Esoteric Buddhism had presented itself as a method of realizing people's worldly wishes.

Uchimaro, pleased with the prompt answer he received, requested Kūkai to bring into being both the image of the Kannon and the hall to house it. He himself was to die of old age very soon. So his eldest son, Fuyutsugu, who had been active in the government service, approached Kūkai to carry out the intentions of his deceased father. Kūkai spent a great deal of time and energy, carving the image of the Kannon, designing the hall to house it, then supervising its construction work on his way to and from Tōdai-ji that he visited whenever duty called. Never before had he so completely committed himself to building and furnishing a place of worship, which, though small in scale, was a place appointed solely for the celebration of Esoteric Buddhism, the first of its kind in Japan. On entering the hall, one saw the main image of Fukū-kenjaku-kannon in the center and the portraits of forefathers of Esoteric Buddhism—Subhakarasimha, Xuanzang, Vajrabodhi, Amoghavajra, Yixing and Huiguo—beautifully displayed on either side.

From about this time when the Nan'en-dō hall was finished (813), the fortunes of the Fujiwara Hokke began to improve to a remarkable extent. This was probably due to Fuyutsugu, a man of unusual ability in politics. But people at large attributed it to the divine favors they received through their devotion to Fukū-kenjaku-kannon at the Nan'en-dō hall. The Fujiwara Hokke's reverence for Kūkai increased, even though Kūkai himself was careful enough not to form any special connection with any of the powers of the time lest he should become another Gembō.

XXIV. The Logic for Attaining Buddhahood by Means of True Wisdom

ON November 25, 813, Saichō requested the loan of *A Commentary on the Rishu-kyō Sutra*. Eight years had passed since he began studying Esoteric Buddhism. Had his knowledge of Esoteric Buddhism reached such a high level as the study of *A Commentary on the Rishu-kyō Sutra*? I am not certain about this, seeing that the first titles he gave in this letter were the *Shinsen Monju-san Hosshin-rai & its Hōen-zu & their Commentaries* (see Note 5 for XXVI), and then came *A Commentary on the Rishu-kyō Sutra*. Did he add it on the spur of the moment? But the postscript he wrote in a blank space can be taken seriously: "Saichō, your disciple, has no treacherous intention, as every Buddha knows. I shall be pleased if you will kindly grant my request." Even if this was just another example of his excessive politeness in writing, "no treacherous intention" does not sound like a normal phrase in declaring one's innocence.

The *Rishu-kyō* sutra, known for the radical glorification of sexual desire as mentioned in Chapter VI, has traditionally been placed among the most valued sutras of Esoteric Buddhism. At least in Lamaism in Tibet, this sutra seems to be placed above the *Mahavairocana Sutra* that had come into being earlier. *Rishu* means logic. Then the formal title of this sutra—*Tairaku Kinkō Fukū Shinjitsu Sammaya-kyō* or *Hannya Haramita Rishu-bon*—means "the logic for attaining Buddhahood by means of true wisdom." Kūkai, having given priority to this sutra for some reason probably different from the reason Lamas would assign it, decided that it should be recited daily and nightly at every temple of his religion.

But this sutra itself must have been the last one he was willing to lend to Saichō or anyone else who had not acquired access to Esoteric Buddhism through the regular channels. Kūkai feared that if read casually or without submitting to the indispensable practice of fusing one's own three mysteries into Buddha's in order to attain Buddhahood in this very existence, the sutra he regarded as the hidden core of his religion might quite possibly lead one to a terrible misunderstanding of his religion. This apprehension on his part was not necessarily groundless, when we consider the history of Esoteric Buddhism in India, Tibet and Japan.

In India about that time, Brahmanism blended with lascivious popular beliefs—Hinduism—was on the rise, and Esoteric Buddhism, influenced by Hinduism, began to assert a marked trend toward the cult of sexual desire. By and by it was brought to Tibet and became Lamaism there. This explains why Lamaism is so rigorous in its expression of the universal principle through sexual intercourse.

But as the Esoteric Buddhism brought to China and then to Japan had not yet been affected by Hinduism, it was quite different from Lamaism in the expression of mysticism. Even though it did share the same thought, it had never shown any sign of lapsing into a cult of sexual desire, as its whole logic still remained youthful, muscular and vigorous. But not many centuries after Kūkai's death, his religion was also denatured when a sexual cult known as Shingon Tachikawa School gained power particularly during the period of the Northern and Southern Courts (1331–1392), when Monkan, the then leader of the Shingon religion, took up this cult and was revered by the Tennō Godaigo of the Southern Court. This fact does suggest that Kūkai's religion, unless it were treated with true respect, could lead to a cult of sexuality.

Shingon Tachikawa School cited the *Rishu-kyō*, the *Yuga-gyō* and the *Bodaishin-ron*, all of which had been introduced by Kūkai, to authorize their philosophy. What Kūkai thought about this matter—the positive view of sexual desire—is unknown because no reference to it can be found in any of his writings. If asked, what would he have answered? To my mind, he would not have said that it should be taken only as a metaphor, as asserted by those who were against the Tachikawa School. Nor would he have said, as the Tachikawa School argued, that sexual intercourse itself could be a discipline through which to attain Buddhahood. The logician Kūkai would have naturally used sexual desire as one of the materials with which to build up his logic, but would not have treated it as a ready-made independent principle.

The opening of Kūkai's answer to Saichō's request for the loan of *A Commentary On the Rishu-kyō Sutra* reads like a model of the fashionable style of his days:

> Your letter has given me the profoundest comfort. It is snowy and cold, but I am glad to know that you are as healthy as ever. Many years have passed since we began to enjoy our friendship, whose closeness could be compared to glue and lacquer, whose evergreenness to pine and oak, whose milk-like aroma to ever-increasing incentives one receives from the good and virtuous. How could I forget or hide the pleasure of this worthy relationship?

But inside this robe covered with jewels of rhetoric had he held a dagger with which to point out what Saichō should do:

> You are the only person responsible for and capable of establishing the Tendai religion in this country. As for Esoteric Buddhism, I have pledged myself to make it take roots here. What better course could we take than to proceed each in his own way?

Kūkai is now trying to check Saichō's advance. Otherwise, he would be misled into a terrible misunderstanding of his religion. Kūkai goes on:

> You may think it possible to absorb the *Rishu-kyō* sutra as long as you have its commentary to guide you. But do you know that the sutra consists of numerous chapters? I wonder what chapters you would like to have.

His tone is serious, too serious to be taken as a mockery of Saichō's ignorance.

> In fact, what the *Rishu-kyō* sutra deals with is so vast that neither heaven nor earth can accommodate it. It is impossible, therefore, for anyone to grasp the whole of it by just selecting only a portion of it.... Because I am not equal to giving you good instruction, I should like to repeat what my master told me. I do hope you will

put your thoughts in order, cleanse them of your preoccupations, listening and learning what *rishu* and the long-treasured tenet of Esoteric Buddhism mean.

The gist of *rishu* is that there are three kinds of *rishu*: one is obtainable by hearing, another by seeing, the other by contemplation. If you wish to obtain the first, all that you have to do is listen to your own voice, that is, the speech that comes from your own mouth, for your voice is the abode of your mystery. If you wish to obtain the second, look at everything you see around you. More concretely, look at your own body, not any other's, for your body is where another of your mysteries resides. If you wish to obtain the third one, you will find it in abundance in your own thought, not in any other's.

Then he gives another trio of *rishu*—the *rishu* of human mind, of Buddha, and of all living things.

If you seek for the *rishu* of human mind, you will find it in your own mind, not in any other's. For the *rishu* of Buddha, you should turn to a Buddha that exists in your own mind.... For the *rishu* of all living things, you will find it in the innumerable people and living things you hold in your own mind.

As to how to obtain the *rishu* in one's own self, Kūkai stresses the need to exercise one's own three functions—physical, verbal, spiritual—until they come into communication with the three mysteries of the universe, thus attaining Buddhahood by actually merging oneself with the universe. This combination of thought and discipline, invented by Kūkai, does explain what Esoteric Buddhism is.

You may ask for the loan of *A Commentary on the Rishu-kyō Sutra*. But are not the three functions or the three mysteries you yourself possess the *rishu* you are asking for? By the same token, the three mysteries I find in myself are the commentary on *rishu* I provide for myself. Just as I cannot possess your body and *rishu*, you neither can possess mine. This is also the case with *A Commentary on the Rishu-kyō Sutra*. In other words, your *rishu*

and mine are different. If you want your own *rishu*, you must go
straight to your own self, not to any other's.

As his eyes ran over these lines, Saichō may have buried his head in his
hands, saying: "Yes, master, that suffices. Thank you!"
Kūkai goes on:

What do I mean by one's own self? It has two kinds: the one
consisting of five elements (form, sensation, conception, volition
and consciousness) is mortal and temporary; the other is the
larger self residing in selflessness. What if one tries to see *rishu*
in the former or so-called lesser self? One will get nowhere
because from the outset the temporary, lesser self has nothing to
offer. Whereas the latter or larger self will lead one to the three
mysteries of Mahavairocana, if only one invokes one's own three
functions, not another's.

Kūkai gives further explanation about this matter as if he were talking to
a novice. In fact, this letter can be read as a lecture on Esoteric Buddhism
rather than a private letter. In Esoteric Buddhism, the principle of the
universe is adored as Mahavairocana, and billions and trillions of natural
beings that exist and move according to that principle are all considered
Bodhisattvas. Human beings as part of natural beings, therefore, are
naturally pure in themselves, even though their purity may be clouded by
their lesser selves. If they succeed in uniting themselves with the principle of
the universe—by exercising their three functions—they will regain their lost
purity as well as their lost Buddhahood. Exercising the three functions,
therefore, is essential in Esoteric Buddhism. Curtailing this process—by
resorting to book-reading only—is abhorred as an infernal deviation from
the right path.
Kūkai now reminds Saichō of his deviation, but he still sounds as if he
expected Saichō to mend his ways when he writes:

The destiny of Esoteric Buddhism depends only on you, and on
me. Therefore, I beg you to keep to the right path. Otherwise, it
will do no good either to the initiator or the initiate. What if I

were to initiate you despite your transgression? Those who come after us will be deprived of their only opportunity to learn what the pursuit of the truth really means. Initiating a person who is in the wrong is allowing him to "steal" the principle. Thus both the initiator and the initiate will be deceiving Mahavairocana. Do keep it in mind that the innermost truth of Esoteric Buddhism can be obtained not by book-reading, but only by a master's direct instillation of the principle into his disciple.

What one acquires from book-reading is nothing but chaff and bran, or piles of broken tiles. If preoccupied by trash and rubbish of that kind, one is sure to lose an opportunity to obtain the supreme fruit of truth and purity.

Kūkai even quotes from Confucius, hinting at Saichō's perversity:

In former days it was for the sake of truth alone that one sought after truth, but nowadays it is for the sake of fame. One who seeks after fame has already loosened one's hold on one's initial intention, while one who seeks after truth has forgotten oneself in pursuing one's initial intention.

It may have been impolite of Kūkai to admonish Saichō, his senior, by citing Confucius, a secular moralist. But the logician in Kūkai may have been asserting himself, for he gives another quotation from Confucius:

Confucius deplored human weakness, quoting the saying of 途聞 途説 (*to-bun to-setsu*: Whatever good words one may hear, one will just pass them on to others instead of keeping them in mind to nourish oneself with them).

In his eagerness to compose his logic, Kūkai fails to check the original in *The Analects of Confucius*, which was 道聴塗説 (*dō-chō to-setsu*) even though the meaning itself was exactly the same. But this lapse of the brush that may reveal the irritated impatience with which he was writing this letter makes me feel as if I could hear him breathing hard on this passage.

Kūkai then urges the importance of having faith first, with his indignation throbbing between the lines:

> Without faith, one cannot vanquish the three evils that poison
> human mind (covetousness, anger and delusion) whatever amount
> of Buddhist literature one may discuss (as you do.)... Without
> faith, and without practising one's three functions in good faith,
> whatever one learns will lead one nowhere or do one no good.

Whatever Kūkai had to say in this letter, his intention was by no means to suspend his relationship with Saichō, as is apparent by the two rhetorical questions and a word of encouragement he wrote in the closing paragraph:

> How can I be the jealous guardian of this principle of mine? How
> could I want to keep it to myself if only you will follow the
> precepts required by this doctrine? ...I do hope you will do your
> best, taking good care of yourself.

There is no knowing what Saichō's reaction to this letter was, because his answer to it has not survived. But the short entry found in the preface to the *Ebyō Tendai-shū*[1] may suggest something he had in mind:

> ... The new authority on Esoteric Buddhism has subverted the
> Japanese tradition of learning things by book-reading.

The objectivity with which Saichō calls Kūkai "the new authority on Esoteric Buddhism" seems to betray his emotion. "The new" might suggest that he regarded himself as "the first" to bring in Esoteric Buddhism. It was true that Japan had learned many things by book-reading, and here Saichō deplored Kūkai's defiance of that tradition, and remained impervious to or unaffected by whatever Kūkai had to say about it. In the end, the admonishment Kūkai had proffered in that long letter was totally lost on Saichō. This proves that Saichō's ego was also strong and fierce.

But Saichō accepted at least one point Kūkai had suggested at the opening of his argument: that he should apply himself only to the exoteric religion of Tendai. Thus he tacitly and sensibly ceased to be "a disciple" of Kūkai, though he remained a friend of his for a few more years.

*   *   *

On March 17, 815, when the tenth anniversary of Kammu's death was solemnized, the seven copies of sutras of the Tendai religion were distributed to the seven major state temples of this country. Since the copying had begun by the Imperial order of Kammu himself, everything was done at the cost of the state.

About the same time, Kūkai, who had "kept my religion to myself as long as ten years[2] since I returned home," finally started propagating his religion by sending a prospectus known as *Kan'en no Sho (An Invitation to the Shingon Esoteric Buddhism)* to many temples: the seven state temples in Nara, Kanzeon-ji in Tsuknshi and Yakushi-ji in Shimotsuke Province, and all the Kokubun-ji and Kokubun-niji temples of this country. He also sent it to "individuals who were interested in my religion, whether men or women, clergy or laity."

In the prospectus he explained the difference between exoteric Buddhism and Esoteric Buddhism: "The doctrine revealed by Sakyamuni is exoteric; it is accessible, simplified, and adapted to the needs of the time and to the capacity of the listeners. The doctrine expounded by Mahavairocana[3] is esoteric; it is secret and profound and contains the ultimate truth." Thus he recommended them to "form a connection with the latter by copying the thirty-six volumes of sutras I had selected for you so that you could recite the sutras, perform the practices prescribed for you, and come to contemplate according to the instructions presented." Unlike Saichō, who had all the expenditure paid by the state, Kūkai requested the people to pay their own expenses for paper, ink and brushes needed for copying.

This prospectus was soon to develop into several of his representative works on his own religion:[4] *The Difference between Exoteric and Esoteric Buddhism* (two volumes), *The Transmission of the Legitimate Heritage of Esoteric Buddhism* (two volumes), *The Attaining Buddhahood in This Very Existence* (one volume), *The Meanings of Sound, Word and Reality* (one volume), and *The Meaning of the Word Hum* (one volume). They were produced through his sincere efforts to try to give convincing answers to various questions he received from those who had read all the sutras he had recommended in that prospectus.

XXV. What Separated Kūkai and Saichō

IN Sakyamuni's Buddhism love is not necessarily considered a noble emotion. What is valued in Buddhism is mercy, the universal spirit that has been extracted and sublimated from love, while love as such is generally rejected, sometimes violently denied, because it is considered to be analogous to voracity, deep-seated delusion or the sexual passion that makes man and woman unite in a firm embrace.

But love is an emotion inherent in humanity. Saichō, who was born richly emotive, must have been endowed with a greater amount of love than is common in ordinary men. But he, as a Buddhist monk, could have no chosen woman to satisfy his instinct. What was more, one of the aims the Buddhist monk was expected to achieve in his life was the purification of that sort of instinct. It was impossible, however, for Saichō—or for anyone else—to put away the great force of love within him as easily and casually as some minor impediment to be shelved for the time being. Then was it not quite possible that he came to find in someone like Taihan an object for his love, even though he himself was not so clearly conscious of it? Was it rather akin to sexual love, that tender emotion and deep attachment Saichō dedicated to Taihan? Or was it genuinely his sense of mission that had made him see in Taihan someone who could not be replaced by any other?

Taihan had been away from Mount Hiei for five years, when on May 1, 816, he received a letter from Saichō, which includes the following:

> I am in my fiftieth year. It will not be long before I depart this life (he had only six years before him, as he then foresaw.) But I regret to say, I cannot tell who will take care of this institute when I am gone. With each one persevering in his own view, there is no peace or friendship to be enjoyed here.

To make matters worse, there were few distinguished scholars on Mount Hiei at that time, as Saichō had occasionally complained in his letters to Taihan. Ennin, who was to become the third patriarch after Gishin[1] and succeeded in making the Tendai religion and Esoteric Buddhism take root, was still only twenty-three years old and had just received the first set of precepts; Enchin, a son of Kūkai's sister or niece, who was finally to fulfill Saichō's wish to reinforce their Tendai religion with Esoteric Buddhism, had just entered his third year at his home in Sanuki. That was why Saichō had to compare himself to a lonely peddler with all his wares on his back.

Recently Saichō had been traveling far and wide. In order to make it clear that his new religion was different from and independent of the old Buddhism in Nara, he had intended to obtain official permission to establish his own ordination platform on Mount Hiei. As this required more supporters, he first traveled around *Kyūshū* with Kanzeon-ji in Tsukushi as his missionary base, and then proceeded east, campaigning in and around Yakushi-ji in Shimotsuke Province. Saichō goes on:

> I never mind wandering around like this, but how I regret that you are no longer with me. Do you remember how we promised each other to devote ourselves to establishing a new Buddhism in this country? Now I am pleased to say that as our Tendai has gained official approval, we are able to have two students every year, while the long series of lectures on the *Hoke-kyō* sutra has become an annual event. Without your help, we could not have enjoyed all these advantages, as we do now. I often recall how we, in the spirit of like-mindedness, received the same baptism at Takaosan-ji, expecting to pursue the same religion and to share the same fruit. How could I imagine then that you would give up your initial intention, so that we were to live apart for so many years? Indeed, this was the last thing I could possibly imagine...though it is only natural that one should take a better one. But in comparing Tendai and Shingon, there is no placing one above the other.

What he mentioned in the last sentence was what he firmly believed all his life, and this was the very point that made Kūkai disagree with Saichō, as will be discussed later. In the closing paragraph Saichō gives his idea of ideal friendship:

The best friends will follow the same path, upholding the same principle, exchanging their loving friendship, until they come to join Maitreya at the end of their life's journey. If we are united by such profound bonds, I should like to walk beside you whether in life or in death, bringing salvation to all the people we come to. Next spring I shall set out on a long journey again. But after that I am going to settle on Mount Hiei and await the end of my days....

The letter was accompanied with ten *kin*[2] of tea, when tea was as precious as gold dust.

Another letter, undated but seemingly sent soon after, sounds even more pathetic because of the closing passage that reads:

Thinking about you, I often have sleepless nights. You are the only friend I have ever had in my cloistered life, even though you have long been away from me for a reason totally unknown and incomprehensible to me. My end is approaching.... Please let me remind you of our noble intention. Please do come back to me so that we may share the sweetest fruit of Buddhism either in joy or in sorrow. Please do come back without delay. Otherwise, you will lose something very important to you. Never, never desert this old man. Anxiously waiting for you,

SAICHŌ

Then he gives abrupt orders in a postscript:

Something of paramount importance has come up. Come straight back this very day. Make no delay.

Undoubtedly Taihan was fascinated by Kūkai. What was it in Kūkai that had attracted him so much? His personality? His principles? To Taihan, both must have been inseparable. In Esoteric Buddhism, what one seeks is to be found in one's own body and in one's own experience, as Kūkai wrote in his letter to Saichō, while one's master is the principle or Mahavairocana itself. Kūkai then, the one and only person in Japan who embodied the principle of Esoteric Buddhism, was to be worshiped by all those who were seeking salvation by Esoteric Buddhism. Taihan, who had been a model ascetic of Esoteric Buddhism under Kūkai for four years, would naturally have made himself a typical worshiper of Kūkai, feeling himself inseparable from his adored master. That adoration may have been transformed into love. But in Esoteric Buddhism, unlike Sakyamuni's Buddhism, love is interpreted as nature itself and is considered to be worthy of the rank of Bodhisattva. Even if Kūkai felt like returning love for love, it would not have contradicted his principle as long as it was taken as a manifestation of the working universe.

What sort of person was Taihan? Considering the unusual eagerness with which Saichō sought after his help, he was obviously a man of ability. But after all he did not turn out to be as talented as Saichō had expected. He achieved nothing outstanding even after he turned to Kūkai. Of all the archives on Kūkai's side, only two entries carry his name: one reports that he was of some help when Kūkai opened Mount Kōya in 816; the other is in the mere list of fifty Shingon priests who were assigned to reside in Tō-ji, a state-owned temple offered to Kūkai in 823 by the Tennō Saga. Had his spirit shriveled when he abandoned Saichō? Or had Saichō made a little too much of him? Or should this be attributed to the influence of a love beyond the categories of logic or reason?

What could Taihan make of Saichō's order to "come straight back this very day"? Morally he was obliged to work out any solution all by himself, however difficult it might be. At least, he should not have told it to Kūkai. It is uncertain whether Taihan always told Kūkai everything that happened to him or Kūkai requested him to do so. The fact was that Taihan then allowed Kūkai to read that letter from Saichō. Kūkai's reaction is quite imaginable, considering what he did after reading it: Kūkai said in disgust, "What nonsense he talks! Now Taihan, you had better break with him, giving the reason why.... But I'm afraid you will find it very difficult because of the many kindnesses you have received from him so far." Then he offered to write for Taihan, and he actually wrote the draft to the embarrassment of his followers of later ages, especially of the Edo Period (1603–1867), who generally took it—as they still do—as vulgar in taste, even though his immediate disciples had simply put it in the collection of his literature,

Shōryō-shū, under the title of *An Answer to a Letter from Priest Saichō*. The letter begins with formal greetings:

> I deeply appreciate the kind admonition I received from you on the first day of this month, which at first gave me the shivers, though it turned out comforting after all. It was extremely generous of you to let me have so much tea. I cannot find proper words to express my great gratitude for it. The rainy season has set in. I do hope this humid heat will not affect your health.

Then he talks about himself: on the ninth he returned from Tajima Province; on his way home he paid a call at Otokuni-dera only to find Saichō who had been staying there had just left for Mt. Hiei; he felt like following him but could not, as he was too tired. Then comes something like a prelude to the main subject:

> I am greatly impressed by your kindness in inviting me to walk together with you whether in life or in death, bringing salvation to all the people we come to by propagating the Tendai religion all over the country. But the noble vision you kindly outlined for me seems simply too good for such an insignificant person as I am. Were I to follow your lead, like a scale on a dragon's tail or like a feather on a phoenix's wing, I should be able to rise even to Heaven's River without any difficulty and drink from the pure stream without doing anything worthy of it. But for me, a humble creature like a mosquito or an earthworm, just receiving such a kind invitation is more than I could wish, although I appreciate it all the same.

Then Taihan (Kūkai) enters into the very core of his answer, referring to what Saichō had written in his letter: "... in comparing Tendai and Shingon, there is no placing one above the other." Kūkai's tone sounds fierce:

> As I know very well, I am so foolish, I cannot tell beans from barley, much less gems from pebbles. But I cannot remain silent when I am told that, in comparing Tendai and Shingon, there is no placing one above the other. I shall be greatly honoured if you will kindly allow me to deliver my humble opinion.

As I have always found, comparing Buddhist teachings is a very hard thing to do. Sakyamuni suited his speech to the person he was then speaking to. As different people have different characters and different intentions, the teachings they receive, like the medicines prescribed by doctors, will be of infinite variety. That is why both Mahayanist Buddhism and Hinayanist Buddhism have good reasons for existence. Likewise the teachings of the one vehicle[3] and the three vehicles[4] are also in emulation of one another, trying to guide people to Buddhist enlightenment. For this reason, it is hard to tell which of the teachings is the real truth or a temporal truth. By the same token, it would not be easy to draw a dividing line between a variety of exoteric religions and Esoteric religion, unless one had mastered all of the Buddhist teachings.

The last sentence implies a question: "Have you mastered all of the Buddhist teachings?" while hinting with proper pride that he himself, having mastered all of them, may be able to distinguish between them, whereas Saichō is unable to do so.

And yet there is a sharp distinction between the real Buddha (the personification of the principle itself: dharmakaya Buddha) and potential Buddhas (everchanging metamorphoses of the real Buddha: nirvanakaya Buddha) who impart approximate truths to people according to their needs. Esoteric Buddhism is founded on the former, exoteric religions like Tendai on the latter. The former offers the teachings of real truth, the latter those of temporal truth. Speaking for myself, I am now enjoying the supreme taste of the former—so much so that I have neither need nor occasion to swallow the cure-alls offered by the latter.

As for the kind invitation to join you in benefiting others, I cannot accept it because I am far from equal to that noble task. For the present, I must train myself in accordance with the precepts so that I can reach the stage in which the six senses[5] of my own body have been freed from any attachment, when I shall finally be able to illuminate others. So I implore you to go on your way without me. I shall be immensely relieved if you will

253

kindly forgive me for not being able to live up to your expectations.

His wording becomes gentle again in the closing paragraph:

> I know very well how you made up your mind to establish the Tendai religion so that you might share your adoration for it with many people. Now I can see how perfectly your noble idea has been realized by the grace of all Buddhas, as the sovereign himself reveres that religion, all the Court officials follow his example, and many others, both clergy and laity, devote themselves fervently to it. Indeed, this is a matter for jubilation and congratulation.

The closing passage that follows, though mildly phrased, consummates his declaration of parting from Saichō:

> As for myself again, I am still lagging behind and I must now diligently apply myself to my practices, day in and day out. So you will be doing me a great favour by simply not blaming me for my maniacal tenacity to embrace Shingon Esoteric Buddhism.
> Even though I confine myself to the mountain, I shall always keep sending you my best wishes.
>
> Your disciple, TAIHAN

This single letter did separate Taihan and Saichō. Saichō, who could easily tell who drafted this letter, would have taken it as Kūkai's declaration that he wished to put an end to their relationship, too.

This incident drove Saichō to sectarianism. In order to prevent the drain of his disciples, he dictated regulations and conventions, which were to turn Mount Hiei into a high-walled religious fortress. The Buddhist denominations Saichō and Kūkai had encountered in both China and Japan had been practically free from any sectarianism, because different denominations simply signified the different systems they offered. Temple doors wide open, priests were free to come and learn any systems they liked and as many systems as they pleased. But Saichō's enclosure of his institute on Mt.

Hiei was to start a new tradition of sectarianism as we see it today. Thus Taihan, though he remained obscure all his life, was by no means an insignificant figure in the history of Japan's Buddhist denominations.

XXVI. CALLIGRAPHY

K AMITSUKASA Kaiun, an elder priest of Tōdai-ji recently died. It was from him I learned that the *Rishu-kyō* sutra is still being recited every morning and every evening before the Giant Buddha or Virocana as the overriding symbol of the Kegon world. I still remember the astonishment with which I learned of this unmistakable trace that Kūkai had left at Tōdai-ji, an astonishment even more intensified by the casual tone in which he talked about it, as if Kūkai were still there, sitting beside him, allowing me to hear his breathing through that telephone line.

On a cold day in mid-February, his funeral was held at the headquarter temple of Tōdai-ji. The portrait of the deceased was placed between a couple of vases holding sprigs of *ume* with white starry blossoms just beginning to bloom. The hall was packed with attendants quietly seated in serried ranks, when the chanting of the *Rishu-kyō* sutra began to permeate the air like audible incense. When it flooded every corner of the hall, I keenly recalled how the deceased priest answered my questions on the telephone.

After the service was over, the attendants walked out into Nara Park, where miniature snow storms occurred here and there even when the sky above was clear and blue—a strange phenomenon often seen in Nara in winter. The person I soon fell into company with was an avant-garde calligrapher, Sakaki Bakuzan, who just began to talk about Kūkai's calligraphy, making a comment I felt very interesting.

"His brushwork is very photogenic."

We had been friends for about twenty years but had seen nothing of each other for about five years. Then was this meeting of ours not the Reverend Kamitsukasa Kaiun's post-mortem kindness to us? The calligrapher went on:

"Some women photograph very well, you know. The same thing happens in Kūkai's calligraphy. This is especially the case with *Fūshin-jō*,[1] I think. Another thing I have noticed about his handwriting is that his, unlike

256

Saichō's, is very hard to define because of the infinite variety of types and styles he adopted each time he took up his brush."

The last mentioned was what had long been pointed out by many. But when I heard it mentioned by the professional, it seemed to assume a new meaning, incidentally leading me to the idea that it would be impossible for anyone to define Kūkai from his calligraphy—or from any other field of his activity.

*   *   *

Since the Nara Period (710–784), the Japanese have been writing after the style of a Chinese calligrapher, Wang Xizhi (307–365). Nobly born, Xizhi followed his career as a high official of the Eastern Jin Dynasty established in Jiankang (present-day Nanjing) and spent most of his retired life amid the beautiful nature of Mt. Guiji. His life, which might have been regarded by Taoists as approaching the ideal, must have contributed to making his calligraphy famous for its refined quality—elegant and exquisite, properly tinged with delicate variations, decorous and clear, but accented with a touch of melancholy. Indeed, it presents a perfect example of what calligraphy should be. But what if one sees it as a work of art, rather than as a mere means of communication or recording, expecting to find in it something specifically artistic? One might feel a sort of deprecation akin to the envy one might feel for something totally free from any fault.

Wang Xizhi lived long enough to see himself recognized as an authority on calligraphy. Then three centuries later, the Second Emperor Taizong (reign: 626–649) of the Tang Dynasty, became obsessed by Wang Xizhi and collected as many as three thousand pieces of his brushwork. To the Emperor, who did not think much of the foreign elements in the culture of the Northern Dynasties, Wang Xizhi's calligraphy must have seemed to represent or symbolize the refined culture of the Southern Dynasties which he appreciated as a legitimate inheritance from Chinese culture. Thus the personal taste of that Emperor was accepted by the Japanese in the Nara Period. This may provide a typical example of how things Chinese, political and cultural, were being accepted by the peoples in lands around China.

* * *

In June 7, 812, Kūkai presented the Tennō Saga with four writing brushes, as he had been requested to do so. Three of them were for three different types of writing—block script, semi-cursive script and cursive script—and the fourth was for sutra-copying. Then, requested by the Crown Prince, Kūkai made another set of brushes and presented it to him, too. In the letters he wrote to them on those occasions, Kūkai points out the importance of using a good brush:

> As good craftsmen give priority to improving their skills, good calligraphers make a point of using a good brush.

Then he stresses the need to change brushes in accordance with what one is writing—seal script, scribe's script,[2] block script, semi-cursive script or cursive script.[3] Pernickety as this may sound, it reveals his habit of mind: whatever he might do, he did it not on the spur of the moment, but according to a principle he had invented or developed himself, and if necessary, by using tools of his own making.

In producing the brushes he presented to the Tennō and the Crown Prince, Kūkai taught professional brush-makers—Sakanai no Kiyokawa for the Tennō's and Tsukinomoto no Koizumi for the Crown Prince's—how to make them, and directed the work all the time, as he wrote in the same letters. This might be taken as yet another example in confirmation of his versatility. But it seems to me that such conduct was also consistent with his thought as an Esoteric Buddhist.

Another thing that needs some consideration is that those brushes were made of racoon dog's bristles. Writing brushes that had been used in Japan so far were exclusively either of sheep's wool or of hare's fur, as was made clear by the historical scientist Kuroita Katsumi (1874–1946) by examining all the brushes that had been preserved in the Shōsō-in Treasure House of Tōdai-ji. Those soft brushes were obviously suited for writing Wang Xizhi's style, whereas the hard brushes made of racoon dog's bristles might have been suited for writing a different style, such as Yan Zhenqing's. So I imagine that, before presenting the new type of brushes, Kūkai had informed

Saga of a new calligraphic trend in China, saying: "Wang Xizhi is no longer unrivaled, now that we have Yan Zhenqing, as great as Wang Xizhi."

In fact, Kūkai's appraisal of Wang Xizhi was made explicit in the letter he sent to Saga on August 15, 816, along with the requested calligraphic work he had done on a brocaded screen: "Wang Xizhi practised so hard, so long, but there is still something lacking in his calligraphy."

Unlike Wang Xizhi who belonged to the distant past, Yan Zhenqing (709–785) could roughly be regarded as a contemporary. A native of Chang'an, he entered the government service in his twenties. In 755 when An Lushan rose in revolt, he who had been a civilian provincial governor organized a patriotic army and fought many a battle. This persuaded other provincial governors to follow his example. It proved to be very helpful to the Tang Dynasty which was trying hard to seize a chance of victory. Naturally he received exceptional promotion when he returned to the capital after the revolt was quelled. But he had to suffer the envious opposition of certain powerful courtiers, and as a consequence had to be demoted again and again. In the end, he was sent to Huaixi by his political opponents on the pretext of dissuading its governor from revolting against the central government. No sooner had this honest man reached there than he was trapped only to be put to death after three years' imprisonment, to the great regret of the Emperor Dezong, who gratefully conferred on him the posthumous name of Zhong-Lie (Intense Loyalty).

As a calligrapher, Zhenquing, a member of the Yan family that had been producing many great calligraphers for several generations, established his own style of virile strength, in reaction against Wang Xizhi's style that tended to favor superficial beauty. Because of the striking contrast between them, they began to be called by contrasting appellations: "the southern copy-book style" for Wang Xizhi and "the northern monument style" for Yan Zhenqing, not that the latter was from the north but that he was greatly influenced by the calligraphy seen on many of the stone monuments carved by northerners.

In writing in Yan's style, one must use one's arm, with the elbow spreading out, the brush pressing the paper at right angles. Yan's style, best demonstrated in the writing of large-sized block script, has been described thus: "The dot (、) looks like a falling stone, the line (一) summer clouds, the hook (亅) a bent metal bar, the halberd (戈) a huge bow drawn to its full extent." In performing such vigorous brushwork, Chinese calligraphers would have chosen a hard brush of racoon dog bristles. It seems, however, that nobody in Japan had ever heard of Yan's style until it was introduced by Kūkai. In Chang'an he would have seen much of Yan's calligraphy. At least, he would have had ample opportunities to acquaint himself with Yan's style because many people were learning that style even though Liu Gongquan, who was soon to be known as a master of Yan's style, had not yet come to the forefront.

In Japan, Saga would naturally have been impressed by Kūkai's having mastered that style, which may have persuaded Kūkai to make use of it in changing something in the current of the times. Kūkai, who was going to propagate a new religion in this country, had naturally been aware of the need to renew all her former spiritual and cultural climate by inspiring her with the refreshing sense that a new era had started. As calligraphy was the base of all spiritual culture in China and her satellite countries, creating a new situation in calligraphy—by bringing in Yan's style—was to become very important to him. Perhaps Kūkai recommended Yan's style to Saga who had a tremendous influence upon patrician society in Japan, even though Kūkai himself was not so clearly conscious of his political intent, as he himself was not whole-heartedly devoted to Yan and was not actually intending to defy the authority of Wang. He was acting, probably by instinct, according to a motto he seems to have been born with: "Things are always changing, so do not stick to one thing only: just perform the right action at the right time; do the right thing in the right place; offer the right person the right thing."

Kūkai's calligraphy itself seems to have been created in accordance with these precepts. He adopted different modes of writing for different persons he wrote to; for example, in writing to Saichō, his calligraphy was largely in Wang's style. Kūkai's letters to Saichō must have amounted to a large number, but only three remain, preserved under the title of *Fūshin-jō*. As for the style, different people offer more or less different opinions. But as a whole, many agree that it tends toward Wang's. Another manuscript Kūkai left is *Kanjō-ki* (a list of those who received *abhiseka* baptisms from him at

Takaosan-ji in 812 and 813). As it was just a personal memorandum, he wrote very casually. The style is unmistakably Yan's. Then what was it that made Kūkai choose Wang's style when writing to Saichō? Probably it was his knowledge that Saichō was master of that style, though I do not think that Kūkai intended to demonstrate his ability in writing that style. Whatever the reasons were, *Fūshin-jō* does allow us to imagine that Kūkai changed his mode of writing according to whom he wrote to. If Saichō had noticed this fact, the good-natured person would not have dreamed of using it as an excuse to discuss Kūkai's personality.

The following is a legend about Saichō as a calligrapher:

> When Saichō was in China—on Mt. Tiantai or in Yuezhou or Mingzhou—he happened to meet a priest-calligrapher named Huaisu, the greatest master of cursive script that Tang China had ever produced. According to his *Autobiography*, he met Yan Zhenqing in 777 when he was in Luoyang. Now Huaisu, amazed at a fine handwriting Saichō had produced, asked him what was the secret of his handwriting. Saichō, who was extremely modest and reluctant to show off his talent, shook his head calmly and said: "I just see to it that I do not make a wrong stroke."

Saichō really meant what he said. To his mind, calligraphy was not art but a mere means of communication. Never had he dreamt of using it as a means of self-demonstration. True to his word, he was simply mindful not to make any wrong stroke in his writing. That was probably why he seems to have spent much time even on a short letter. The elegant serenity we perceive in his calligraphy may be attributed to this utmost sincerity with which he wrote.

Saichō's calligraphy never changed, as is seen in *Nittō-chō* (the copy of the official document for allowing him to go to Tang China), *The List of the Items introduced from Yuezhou*, a copy of *The List of the Items Introduced from China* by Kūkai, *Kyūkaku-jō* (Saichō's letters to Taihan), *The List of Karma-vajra-sticks*, and *Tendai Hokke Nenbun Engi* (the record of how the Tendai religion had its annual ordination started). It is gracefulness itself, and even just to gaze upon it makes us feel as if our soul were being cleansed by it. Certainly, his style was undeviatingly Wang's. But having been so firmly established and having developed far beyond the stage of imitation, it could rightly be called his own style, one that reflected his own personality. In China Saichō would have seen Yan's style being eagerly adopted by many. If he met Huaisu, as the above-mentioned story goes, he would have heard of Yan Zhenqing and probably seen Huaisu's own calligraphy best known for "the wildest cursive style" he had created. But whatever he might have come across in China, he just went on keeping to Wang's or his own style. To such a devotee of Wang Xizhi, Kūkai chose to write in Wang's style, occasionally bringing in Yan's, as we see in *Fūshin-jō*. The contrast we see in it—sporadic strong strokes of Yan's style seen in the fluent flow of Wang's—does produce a brilliant beauty as if the diffused reflection of light were flooding all over it.

On the other hand, *Kyūkaku-jō*—Saichō's letter to Taihan, dated November 25, 813—is honesty itself. Saichō had recently received from Kūkai a poem celebrating his own fortieth birthday.[4] He naturally wished to compose a poem in reply, but he would not do so until he had understood everything written there:

> I have not heard from you for a long time, despite my unceasing longing for you. So it was some comfort for me to hear that you had been doing well all this while. Now I should be very pleased if you will kindly do something for me. I have recently received a poem which the Great Master (Kūkai) himself wrote in commemoration of his having reached his fortieth year. I appreciate that poem, but not fully, because I cannot understand what he meant by what he had written in the prelude: 一百廿礼仏 竝方円図竝註義.[5] Please ask him what it means and let me know. Otherwise, I cannot make a reply in verse. Errors once made in writing will never be corrected. I shall be very grateful if you will kindly help me.

His calligraphy, quite suitable to the contents, honest and modest exactly as he was, does make us feel as if he were seated here, his head bent over this letter. Even after the death of the Tennō Kammu, the Court remained reverent to Saichō. But he was too busy to keep in close contact with them. Fighting alone against the old Buddhism in Nara, he had to teach and train his disciples by himself, while trying to establish his religion alone, and making solitary missionary tours around the country.

On the other hand, Kūkai was free from any such difficulties or sorrows in the latter half of his life even though in the first half he was a lonely beggar as was described in *The Indications of the Three Teachings*. Kūkai now had won the Tennō Saga as his patron; he never thought of paying court to him but the Tennō himself tried to please him. It was almost touching how Saga idolized Kūkai even though he himself was always treated by Kūkai as inferior, or at best, as an equal.

In spring, 814, Saga sent to Kūkai a poem as the season's greetings together with one hundred bundles of cotton. Cotton was very precious in those days. According to an official record, "three hundred rolls of cotton" was among the items Japan presented in 759 to the envoy from Bohai. Then the one hundred bundles of cotton Kūkai had received must have made an extravagant gift even if the presenter was the Tennō. The poem Saga sent to Kūkai on that occasion may suggest the nature of their friendship:

> My respected priest has long been living
> upon the lofty summit muffled in clouds.
> Viewing it from afar, I suppose the spring
> up there is still being gripped with cold.
> Befriended by pines and oaks of profound
> silence or dining on smoky mist for years,
> he has recently forgotten to write to me.
> Here in the capital, flowers and willows
> are budding. I pray that my Bodhisattva
> may not frown at this small gift but save
> its sender and his people from misfortunes.

The following poem also by Saga is undated but presumably was made when their friendship was well ripened:

We have been following different paths for years.
But on this autumnal day, we have had a happy reunion,
talking over many a cup of fragrant tea until at last
we have to pause and watch the day fading.
After a profound bow of sad parting,
I gaze upon the smoky cloud
that blurs my sight.

Saga's calligraphy was greatly influenced by Kūkai's. As is typically seen in *Kōjō Kaichō* (the certificate of Saichō's disciple Kōjō's having received the precepts) which is considered to be of his own writing, Saga has already got over the classical respectability of Wang Xizhi and acquired the complete freedom Kūkai showed in his *Fūshin-jō*, relaxing elegantly, occasionally taking a pleasant turn into vigorous virility, thus making the whole sheet as impressive as if it were a sort of visible music.

At one time, Saga decided to renew all the tablets hung on the gates of the Imperial Palace. The Palace itself having been there only for a quarter century, all the tablets still appeared fairly presentable, with characters on them quite clear. But in the eyes of Saga, the calligraphy itself might have seemed far from satisfactory. Then he chose two calligraphers—Kūkai and Tachibana no Hayanari—to help him with this task. This does indicate how Saga was enjoying their company. According to *The Record of the Kampyō Era*,[6] Saga wrote on the six tablets for the three gates in the eastern wall and in the western wall respectively; Kūkai on the four tablets for the three gates in the southern wall (the front wall) and for the Ōten-mon gate (the central gate in the inner front wall); Tachibana no Hayanari on the three tablets for the three gates in the northern wall. "*San-pitsu* (the Calligraphic Trio)"—the nickname by which they were later called to share the immortal fame—must have originated from this calligraphic event they joined in on that occasion.

Tachibana no Hayanari, a cousin of Saga's first consort Kachiko, remained low and obscure all his life, partly because he was a most difficult person to work with, and partly because almost all the important posts at Court were occupied by the Fujiwaras. All that is known about his official career is that two years before his death he was appointed as the Supernumerary Provincial Governor of Tajima Province with the junior grade of the fifth court rank. Who could believe that in Chang'an he used to be called "Ju, the talented"? Kūkai remained his constant friend, as may be imagined by the fact that Hayanari was invited by Saga for the calligraphic event mentioned above. Indeed, why Hayanari who was recorded as "a dare devil at Court" should have been treated as an important member only in Saga's salon was probably because he had been unfailingly befriended by Kūkai, though of course his talent itself was far from mediocre.

Of "the Calligraphic Trio," Hayanari lived longest. Kūkai died in 835, followed by Saga five years later. Only a couple of months after Saga's death, a plot was discovered at Court. Hayanari was involved in it and was sentenced to exile to Izu Province, though he died of illness on his way there. Hayanari had a daughter, who followed her father as he was being carried in a cage; she never deserted him even after he died. When the men in charge scolded her, she disappeared, but when night fell, she came back and watched over the cage with his body in it, until one day she went to a nunnery and became a nun. Only the death of Saga could have occasioned such grief in Hayanari and his daughter.

*   *   *

The only tribute I can think of in paying Kūkai's calligraphy is "brilliant." Shinzei, a compiler of *Shōryō-shū*, the collection of Kūkai's literature, has given in its preface a crisp description of his master:

> Heaven favoured our master by equipping him with a variety of
> artistic talents.

Shinzei observes that of all his accomplishments in the arts he was most proficient in calligraphy, especially in "grass hand," whose inspired wildness would surely make him "the master of masters of grass hand." Legend has it that while in China he learned calligraphy under Han Fangming. But this seems improbable, considering how many things he had to do in such a short period of time when he was there. Kūkai himself has never mentioned Han Fangming in any of his writings. The only entry he wrote about how he learned calligraphy in China is found in the letter he sent to Saga on August 15, 816: "I happened to meet a good teacher of calligraphy, who kindly instructed me on the vital points in handwriting." Probably this was actually how he learned it. But somehow or other he became the only Japanese who possessed a free, bold hand in all types of writing. He wrote a large hand, too, when all others were writing only in small size.

As for his own idea about calligraphy, he wrote in the same letter:

> As ancient calligraphers said, calligraphy is an art of self-dispersion. That is to say, the secret of calligraphy is to give oneself to nature, heart and soul, thus to liberate oneself fully so that one may imbue one's strokes with what one sees in nature. Correctness is not everything. What is imperative is to concentrate one's attention upon things in nature, to give one's whole self to them, and then to let your strokes go and grasp seasonal scenes or objects, letting each character you are making assume a form one has caught in nature.

Then he cites two calligraphers to illustrate this statement:

> Wang Xizhi once made an excursion up to Mt. Tiantai. While travelling around Lake Dongting on his way home on Mt. Guiji, he was invited by someone to adorn a pillar in his mansion with some calligraphy. His mind then having been intensely filled with an image of a flying dragon with its claws tearing at the air, the character he made—飛 (flight)—did take on a superb form— the claws of a dragon taking its vigorous flight from the lake.

> Tang Zong who lived in the land of Lu once had a dream in which he was being caught in the coils of a serpent. On waking up, he just took up his brush and produced the fine character of 蛇 (serpent).

Kūkai's comment on these episodes is: "Both of them, strongly impressed by something from nature, were inspired to produce a masterstroke."

The same thing can be said about Kūkai and his calligraphy which was an outcome of the profound admiration he felt in the nature he had around him. In the end, Kūkai's calligraphy does not belong in any category. This may be attributed to what he was born with. But to my mind it is closely connected with his Esoteric Buddhism that detects infinite divinity in nature itself: nature's essence and principle and function are all represented by Mahavairocana, which is numerically zero but contains all things that exist in the universe; and unifying oneself, just as one is, with that zero is fulfilling the ultimate aim of Esoteric Buddhism: the attaining of enlightenment in this very existence. If he had already attained that level or the Buddhahood of Mahavairocana, as he declared he had done, it would be inconsistent if he were to hold on to Wang's style or anyone else's. Indeed, the style he adopted according to whom he wrote and what he wrote were so infinitely varied that it would naturally follow that defining his calligraphy is practically impossible, as Mr. Sakaki told me the other day. But this, I now realize, will best prove that he had been living up to his own religion even to the peak of perfection.

Kūkai's calligraphy is said to accommodate his own spirit. Even if he himself cannot be found anywhere in his calligraphy because of its ever-changing nature, still his brushwork gives a trace of his spirit carried within it. That may be the most appropriate way for him to present himself. Conversely, when I imagine what he was through his calligraphy, I should say that Kūkai was so perfectly suited to the thought of Esoteric Buddhism that he could not possibly make himself anything but the incarnation of that thought. If his calligraphy really carries his spirit, that will be the one and only entity that makes the essence of Kūkai.

XXVII. How Mount Kōya Started

O NE summer in the middle of the Pacific War (1941–45), I traveled on foot with two friends of mine. As we were told that we students would also be sent to the front before long, this hiking, we thought, would be the last opportunity for us to be able to enjoy any freedom. We planned to start from Yoshino and cross the mountain mass of Kumano to reach Cape Shio-no-misaki at the tip of the Kii Peninsula to enjoy a commanding view of the ocean.

Starting from a small railroad station of Shimoichi where we gathered, we soon found ourselves in a mountain forest. One of my companions was carrying a short sword with him "in case we are attacked by bears," which was always the subject of joking remarks every time we recalled it later.

At first we walked in the daytime and slept at night. But soon the unbearable heat in the daytime made us hit on the notion of making a nocturnal march in a starlight and sleeping in the daytime at a small Shintō or Buddhist shrine, or at a vacant charcoal burners' hut. This shift, as we soon found, was much better and less tiring. None of us carried any map to guide us. Commodities had already been scarce and no map was on sale, I suppose. But we did not mind, as we believed that we should surely come to the land's end as long as we were proceeding south.

We passed Kurotaki Village on a dark night. From Tenkawa Village we walked up along the Ten-no-kawa river for a few nights until we came to Ōtō Village, where we were fortunate enough to have a day's lodging at a Buddhist temple. Then we resumed our way along the river, expecting to reach the Totsu River. As it was, we were following a wrong stream, which became narrower, and the paralleled path gave way to an animal trail lined with shrubbery. It was an extremely hard climb but we had no other idea but going on and on. Then all of a sudden, a sight of a lighted town popped into our eyes. Were we bewitched? Feeling as if in a dream, we hobbled up to a lighted window under the low eaves of a building and asked where we were.

To our astonishment, we were told we were on Kōya-san (Mount Kōya), a religious town Kūkai started on top of Mt. Kōya. I now realize that that astonishment I felt then at the entrance to Kōya-san was the dawn of my interest in Kūkai, which, thirty years later, makes me follow his trail like this.

* * *

Mt. Kōya in Kūkai's days, hidden under the sea of foliage that drowned the Kii Peninsula, remained unknown even to the local hunters. Then those who informed Kūkai of Mt. Kōya as "a singular mountain deep in the Province of Kii" would have been mercury miners who called themselves Niu after the place name Niu, which means "where cinnabar comes from." The sulfurated mercury or cinnabar they produced was used in a variety of ways. During the Tumulus Period, it was packed into coffins as an antiseptic. In the ensuing era during which Kūkai lived, it was in great demand not only for the painting of temple buildings, official buildings and palaces and mansions for the wealthy and powerful, but also for the production of lacquer ware, pigment and stamp ink.

There are several kinds of legends that tell how Kūkai came to know Mt. Kōya. According to *The Memoirs of Our Master*, Kūkai once climbed this mountain, when Niutsu-hime-no-mikoto, the guardian goddess of mercury miners, took possession of a local Shintō priest and gave an oracle to Kūkai: "I have long been waiting for a Bodhisattva like you. Now that you are here, you shall have this mountain." In a practical context, it may have been that the native mountain folk told Kūkai where Mt. Kōya was and allowed him to take possession of it.

The Record of How Kongōbu-ji Was Brought into Being gives a story that preceded the story above:

> One day in summer in the seventh year of Kōnin (816), Kūkai was travelling across Uchi County in the Province of Yamato, when he met a hunter accompanied by a couple of dogs, a white one and a black one. Unlike any other hunters he saw in the neighbourhood, he was red-faced, eight feet tall, clad in blue, with a huge bow in his hand. Impressed by his appearance, Kūkai

asked him who he was. The hunter said: "I am Inukai (Dog Keeper) living in Nan-zan (Southern Mountains). Among the numerous mountains I possess, there is a very singular mountain; its lofty peak, flat and spacious, does provide a place of perfect quietude and frequent auspicious signs."

The man disappeared before Kūkai made any response. That night Kūkai took a night's lodging at a Niu family living in a village named Kudoyama[1] by the Yoshino River. When he told his host about a strange hunter he met that day and "a very singular mountain" he talked about, Mr. Niu said: "I believe he was talking about Mt. Takano (Kōya). Certainly it has a flat peak with streams of ample water all running eastward. In the daytime it is wrapped up in towering clouds of unusual beauty; at night it is illuminated with mysterious lights."

The next day Kūkai was on his way to that mountain, when he met a Shintō priest and received a message from Niutsu-hime-no-mikoto, as mentioned before.

Certainly these are mere legends. But considering Kūkai's situation at that time, it is quite probable that he who had long planned to build a religious center of his own was searching for a mountain whose top was flat and spacious enough to accommodate such an institute.

Mt. Kōya he was allowed to possess in 816 by the Tennō Saga was certainly very notable for the flat plain that crowned it. Shin'ei, one of the disciples who first surveyed this mountain on Kūkai's orders, aptly described the place: "Vast was the land that stretched before our eyes. It could be the seat for a county," as is recorded in *The Honourable Life of Kōya Daishi*.

"What was it that made Kūkai build such a religious town like this up here?"

I, a student hiker who had just scrambled up the thorny mountainside to find myself quite unexpectedly on the edge of the elevated town of Kōya-san, could not help repeating this question to myself while walking along the lighted streets in the town. My knowledge of Kūkai was so limited at that time, I was happily able to give full rein to my imagination, which is now sadly impeded by all those scraps of information I have collected. The sight of the towering gate that marked the western end of this town—the two-storied structure whose tiled roofs were glimmering in bluish sulfurated silver against the night sky—did induce me to imagine that: when it was new with all those pillars shining in cinnabar red, it would have looked exactly like the Chunming-men gate through which Kūkai entered the Chinese capital of Chang'an; what was seen inside the gate—a wide street lined with fine buildings—would have also been similar to what Kūkai had seen in Chang'an.

This idea of mine had obviously been prompted by a newly published book I was then reading with great relish—*Spring in Chang'an*. Having read it over and over again, poring over the map it contained, I could almost see the streets in Chang'an ringing with the busy traffic, especially the streets in and around the Qinren-fang block where An Lushan used to have his residence or the Jing'an-fang block where a poet official Han Yu (788–824) was living. In other words, I was feeling as if I had always been there, and this made me feel as if I could tell what Kūkai back in Japan was feeling: "He missed Chang'an—so much so that he hit on the idea of building his own Chang'an on top of Mt. Kōya and tried to realize it...."

We can imagine how Kūkai, lying leisurely in his hermitage on Mt. Kōya, was gazing upon the shining rain of early summer gently washing the brightly-painted buildings, occasionally feeling as if he were back in Chang'an again. This would not detract from the grandeur of his thought. Nor would it detract from the charm of his personality even if the idea of having such a religious town had been motivated by his own personal pleasure at having a replica of the Chang'an he loved. Rather it would help illustrate the greatness of Kūkai who still remains unparalleled in the cultural history of Japan—a greatness that seems to have been manifested best in the ease or in the pleasure with which he produced the fruits of his versatility.

Gratified by this idea of mine, I confided it to a steward priest who had been taking care of us at a temple inn where we were allowed to stay for the rest of the night:

"... So I think O-Daishi-san was taking a great pleasure in bringing Kōya-san into being. Don't you think so?"

271

The priest, who had been sipping *sake* (rice wine) in great good humor, suddenly put on a stern expression and warned me, to my horrified amusement: "You should be more careful in talking about O-Daishi-san, if you wish to return safe from the front."

But I could not dismiss this idea as if it were a puff of red smoke blown into my brain.

Certainly Kūkai back in Japan was extremely busy. Believing himself a reincarnation of Amoghavajra, Kūkai would have naturally pondered over the life of Amoghavajra, intending to lead the same kind of life as he did, a non-Chinese who dedicated himself to the transplantation of Esoteric Buddhism in the soil of China, while doing everything he could in his attempt to protect the state or to introduce Mahavairocana's Land there. Kūkai, whose rich culture and intellect had made him feel at home in Chang'an, had to feel in Japan as if he were an alien. Then, even before returning to Japan, he would have been prepared to accept his fate to go on staying in Japan, doing everything he could to introduce Mahavairocana's Land there.

In fact, what Kūkai did in the latter half of his life or after he returned home was so varied and so thoroughgoing that it seems as if he had established the most important part of Japanese culture all by himself. As a thinker he produced over fifty volumes of writings, including *The Ten Stages of the Development of Human Mind* (ten volumes) and its sister version of *The Precious Key to the Secret Treasury* (three volumes), Japan's first great books of philosophical thought. As a religionist, he organized the order of his Shingon religion, though this was not necessarily what he intended for the reason to be mentioned in the final chapter. As an artist, he produced, or taught others how to produce, a large number of things indispensable to his religion, such as paintings, sculptures, architectures and a variety of ritual objects, while laying down detailed rules in the making of them. As an educator, he founded in the capital Shugei-Shuchi-in,* a university open to the common folk, the first of this kind in Japan. As a man of literature, he wrote *An Introduction to Literature* (six volumes), inviting more people to make poetry and prose, thus exerting considerable influence on a Japanese literature still in its germinal stage. He also brought out thirty volumes of

Ten Rei Banshō Meigi, the first dictionary Japan had ever had. As a civil engineer, he built a dam for Mannō-ike reservoir in Sanuki Province; he contributed to the completion of Masuda-ike reservoir in Yamato Province, too, though he had no time to come down to direct the construction. Even if I left out the popular belief that he invented *kata-kana* (the Japanese phonetic syllabary) and *hira-gana* (another kind of syllabary),[2] what Kūkai did during the latter half of his sixty-two year life was almost super-human both in quality and in quantity.

Even though these things kept him unusually busy, the loneliness he must have felt in Japan might have remained unrelieved. In Chang'an, where the Tang culture had reached its full maturity, Kūkai was always surrounded by those whose intelligence and intellectual curiosity were of about the same level as his own. Widely and highly reputed, he had many others who had come over to make friends with him. If one of the pleasures in life is to keep company with those whose intellectual level is as high as one's own, Kūkai in Japan was sadly deprived of this pleasure. Japan in Kūkai's days, except for a very limited section of the capital, was still very backward and impossible to be compared to China. Literature, for example, was still in an embryonic stage, and that was why Kūkai had to write *An Introduction to Literature*. A modest group of literati in the Court could not possibly be compared with such fine coteries as Kūkai used to know in Chang'an. Even the Tennō Saga who represented Japan's intellectuals always remained his student, instead of being a friend who would supply him with intellectual pleasure and excitement.

* * *

In 816, when Kūkai was forty-three, he presented a memorial to Saga, asking for the possession of Mt. Kōya. The following entry in the memorial may suggest when and how he came to know that mountain:

In my boyhood I was very fond of ranging over mountains, and ...

Kūkai in his youth may have found himself on top of Mt. Kōya. He seems to have taken almost the same route as we three happened to take on

273

that summer excursion:

> ... Starting from Yoshino, one day's southerly hiking and two
> days' westerly plodding brought me to a secluded highland, aptly
> named Kōya (Elevated Plain), located south of Ito County in the
> Province of Kii.

As for the mountain itself, he says:

> It commands lofty peaks all around; no beaten tracks lead to the
> top.

Then he explains why he needed that mountain:

> It is deeply regrettable that in Japan very few could achieve
> emancipation through the practice of meditative concentration.
> The reason was because there was no proper monastery suited to
> it on the lofty peak of a secluded mountain.

As to the merits of the lofty peak of a secluded mountain, they are
propounded as follows:

> The clouds and rain that accumulate on high mountains are
> beneficial to vegetation there, while the abundant water there
> attracts fishes and dragons. Likewise, Mt. Grdhrakuta in India
> (where Sakyamuni often preached) preserves the everlasting
> grace of Sakyamuni, and Mt. Potalaka on the southern coast of
> India is known for the marvelous efficacies of Kannon
> Bodhisattva. Those mountains are so made from the very
> beginning to serve such sacred purposes. In China, too, they have
> such mountains as Mt. Wutai always visited by a host of
> meditators and Mt. Tiantai ever crowded with contemplative
> ascetics. They are all national treasures, since they provide
> people with precious bridges to emancipation.

These references to the sacred mountains in India and China may suggest
where his idea of Mount Kōya came from. But considering the way of
writing of his days, he had to draw on classics or historical events, giving
impressive illustrations in pairs, if he intended to compose a stately

memorial to the Tennō. In persuading the Japanese Court to help, nothing would have been more effective than presenting the exemplars of India and China. On the other hand, Saichō's Mount Hiei might have provided a precedent. Most probably Kūkai, having started his career as a mountain ascetic, would have naturally been led to an idea of having a mountain monastery so that his disciples and followers might have a proper place to pursue the first tenet of Esoteric Buddhism: attaining Buddhahood in this very existence.

But considering the overflowing richness of his sensibility, it does not seem wholly correct to think he wanted Mt. Kōya to emulate Mt. Tiantai, Mt. Wutai or Mt. Hiei. That is why I still prefer to imagine that Kōya-san on Mt. Kōya would be a replica of Chang'an which Kūkai built on that mountain not only to provide a seat for his religion that would appeal to anyone who lives at any time in history and in any place in the world, but also to appease his undying longing for Chang'an as a truly international metropolis.

As it was, Kūkai did not live to see even one hundredth of what Mount Kōya was when it was completed in the sixteenth century. His appeal for the possession of Mt. Kōya was granted in the same year (816). Nineteen years remained before his death. But the progress in building a monastery was very slow. As it was a private institute, he could not expect even one *sen*[3] from the national treasury. This made him turn to the powerful and wealthy in the capital. But since agricultural productivity at that time was still very low, even the most influential Fujiwara clan could not possibly be called plutocratic. Then all that he could realize on Mt. Kōya would have been only a tiny fraction of what he had had in mind whether it had been a Japanese version of Mount Tiantai or of Mount Wutai.

Those who proved to be of the greatest help to Kūkai were not the distinguished few in the capital but the unknown local powers in the vicinity of Mt. Kōya in Kii Province, as is known by many letters he sent to them, asking for contributions or acknowledging what help he had received from them. In one of those letters, which are included in *Kōya Zappitsu-shū*, Kūkai reminds Ōtomo *uji* in Kii Province, of their common ancestry by referring to the Ōtomo clan in the capital:

... Let me invite you to help me for kinship's sake. I shall be very, very pleased if you layman will thoughtfully cooperate with us in upholding Buddhism....

There is a pathetic letter sent to an unidentified person:

... Having no nails, carpenters cannot go on with their work. We shall be very grateful if you will kindly send us some nails as soon as possible....

In another letter he thankfully wrote:

... We greatly appreciate your kindness in sending us so much rice and oil, which literally made us jump for joy....

Food was very scarce, as may be imagined by what he wrote in another letter:

... It is very hard to supply food for so many people working here....

Kūkai in his lifetime had not yet gained the fame as he was to enjoy in ages to come. Otherwise, he could have easily collected whatever funds he needed. At least, the powerful and the wealthy in the capital would have vied with each other in backing him up. What made Kūkai turn almost exclusively to the provincial clans was not necessarily his people-oriented thought, but probably the fact that they were the only people he could ask for help by addressing them as follows:

Each of you shall help us with one *sen* and one grain of rice....
The merit of such deeds done by parents will endure and expand
to all the generations that follow them.

Building a private temple in this way was unheard of in those days. But this persistent appeal Kūkai made to gain "one *sen* and one grain of rice" did much in bringing Mount Kōya and common people closer together, thus eventually forming the distinct character of Mount Kōya as sharply contrasted to that of Saichō's Mount Hiei, which was a national institute from the very beginning and was destined to remain more or less aloof from the common folk. As for this contrast between Mount Hiei and Mount Kōya, the thoughts of the founders—Tendai and Shingon—should be taken into consideration, and the missionary activities of Kōya *hijiri** itinerant monks in later ages should not be overlooked. But it was what Kūkai did for the genesis of Mount Kōya that must have been most decisive in molding its character.

XXVIII. Consummating His Thought and Action

IN 818 the bank of Mannō-ike reservoir in Sanuki Province was broken, inflicting serious damage on the fields and villages below. The provincial administrator tried hard to mend it, but without success, even after spending three years on it, since the bank was completely washed away every time the rainy season came round. The only possible way to deal with this situation was to rely upon "the honourable Bodhisattva" who had come from Tado County. Here I must remind the readers that Mannō-ike, Japan's largest reservoir, was so located as to irrigate the Mano Plain below, which was later administratively divided into two counties—Naka County and Tado County.

Now the people of the two counties made an earnest appeal to the provincial administrator, asking him to invite Kūkai to direct them in the repair of the bank. In the petition he sent to the central government, the provincial administrator described the eagerness of the people's wish to have Kūkai sent to them so that he might help them out of their difficulties:

> ... The people are longing for him as if he were their father or mother.

In 821 the petition was accepted and Kūkai was to come down to Sanuki as "director especially appointed by Imperial order." Before his departure for Sanuki, the Council of the State issued orders that Michi no *mahito* Hamatsugu, who had been supervising the work on the pond since the year before, should come up to the capital to meet Kūkai and guide him all the way to the reservoir in Sanuki, and that the administrators of the provinces through which Kūkai and his suite would travel should provide them with meals and lodgings, post-horses and boats. But Kūkai's suite itself was a very small one: a young man who had just been admitted to be a novice and four young boys who were to carry a few young Chinese quince trees.¹ The descendants of those trees which had been presented by Kūkai to the Yabaras with whom Kūkai and his suite were staying while they were in Sanuki are still to be seen growing in large numbers in the neighborhood.

As was expected, Kūkai, a magnetic personality, had attracted tens of thousands of people from all over Sanuki Province all wishing to lend a hand to their adored Bodhisattva. Soon he could be seen climbing up on to a giant rock projecting into the pond. He built a special altar there and performed an Esoteric Buddhist fire rite known as *homa*, thus inviting the help of all the Buddhas and deities concerned in that work. Those who were watching the *homa* would have felt a strange sensation as if they were witnessing a rebirth of heaven and earth. When the rite was over, Kūkai rose to his feet, and addressed the crowds intently gazing up at him:

"Now I have invited all the Buddhas and Deities concerned, so that they may help us build a dam that will last for ever. All that remains for you now is to do your very best."

All the people threw themselves to the ground, thus expressing their awe and inspiration. That inspiration worked, for the dam, upon which years had been spent in vain, was successfully repaired in a few months.

Though this was among the best-known acts he had performed to bring happiness to people, there are numberless legends about his having invited rain, dug wells, detected springs or hot springs, introduced new foods and plants, all suggesting that he was always intent on improving the welfare of people. His knowledge of medicine is also known to have cured many people of a variety of illnesses.

* * *

In 822, the Abhiseka Seminary—popularly known as Shingon-in—was founded by Imperial order in the precincts of Tōdai-ji that had still remained the core of Japan's Buddhism, not just of Nara Buddhism, so that Kūkai could regularly offer the prayer there for the peace and security of the state and for the welfare of the people. Shingon-in temple is still there, gracefully laid out just outside the main gate to the main hall that enshrines the giant statue of Vairocana Buddha.

In the following year or in the last year of the Tennō Saga's reign (809 –823), Saga offered Kūkai Tō-ji so that he might transform it into a seminary for his own religion. Tō-ji, originally built as a reception hall to accommodate guests from abroad, was suitably situated to the east of Rajō-mon Central Gate in the capital. Naturally it was, and still is, a spectacular landmark in the neighborhood.

While propagating his religion, Kūkai had been feeling the absolute necessity of having his own temple dedicated to Esoteric Buddhism, since it was originally conceived to express itself through paintings and sculptures. Kūkai had probably been persuading Saga to help him along these lines. But something may have prevented Saga from granting this request so soon.

Now his being allowed to have Tō-ji meant that he was able to transform it into his religious headquarters at national expense. This might have been good for him, but not quite good, for what he really wanted to have was a temple that had been built exactly on his own authority, including its location, layout, buildings and furnishings, so that it might be an expression or embodiment of his own thought. This was something unheard-of either in India or in China. Even Qinglong-si temple which his master Huiguo had presided over was just one of the numerous facilities the Chinese government had provided for religionists. Esoteric Buddhism in China had hardly established itself as an independent religion, and it was generally regarded as a specialist element in invocation only recently introduced into the established denominations of Buddhist religions. But Kūkai, since returning to Japan, had been assiduously developing it into an independent religion. When he succeeded in creating one, he called it Shingon Esoteric Buddhism, and regarded it as opposed to all other Buddhist religions, which he proclaimed exoteric and therefore inferior, as he was soon to verify in *The Difference between Exoteric Buddhism and Esoteric Buddhism.*

Now he was moving further on, trying, as he was typically trying to do on Mt. Kōya, to bring into being a temple that would become a palpable version of his own thought, thus consummating the purification and synthesis of his own religion.

Tō-ji was renamed Kyō'ō-Gokoku-ji (Temple for Teaching the King and for Protecting the State) after the *Kyō'ō-Gokoku-kyō* sutra. Obviously Kūkai was going to make it a place where he would realize another tenet of his Esoteric Buddhism: the inviting of the Mahavairocana's Land by keeping the peace and security of the state for the welfare of the people.

The Tennō Junna who followed Saga proved to be willing to help him, too. In 824 Junna issued an Imperial edict that Kyō'ō-Gokoku-ji should have fifty Shingon priests under Kūkai's guidance and supervision. Also in the same year when Wake no Matsuna and his brother Nakayo presented a memorial to the Tennō, offering their Takaosan-ji to the state so that it might be turned into a seminary for Shingon religion, the Tennō was ready to allow it to have fourteen Shingon priests. This temple, renamed Jingo-ji (Divine Protection Temple), was also expected to be a medium for Kūkai to introduce the Mahavairocana's Land.

The first thing Kūkai did at Kyō'ō-Gokoku-ji, or Tō-ji, as has popularly been called even to this day, was to build a hall to house the twenty-one sculptural images that were intended to constitute a mandala that would represent the concept of his own religion: they were five Buddhas, five Bodhisattvas, five Vidyarajas[2] and six Devas,[3] all placed in their ornamental settings, and all carved in conformity with established rules. The ritual implements to invoke their power were also produced in accordance with the traditional rules. Then he built a hall for *abhiseka* baptism, a belfry, a sutra library and a five-storied pagoda. The last mentioned was such a magnificent structure that he had to collect special funds to cover the deficit.

*   *   *

It was also about this time that Kūkai founded a university, named Shugei-Shuchi-in, for those who were really eager to learn, no matter what their social status or economic situation was. It was the first of its kind in the world. The land and buildings of the university were presented by Fujiwara no Mimori, the former Great Councilor, who had been friendly toward Kūkai.

Unlike the old state-owned university as the nursery of government officials, the new university offered not only a course in Confucianism but also courses in Taoism and Buddhism, so that students could study any of the three major intellectual disciplines known in the East at that time. In fact, "Shugei-Shuchi" meant "synthesis providing seeds of wisdom." In the course in Buddhism, both exoteric Buddhism and Esoteric Buddhism were taught impartially. In the courses in Taoism and Confucianism, history in general, culture as learning and literature of various kinds were also taught. Students were recommended to take several subjects in the other courses. The teachers were of two types—specialists and generalists. Both students and teachers were provided with food, clothing and housing, if necessary. The expenses needed to run the university were paid by what was gained from the rice paddies that Kūkai had received from those who were invited by Kūkai to help him in this enterprise. This is said to be the first trust company that Japan had ever seen.

XXIX. THE BELIEF THAT THE DAISHI STILL EXISTS ON EARTH

I HAD intended to pay another visit to Mount Kōya before I settled down to write this chapter. But I failed to do so because of the fatigue I suffered from after a journey I had recently made around China, including Luoyang and Xi'an. In Luoyang, I was pleasantly astonished to find that the peony fever I wrote about in Chapter XIII still prevails among modern Chinese. In Xi'an the air was thick with the fluffy seeds of willows.

The ancient site of the Imperial Castle of the Tang Dynasty is included in the city of Xi'an, and what Chang'an used to be has long since gone, except for a couple of stupas: the Big Wild-Goose-Pagoda and the Little Wild-Goose-Pagoda.[1] For gentlemen in Chang'an it was an annual event in early spring to climb to the top floor of the former—a sixty-meter-tall and seven-storied brick building—in order to enjoy the unmistakable harbingers of spring beginning to tinge the pastoral scenery of outlying districts. As Kūkai must have climbed up there, I wanted to climb up there, too. But the more I climbed, the more impossible it seemed to me to go on climbing up those seemingly endless stairways. Breathing hard, I often thought of giving up, but somehow or other I dragged myself up to the top floor. I could not help thinking of Kūkai, young and vigorous, a well-trained mountain ascetic, who must have been dancing up these steps on sprightly feet, as if borne up by a gentle wind.

*　*　*

Mount Kōya is where Kūkai spent the last months of his life and where he died. But somehow or other, those who live in Mount Kōya and many others all over this country believe that the Daishi (Kūkai) did not pass away but has been abiding in the underground stone vault of the innermost shrine on Mount Kōya, ever since he "entered into a supreme plane of meditation"

KŪKAI THE UNIVERSAL

there on March 21, 835. They believe he is ready to return to us whenever he is called upon for help, as is illustrated in the following story which a friend of mine recently told me:

> Not long ago, an acquaintance of mine, who teaches Japanese literature at Kōya-san University, was climbing Mt. Kōya by an old disused path together with his students. He made a false step on an overhanging patch of grass, and fell to the bottom of a ravine, where he lay unconscious for a while. As he was gradually coming to his senses, he found himself being vigorously embraced by his students who were repeating in a desperate chorus the prayer of *"Namu Daishi Henjō Kongō* (I put my faith in Daishi, the Universal Adamantine Illuminator)." "The Universal Adamantine Illuminator" was the Esoteric Buddhist name which Kūkai received from his master Huiguo, and in Japan it has long been used when addressing Kūkai in prayer. The students, trying to bring their teacher back to life, were thus seeking his help by incessantly calling upon him by that auspicious name.

Even today this kind of cult of the Daishi has been firmly maintained not only on Mount Kōya but also on the Shikoku Pilgrimage that annually attracts hundreds of thousands of people from all over the country. This cult dates back to the middle ages (1185–1573) when it was widely propagated by those engaged in the logistics of Mount Kōya: Kōya *hijiri* (a group of itinerant monks who traveled all over the country, soliciting funds to maintain Mount Kōya) and Kōya *gyōnin* (another group of humble monks who took charge of the mundane business of Mount Kōya). The former, traveling far and wide, played an especially conspicuous part in contributing to the popularization and even vulgarization of Mount Kōya. But apparently Mount Kōya still retains its aura of devoutness, as is revealed in the story above.

I once asked a question of the Reverend Wada, the head priest of Seinan-in temple on Mount Kōya: "Could you tell me about that aged priest on Mount Kōya, who assumes a very important role at every service held here, and who is practically as important as its chief abbot, but is always dressed

284

in a plain, yellowish robe, not in a surplice of gold brocade as is worn by other high priests?"

"I think you are talking of 'the man in yellow'," said the Reverend Wada, adding that the priestly robe in Kūkai's days was generally yellow. "We call him *Ina-san*. *Ina* is the official title of the superintendent of the innermost shrine of Mount Kōya. He is the only person who is allowed to take care of O-Daishi-san (Kūkai) in his sanctuary, changing robes and serving two meals a day, just as his servants used to do in his lifetime. That is why *Ina-san* is always dressed in yellow exactly as his servants were long ago."

I had once been told that on Mount Kōya successive *Ina-san* have never told anyone anything about what he saw in that sanctuary; so even on Mount Kōya no one but *Ina-san* knows whether it is Kūkai still seated there, rigid and motionless, or it is only his wooden image that is placed there, or what is enshrined there is only a sacred enclosure. I still remember the cheerfulness with which a young priest smilingly evaded my question, saying: "Well, I don't know. There is no need to know that."

I cannot think of Kūkai's sanctuary without being reminded of a story contained in *Tales of Times Now Past* which came into being early in the twelfth century. The incident is supposed to have taken place about seventy years after Kūkai's death, when Mount Kōya was being left unattended. Such an unusual situation had been caused by a dispute between Mount Kōya and Tō-ji over the possession of *The Thirty-Fascicle Manual for Ritual Rules*. A variety of hands seen in that collection imply that Kūkai, pressed in time, not only hired transcribers but also asked Hayanari to come and help him. Back in Japan, he must have turned its pages every time he prepared to perform a ritual. In his later years, he used to keep it in the library hall of Tō-ji. After his death, Shinzen, the second chief abbot of Mount Kōya, borrowed it but died before he could return it to Tō-ji and it was to remain on Mount Kōya, even until Mukū, the fourth chief abbot, came to take office. Kangen, the then patriarch of Tō-ji, urged Mukū to return it again and again, but to no avail. Kangen may have found it impossible or next to impossible to perform some rituals properly without that manual. But apparently he went too far when he approached the retired Tennō Uda (reign: 887–897) and asked him to issue a decree that the manual should be returned to Tō-ji. On receiving this command, Mukū became more obstinate than ever, and chose to leave Mount Kōya for good and go into hiding with that treasured manual. As all his disciples followed him, Mount Kōya was inevitably brought to ruin and even "Kūkai in his sanctuary" was left unattended.

After much parleying, the manual was returned to Tō-ji, and Kangen, who had temporarily taken over the chief abbacy of Mount Kōya, paid a formal visit to the sacred mountain. The incident that appears in *Tales of Times Now Past*—under the title of *How Kōbō Daishi Started Mount Kōya* —took place when Kangen on his inspection tour around the institute dared to enter the forbidden sanctuary where Kūkai was believed to be seated on the plane of supreme meditation.

The Hall dedicated to Kūkai, as we see it today, is a wooden structure crowned with a pyramid-shaped roof thatched with layers of cypress bark, though it is not known if this was the original style carefully preserved every time it was reconstructed. It houses a five-pieced tombstone,[2] under which a cellar is supposed to exist.

What Kangen saw on that occasion is described as follows:

> ... He opened the door to the sanctuary. It was so misty and pitch-dark inside that nothing was to be seen at first. When the mist lifted after a while, he saw the air was full of dust, which he soon found came from torn fragments of the decayed robe of Daishi blown up by a puff of wind coming from the open door. When the dust settled, there loomed the figure of Daishi, his hair grown as long as one *shaku* (thirty-three centimeters). Kangen left the place, washed himself clean, changed into new clothes, and returned to Daishi to shave him carefully with a new razor. He collected the crystal beads of Daishi's rosary that lay scattered all over the floor. He strung them on a fresh string and hung it gently on Daishi's hands. Then he took up a new robe he had brought with him and dressed Daishi carefully in it. Since everything was made clean and orderly, Kangen was about to leave, when he suddenly found himself weeping bitterly as if he were going to part from Daishi for the first time in his life. Never again would he have the temerity to open the door to the

sanctuary.

If we take some other research materials into consideration, it seems true that Kangen entered the sanctuary, even though it is doubtful that what he saw there was exactly what is recounted in the story above. As for the cellar that constitutes the sanctuary, what is recorded in *Gempi-shō* and *Kōya Hiki* (historical records on Mount Kōya) seems fairly believable: underground about five meters deep lies a cellar, made of stone, about 1.8 cubic meters in size, containing a cabinet with Kūkai on a supreme plane of meditation; the ceiling of stone about one meter thick is covered with a layer of earth upon which a five-pieced tombstone stands; the whereabouts of the entrance door is unknown, though it existed when Kangen entered the place; after Kangen closed the door for the last time, it was locked and buried forever so that no one could enter it again.

As to the belief that Kūkai is still there on a supreme plane of meditation, it does not seem to have been challenged, even by his modern disciples. Even in the case of the authors of *The Life of Kōbō Daishi* (edited by Hasuo Kanzen, published in 1931), who have won a reputation for precise narration, their tone subtly changes into a pious one when it comes to that point:

> Entering into a supreme plane of meditation is one thing, entering Nirvana (Buddhist Beatitude) is quite another. Daishi chose the former, not the latter.

It would have been difficult for the pious to make a factual investigation, but they tried to confirm their view with the help of research materials and even went so far as to give a statement to the effect that if one attains *samadhi* (the height of meditative concentration), one is able to control even one's death as well as one's life. But they do not speak with confidence about another relevant belief that his body remains intact. Does this mean that he mummified himself just as several ascetics did in later ages?[3] Or does he still remain as uncorrupted as he used to be in his lifetime? As for the precedent for "entering into a plane of meditation with one's body kept intact," they report that there had been no examples of this either in Japan or in China, though one or two cases had been reported in India.

Moriyama Shōshin, a great scholar and the author of *The Life of Kōbō Daishi Viewed from the Standpoint of Cultural History*, published in 1933, does not take a mystic view but says: "Daishi entered Nirvana." But he makes an additional statement: "... but Daishi himself, having believed in the possibility of his entering into a supreme plane of meditation, believed that he had succeeded in doing so." The research materials to support this conviction are very slight, but the author, a priest of Shingon religion may have refrained from defying the sacred belief any further.

If we consider this matter from the standpoint of Kūkai himself, those beliefs have nothing to do with the thought he upheld; to Kūkai, whose view of the universe was "everything is zero and zero includes everything," those beliefs may be an unnecessary tribute to him. To my mind, Kūkai died an ordinary death. As is often pointed out, those beliefs would have come into being one or two centuries after his death to be maintained throughout the ages to come.

XXX. The Wood Has Run Out

KŪKAI in his closing years still remained steadfast, always looking calm and dignified. A few years before his death, he knew his time was approaching and foretold when it would come, not because he wanted to demonstrate his ability to do so, but because he wanted to keep his disciples alert and aware enough to help him accomplish everything he thought should be done before his passing.

In August, 831, four years before his death, he wrote to the Tennō Junna, expressing his wish to be relieved of the post of *Dai-Sōzu* or the highest-ranking *Sōzu* (see Note 2 for XXI), which he found too hard to administer because of his illness:

> Since the end of last month, I have had a virulent abscess, which shows no signs of getting better. I shall be very grateful if I am allowed to resign my office at Court so that I may be free to spend the rest of my days in devotion only to the religious truth (*dharma*).

According to *The Record of the Daishi's Deeds*, he had been afflicted with carbuncle since around June, 831. In those days, carbuncle—a cluster of small furuncles breaking out on hypodermic tissue—was dreaded as a boil of the worst type. It could be fatal if it broke out on some parts of the body. In Japan it was not until Dutch surgery was introduced in the eighteenth century that the death rate from this type of boil began to diminish. The carbuncle which Kūkai suffered from at that time is generally believed to have been the cause of his death. In *The Life of Kōbō Daishi Viewed from the Standpoint of Cultural History* mentioned in the previous chapter, the author Moriyama Shōshin reasons, after examining the data he collected for diagnostic purposes, that Kūkai died of a carbuncle and some other disease like kidney trouble that he had to endure concurrently.

But why is there no material, such as records of prayer services performed for his recovery, which would prove that this carbuncle persisted for four years until it finally brought about his death? On the other hand, the following entry found in *The Record of the Daishi's Deeds* suggests his having recovered:

> ... His disciples saw a strange ascetic come into his sickroom. It was Huiguo. How pleased Daishi was to see his old master again! Then Huiguo began to recite the mantra of Acala.[1] After reciting it several hundred times, he bent over the patient and pulled out the root of his carbuncle, thus restoring him to good health.

This story is too far-fetched to believe. But it may encourage us to assume that at least once he made a miraculous recovery. If so, it was probably why, his wish to resign his post of *Dai-Sōzu* not having been granted, he was kept busy working around Kyōto and Nara, as is reported in many documents.

In 833, two years before his death, Kūkai, a man of action and enterprise, thought of carrying out what was to be the last undertaking in his life. That was to be the first annual event he called *Mandō-e* (Ten-Thousand-Lantern-Offering Festival). Even to this day, the event is held annually on April 21[2] at the Lantern-Offering Hall of the Innermost Temple dedicated to Kūkai. The sight of more than ten thousand lanterns hung round that hall being lit all at the same time to blaze on the surrounding darkness carries us back to the resplendent magnificence ancient people were treated to on that special night. When 'night' was synonymous with 'darkness,' how very impressive this pageant of lights could be!

Now Kūkai told his disciples the significance of the event, and how it should be performed, then ordered them to do their best to make it successful. Oil was very expensive in those days. In order to collect funds for it, Kūkai wrote to the wealthy and the powerful, asking for contributions.

The prayer Kūkai wrote for the Festival which occurred on August 22 begins as follows:

> Darkness is the source of life and death; illumination is the origin of Buddhahood....

In extrapolation of this proposition, he explains the necessity of holding a festival for the illumination of so many lanterns. It sounds rather exaggerated. But we must remember that religious rituals were always based on something more or less elaborate or fanciful, and that the aesthetic creed of his days was "the more magnificent, the better." This letter, which proved to be one of the most impressive literary pieces he produced in his life, includes the following:

> ... Should all space have come to an end, should all lives have come to an end, should all Buddhahood have come to an end, then, only then, my prayer for universal enlightenment would come to an end, too.

His current state of mind that had explored the very depths of his existence would seem to be revealed in this passage. He who once entertained a permanent conviction that he would live to be a centenarian now abandoned it, sublimating it in prospects to brighten the last stage of a life that was turning out to be unexpectedly short—sixty-one years, nine months and six days. Gazing upon his solitary figure in my imagination, I cannot help perceiving in it something unfathomably significant—the real Bodhisattvahood that had made him express this eternal wish.

Whether he recovered completely or not, his life in those years was a very active one. In January, 834, fourteen months before his death, he offered the Seven-Day Prayer for the New Year[3] at the Department of Central Affairs in the Court. On February 11, he went to Nara at someone's request to officiate at a sutra-copying service, for which he wrote a prayer, too, as he did on many other such occasions. Then he went to Tōdai-ji and gave many lectures, including a lecture on the *Hoke-kyō* sutra which he gave at his own temple—Shingon-in. In preparation for it, he was so intent that he even wrote a specific text, *A Commentary on the Hoke-kyō Sutra*. The *Hoke-kyō* sutra, upon which Saichō's Tendai religion was founded, would seem to have been the last sutra Kūkai would choose for his lecture theme. By that time, however, Kūkai had grown out of his former rigorism, as he finally found that Esoteric Buddhism *is* within exoteric Buddhism, too,[4] and that his Shingon religion *can be* the synthesis of all other Buddhist religions and teachings.[5] Now he went so far as to say to his own disciples: "You must learn exoteric Buddhism as well, though you must not forget that Esoteric Buddhism forms the central core, exoteric Buddhism external structure."

According to *The Annals of Tōdai-ji*, it occurred in the same month that Kūkai had one of his major disciples, Dōshō, give a lecture also in Tōdai-ji on *The Secret Key to the Hannya-shin-gyō Sutra*, which was actually a concise version of *The Precious Key to the Secret Treasury*.

Now he had less than thirteen months to live. But *The Record of the Successive Abbots of the Tendai Religion* contains an entry that on March 31 Kūkai went up to Mount Hiei in obedience to an Imperial order. Saichō had been dead for twelve years. Kūkai, together with his best six disciples, attended the ceremony to celebrate the inauguration of Saitō-in, a newly-built temple there, and performed his duty as the leader in prayer. It required a great deal of energy. If he still suffered from the carbuncle complicated by some other illness, as was probable, the spiritual power he showed on that occasion must have been really amazing.

What was even more amazing was the fact that he had not partaken of anything nutritious, as is reported in *The Memoirs of Our Master*:

> One day he said: "As you all know, since November 12 of the year before last (832), I have taken an intense dislike to cereals, though developing a greater liking for meditation."

A very unusual statement, indeed. Was it his disease that made him dislike cereals such as rice, barley, millet and beans? Seeing that he had been very active all this while, he must have had some other things to eat, but there is no entry about them in any of the reference materials. As for the reason why he abstained from cereals, he explains:

> "My abstinence from cereals will be a wise policy to give our religion an eternal life; it will also do good to all the disciples and followers of all times. Now listen to me, listen to me, my dear disciples. I shall soon be going. But never fail to lead a good life, faithfully acting up to the teaching and doctrine, even after I have gone to the mountain (probably Mt. Kōya) to abide there long."

No account is given as to why his abstinence from cereals would be so beneficial to his religion and his disciples and followers of all times. To my mind, not all that is recorded in *The Memoirs of Our Master* should be taken too literally, for it was produced not by Kūkai himself but by his disciples who wrote several different versions from memory, interpreting their master's speech in their own way. But this passage has long been cited as a positive proof of Kūkai's having entered upon the plane of meditation on Mt. Kōya, further persuading his followers that Kūkai's intention to keep his body intact made him abstain from grains. Even if Kūkai should have intended to do so, how on earth did he obtain the knowledge that abstinence from grain would enable one to achieve successful mummification or preservation of one's body?

To my mind, Kūkai was probably thinking of dying a natural death. He pondered on his disease and the time of his death, and he, the excellent planner and outstanding man of action, was steadily making preparations for his end, so that it might be an impressive one. By denying himself cereals, he may have been expecting a smooth debility of his body. Aging is a solemnization of life. Imaginably, Kūkai was living up to his own idea that if an old man were to defy this providence of nature and take nourishing food to feed what little vitality remained in him, his disease in metamorphosis of that vitality would also be fed, turning his body into a battleground between life and death, thus eventually bringing him to an unsightly end.

As is reported in a certain version of *The Memoirs of Our Master*, one of his disciples once tried to expostulate with him on his having abstained from cereals, saying: "Eating properly will do good especially to the aged. Not eating any grain is probably the last thing you should do." But the answer he got was: "Life is limited. So one should not struggle to make it longer. All I want to do is to wait calmly for my last moment." There is a command given by him in the same situation: "Stop. Stop that nonsense." Indeed, his attitude toward death was really firm and resolute.

On the last day of May, 834, Kūkai, who had recently returned from Nara to Tō-ji or Mount Kōya summoned his disciples and read them his will, which was later known as *Nine-Point Will*. By that time he had already

293

decided who should succeed to his presidency at Kōya-san, Tō-ji, Shingon-in of Tōdai-ji and Jingo-ji on Mt. Takao.

Jichie was appointed to be the head of these successors of Kūkai. Seeing that Jichie also came from Sanuki and his secular surname was Saeki, he may have been related to Kūkai. According to *The Record of Kūkai's Disciples*, Jichie in his nineteenth year (804) received Buddhist confirmation at Kaidan-in of Tōdai-ji. Until then, he had been learning *Consciousness-only* at Daian-ji, where quite probably Kūkai met him for the first time, and found in him a comrade. Jichie, who must have seen Kūkai off at Naniwa-zu port when he left for China, was the first to come to see him at Makino'o-san-ji, as is suggested by several reference materials. Probably it was then and there that Jichie offered himself as a disciple of Kūkai. How deeply Kūkai came to trust him is testified in the following words recorded in *The Memoirs of Our Master*: "After my entering into Nirvana (he did not say "my entering upon a plane of meditation,") Jichie shall be the mentor for all my disciples to turn to."

Sometime after that, Kūkai settled down at Mount Kōya. On November 15, when Mt. Kōya was beginning to be covered with snow, Kūkai called up his disciples again and announced the date and hour of his death: "I shall enter Nirvana (again he does not say "I shall enter upon the plane of meditation") around four on the morning of the twenty-first of next March. My dear disciples, do not cry so much."

It is rather horrifying to read what is recorded in *The Life of Priest Kūkai*: "One day in the new year season of his last year, he began to deny himself anything to drink." What made him do so? His disease or his express purpose? I suspect it was part of the self-control he exercised in separating himself smoothly from his body, which was, according to his thought, nothing special but something common to all human beings on earth.

On January 22, he presented a petition to the Court, requesting that his religion should be allowed to have "three students to be ordained annually." Had he not yet had any students to be ordained annually? No. Unlike Saichō who was eager to organize the order of his own religion as soon as possible, Kūkai was not so much interested in forming the order of his own religion as in organizing all the Buddhist religions into a synthetic order, thus to realize his ultimate thought: Esoteric Buddhism is within exoteric Buddhism and his Shingon religion can be the synthesis of all the Buddhist teachings. But now in his deathbed, he saw he was no longer able to go on seeking the way to realize this conviction.[6] This made him decide to ask for "three students to be ordained annually" so that his religion could go on existing even after his death. His petition was immediately granted by the Court and his Shingon religion finally became the eighth acknowledged Buddhist religion in Japan.

Toward the end of February, Kongōbu-ji or the temple Kūkai was building on Mt. Kōya was offered "regular protection from the State," imaginably to the great relief of Kūkai.

On March 15, six days before his death, Kūkai called Jichie and several other disciples to his bedside and said: "My days on this earth are numbered. I shall soon be in the Tusita Heaven to wait upon Maitreya."

This image of himself as the one who, at the end of his life's journey, would arrive at the Tusita Heaven, does correspond to what he pronounced through the mouth of the Beggar Boy, the hero of *The Indications of the Three Teachings* that marked the starting point of his career. This correspondence also manifests what his sixty-two-year life was and what it was for.

Kūkai on his deathbed had some other things to say:

"Even when I am in the Tusita Heaven, I shall be always gazing down upon the earth from between the clouds, watching what you are doing. I shall return here when Maitreya descends. Then I shall revisit my old places and those who have been in good faith will be saved; those in bad faith will not, to their eternal regret."

I believe this statement recorded in *The Memoirs of Our Master* was exactly what Kūkai said to his disciples, because in teaching them he had always been consistent and thorough as no other master could be. He held on to his thought, because he knew it was not just a thought but the truth of the universe. This naturally decided his attitude toward his disciples: in transmitting it to them, he always endeavored to insert it into the very marrow of their being; it needed the sort of skill that is required of a good surgeon. To him this was the one and only reliable method, while book-reading and self-seeking were of secondary importance. Thus Kūkai was fated to remain an omniscient master to his disciples even to the very end of his life.

As for when and where Kūkai died, it would be most sensible to rely on the official record of *Shoku Nihon Kōki*. As is to be expected from a document of this kind, its entry is very concise:

> On March 21, 835, the *Dai-Sōzu* and *Dentō Dai-Hōshi*[7] Kūkai
> passed away at his own temple in the Province of Kii.... He had
> predicted the date and the time of his death.

The last mentioned shows that this matter had also come to the knowledge of the recording secretaries at the Court. In a different section in the same book, there is an epistle sent from the former Tennō Junna (reign: 823–833). Naturally it is properly emotional in tone. It is dated March 25, suggesting that it took the messenger four days to travel from Mount Kōya to the Court. On receiving the news, the then Tennō Nimmyō (reign: 833 –850) sent to Mount Kōya his messenger whom the former Tennō Junna had entrusted with his letter. In the letter Junna calls Kūkai "the greatest master of Shingon, the Patriarch of Esoteric Buddhism" and expresses his condolence: "How could I conceive of his passing away so soon?" and "since Mount Kōya is far away, the news arrived here too late for us to go there to attend his *dabi*."

The word '*dabi*,' originally a Pali word[8] '*jhapeti*' that means 'cremation' or 'burning oneself to death,' had been used in Japan since the advent of Buddhism in the first half of the sixth century. Considering that the Japanese at that time generally took a great interest in how to treat a dead body, the messenger sent to the Court could not have failed to report the way Kūkai's body was treated, which would have led the former Tennō to mention '*dabi*' in the letter he sent to Mount Kōya, thus incidentally providing us with the fact that Kūkai's remains were cremated.

In India, cremation is regarded as an expression of Buddhist thought, and it was, and still is, practiced mainly among believers in Buddhism. When that custom was introduced into Japan along with Buddhism, it was accepted so widely that the native custom of building burial mounds was soon to be discarded, thus putting an end to what is called the Tumulus Period. Kūkai, who regarded Esoteric Buddhism as a development of Buddhism, would have naturally liked to follow the Buddhist custom of cremation or *dabi*. Indeed, *dabi* seems to suit his vigorous spirit that manifests itself so vividly in his literary writing as well as in his calligraphy.

Jichie took great pains in sending a letter to Qinglong-si temple[9] in Chang'an, China, informing them of his master's death. This sort of thing had never been done before or since. What made him do so? Had Kūkai asked him to? Or Jichie could not help doing so when he thought of his master's undying longing for Chang'an?

In the letter which was to be offered before the tomb of Huiguo, Jichie wrote about what Kūkai did after his returning home from China, enumerating his achievements, and describing how perfectly he had accomplished them, thus proving himself worthy of the confidence his master Huiguo had reposed in him. Then Jichie recounts how Kūkai realized his wish to have a place dedicated to his religion—how he divined its site on Mt. Kōya, built a temple there, named it Kongōbu-ji (Vajra Summit Temple), and spent his last months there after leaving the capital around the middle of the year before. As for his death that occurred "in late spring in 835," Jichie wrote:

> The wood has run out, and the fire has died. It was in his sixty-second year.... What grief we have to bear!....

Those who argue that Kūkai's remains were cremated take this reference to 'wood' and 'fire' as one of the evidences to support their opinion. But to my mind, this does not describe the scene of cremation. In Buddhism, the human body is considered to be composed of five elements—form, sensation, conception, volition, consciousness, and it is aptly compared to firewood: while wood is burning, it is in life; when fire has gone out, it is reduced to ashes. Now Kūkai's wood had run out and his fire had died.

On receiving this letter, the whole of the Qinglong-si temple in Chang'an was struck into silence and everyone, dressed in white, mourned the death of their revered priest.[10]

NOTES

Notes for I. THE BACKGROUND

1) the Jōmon Period:

Recent archaeological findings suggest that the period started much earlier and ended earlier and that agriculture (including dry-field-rice farming) and trading were part of their life especially toward the end of the period.

2) the Yayoi Period:

This period may have started earlier if the preceding Jōmon Period ended earlier, as mentioned in the note 1. As for the immigrants from China, what was happening in China may explain that: Toward the end of the Warring States Period (403 B.C.–221 B.C.), one warlord after another surrendered to the king of Qin, producing more and more refugees, until 221 B.C. when the First Emperor, Ying Zheng, united the whole land of China.

☆ The immigration from South India (600 B.C.–100 B.C.) can be explained by the linguistic analogy between ancient Tamil and ancient Japanese, as is typically seen in the paddy-rice-growing terms. Probably driven by the Aryan movement down the sub-continent, the natives might have left home and sailed up the Southern Sea, the East China Sea, the Yellow Sea, even as far as the Bohai Sea. ŌNO SUSUMU, *Nihongo no Kigen* (The Origin of Japanese Language).

3) the tennō:

The Japanese word "tennō" by which the monarch of Japan has been called is an honorific title of "emperor." The first person who used this word is considered to be Prince-Regent Shōtoku (574 –622), an ardent believer in Buddhism, who intended to rule the country as a bodhisattva (one who seeks enlightenment not only for himself but also for others). During his regency, he sent the first envoy to Sui China. According to *The Chronicles of the Sui Dynasty*, the letter sent in 607 by Prince-Regent Shōtoku to the Emperor Yangdi began: "The Ruler of the Land of Sunrise sends his message to the Ruler of the Land of Sunset."

To the Chinese Emperor, who regarded himself as the supreme ruler of the universe, this tone of equality and the contrast between Sunrise and Sunset sounded like the height of insolence. In his reply, therefore, the Emperor wrote at the opening, intending to show how the Prince-Regent should address to him: "The Emperor speaks to the Prince of Yamato (Japan)."

But the Prince-Regent, who insisted on terms of equality, ignored this and just wrote in his next letter to the Chinese Emperor: "The Tennō (the Ruler of the Heaven) of the East speaks to the Emperor of the West." What was the reaction of the Chinese Emperor was unknown because the envoy had "lost his answer on his way home." But it was quite imaginable that the Chinese Emperor again showed his displeasure at the word "Tennō." In 630 when the sending of envoys to Tang China began, the Japanese government thought it wiser not to bring any such royal message to the Tang Emperor.

Certainly the Prince-Regent might have gone a little too far when he adopted an honorific title of emperor in naming the king or the queen of Japan. But this manifests his firm conviction of the equality of nations in the light of Buddhist faith.

Chinese emperors and Japanese tennōs were totally different in function, too. Successive tennōs (who were essentially none but priests of the rice-culturing rites) reigned but did not rule, their actual ruler being brother, prince, consort, regent, chief councilor or shōgun (hereditary commander-in-chief and virtual ruler in the feudal ages that lasted from 1185 to 1867). There are only two exceptional periods in which the tennō himself ruled or supposed to rule: one was in the eighth century when the new political structure inaugurated after the Taika Reform (645)* was vigorously carried out under the tennō's direct dictatorship; the other was when modernized Japan turned to militaristic fascism (1889–1845) under *The Imperial Constitution of the Japanese Empire*.

☆ In ancient times there were several female tennōs, too.

4) *Kojiki* and *Nihon Shoki*:

Kojiki (three volumes), finished in 712, records all the tennōs' genealogies and successions as well as the myths and legends transmitted by the Imperial Court and major clans. *Nihon Shoki* (thirty volumes), the first official history of Japan, compiled in 720 after the model of the Chinese histories, mainly relates events from the age of the myths to the reign of the forty-first female tennō Jitō (reign: 690–697). Both were written in Chinese.

5) Chinese characters:

After the destruction of the Chinese colony Lelang Commandery* in northern Korea (313), some Chinese took refuge in Japan. Through the Chinese literature they brought with them, the Japanese began to learn Chinese characters and finally adopted them. But this does not mean that the Japanese adopted the Chinese language as a whole, for the Japanese went on speaking their own language totally different from the Chinese language in phonemics, vocabulary and grammar. For the Japanese to maintain this duality was not easy but their brains just bore that burden. That was why all the books and records written by the ancient Japanese, including Kūkai, were written in Chinese. At some time in the ninth century, their efforts to bridge the gap finally led them to complete their own phonetic syllabaries (*hira-gana* & *kata-kana*: see Note 2 for XXVII), which eventually enabled them to write their own language phonetically.

6) the title system:

The official titles created then were *mahito, asomi, sukune, imiki, michinoshi, omi* and others. The highest one, *mahito*, was conferred only on relatives of the tennō.

7) The Taika Reform (the Great Political Reform):

Before 645 when the Taika Reform was carried out, many mighty clans, central and local, were in constant strife over their arbitrary possession of land and people. To correct this situation a new rule was sought after. In Sui and Tang China (581–618 & 618–907), they had established the centralized government with a political structure based on a penal code and a civil and administrative code. When this system was adopted in Japan through the efforts of those who had studied for decades in Sui China, it accelerated political reforms that were consummated in the Taika Reform.

The main points of the Reform were: the land and people, so far possessed by local magnates, shall be the property of the tennō; the land shall be divided into about sixty provinces to be controlled by the Provincial Administrator sent from the central government; all people shall be allotment-farmers; they shall pay three kinds of tax: land tax paid in rice, labour tax, and produce tax paid in commodities other than rice. But it was not until 701 that these points were formally codified in the form of the six volumes of the penal code and the eleven volumes of administrative code, because the government was beset with troubles both at home and abroad.

Certainly the Reform succeeded in establishing the centralized government that conformed to imperial rule, but as the land-allotment system that supported that political structure demanded more and more land, a law promulgated in 743 had to recognize perpetual ownership of newly-reclaimed land if some conditions were fulfilled. Thus the land-allotment system soon began to deteriorate to be replaced by the manorial system.

8) Their request was conceded:

This meant that they were allowed to have a new post, too, appropriate to the holder of the title of *sukune*. In fact, in the following year they left Tado County in Sanuki for good, as the head of the family was given a place at the Metropolitan Office in the capital.

9) O-Daishi-san:

In 921 Kūkai was posthumously canonized as Kōbō Daishi. "Daishi" means "Great Saint," a title bestowed by the Imperial Court upon Buddhist priests of the highest virtue. "Kōbō" means "to spread widely the Buddhist teachings." There are twenty-three saints on whom the title of Daishi has been conferred. But as a popular saying goes, "Kōbō made off with the title of Daishi." That is, when one speaks of *the* Daishi there is no question whom one means. Those who come from Shikoku, to say nothing of his followers or pilgrims that travel around Shikoku, often call this saint of saints "O-Daishi-san" (O- = a polite prefix; -san = originally an honorific suffix used after a person's name, but today it is used after everyone's name), as if he were one of their neighbors, demonstrating their affectionate love for him.

☆ Besides Kūkai, three Daishis came of the Sanuki Saeki: Hōkō Daishi (Shinga; Kūkai's younger brother), Chishō Daishi (Enchin; Kūkai's nephew, or some say Kūkai's neice's son), and Dōkō Daishi (Jichie). They will all be mentioned in later chapters.

☆ The other Daishis also mentioned in this book are: Dengyō Daishi (Saichō), Jikaku Daishi (Ennin), Kōkyō Daishi (Kakuban), Kenshin Daishi (Shinran), Shōyō Daishi (Dōgen), and Risshō Daishi (Nichiren).

10) Kōya-san on Mt. Kōya:

In China many of the Buddhist temples used to be built on the mountains and the name of the mountains were always referred to in mentioning the temples until the names of the mountains just represented the temples or temple complexes. Because of this tradition introduced into Japan, Kongōbu-ji or the temple complex that Kūkai started on Mt. Kōya, for example, is often simply called Kōya-san (Mt. Kōya), just as Enryaku-ji or the temple complex on Mt. Hiei is called Hiei-zan (Mt. Hiei). In this book. "Kōya-san" or "Mount Kōya" and "Hiei-zan" or "Mount Hiei" are used for those temple complexes.

11) Kokubun-ji and Kokubun-niji:

In 741 two Buddhist temples—one attended by official priests and the other by nuns—were established in each province by the order of the Tennō Shōmu (reign: 724–749). They served as centers not only for religious observance of prayer for the security of the state and the harvest of abundant crops but also for social work, especially of medical care.

12) Zentsū-ji temple:

According to *The history of Zentsū-ji* (edited and published by the Publishing Department of Zentsū-ji in 1972), Zentsū-ji temple Kūkai built in 813 was named after the Buddhist name of his father, Zentsū, who dedicated both the site (about three times today's area) and the buildings of the temple.

13) some newly reclaimed land:

See the final paragraph of Note 7.

Notes for II. BOYHOOD

1) *The Memoirs of Our Master***:**
There are several versions under the same title, since Kūkai's major disciples wrote their own versions from memory or with reference to Kūkai's own *Memoirs.*

2) Sugawara no Michizane (845–903):
A distinguished scholar and Court official. He was once raised as high as the Minister of the Right (see Note 4) but was soon brought low by his envious rivals and died a lonely death in the remote province of Tsukushi. As a series of natural disasters that attacked the capital after his death were attributed to his revengeful soul, his lost position and honor were restored (923), and later (993) even the highest post of the Chancellor (see Note 4) with the highest court rank was offered to him. In the meanwhile, people dedicated a shrine to him, calling him Tenjin (Heaven's god) by his Shintōist title, and worshiping him as a guardian deity for students and scholars.

3) Confucius (551 B.C.–479 B.C.):
A Chinese thinker. His thought, as is recorded in *The Analects of Confucius,* was first officially approved in 136 B.C. by the Emperor Wudi of the Han Dynasty, to be retained as their guiding principle by all the ensuing dynasties of China, including the last dynasty, the Qing, that was brought to an end in 1911.
The core of the principle was 仁 or *ren* in Chinese, which means, in a narrow sense, benevolence, in a broader sense, a compound of all virtues including justice, propriety, intelligence, faithfulness and harmony. As for the access to *ren,* sincerity and sympathy are recommended.
Confucius, though orphaned when very young, grew up to be a minister of the Land of Lu. But at fifty-six he resigned his post and went on a speaking tour around twelve other lands, including Qi and Chu, with little or no success. Fourteen years later, he returned home and engaged in educating his disciples and followers, who are said to have amounted to three thousand in number.

4) the court rank:
The eight court ranks conferred on the officials according to the importance of the posts they held in the Council of State were as follows:

Chancellor
(Number of persons: 1, Court Rank: first)

Minister of the Left (1, second)	Minister of the Right (1, second)
Great Councilors (4, third)	Minor Councilors (4, third)
Controllers of Four Departments of Central Affairs, Ceremonial, Civil Administration, Popular Affairs (4, fourth)	Controllers of Four Departments of Military Affairs, Justice, Treasury, Royal Household (4, fourth)
Vice-Controllers (4, fifth)	Vice-Controllers (4, fifth)
Secretaries (4, sixth)	Secretaries (4, sixth)
Minor Secretaries (4, seventh)	Minor Secretaries (4, seventh)
Recorders (4, eighth)	Recorders (4, eighth)

The third court rank and above were constituted as peerage. In the case of the university under the control of the Department of Ceremonial, the pesident and professors of literature held the fifth;

professors of Chinese classics held the sixth; professors of Chinese pronunciation, calligraphy and mathematics held the seventh.

The holders of these ranks were granted stipends. In the case of Ato no Ōtari whose court rank was the junior grade of the fifth, 2,000 *koku* was granted a year. One *koku* was about 180 liters of rice or the amount of rice to feed a man for one year.

5) Shintō:

The indigenous religion of Japan, based on animism and nature-worship, was an unorganized religion, and not until the sixth century when Buddhism was introduced into Japan did the Japanese begin to perceive it as something peculiar to themselves. The word of Shintō (the Way of Deities) was then invented, while the cult of heroes and ancestors was more or less clearly defined. As tribes and clans were gradually amalgamated by a ruling clan that founded the Yamato Court, the Sun Goddess revered by them as their ancestor was made the supreme deity of Shintō. This cult of the national gods, including the worship of the clan and communal deities, remained comparatively free from Chinese influence. That explains why the National Cult Department was independent of the Council of State as the supreme organ of government.

6) Tōdai-ji temple & the Giant Buddha:

The Tennō Shōmu who erected Kokubun-ji in each province thought of building their headquarters temple, which materialized in the form of Tōdai-ji. In other words, by building this edifice as a symbolic display of the Buddhist ideal of universal spiritual communion centered in the person of Buddha, parallel to the political unity of national life centered in the monarch, the Tennō, a devout Buddhist, consummated the close connection between Buddhism and the state.

In 752, the main hall was completed and dedicated to Vairocana Buddha as a heavenly manifestation of the Buddha Sakyamuni, which was believed to have appeared when he was still in spiritual rapture after having attained supreme enlightenment under a bo tree, as is stated in the *Kegon-kyō** sutra.

The casting of that bronze statue popularly known as the Giant Buddha, 14.9 meters tall, seated on the pedestral about 2 meters high, had been finished in 749. The reason why the Buddha was made so huge was because he represents 10,000,000 Sakyas who are to save as many worlds by the power of the *Kegon-kyō* sutra, as we know from what was carved in the lotus petals on the pedestral.

☆ The headquarter temple for Kokubun-niji nunneries was the Kokubun-niji of Yamato Province. Originally it was the residence of Fujiwara no Fuhito (see Note 8). After his death, one of his daughters who had been the queen consort of the Tennō Shōmu dedicated it to found the Kokubun-niji or Hokke-ji in Nara.

7) the Fujiwara clan:

Nakatomi no Kamatari (614–669), who played a prominent part in inaugurating the Taika Reform (645), was allowed to have a new family name—Fujiwara—after the place name of his residence in Yamato Province. The Nakatomis had long been known as a family of Shintō priests, but by the time of Kamatari, they had adopted Buddhism and began to distinguish themselves in politics as ministers of the state and majordomos of the Imperial family.

Kamatari's son, Fujiwam no Fuhito, who did a great deal in compiling the penal and administrative codes (701), was strengthening his ties with the Imperial family by arranging his daughters' marriages to the tennōs. As for his four sons, he established them in their own families—Fujiwara Nanke, Fujiwara Hokke, Fujiwara Kyōke and Fujiwara Shikke. The rivalry among them was such that it often led to political disturbances in the years to come.

8) *A Collection of Ten Thousand Leaves*:

Japan's oldest remaining anthology of poems in twenty volumes, with the oldest poem written in the mid-fifth century and the latest one by Ōtomo no Yakamochi in 759. It contains about 4,500 poems of various types (long epics, short verses of various forms, ancient popular songs and others). The poets are varied, too, from monarchs to humble, nameless people like enrolled soldiers for the defense of western Japan. Poems are written in *man'yō-gana* (Chinese characters used as phonetic symbols: e.g. a = 阿, 安 or 足).

9) the Great Healer:

The Buddha of Healing or the Lord of the World of Pure Emerald in the East. Because of his vow to cure diseases, he is among the most popular of the Buddist pantheon. He and his followers (Sunlight Bodhisattva and Moonlight Bodhisattva) are called the Trio of Healers.

10) Bodhisattva:

In Mahayana Buddhism,* the *bodhisattva* indicates one who practices the teaching of Buddhism in both other-worldly and secular ways of life. Instead of becoming a Buddha immediately, he or she vows to save all beings and works with compassion for suffering beings. In Hinayana Buddhism,* the Bodhisattva indicates Sakyamuni practicing austerities before his emancipation or before his appearance in this world.

11) an Eleven-faced Kannon Bodhisattva:

One of the seven Kannon Bodhisattvas of great compassion who attend the Amida Buddha.* The eleven faces of an Eleven-faced Kannon represent the same number of talents he or she possesses as a savior (see Note 4 for XXIII).

12) the poetry-making party on the water:

One of the annual events of the Court of the ancient times. One day early in March, the holders of the third court rank or above, who had been invited to the party, were seated along the edge of a stream or a pond. Meanwhile a flat cup of *sake* was placed upstream. What each of the participants was expected to do then was to improvise a poem by the time the cup floated down before him, to lift the cup to sip some *sake* and to place it on the water again so that it would go down to the next. When the last person emptied the cup, they all came to a banquet to be held in a different place, where each of them sang out the poem he had just composed. Reportedly it originated in China.

13) Imperial palaces:

In the earlier days, tennōs often had their palaces built in a new place according to their Shintōist idea that a place that had death in it is desecrated and therefore must be abandoned.

14) *nusa*:

A Shintōist symbol of sanctity, made of a stick and a piece of paper or cloth.

15) Naniwa-no-miya:

Like Kōga-no-miya, which was mentioned earlier in the same chapter, this was one of the several imperial palaces which the Tennō Shōmu had built and abandoned before 744 when he finally returned to the capital of Nara."Naniwa" is the ancient appellation of present-day Ōsaka City and its neighborhood.

Notes for III. AT THE TURNING POINT

1) *Shoku Nihon Kōki*:
One of the six historical books compiled by Imperial orders during the Nara Period and the early part of the Heian Period. The six historical books, which are referred to in this book, are as follows:
  (a) *Nihon Shoki* (30 volumes) covering from "the age of the gods" to 697.
  (b) *Shoku Nihon-gi* (40 volumes) covering from 697 to 791.
  (c) *Nihon Kōki* (40 volumes) covering from 792 to 833.
  (d) *Shoku Nihon Kōki* (20 volumes) covering from 833 to 850.
  (e) *Montoku Jitsuroku* (10 volumes) covering from 850 to 858.
  (f) *Sandai Jitsuroku* (50 volumes) covering from 858 to 887

2) the Six-Dynasties style:
An extremely ornate style of Chinese prose widely adopted from the era of Six Dynasties (220–581) through the Tang era (618–907). Regulated by a couple of phrases of 4–6 characters, it was characterized by parallelism and frequent references to classics.

3) Yamanoue no Okura (ca.660–ca.733):
A distinguished poet whose poems are well represented in *A Collection of Ten Thousand Leaves*: ten long epics and fifty-one *tanka* (thirty-one-syllable verses: see Note 2 for XIX). His poetry, which exclusively deals with people including his own children and allotment farmers suffering from the penal and administrative code systems, appeals to modern people as well. As a good scholar who had been in Tang China as junior secretary, he had been appointed tutor to the crown prince who later became the Tennō Shōmu.

4) Not of noble lineage, Okura was usually left out of promotion....:
There was a custom that would have been very discouraging to those who were not of noble lineage: all youths whose father or grandfather retained the fifth court rank or above, whether they had attended university or not, were automatically granted the junior grade of the fifth court rank (or above) when they reached twenty-one.

5) Sakyamuni (ca.560 B.C.–ca.480 B.C.) and his thought:
Though the father of Buddhism is often called Sakya or Sakyamuni, Sakya was originally the name of the land he was born in or of the tribe he belonged to, and Sakyamuni means the Sage from the Land of Sakya—a small country that existed at the foot of the Himalayas. His father, a man from the Gautama family, being the king of the Land of Sakya, Sakya (or Siddhartha as he was named by his parents) was brought up at the capital called Kapilavatthu Castle.
  At twenty-nine, after having fulfilled his duty to have a son to keep his family name, he left his home for good to lead an ascetic life in the Himalayas under the guidance of Brahmans. But it was not until he left there at thirty-five and came to Buddhagaya that he realized, while meditating under a bo tree or a *bodhi-druma*, the truth of the universe, which he called **karma doctrine**: everything that occurs in the universe has a long chain of causes.
  He spent the rest of his life propagating this doctrine, attracting a large number of people from all over India, high and low, good and wicked. No matter which of the four classes of Indian society they might belong to, they were treated as equal with all others as long as they adhered to his order, for he said: "the different waters of the four rivers of India just flow into one and the same entity called sea." He had two kinds of followers—clergy and laity. They helped each other, the former engaging in illuminating people, the latter supplying the former with food, clothing and temple buildings to house Sakya's teachings.

Though the doctrine of karma was his own discovery, he did not necessarily consider himself the originator of a new religion, but rather as a new type of rational interpreter of the ancient Brahminism. In conveying his thought, he never allowed his disciples to use the highly polished language of Sanskrit in which Brahmin scriptures were written, but insisted on using popular, local colloquialisms on all occasions. During his lifetime and even after his death, therefore, there was no Buddhist scripture written in any language, all his teaching having been retained and transmitted orally. It was not until four or five hundred years later that his speeches began to be recorded in Sanskrit.

The gist of his first speech, that later became the base of all forms of Buddhism, was as follows: "I had lived two contrasted lives—a pleasure-seeking life and an ascetic life. But as neither of them brought me profound satisfaction, I decided to follow the Middle Way, which, through the Eight Righteous Steps, finally led me to a supreme enlightenment that eventually brought me great satisfaction." As for the rationale of this process, he gave five elements for human existence—form, sensation, conception, volition, consciousness—which, when touched by desire, produce mental distress; to conquer that desire, therefore, is to reach enlightenment. To conquer that desire, he says the first step is to realize that everything is ever-changing because the five elements mentioned above are incessantly working in infinite variety according to the doctrine of karma.

6) Taoism:

The whole complex of beliefs and worship known by the name of Taoism may be called the national or indigenous religion of China. There are two types of Taoism; one is an organized religion, the other a folk religion. The former came into being, stimulated by Confucianism, when it was officially adopted by the Emperor Wudi of the Han Dynasty (136 B.C.) and then by Buddhism introduced into China toward the end of the same dynasty around the turn of the first century. In China, this type of Taoism has traditionally been compared with Confucianism and Buddhism. The latter type of Taoism, based on animism and nature-worship, has profoundly influenced the culture and emotional life of the Chinese.

Notes for IV. BEGGAR BOY

1) Kimō & Tokaku:

They come from a set phrase: Kimō-Tokaku 亀毛兎角, meaning "Hair of Tortoises" and "Horns of Rabbits." A figurative phrase to show that one sees something where nothing really exists.

2) the Nine Chinese Classics:

The Analects of Confucius, The Great Learning, The Spring and Autumn Annals, The Book of Songs, The Book of Documents, The Book of Changes, The Book of Rites, The Works of Mensius, The Doctrine of the Mean.

3) the Three Great Books of History:

The Record of the Historian, The Chronicles of the Han Dynasty, The History of the Later Han Dynasty.

4) *The Memoirs of the Three Emperors*:

The book on the three legendary Emperors of China of the earliest times: Fu Xi, Shen Nong and the Yellow Emperor.

5) Shun and Yao:

Legendary kings of China of the earliest times. Their virtuous rules are considered to be a paragon of righteous government.

6) mandala:

Since Esoteric Buddhism embraced deities and demons, saints and goblins, Hindu, Persian, Chinese and others, all interpreted as manifestations of one and the same Buddha called Mahavairochana (Great Illuminator), various diagrams were invented to show where they stood in that Buddhist pantheon or how they work cooperatively. There are a variety of mandalas, and they all work as visual aids for those who are seeking enlightenment. The most representative are a pair of mandalas; one representing the ideal side of the world which is called "the Realm of the Indestructibles" (Skt., *Vajra-dhatu*; Jan., *Kongō-kai*) in which the basic and indestructible ideas are present in the all-comprehensive soul of Mahavairochana. All of these indestructible potential ideas are destined to manifest their activities, which make up the dynamic aspect of the universe, as is represented in the other graphic scheme called "the Womb-store" (Skt., *Garbha-kukshi*; Jan., *Taizō*), where the manifold groups of deities and other beings are arrayed according to the kinds of powers and intentions they embody. MASAHARU ANESAKI, *History of Japanese Religion.*

7) Mahayana Buddhism:

Around the turn of the first century there arose in India a movement of Buddhist reformation. Since the death of Sakyamuni (ca.480 B.C.), his disciples had been trying to organize his teaching into a unified system of religion in their own way. The conservatives, thinking highly of disciplines, concentrated their attention on attaining Buddhahood through asceticism. The progressives made much of carrying Sakyamuni's precept into practice through working for people in society, calling their people-oriented principle Mahayana (the GreaterVehicle), as they thought it more efficient in bringing a large number of people to Buddhism than the conservative's self-centered principle which they called **Hinayana** (the Lesser Vehicle). By the turn of the sixth century, Mahayana Buddhism had produced a large number of scriptures, including *Kegon-kyō*, *Hannya-kyō*, *Yuima-gyō*, *Hoke-kyō*, *Rishu-kyō*, *Dainichi-kyō* (*Mahavairocana Sutra*), *Kongōchō-gyō* (*Vajrasekhara Sutra*) and *Konkōmyō-kyō*, which are all mentioned in later chapters.

8) amateur Buddhist practitioners:

One of the stories in *Nihon Ryōiki*, Japan's oldest collection of Buddhist fables edited by Priest Keikai about Kūkai's time, depicts a scene in which a wealthy man calls in a traveling monk and asks for a lecture on the *Hannya-gyō* sutra, only to receive a disappointing answer: "A beggar monk such as I am cannot do such a difficult thing. All I can do is chant a *dharani* of the *Hannya-gyō* sutra."

☆ *Dharani*-chanting was a kind of mnemonics or rather an incantation for memorizing sutras in the early days among non-Buddhist ascetics in ancient India. In Japan at that time *dharani*-chanting, believed to invoke the mysterious power of the sutra it represented, was being much sought after, so much so that it allowed even a large number of unofficial monks to make a living by *dharani*-chanting alone. As for *dharani*, see Note 4 for V.

9) encouraging people to look down upon those ... as abominable:

The following story from the collection mentioned above tells what happened to Inukai no *sukune* Maoyu, who had taken an intense dislike to such beggar monks:

> One day a beggar monk came round to Maoyu's residence and asked for food. Maoyu just caught him, tore off his robe, almost throttled him with the collar of his underwear, and snarled: "Tell me who made you a monk!"
> " ... I myself...."
> The beggar gasped, struggling for a breath. But Maoyu would not release him until

he gave him a good beating.

That evening Maoyu prepared jelly from carp, intending to eat it next morning. But next morning, no sooner had he tasted a mouthful of it and raised a cup to take a sip of *sake* than he spat black blood until he was dead.

The editor closes the story with a moral:

A wrong view is a sharp-edged sword to destroy yourself. Anger is an evil spirit that invites misfortune to yourself. Covetousness leads you to the world of Pretas (the Buddhist inferno of starvation). If you have a beggar at your door, you should not let him go empty-handed.

Notes for V. THE MORNING STAR FLEW INTO HIS MOUTH

1) Jianzhen (688–763):

A Chinese Buddhist priest. In 742, eagerly solicited by some Japanese priests who had been in China, he decided to come over to Japan. But the following twelve years saw him attempt five voyages without success mainly because of unfavorable weather. Though one of the voyages had cost him his eyesight, he fulfilled his promise in 754 when at sixty-six he arrived in Japan by taking advantage of the return journey of the Japanese envoy to China. He brought with him three thousand pieces of Sakyamuni's relics and many Buddhist scriptures. As a master of the Disciplinary School, he introduced a system of monastic discipline (*ritsu*) and built some ordination platforms, firstly at Tōdai-ji in Nara, then at Yakushi-ji in Shimotsuke Province in the east, at Kanzeon-ji in Tsukushi Province in the west and at his own temple Tōshōdai-ji in Nara. His knowledge of medicine, architecture and sculpture also made him a memorable contributor to the development of Japanese culture.

2) Bodhisena (704–760):

A Brahman from South India. In 733 he came over to Japan, after he was invited to do so by the Japanese envoy he met in China. Several learned monks and musicians from Indo-China and China he brought with him also served Buddhism in Japan. The highlight of the latter half of his life he spent in Japan occurred in 752 when he administered the ceremony consecrating the newly-cast image of the Giant Buddha of Tōdai-ji in Nara (see Note 6 for II).

3) Jetavanavihara Monastery:

When Sakyamuni was attracting a large number of followers, wealthy merchants dedicated temples and monasteries as an act of charity or faith. This monastery was one of the two largest ones built at that time.

4) "mantra-reciting for invoking Akasagarbha":

The mantra used for this asceticism is considered to be the essence of the sutra entitled 虚空蔵菩薩能満諸願最勝心陀羅尼求聞持法, which in 717 Subhakarasimha* translated into Chinese. The asceticism as well as the sutra itself seems to have been introduced into Japan in 718, when Dōji, a priest of Daian-ji, returned to Japan after studying in Tang China for eighteen years.

☆ A comparatively longer mantra like Akasagarbha's mantra is often called *dharani*, and it is usually regarded as the quintessence of a sutra.

5) dharmakaya Buddhas:
Sakyamuni is called Buddha. But in Mahayana Buddhism there are numberless Buddhas, and they were divided into three kinds: dharmakaya Buddha as the principle of the universe (like Mahavairocana), nirvanakaya Buddha as a condescending manifestation of Buddha (like Sakyamuni), and sambhogakaya Buddha as an ideal unity of the eternity of dharmakaya Buddha and the concreteness of nirvanakaya Buddha (like Amida Buddha: see Note 4 for XVIII).

6) En no Ozunu (?-701):
Since Japan became a paddy-rice growing country, mountains as a source of irrigation had been looked upon as sacred places or abodes of the mountain gods. Ancient people drew no hard line between such gods and their own ancestors who they thought became protective spirits watching over them from on high in the mountains. On the other hand, the asceticism practiced there was believed to be particularly effective. En no Ozunu is known as the pioneer of such mountain asceticism. In the ninth century, Esoteric Buddhism was to reinforce the older beliefs with more complex lore, attracting more and more mountain ascetics to high mountains.

7) transcend humanity and acquire divinity:
This may sound like what Catholics call "the sin of pride," but ancient people in Japan drew no hard line between divinity and humanity, as is mentioned in Note 6 above, or in the paragraph concerning Sugawara no Michizane (see Note 2 for II). Or it may be that Kūkai had anticipated his ability to unite himself with any representative of that Esoteric Buddhist pantheon through performing what he called three mysteries.*

8) Kūkai was probably the last person ... so drained of color:
It is known, however, that Kūkai often inhabited snowy mountains, too, as is known by the letter he wrote to Yan Jimei, as presented in Chapter X.

9) the Shikoku Pilgrimage: (map on page 338)
The pilgrimage circumambulating Shikoku Island via the eighty-eight Buddhist temples designated as the Sacred Sites of Shikoku is meant to follow the trail Kōbō Daishi (Kūkai) walked in his youth for ascetic practice, searching for the truth. That is why authentic pilgrims go on foot as Kūkai did long ago. It takes about sixty days to tread the 1,500 km of the route shown below. As for the origin, it is generally believed that Kūkai's disciples began to make the round of his memorial places in Shikoku. Even today formal pilgrims start from Kōya-san as his burial place, and after making the circuit of eighty-eight temples, will return to Kōya-san via Temple No.1, just as the disciples of Kūkai did long ago. According to the temple legends, many of the temples were founded or restored by Kūkai.

10) what it is in Kūkai that has attracted so many men and women....:
Actually what attracted so many men and women on that day was not only Kūkai but the Yakuō (a bodhisattva who dispenses medicines) enshrined in the main hall, and the other Buddhist pantheon displayed in the pagoda. Each temple on the Shikoku Pilgrimage has at least two halls: the main hall housing the principal image of that temple and the Daishi-dō hall dedicated to the Daishi or Kūkai. This fact may reveal the duality of what the Shikoku Pilgrimage offers: a presentation of a mandala consisting of divinities from the Buddhist pantheon and a cult of Daishi or Kūkai (see Note 6 for XXX). The temple—Yakuō-ji—was named after Yakuō Bodhisattva.

11) the advent of Buddhism:
In 538, Buddhism was presented to the Yamato Court by a delegation sent by the Prince of Paekche* (a principality in the Korean Penninsula). The delegation was accompanied by Buddhist priest, and the objects presented were statues of Buddha and his saints, copies of scriptures, banners

and other articles to be used in rituals.

12) orthodox Buddhism was gradually introduced into Japan:
This occurred through over a dozen student priests sent to the Sui China (581–618) and the succeeding Tang China.

13) the six departments of Nara Buddhism & the temples that accommodate them:
The **Sanron** (Three Treatises) School is based on the two treatises written in India by Nagarjuna and one treatise by one of his disciples. Nagarjuna, a leader of Mahayana Buddhism, philosophically speculated on what Sakyamuni called the Middle Way and denied, unlike the Hinayana Buddhists, not only the five elements (form, sensation, conception, volition, consciousness) but also all the antitheses, such as life and death, Nirvana (Buddhist paradise) and this world caught in the circle of transmigration, people and Buddhas, distress and enlightenment, and formulated the view that they are all essentially the same, calling the wisdom that enables one to grasp this essential sameness Perfect Wisdom. The key to this absolute monism was *kū* in Japansese (Skt., *sunya* or *sunyata*).

Early in the fifth century, the Three Treatises were translated into Chinese in Chang'an, China, by Kumarajiva (344–413; his father was Indian, his mother a sister of the king of Qiuci or present-day Kuqa in the Xinjiang Uighur Autonomous Region. Then they were introduced into Japan by way of Korea. It was in the philosophy of this department that the Prince-Regent Shōtoku (see Note 3 for I) was educated in his youth.

The **Jōjitsu** theology is based on the treatise on Four Noble Truths, a basic concept in Buddhism which explains the cause of suffering and the way of deliverance; one of the first doctrines taught by Sakyamuni after he was enlightened: the first two truths relate to the world of illusion, the second two to the world of enlightenment. The doctrine itself is regarded as the highest point attained by Hinayana Buddhism, constituting the stage of transition between Hinayana and Mahayana. Written by an Indian monk Harivarman around 300, it was translated by Kumarajiva mentioned above. In China it had its own school, but in Japan it was usually studied as part of Sanron theology since it arrived along with the Sanron theology.

The thought of **Hossō** (Consciousness-Only) started in India in the fourth century by Vasubandhu and his brother Asanga, who agreed to Nagarjuna's absolute monism, went further by analyzing human mind and pursuing it through an examination of sensation and apperception to the ultimate soul-entity called Alaya (Store of the Unconscious). An inexhaustible number of seeds stored up in the Alaya-soul will manifest themselves in limitless varieties of phenomena, both physical and mental. To become emancipated from this transmigration, this analytical study of psychological problems is considered a necessary prerequisite and associate of the contemplation called Yoga (the union of the individual soul with the cosmic soul).

This philosophy systematized into *Dharma-lakshana* (the Criterion of Laws and Truths: Hossō), brought back to China to be translated and advocated by the great Chinese scholar priest Xuanzang, became predomenant in Japan throughout the Nara Period.

The thought of **Kusha** is founded on the treatise *Abhidharma-kosha* (the Store of Analysis) written also by Vasubandhu mentioned above. This analytical study devoted to cosmological and psychological problems was also brought back and translated by Xuanzang. In Japan its doctrines were accepted as part of the Hossō school.

The **Kegon** School based on *Kegon-kyō* sutra was founded by the Chinese priest Dushun (557 –640) and was introduced into Japan by the Silla priest Shenxiang (Shimsang in Korean: ?–742), who in 740 gave a long series of lectures on that sutra at Tōdai-ji by Imperial order, thus to be made the first patriarch of the Kegon school of Japan.

The gist of the Kegon doctrine is: all beings have Buddha-nature in them; each phenomenon bears a relation to all other phenomena; each experience contains all experiences within itself in an interdependent, mutually complementary relationship.

The **Ritsu** School devoted to monastic discipline (ritsu) was founded on the basis of Mahayana ethics as systematized in China by Daoxuan (596–667), and was brought to Japan by the Chinese priest, Jianzhen (see Note 1).

The seven temples in Nara that kept these six departments of Nara Buddhism were as follows:

Tōdai-ji for Kegon, Hossō, Kusha and all the rest.

Kōfuku-ji for Hossō and Kusha: The guardian temple of the Fujiwara clan, originally built in Yamashiro Province later to be moved to the Nara Capital.

Gangō-ji for Kegon: The first temple Japan ever had. It was originally known as Asuka-dera, erected in 588 at Asuka in Yamato Province. It was dedicated to the Buddha Sakya by the Prince-Regent Shōtoku who had just defeated his political enemy "with the help of the Buddha." Later it was moved to the Nara Capital, but the original was left there.

Daian-ji for Sanron, Hossō and Jōjitsu: A monastery built in 617 also by the Prince-Regent Shōtoku was made a large state temple—comparable in grandeur with Tōdai-ji—when moved finally to the Nara Capital.

Yakushi-ji for Hossō: It came into being in 680 when the Tennō Temmu dedicated the temple to a group of Great Healers, praying for his consort's recovery from illness.

Tōshōdai-ji for Ritsu: It was built in 759 as the resident temple for the Chinese priest, Jianzhen.

Saidai-ji for Ritsu: Built in 765 by the Tennō Shōtoku, it was comparable in scale with Tōdai-ji. The seven-storied octagonal pagoda that existed there suggests the strong connection it had with Jianzhen and other Chinese priests.

14) some of the legends:

The temple legends of Shōzan-ji and Tairyū-ji (the twelfth and twenty-first temples on the Shikoku Pilgrimage) are best known.

15) the gale was so fierce:

This area, a regular route for typhoons, is the windiest part of Japan, average years having over 180 days with winds of gale force. While staying in Muroto, Kūkai made a poem, which goes as follows:

> I hear Muroto is Buddha-natured, but for me
> Not a day passes without being assaulted
> by waves and winds caused by *in* and *en*.*

☆ *In* is the inner and direct cause by which the result occurs, while *en* means the external and indirect one.

16) sea and sky:

Many people support the notion that Kūkai named himself here in Cape Muroto, since "*kū*" means "sky or void or *sunyata*" and "*kai*" means "*sea*."

☆ The name his parents had given him was Maio, meaning "True Fish."

17) the morning star:

In Buddhism it is considered to be the manifestation of Akasagarbha Bodhisattva.

Notes for INTERLUDE 1. THE ORIGIN OF ESOTERIC BUDDHISM

1) *Sunya or sunyata*:

A fundamental concept of Buddhism that can be translated as 'relativity.' It holds that all existence and the constituent elements which make up existence are dependent upon causation. Since the causal factors are changing every moment, it follows that there can be no static existence. *Sunya*, therefore, denies the possibility of any form of static existence

2) a *cintamani* jewel:

A legendary jewel which is capable of responding to every wish is said to be obtained from the dragon-king of the sea. What is considered to be that jewel can be seen among the ornaments of ritual objects and decorative parts of temple buildings, too.

3) Xuanzang (602–664):

Eager to learn more Buddhism, the twenty-five-year-old Xuanzang left home for India even though the Tang Dynasty at that time prohibited their people from leaving their country. Crossing the many countries in Central Asia, he entered India via Afganistan. After making a pilgrimage around places sacred to Sakyamuni, he studied at Nalanda Monastery, the largest institute for students of Buddhism, while visiting many great scholars in various parts of India. After returning home in 645, bringing with him a large number of Buddhist scriptures and images, he wrote *The Memoirs of the Central Asia and India*. The nineteen years before his death he spent producing excellent translations of *Dai-Hannya-gyō* sutra (600 volumes) and seventy-four other Buddhist scriptures and treatises (1,335 volumes), leading disciples of great intelligence.

4) a chest for Sanskrit texts:

This term refers to the Indian sutras which were written on *tala* leaves and held together by boards, giving the impression of a chest.

5) Chishaku-in temple:

The head temple of Shingi Shingon sect to be mentioned at the final paragraph of Chapter XVIII.

Notes for VI. PREPARATION FOR THE GREAT LEAP

1) Nishida Kitarō (1870–1945) & his philosophy:

A Japanese philosopher whose life-long theme was to compare the oriental way of thinking as is typically found in zen (see Note 2) with the European way of thinking that led contemporary philosophy, thus to form a new system of philosophy. The basic principle he reached was: absolute antitheses identify themselves with each other.

2) zen and Zen:

zen (Skt., *dhyana* = contemplation) is an intuitive method of spiritual training that dates back to the Vedas or India's oldest religious literature made by Aryans. The aim of zen consists in attaining a lofty transcendence over worldly care. Sakyamuni propounded it as the final step of the Eight Steps to Buddhahood. When introduced into China, it was amalgamated with the tranquil temper of Taoist quietism. In Japan, it was introduced from China toward the end of the twelfth century when the military men were rising to be rulers and administrators. They had needed a religion which could fulfil the task of training the ruling class in mental firmness and resolute action and of satisfying their spiritual aspirations. Thus the Zen sects were welcomed and developed by the military men and through them exercised influence upon the people at large.

3) Kume-dera temple:

The temple is said to have been built by a man popularly known as "Kume no Sennin (Taoist hermit living in Kume)." The legend goes as follows:

> Once upon a time, a man secluded himself in Mt. Yoshino and practiced Taoist asceticism until at last he was able to fly in the air. One day he was flying over Kume Village, when a young woman caught his eyes. She was washing taros in a stream. On seeing her while legs showing from the bottom of her clothes well tucked up, the poor man lost his occult power and fell down to the ground. Soon he was seen among the local farmers mobilized for construction work on the imperial palace being built in that neighbourhood. While working very hard, he gradually regained his lost power and when the palace was completed, he who had worked exceptionally well was rewarded with tax-free land, upon which he built a temple which was later known as Kume-dera.

It was a small temple. So if it had "the east pagoda" on its grounds, it might have been dedicated by a high-ranking official who came from that village or a wealthy man living in the neighborhood.

4) the copies were made:

According to *The Documents Kept at Shōsō-in*, the *Mahavairocana Sutra* was copied in 737. Another sutra that constituted the core of Esoteric Buddhism—the *Vajrasekhara Sutra*—which had also been introduced by Gembō,* had been copied in the year before. So it is quite probable that Kūkai had been acquainted with the *Vajrasekhara Sutra*, too, before going to China.

It is also known that *A Commentary on the Mahavairocana Sutra* by Yixing (see Note 3 for XVII) had been imported by Tokusei of Saidai-ji in 778 when he returned from Tang to Japan. Then Kūkai must have read that, too.

☆ Shōsō-in was the treasure-house of Tōdai-ji in Nara, built in 756, in order to house the Tennō Shōmu's property.

5) mudra-making:

Mudra is a sign or gesture which represents the enlightenment or vows of Buddhas, Bodhisattvas or other divinities.

A large number of mudras in Esoteric Buddhism employ virtually all possible movements of the fingers, some being a single gesture and others involving complicated sequences composed of several changing mudras.

(a) *Gasshō* (b) *Chiken-in* (c) *Hōkai Jō-in* (d) *Gōma-in* (e) *Semui-in* (f) *Yogan-in*

Credited to DAIJISEN (Shogakkan, Tokyo, 1995)

Examples:
(a) *Gasshō (the pressing of palms together)*: Held together in *gasshō*, the hands symbolized the unity of the eternal Buddha Realm (right) and the transient world of phenomena (left).
(b) *Chiken-in (the Wisdom Fist Mudra)*: Formed by Mahavairocana in the Realm of the Indestructubles (see Note 6 for IV), this embodies teaching considered among the most secret in Esoteric Buddhism.
(c) *Hōkai Jō-in (Dharma Realm Samadhi Mudra)*: Mahavairocana in the Womb-store (see Note 6 for IV) forms this mudra of dwelling in the enlightened mind of the universal Dharma Realm and the self as one body.
(d) *Gōma-in (Mudra for Subjugating Demons)*.
(e) *Semui-in (Mudra for delivering people from what is horrifying them)*.
(f) *Yogan-in (Mudra for Answering Prayers)*.

Notes for VII. SAICHŌ

1) the Tendai (Tiantai in Chinese) religion:
Its original system was formulated by the Chinese philosopher Zhiyi (538–597), and was named Tiantai after the mountain where he was living then. In 805, Saichō introduced that religion to develop it into a synthetic religion and called it Tendai religion. The Chinese Tiantai and the Japanese Tendai religions, therefore, cannot be regarded as the same, though the Chinese characters 天台宗 are the same.

Saichō tried to keep his Tendai religion independent of the old Buddhism in Nara—especially its Hossō department which, in emphasizing hierarchic degrees of spiritual attainment, was highly aristocratic, for only the select few were supposed to be able to enjoy spiritual illumination; whereas the Tendai doctrine emphasized the universality of salvation, embracing even the most vicious. This strife lasted even to the end of Saichō's life (822) and his wish to be independent of the old Buddhism was posthumously fulfilled, as is mentioned in Note 1 for Chapter XXIV

2) the Korean Peninsula:
Koguryo, Paekche and Silla were the three kingdoms on the Korean Peninsula. When the Sui Dynasty united the whole of China toward the end of the sixth century, they started to invade Koguryo again and again; then the ensuing Tang Dynasty followed the example of the Sui and attacked Koguryo and Paekche until they defeated the latter in 660 and the former in 668. Silla had helped tang China all this while, but abhorring the idea that the whole peninsula would be occupied by Tang China, it launched its attacks against Tang China until it abandoned the conquest of the peninsula (676). Thus Silla became the first to unite the whole peninsula.

3) *Sōgō Bunin*:
A record concerning the hierarchical posts in the Ecclesiastical Office.

4) *Genkō Shakusho*:
Japan's first historical book on Buddhism covers the subjects from its introduction into this country (538) to 1332 when this book was completed. More than four hundred priests are referred to.

5) *obito*:
A title for the Estate Master during the period prior to the Taika Reform (645). His rank was only one degree below that of the Local Chieftain whose title was *atae*.

6) the three worlds:
The three worlds round which the unenlighted must transmigrate: the world of desire-driven beings, the world of beings with form, and the world of beings without form.

7) the *Konkōmyō-kyō* sutra:
This sutra advocates that the four guardian gods will protect the king who rules his country in a proper manner. Together with the *Hoke-kyō* sutra and the *Ninnō-gyō* sutra, it was highly esteemed as one of the three great sutras for protecting the country.

8) *Daijō Kishin-ron*:
This work, translated into Chinese in 550, is very popular both in China and in Japan as an excellent exposition of Mahayana Buddhism, since it maintains that the spirit of Mahayana can be found in the inherent nature of everyone.

9) This place is ideally located:
According to the Way of *Yin* and *Yang* (see Note 10), the place with a stream to the east, a road to the west, a sunken place to the south, a hill to the north, was to bring those who live there wealth, good health and longevity, because it gratifies the guardian god of each direction—Blue Dragon of the east, White Tiger of the west, Vermilion Sparrow of the south, and Fighters represented by Turtle and Snake of the north. The idea of Demon's Entrance in the northeastern corner comes from the same source.

10) the Way of *Yin* and *Yang*:
A Chinese philosophic doctrine according to which two opposing principles, the active (*Yang*) and the regressive (*Yin*), produce all phenomena by their operation upon the five elements (fire, water, wood, gold, earth). It degenerated into a kind of pseudo-science like fortune telling: interaction of the ten calendar signs and the twelve horary signs determined fortune and misfortune, prosperity and adversity. Divination greatly influenced everyday life. Examples are the avoiding of going in an inauspicious direction by the Heian aristocracy and confinement to one's house on unlucky days.

11) the Imperial chapel:
It was founded in 655 in accordance with the belief that the peace of the state and the security of the throne depended upon the guardianship of Buddha and his saints.

12) Usa Hachiman-gū shrine:
Hachiman, the most popular Shintō deity along with Tenjin mentioned in Chapter I, is the semi-mythical fifteenth Tennō Ōjin, who was deified as a guardian god of the Yamato Court. As he proved to be a great protector of the Court and the state, a messenger was often sent there to consult an oracle or to pray for victory or success. Hachiman, the first to be offered the title of Bodhisattva, took the lead in a mixture of Buddhism and Shintōism.

13) the three principal scriptures on the Tiantai principle:
Maka Shikan (a text for *shikan* meditation*), *Hokke Mongu* (*A commentary* on *Hoke-kyō*), *Hokke Gengi* (*The Profound Gist of Hoke-kyō*). All of them were written by Zhiyi mentioned in Note 1.

Notes for INTERLUDE 2. THE ENVOYS TO CHINA

1) the Emperors of preceding dynasties:
    The third Emperor Taiwudi (reign: 423–452) of the Northern Wei and the third Emperor Wudi (reign: 560–578) of the Northern Zhou.

2) the northern route and the southern routes:
    They are shown on the map on page 337.

3) *ri*:
    About 600 meters. But "the three thousand *ri*" is a set phrase that means "a very long distance." Actually the shortest crossing is about 800 kilometers.

Notes for VIII. THE BOATS TURNED BACK AND SET SAIL AGAIN

1) the next:
    It was dispatched in 838, and Kūkai had been dead for three years. This one (the seventeenth embassy) was actually the last one (see Note 9 for XXX).

2) *tan* and *hiki*:
    Tan is a piece of cloth, 34 centimeters wide and 10 meters long, enough to make a suit of clothes; *hiki* is a couple of *tan*.

3) *ryō*:
    38.5 grams of gold.

4) dozens of Buddhist temples:
    Not only many of the Eighty-eight Temples on the Shikoku Pilgrimage but also many other temples on the island have proper authorities or grounds to claim that Kūkai was their founder.

5) *Nihon-kiryaku*:
    A historical book that consists of an abbreviated version of the six historical books that cover from "the age of the gods" to 887 (see note 1 for III) and of the records and diaries kept from 887 to 1036.

6) the Legalists:
    One of the many groups of thinkers who appeared in the Warring States Period (770 B.C.–221 B.C.) in China. Legalists, represented by Han Feizi (?–ca.233), advocated the monarch's strict rule on the basis of law.

7) Laozi (?–?):
    One of the many thinkers mentioned in the previous number. He extolled the merits of returning to nature and doing nothing as the best approach to success in life. Later when the theory made contact with Buddhism, it developed into a philosophy centered around non-existence or pure consciousness required before the acquisition of any form of experience or knowledge. His thought and Zhuangzi's mentioned in the following number were later systematized into Taoism as a

philosophy, not as a religion (see Note 6 for III).

8) Zhuangzi (?-?) :
Around 300 B.C. he unfolded a sort of speculative philosophy, exalting individual freedom, transcendental mysticism and anarchism, while denouncing social conventions and ethical theories.

9) the magnificent ramparts:
Cities and capitals in China were surrounded by magnificent ramparts. That was why they were and still are called mainly in a literary context not cities or capitals but castles, like Chang'an Castle. In Japan, Nara capital and Heian (Kyōto) capital, built after the model of Chang'an Castle, were equipped with ramparts, but they were rather for form's sake. But those of Dazai-fu capital, part of which still remain, were comparatively large as a precaution for defense against enemy attack from aboroad.

10) the school and the hospital:
They used to belong to a large temple. The first great Buddhist institution in Japan, built at Naniwa by the Prince-Regent Shōtoku—Shitennō-ji—was composed of four establishments: the temple proper, an asylum, a hospital and a dispensary, thus creating a model of what temples should be as a group of religious, educational and philanthropic organizations.

11) many an embassy to China set sail in midsummer:
The principal reason why they usually started in summer is considered that attending the New Year celebration at the Tang Court was the highlight of their visit to Chang'an and this made them start earlier instead of waiting until fall.

Notes for X. HIS WRITING SAVED THE DIFFICULT SITUATIONS

1) *Shōryō-shū*:
The ten-volume collection of Kūkai's literary works. The last three volumes were once scattered and lost, but were made up as supplementary volumes.

2) [Kūkai] was able to speak current Chinese fluently:
Kūkai as a mountain ascetic in his youth seems to have had occasional chances to meet and make friends with a considerable number of Chinese technicians who had been engaged in mining and refining a variety of minerals, such as iron sand, copper and mercury. From them Kūkai would have not only learned current Chinese but also acquired the knowledge of minerals and how to process them. The latter would have been very useful later when he came to produce Buddhist images and ritual impliments himself and then to teach others how to produce them.
☆ From this presumption, some people support an idea that those technicians, Chinese and Japanese, had made a great contribution when Kūkai was raising the funds before he left for China.

3) the following poem:
This poem was composed under the impetus of the following poem Kūkai had made for Weishang, a Buddhist monk who came from Shu (present-day Sichuan Province), and whom Kūkai probably met and shared difficult times with on his way to Chang'an:

碪危人難行
石險獸無登
燭暗迷前後
蜀人不得火

The stone steps are too trecherous to climb.
Rocks are too steep even for beasts to crawl.
Lantern lights are too dim to let us go on.
You, coming from Shu, do not carry any fire.

This type of poem is called "character-dividing poetry": 碪 in the first line is divided into two characters 石 and 登 to be used in the second line; 燭 in the third line is also turned into two characters 蜀 and 火 for the last line.

The poem Ma Zong made for Kūkai was:

何乃万里来
可非銜其才
増学助玄機
土人如子稀

This poem belongs to the same type of poem, but not so perfect as Kūkai's: 何 in the first line partly appears as 可 in the second line; 増 in the third line becomes 土 for the last line. Obviously Kūkai's is much better than Ma Zong's.

4) sustaining myself only on vegetables, lying in snow...:

This statement may correspond to the following entry in his autobiographical work, *The Indications of the Three Teachings*:

> ...at one time I had a hard time in the snow that buried Mt. Kimpusen in Yoshino, but this brought me nothing, to my regret; at another time I starved myself on top of Mt. Ishizuchi in Shikoku, but this also turned out to be a sad failure.

☆ Both Mt. Kimpusen and Mt. Ishizuchi were, and still are, among meccas of mountain ascetics. These were also among the mountains known for their mineral products (see Note 2).

5) because of a vacancy that happened to occur before our voyage:

This phrase if probably based on the fact that government students who survived the wreck on the fifth day at the Inland Sea were not allowed to re-join the embassy because it was believed that to send them to sea again would invite further mishap.

Notes for XI. Travel to Chang'an

1) *Wo* and *Wo-guo*:

The Japanese and their country had been called *Wo* and *Wo-guo* by the Chinese since they were mentioned first in *The Chronicles of the Han Dynasty* completed in 82 A.D.

2) Jipang:

Just as the Prince-Regent Shōtoku called his country "the Land of Sunrise" (see Note 3 for I), the Japanese began to write the name of their country in Chinese characters: 日本 (Sun Base), and in 701 it was decided upon by low. "Jih-pen" in northern China or "Yat-pan" in southern China is said to be the origin of Zipangu, Jipangu, Jipang or Japan.

3) many religious practices:

Ablutions in Shintō (see note 5 for II), blended with the Buddhist notion of lustration, produced a variety of religious practices such as purifying exorcism, water ablutions, cold water ablutions and waterfall ablutions. They are still practiced in various situations—in religious ceremonies or in ascetic practices by Shintōist and Buddhist mountain ascetics, and Buddhist monks and laymen.

4) *The Pilgrimage around Tang China in Search of the Truth*:

This journal has been translated into English by Edwin O.Reischauer: *Ennin's Diary, The Record of a Pilgrimate to China in Search of the Law* and *Ennin's Travels in T'ang China* (The Ronald Press Company, New York, 1955).

☆ Ennin (794–864) went to China in 838. While staying there for ten years, he studied on Mount Wutai and then in Chang'an where he was initiated into Esoteric Buddhism, which was more or less different from what Kūkai had been initiated into from Huiguo. (see Note 4 for XVI)

5) [Laozi] is said to have passed this station:

It is said that Laozi wrote what was later know an *Laozi* at this station, as he was requested to do so by the barrier-keeper.

6) "the four distinguished lords":

Mengchang-jun of Qi, Pingyuan-jun of Zhao, Xinling-jun of Wei, and Chunshen-jun of Chu.

7) Bai Letian (772-846):

Letian is the style for Bai Juyi. His poetry, plain and elegant, was loved and recited by many including the Japanese. The epic mentioned here, *A Song of Everlasting Sorrow (Chang Hen Ge)*, written in 806, was to have a great influence on Japanese literature in the Heian Period. Lady Murasaki (?–ca.1016), the author of *The Tale of Genji*, the world's oldest long novel, is said to have been a great reader of this work.

Notes for XII. SPRING IN CHANG'AN

1) those who have been to the Apricot Garden:

Those who had recently passed the higher civil service examination were invited by the Emperor to the banquet held at Xing-yuan (Apricot Garden). For many high-ranking officials who attended that annual event, it was a very good opportunity to seek for eligible young men for their daughters.

2) fragrant dust:

In March, April and May a tremendous amount of dust is raised from the deserts in the northwestern part of China to be blown east, sometimes as far as Japan. In Chang'an it was made fragrant as it passed through the germinating fields and hills in the suburbs.

3) [they] broke off sprigs of the willows:

The Chinese had observed the fact that willows have amazing vitality. This led them to think that they had a magical power to protect them from evil. Another fact that the sprig is so supple that the two ends easily meet was also used to express their wish to meet again soon.

4) Bohai:

The influential that had survived the fall of Koguryo (668) founded their own country (698 –926) together with a Tungus in the eastern part of northeastern China. Since 727, it had kept friendly relations with Japan.

5) Wuling:

"Wu-ling" means "five Imperial mausoleums," which were dedicated to the five Emperors of the Han Dynasty.

6) *The Memoirs of the Central Asia and India*:

The most comprehensive and important record of travel to India ever written in the Orient, and is also an incomparable reference work in the field of Indian History. *Monkey* (*Xiyou-ji*) is its popularized version written by Wu Cheng'en (1500–1582). (see Note 3 for Interlude 1).

7) a really convincing piece of writing:

Among many other convincing letters Kūkai wrote to the Court for others, the following two are often mentioned: one asking for reduced sentence for Priest Chūkei of Gangō-ji who fell in love with a Court lady; the other for requesting a proper post for Kiyomura no Toyonari who had long been neglected because of his having once been tutor to Prince Iyo (see Interlude 3).

8) a dry mugwort:

Mugwort whose botanical name is *Erigeron acris* seems to represent dry weed in winter.

9) Qingqi-men gate:

Another name of Chunming-men gate. "Those lingering around" this gate were probably two friends, one of whom was going to leave Chang'an by that gate. Apparently they were reluctant to part with each other.

Notes for XIV. THE TWO INDIAN MASTERS AND ABBOT HUIGUO

1) Prajna and Munisri:

They are usually called the *Tripitaka* Prajna and the *Tripitaka* Munisri. "*Tripitaka*" was an honorific title conferred on a Buddhist priest who was both highly virtuous and well-versed in the *tripitaka* (sutras, rules of discipline and commentaries on doctrines). The most famous person with this title is Xuanzang, who is often called just "the *Tripitaka*."

2) the *Roku-Haramita-kyō* sutra:

The sutra expounds the six kinds of practice by which bodhisattvas are able to attain enlightenment: donation, keeping precepts, forbearance, assiduity, meditation, and wisdom.

3) Dongta-yuan temple:

One of the several temples that were included in the temple complex of Qinglong-si. Large temples in China had many temples in their spacious compounds, as in the case of Tōdai-ji in Japan, which encompasses thirteen temples. In China, "-*yuan*" is added to the end of these temples' names, while in Japan the suffix is "-*in*."

Notes for XV. THE EIGHTH PATRIARCH OF ESOTERIC BUDDHISM

1) the Four Guardians of Buddhism:
The quartet of the Twelve Guardians, who control the four directions

2) a tendency to self-glorification:
Probably it would have been his disciples who intensified the glorification of their master when he once told them this episode, for in the level of daily life Kūkai had brought himself under the following mottoes given by Cui Ziyu, a Confucian, who lived during the Earlier Han (202 B.C.–8 A.D.)

Do not speak of other people's faults.
Do not talk of your own merits.
Do not think much of what you have done for others.
Do not forget what you have received from others.
Worldly honour does not deserve your aspiration.
Let the virtue of *ren** alone guide your way.
Good consideration first; action second.
Then whatever others may say will not affect you.
Do not let your reputation surpass what you are.
The saints always keep themselves low.
Precious is the immaculate in ditch mud.
Keep your appearance dim, your inward brilliant.
The gentle and weak will go on living.
Lao-zi remonstrated against the harsh and strong.
The uncivilized will aspire to be sturdy and strong.
Unfathomable is the one who is calm and quiet.
Use prudence in speech; use moderation in eating and drinking.
Learn to be contented, and you will be able to hold disasters in check.
If you always keep these in mind and act accordingly,
Your fragrance will surely be immortal.
*(see Note 3 for II)

3) *kana*:
Kana were brought into being while the Japanese were trying to write their own language phonetically (see Note 5 for I & Note 2 for XXVII). Here Kūkai incidentally warned against reading only the phonetic transcriptions in *kana* written at the side of each Chinese character instead of reading the Chinese characters themselves.

4) the Five Wisdoms:
The Five Wisdoms to be attained through persuing Esoteric Buddhism are as follows: (1) Subjective wisdom in relation to every element. (2) Wisdom which reflects all phenomena of the world as clearly as a mirror. (3) Wisdom which observes the equality of everything after denying the difference of phenomena. (4) Wisdom which recognizes the elements of the world and observes the various faculties of sentient beings in order to establish a standard of preaching and resolve

various doubts of the people. (5) Wisdom which enables one to develop the elaborate faculties of benefiting both oneself and others.

5) the Chinese aniseed tree:

A fragrant tree about three meters tall. Its sprigs placed in vases make an offering in Buddist services. Its leaves and bark are made into incense sticks and powder.

6) *kan-mon*:

One *mon* made one coin or one *sen*; one thousand *mon* makes one *kan* or one *kan-mon*.

Notes for XVI. LEAVING CHANG'AN

1) military expeditions:

The subjugation of Ezo had been carried out from ancient times, as mentioned in Chapter I, and it was intensified after the Taika Reform (645). But in 802, when Commander in Chief, Sakanoue no Tamuramaro,* succeeded in building a fortress in Izawa in northern Japan, it was tentatively brought to an end.

2) Ju:

The family name of Hayanari was 橘, which is pronounced *Tachibana* in Japanese, and *Ju* in Chinese.

☆ In adopting Chinese characters, the Japanese used two ways in reading them: they read them phonetically as the Chinese do or in their own pronunciation by translating them into Japanese. The result is that one Chinese character can have several readings of each type.

3) a mole cricket:

The insect, about three centimeters long, resembles the cricket in shape, but unlike the cricket it digs with its wide forelegs, as the mole does.

4) Enchin (814–891):

His forefather was the District Administrator of Naka District seated in Mano Plain. His birthplace is perpetuated as Konzō-ji, the seventy-sixth temple on the Shikoku Pilgrimage route. Enchin as a boy went to Mount Hiei, as someone of his family had already been there. In 853 he visited Mount Tiantai in Tang China and then proceeded to its capital to be initiated into the revised version of Esoteric Buddhism by Faquan of Qinglong-si temple. After returning home in 858, he successfully expounded its superiority to Tendai religion to Ennin (see Note 4 for XI) who had finally established not only Tendai but Esoteric Buddhism as well. After Ennin, Enchin became the chief abbot of Mount Hiei. Thus they established a tradition that the chief abbacy on Mount Hiei should be conferred to the one who obtained the complete mastery of both Tendai religion and Esoteric Buddhism. When those on Mount Hiei began to name their Esoteric Buddhism Tai-mitsu, the one established by Kūkai began to be called Tō-mitsu (the Esoteric Buddhism offered at Tō-ji*).

Notes for XVII. RETURN TO JAPAN BY WAY OF YUEZHOU

1) that famous rivalry:

Their fierce rivalry lasted two generations. In order not to forget their original intention to gain the better of the other, the king of Wu made it a rule to sleep on firewood, and the king of Yue to occasionally taste liver so that its bitterness might give hime fresh determination. Their rivalry, which ended in 472 B.C. when Wu was overthrown by Yue, was to be perpetuated by famous set expressions such as: 臥薪嘗胆 (Lying on firewood and licking liver) and 呉越同舟 (Wu and Yue, or cat and dog, in the same boat). Mt. Guiji, where the King of Yue was once defeated by the king of Wu, is also referred to in the phrase of 会稽恥 (the unforgettable humiliation as the King of Yue had to suffer on Mt. Guiji).

2) a rubbing of the epitaph created by the Emperor Xuanzong himself:

It was Kūkai who had handed this rubbing to the envoy Fujiwara, hoping that it would help Kammu understand what the purpose of his visits to China was. As for how he got it, it is unknown but an admirer of Yixing might have presented it to Kūkai as a token of their friendship.

3) Yixing (683–727):

A Chinese Buddhist priest. He had been versed in zen meditation, Buddhist precepts and the Tiantai religion before he studies Esoteric Buddhism at first under Shubhakarasimha and then under Vajrabodhi, thus to be initiated into the two different currents of Esoteric Buddhism. When Shubhakarasimha was translating the *Mahavairocana Sutra* into Chinese, he helped him in writing it. Then he wrote *A Commentary on the Mahavairocana Sutra* by not only compiling what he had learned from Shubhakarasimha but also incorporating his own thought he came to embrace through studying other Mahayana sutras. Thought he left no direct successor, he is placed among the eight patriarchs who transmitted Esoteric Buddhism: Nagarjuna, Nagabodhi, Vajrabodhi, Amoghavajra, Shubhakarasimha, Yixing, Huiguo and Kūkai.

He was also good at mathematics and calendric science and became famous for his creation of a new calendar, which was adopted in 728 by the Emperor Xuanzong.

4) Students to be ordained annually:

They were to spend several years as a novice before they were actually ordained.

5) *Zhuangzi*:

The work produced by Zhuangzi, together with *Laozi* by Laozi (see Note 5 for XI), represents Taoism as philosophy (see Note 6 for III).

6) *The Sequel of the Topography of Chikuzen Province*:

The Topography of Chikuzen Province was one of the local histories written in compliance with an Imperial edict issued in 713. Its sequal was compiled about a millennium later at the command of the Provincial Lord.

7) he was making a thanks-giving pilgrimage around the Shintō shrines:

Kūkai's Esoteric Buddhism was so comprehensive that the native gods of Shintō (see Note 5 for II) were never to be rejected but respected as the guardians of the local places, as was seen in the case of opening Kōya-san or building a dam for Mannō-ike reservoir.

8) the *Hannya-shin-gyō* sutra:

A compendium or a summary of the *Hannya-gyō* sutra (*The Wisdom Sutra*). The Sanskrit text was published by M.Müller and an English translation can be found in *The Manual of Zen*

Buddhism by Daisetsu T. Suzuki.

Notes for XVIII. Two Years on Mt. Makino'o

1) the Shingon Ritsu sect:
A sect which harmonizes the doctrines of Shingon Esoteric Buddhism and the Hinayana and Mahayana precepts. In 1895, it became independent of Shingon religion.

2) at his hermitage there:
As to where this poem was made, different people give different places, including Mt. Takao and Mt. Kōya.

3) Kamakura Buddhism or Buddhism during the Kamakura Period (1185–1333):
The establishment of the new military government (Shōgunate) under the dictatorship of the Minamoto clan in 1185 marked an epoch-making change in the history of Japan. Their firm military rule extending over the whole country from their headquarters in the east, at Kamakura, was in strong contrast to the luxurious life and lax administration of the court nobles in the Heian (Kyōto) Capital.... It was not a mere political revolution, but social, moral, and religious at the same time.... The Buddhist religion of the new age was not one of ceremonies and mysteries but a religion of simple piety or of spiritual exercise. Dogma gave way to personal experience, ritual and sacerdotalism to piety and intuition, and this new type of religion exerted its influence beyond class limits.

We may distinguish three forms of Buddhism which signalized the change and then ruled the people's faith during the warlike ages between the thirteenth and sixteenth centuries. The first was the pietist faith of Amida-Buddhism (see Note 4). Its leader was **Hōnen** (1133–1212), a remarkable representative of pious devotion. The second was the intuition of Zen, a new form of Buddhism introduced from China by the puritanical mystic, **Dōgen** (1200–1253). The third was the revivalism of Hokke Buddhism propounded by **Nichiren** (1222–1282), a militant propagandist of prophetic ardour. Masaharu Anesaki, *History of Japanese Religion*.

As for **Shinran**, see Note 4.

4) Jōdo pietism:
.... this worship of Buddha Amida, the Lord of Infinite Light, set a stream of pious contemplation flowing in Buddhism through its history in India and China. The belief was that he had once been a royal prince and then a monk, who out of compassion for his fellow beings, took a vow to dedicate all the merits of his long, strenuous self-training to their spiritual benefit. By the mysterious virtue of his meritorious work, he finally accomplished the task of establishing a paradise, the Land of Purity (Jōdo in Japanese), located "far beyond millions and billions of leagues in the west," where he could embrace the pious souls who would call upon his name. He is believed to be residing there even now and working perpetually to save even those who are not capable of learning and discipline....

There were in India and China some reclusive monks devoted to meditation on the Buddha Amida and to invoking his name so as to be received by him in his paradise. In the earlier stage of this form of Buddhism in Japan, Amida was worshipped as one of those innumerable deities in the Shingon pantheon....

The briefest confession of a pietist saint (Hōnen) includes: "When we invoke Buddha and say *'Namu Amida Butsu'* (Adoration to the Buddha of Infinite Life and Light) with the firm belief that we shall be born in Buddha's paradise, we shall surely be born there."

Shinran (1173–1262) was converted to Hōnen's religion. His personal contact with the master lasted only six years.... Thus Shinran carried the idea of Buddha's grace to extreme conclusions.... and founded an independent branch of Jōdo Buddhism now known as Jōdo-shin-shū (True Doctrine).... A saying of Hōnen runs—"Even a bad man will be received in Buddha's Land, so how much more readily a good man!" Shinran turned this to—"Even a good man will be received in Buddha's Land, so how much more readily a bad man!" In short "neither virtue nor wisdom but faith" was his fundamental tenet, and faith itself has nothing to do with our own intention or attainment but is solely Buddha's free gift.

Kakuban combined the invocation of Amida's name with his Shingon mysticism. Here in his case, the mystery of "Calling the Name" was identified with the mystery of the "Word," as stated above in considering the three mysteries* taught by Shingon Buddhism. MASAHARU ANESAKI, *History of Japanese Religion.*

Notes for INTERLUDE 3. THE THREE IMPERIAL PRINCES

1) Yamaga Sokō (1622–1685):

A scholar who represented a school of Confucianism during the Edo Period (1603–1867). Rejecting the later interpretations and dogmatism of Chinese Confucians, Chu Hsi [Chu Xi] (1130 –1200) and Wang Yangming (1472–1528), this school directly investigated the original meaning of Confucius and Mencius and imitated the way of the ancient sages.... This revival of the ancient interpretation and new study of the classics influenced the study of Japanese classical literature. JOSEPH M. GOEDERTIER, *A Dictionary of Japanese History.*

2) Motoori Norinaga (1730–1801):

A scholar of *Kokugaku* or a school of learning which originated during the middle of the Edo Period. From the previous ages, a distorted and dogmatic Buddhist and Confucian interpretation was given to poetry, *Kojiki, Nihon Shoki, The Tale of Genji,* etc. Against this interpretation and against the tendency to communicate this interpretation secretly, *Kokugaku* studied the classics to learn the orthodox meaning of the ancient terminology and brought to light the spirit prevailing in ancient days. Rejecting Confucian virtues, this school stressed ancient morality which preached Japanese virtues.... It reached its climax under Motoori Norinaga. He spent half his life writing *A Commentary of Kojiki,* which was not merely a commentary on a classic but a study of antiquity carried out with all the knowledge available at that time. JOSEPH M. GOEDERTIER, *A Dictionary of Japanese History.*

3) Hirata Atsutane (1776–1843):

When *Kokugaku* (see Note 2) further developed under Hirata Atsutane, it became a fanatic kind of revived Shintō which evolved into the leading political principle of the Meiji Restoration. The ideology came to standstill on its contact with European and American ideologies, but, together with Confucianism, *Kokugaku* survived for a long time as the keynote of ultranationalism. JOSEPH M. GOEDERTIER, *A Dictionary of Japanese History.*

4) Saigō Takamori (1827–1877):

An activist in the revolutionary era of Japan. He who was once a warrior from Satsuma (present-day Kagoshima Prefecture) made a great contribution in carrying out the Meiji Restoration (1867: a political revolution which resulted in the abolition of the feudal system of the Edo Period and the establishment of a new form of government). After the restoration, the modernization policy adopted by the government resulted in the loss of feudal privileges of the warriors. In order to soothe their discontent, the government was planning to invade Korea, as advocated by Saigō. But when it was opposed by those who had just returned from an inspection tour round Europe and the United States, Saigō resigned from the cabinet and returned home (1873). At home he was to lead the Seinan War: the last and worst warriors' revolt against the government. His troops fought fiercely, but when their stronghold at home was attacked by the government troops, they had to withdraw and Saigō committed suicide.

5) Uchimura Kanzō (1861–1930):
A non-church Christian and critic. Though strictly educated in accordance with Confucianism, he turned Christian at seventeen. After finishing his education at Amherst College and Hartford College of Theology in the United States, he taught at several missionary schools until he began to devote himself to writing. As a pacifist, he advocated renunciation of war before and during the Russo-Japanese War (1904–5), mainly through *A Study of the Bible*, a periodical he issued. This periodical and his seminar continued even in his later years, having great influence upon many literature young men and women at that time.

6) Yoshino Sakuzō (1878–1933):
A Christian scholar of politics. In 1906, after finishing the graduate school of law of Tōkyō Imperial University, he went to China to spend three years there as the tutor to the eldest son of Yuan Shikai, who was to be the first President of the Republic of China (1912). After returning home, he soon left for Europe and the United States to spend another three years in finishing his own education. After returning home again, the professor of law began to publish his opinions, criticizing China's restoration of the Imperial rule (1915) and Japan's dispatch of troops to Siberia (1918–22). Thus he made himself a virtual leader of what it is now known as "democratic movement in the Taishō era (1912–1926)."

7) to make use of the Tennō as a tool to serve his missionary purpose:
This may not necessarily be true, when we see what he did in propagating his religion or in bringing Mount Kōya into being, as is recounted in later chapters XXIV and XXVII.

Notes for XIX. Those Who Sought His Help

1) there were no temples available in and around the capital:
Nara Capital had many large state temples in and around it and this led Nara Buddhism to interfere with politics sometimes to an undue extent. This made Kammu decide not to have any Buddhist temples in and around his new capital, except for Tō-ji and Sai-ji, which were intended to be Reception Halls rather than Buddhist temples.

☆ The suffix *-ji* (*-si* in Chinese) used to have two meanings: Buddhist temple and government office.

☆ All those Buddhist temples that one sees in the city area of present-day Kyōto were originally either temple-residences for Imperial family members (retired tennōs or princes or princesses in holy orders) or were privately founded by pious individuals or political powers in later ages.

2) A Collection of Waka Ancient and Contemporary:
As its original title, *Man'yō-shū: Second series*, suggests, this was practically a sequel of

Man'yō-shū or *A Collection of Ten Thousand Leaves* (see Note 8 for II). But this new anthology was written in *kana*, not in *Manyō-gana* which were actually Chinese characters. The type of poems most favored by the one hundred and twenty poets that contributed to it was thirty-one syllable verse (5-7-5, 7-7), which was to be favored by many even to this day. Formerly *waka* meant "Japanese poems of various types as were seen in *A Collection of Ten Thousand Leaves*" in contrast with Chinese poems. But today *waka* or *tanka* (short verse) means thirty-one syllable verse only.

3) Ninna-ji:

It was completed in 888 by the Emperor Uda. After entering priesthood of Esoteric Buddhism (after descending the throne in 897), he came to reside there, thus starting a tradition of having a member of the Imperial family as its chief priest (see Note 1).

4) *Acalaceta*:

Acala (see Note 1 for XXX) in the form of a boy.

5) [the Tennō Saga] allowed me to propagate my religion:

Despite this permission, Kūkai would not propagate his religion at once. The reason will be mentioned in Chapter XXIV.

6) *O-mizutori*:

O-mizutori is the highlight of the greatest annual event of Tōdai-ji: the *Shuni-e* Ceremony, which is held at Nigatsu-dō or Second Month Hall during the first half of the second month of the lunar calendar. It dates back to 752. Its purpose is to offer repentance to the main image there—the eleven-faced Bodhisattva—for all the sins committed during the past year, and to pray for happiness in the coming year and for the peace and security of the state and a harvest of abundant crops. *O-mizutori*, in which "fragrant water from the spring" is offered to the Bodhisattva, is a popular appellation for the whole ceremony.

Notes for INTERLUDE 4. THE KUSUKO AFFAIR

1) he changed his residence as many as five times:

This fact shows that like many of the Heian aristocracy he was a great believer in the Way of *Yin* and *Yang*. According to that system of divination, interaction of the ten calendar signs and the twelve horary signs determined good luck and bad. So if he wanted to avoid departing in an inauspicious direction or on unlucky days, he might spend many months before he reached his destination. This made him change his residence so often.

2) the new office he had started under his direct control:

Though Japan adopted a Chinese political structure based on the penal code and the civil and administrative code, the supreme organ of administration was not the tennō but the Council of State, because the tennō in Japan reigned but did not rule, quite unlike the emperor in China. But in 810, the Tennō Saga started an extralegal office under his direct control to cope with the Kusuko affair.

3) his lineage (Fujiwara Hokke) was to retain their power even to the end of the Edo Period (1867):

In 858, during the reign of the Tennō Seiwa (850–880). Fujiwara no Yoshifusa, a son of

Fuyutsugu and Seiwa's maternal grandfather, was made regent. Since then the Fujiwara Hokke who monopolized the office of regent or chief councilor to the tennō became the real power behind the throne. Throughout the ensuing eras, even after the family was split into five branches, that office was alternately assumed by a member of one of these branches.

4) Heizei chose to accept that proposal:
Even after he took the tonsure, he went on living in that palace, which in 847 was turned into a temple (present-day Futai-ji of Shingon Ritsu). In 821 Heizei received *abhiseka* baptism from Kūkai.

☆ In 822 one of his sons named Takaoka (?–ca.865), who had once been the Crown Prince of Saga though he had to be deprived of that post because of his father's misconduct, also entered priesthood. After learning Sanron at Tōdai-ji, he became a disciple of Kūkai—now known as Shinnyo, one of the Ten Great Disciples of Kūkai. Before his master's death that occurred twelve years later, he was to produce a portrait of Kūkai by copying what Kūkai himself had made his portrait. This became the prototype of all the other portraits of Kūkai.

In 862, when he was nearly sixty, Shinnyo went to Chang'an, China, in search of someone who would answer his doctrinal questions. But unable to find anyone who satisfied him, he left for India only to die on his way there.

Notes for XX. HIS NEWLY-ACQUIRED SELF-IDENTITY

1) An Lushan (705–757):
His father was Soghd, his mother Turkish.

2) the *Daijō Mitsugon-kyō* sutra:
This sutra was first translated into Chinese by an Indian priest, Jivakara. He presented his idea of Mahavairocana's Land while discussing the question of rebirth there. Amoghavajra, who had been working hard to obtain official recognition for his religion, took a particular interest in that idea and produced his own version of the same sutra. Another Esoteric Buddhist priest who made a study of this sutra was Yixing (see Note 3 for XVII), who also expounded Mahavairocana's Land in his *Commentary of the Mahavairocana Sutra*.

3) the seven evils:
Extraordinary phenomena in the sun, the moon and the twenty-eight constellations, calamities caused by fire, rain and wind, illnesses, and threats to peace and security of the state.

4) the Southern Court:
After the Kamakura shōgunate (feudal government) was destroyed in 1333, the imperial restoration was inaugurated and soon had two tennōs (the Southern Court in Yoshino and the Northern Court in Kyōto). This abnormal situation lasted from 1336 to 1392 when the Muromachi shōgunate brought about the unity of the two lineages of tennōs.

Notes for XXI. At Otokuni-dera Temple

1) *Jū Nyoze*:
According to the *Hoke-kyō* sutra, the ten factors of existence (*Jū Nyoze* 十如是) are: form, nature, substance, power, activities, primary causes, environmental causes, effects, rewards and retributions, and the totality of the above nine factors.

2) *Sōjō*:
The three major controllers of the priesthood who served at the Ecclesiastical Office were *Sōjō*, *Sōzu* and *Risshi* in descending order of rank, each divided into three or four ranks according to the order of importance: e.g. *Dai-Sōzu > Gon-no-Dai-Sōzu > Shō-Sōzu > Gon-no-Shō-Sōzu.*

3) *Dai Nihon-shi*:
A work on Japanese history. Its compilation was begun in 1657 by Tokugawa Mitsukuni, the Lord of Mito, and was completed in 1906 after the constant commitment of successive generations of the Mito clan. Their feudal moralism, whose backbone was the Confucian theory of the legitimacy of the ruler and of duty toward the sovereign, was to deeply influence Imperialists in the closing years of the Edo Period.

4) Saga, who intended to appease the Crown Prince's furies:
Later Saga was to ask Kūkai to do the same thing at Kawara-dera in Yamato Province, where in the second year of Heizei the Prince Iyo and his mother had been forced to kill themselves. Then the temple (present-day Gufuku-ji) was to be given to Kūkai by Saga.

5) a series of lectures on the *Yuima-gyō* sutra annually given at Kōfuku-ji temple:
It was, and still is, held from October 10 to 16 for the anniversary of Fujiwara no Kamatari's death. Kōfuku-ji, founded by Kamatari's wife, later became the guardian temple of the Fujiwara clan.

The *Yuima-gyō* sutra relates how Vimalakirti (Yuima), a lay follower of the Buddha, refuted the Hinayanist disciples of the Buddha by basing himself upon the concept of *sunyata*. Many found it interesting to see how the Buddhist laymen acted at a time when Mahayana Buddhism was evolving.

6) the sacred teaching:
It came from *The Yellow Emperor's Canon of Internal Medicine* (*Huangdi Neijing*), the oldest medical book written in China sometime during the Han era. Its commentary that appeared during the Tang era had already been introduced into Japan.

Notes for XXII. Their Expectations Turned Out to Be Unfulfilled

1) a real master:
Officially, Saichō had already been made the supreme master of Esoteric Buddhism by the Tennō Kammu, as mentioned in Chapter XVII.

2) that teaching must be transmitted directly from master to disciple:
They believed the most important and delicate thought must be transmitted by means of

immediate commumication from one mind to another, instead of delivering it on paper, sheepskin, wood or stone.

Notes for XXIII. How to Approach the Truth of the Universe

1) Engaku:

The teaching that helps one attain enlightenment for oneself by perceiving the Buddhist doctrine of *in* and *en*. *In* is the inner and direct cause by which the result occurs; *en* is the external and indirect one. According to the Buddhist doctrine, every action occurs in the harmony of both *in* and *en*.

2) Shōmon:

The teaching that helps one attain enlightenment by listening to the Buddha's teaching. Those who have attained enlightenment by means of Shōmon and Engaku are regarded as Hinayanist saints (see Note 7 for IV).

3) when Mount Hiei was attacked by Oda Nobunaga:

Ashikaga Yoshiaki, the last Shōgun of the Muromachi Shōgunate (a military government that lasted from 1392 to 1573), had been backed up by Oda Nobunaga (1534–1582), the strongest civil-war baron who was steadily unifying the country. But when they quarreled with each other, Nobunaga attacked Mount Hiei because they had taken the side of his enemy.

☆ In order to defend their manors against aggression, some temples had had their soldier monks since the latter half of the Heian Period. Soldier monks of Mount Hiei was especially active throughout the civil war period that lasted about a century from the close of the 15th century, but they were exterminated by Nobunaga and his successor, Toyotomi Hideyoshi (1536–1598), who finally succeeded in unifying the country. Mount Hiei itself was gradually restored by Hideyoshi and the Tokugawa Shōguns, who ruled throughout the Edo Period (1603–1867).

4) Fukū-kenjaku-kannon Bodhisattva:

This Kannon Bodhisattva carries a fishhook with which he pulls the fish (all sentient beings, including human beings and animals, that transmigrate around the Six Worlds) from the sea of illusions to the shore of enlightenment.

☆ The images and sutras of these multi-talented Kannons, like Eleven-faced Kannon (see Note 11 for II and Note 5 for XIX) and One-thousand-armed Kannon, had been introduced by Gembō in 735. It was also Gembō who suggested to the Tennō Shōmu and his first consort that they should have the huge images of Fukū-kenjaku-kannon created and enshrined in Hokke-dō of Tōdai-ji and Tōshōdai-ji in Nara. These images and sutras on them were a sort of prelude to the purified Mantrayana Kūkai was to establish.

Notes for XXIV. The Logic for Attaining Buddhahood by Means of True Wisdom

1) *Ebyō Tendai-shū*:

In this work he published in 813, Saichō unfolded his observation that: "Every other sect of Buddhism is essentially founded on the Tendai doctrine," thus leading to the heated dispute especially with those who belonged to the Hossō sect. The preface to this writing was to be added later in 816. This dispute was intensified in 822 when Saichō in his last year sought permissiion to possess his own Tendai ordination platform on Mt. Hiei, so that the Mahayana precepts he had introduced into Japan might be conferred there. What had been conferred on the old ordination platforms in Tōdai-ji and three other temples (see Note 1 for V) were the Hinayana precepts. The Tennō Saga himself was ready to permit Saichō to do as he wished, but because of the opposition presented by the Ecclesiastical Office, the grant was delayed until seven days after Saichō's death.

2) as long as ten years:
The reason was because he was waiting for the right time when people were ready to accept his religion, as is known by the following he wrote in a letter to someone who urged him to propagate his "treasured religion" as soon as possible: "Even the supreme medicine will do harm unless taken at a right time."

3) The doctrine expounded by Mahavairocana:
According to the doctrine of Esoteric Buddhism, Vajrasattva once received the teachings directly from Mahavairocana, compiled them as scriptures, and sealed them in an iron tower in South India. This tower was opened, it is believed, eight hundred years after the demise of Sakyamuni, by Nagarjuna, who then revealed the long-hidden scriptures.

4) his representative works on his own religion:
One can read them in English in some books such as *KUKAI: MAJOR WORKS* by Yoshito S. Hakeda (Columbia University Press, New York, 1972).

Notes for XXV. WHAT SEPARATED KŪKAI AND SAICHŌ

1) Gishin (781–833):
Gishin, who had accompanied Saichō to China as interpreter, succeeded Saichō after his death in 822. But he was not interested in Esoteric Buddhism and the Esoteric Buddhism Course Saichō had started on Mount Hiei was to be totally neglected, as is known by the treatise he presented to the Tennō Junna in 830 (see Note 5 for XXX). In order to improve this situation, dozens of priests from Mount Hiei, including Enchō who was to be the chief abbot of Mount Hiei after Gishin, earnestly requested Kūkai to instruct them by initiating them into the Shingon religion as was extolled in his *Ten Stages of the Development of Human Mind*. Kūkai, though beginning to be afflicted with fatal disease, fulfilled their wish in 831.

2) *kin*:
About 600 grams.

3) the one vehicle:
The one great vehicle which comprises both Hinayana and Mahayana (see Note 7 for IV). This thought is most emphatically stressed in the *Hoke-kyō* sutra.

4) the three vehicles:
Engaku (see Note 1 for XXIII), Shōmon (see Note 2 for XXIII) and Bodhisattvahood or Mahayana (see Note 7 for IV).

5) the six senses:

The six senses of sight, hearing, smell, taste, touch, and thought. When one reaches the stage in which the six senses have been freed from any attachment, one has attained Bodhisattvahood. In the Tendai religion, reaching this stage is considered indispensable before one engages in the way of Bdhisattvahood, which enjoys the two aspects of benefiting oneself and benefiting others.

Notes for XXVI. CALLIGRAPHY

1) *Fūshin-jō*:

An answer to Saichō's letter to him, in which Kūkai says he cannot accept Saichō's invitation to Mt. Hiei because he has had something to attend to, but expresses his wish that they would be able to meet at Mt. Takao some day in the near future, so that they could discuss how to propagate their new Buddhism successfully

2) seal script, scribe's script:

Seal script was first created in the land of Zhou (c.1100 B.C.–256 B.C.), then was simplified in the land of Qin (770 B.C.–206 B.C.). After scribe's script and block script came into being, the old script was used only in seals or in inscription on stone monuments or on temple bells. Scribe's script, which was made by further simplifying the simplified seal script, was to develop into block script.

    (a) seal script
    (b) scribe's script

2) (a)　2) (b)　3) (a)　3) (b)　3) (c)

Credited to DAIJISEN (Shogakkan, Tokyo, 1995)

3) block script, semi-cursive script and cursive script:

    (a) block script
    (b) semi-cursive script
    (c) cursive script

4) a poem celebrating his own fortieth birthday:

A Poem upon the Turning Point of Human Life 中寿感興詩, composed of forty characters, goes as follows:

黄葉索山野
蒼々豈終始
嗟余五八歳
長夜念円融
浮雲何処出
本是浄虚空
欲談一心趣
三曜朗天中

                            Dry
                           leaves
                       are scattering
                all over mountains and fields.
                    How could they remain
                 fresh and green all the time?
             I myself have come to the fortieth year,
                     that leads me to think
                   over the perfect harmony.*
           Where have the floating clouds come from?
              Originally, they are pure nothingness.
             When I want to mention my sentiment,
                 the triple radiants in the skies
                       are cheerfully
                          smiling
                           upon
                           me.

* the perfect harmony = the Buddhist view of the universe: Everything in the universe exists there in perfect harmony with all the others.

5) 一百廿礼仏竝方円図竝註義:
In order to congratulate himself for having arrived at his fortieth year, Kūkai performed the ritual invocation of Monjusri, the Bodhisattva of meditation and supreme wisdom. As he wished to share this happiness with others, he produced a textbook for that ritual invocation—*Shinsen Monju-san Hosshin-rai* (新撰文殊讃法身礼) or briefly *Ippyaku Nijūreibutsu* (一百廿礼仏) along with a couple of mandalas (*Hōen-zu* 方円図) and their *Commentaries* (註義).

On the same day, Saichō wrote directly to Kūkai, too, asking for the loan of that newly-produced text along with the mandalas and their commentaries, as mentioned in Chapter XXIV. Kūkai allowed Taihan to prepare them for Saichō's messenger to bring back. By and by Saichō composed a poem in reply and sent it to Kūkai, though it is lost now.

6) *The Record of the Kampyō Era*:
The historical record of the Kampyō Era (889–898) in which the two tennōs, Uda and Daigo, reigned.

Notes for XXVII. HOW MOUNT KŌYA STARTED

1) Kudoyama:
It was where Kūkai's mother came to live when Kūkai was allowed to have Mt. Kōya. Her hermitage, now turned into a temple named Jison-in, marks the place from which the ascent to Mt. Kōya was made.

2) the popular belief that he invented *kata-kana* and *hira-gana*:
It is quite probable that the foundations of the *kata-kana* (Japanese phonetic syllabary), which is almost identical with the Sanskrit phonetic syllabary, were laid by Kūkai, the first Japanese who had mastered Sanskrit language and phonetics, as stated before.

The *hira-gana* syllabary takes the form of a poem that delivers the Buddhist ethos:

いろは　にほへと　ちりぬるを
わかよ　たれそ　つねならむ
うゐの　おくやま　けふこえて
あさき　ゆめみし　ゑひもせす　ん

Flowers, though fragrant, will soon fade.
Who in this world will remain immortal?
If, today, we pass the inner mountain of
illusions, there will be no more empty
dreaming and no more drunkenness. *Un.*

Many give Kūkai as the poet, but others cite various authorships.

3) *sen*:
1/1000 *kan-mon* (see Note 6 for XV)

Notes for XXVIII. Consummating His Thought and Action

1) young Chinese quince trees:
Kūkai had brought back from China many kinds of seeds of plants. From among the trees he was then growing, he must have chosen Chinese quince trees, whose fruit is still used in making cough medicine.

2) Vidyarajas:
Esoteric Buddhist deities to destroy all kinds of evils by order of Mahavairocana.

3) Devas:
One of the eight kinds of beings who protect Buddhism.

Notes for XXIX. The Belief That the Daishi Still Exists on Earth

1) the Big Wild-Goose-Pagoda and the Little Wild-Goose-Pagoda:
The former was built in 652 by Xuanzang in the precincts of Daci'en-si temple where he resided. It is said that Xuanzang used to keep in it the sutras he had brought back from India. The latter belonging to Dajianfu-si temple was built early in the eighth century.

☆ Legend has it that the original pagoda was built on the eastern peak of Mt. Indrasaila-guha in Magadha, India, to memorialize what happened there: a bodhisattva once sacrificed himself by changing into a wild goose in order to stop the monks from eating meat.

2) a five-pieced gravestone:
A gravestone composed of five pieces piled up one upon another representing, from the bottom upward, earth, water, fire, wind and heaven respectively.

3) several ascetics did in later ages:
It is said that in Japan there are twenty-three mummified ascetics remaining. Mt. Yudono in

Dewa Province is known as their mecca.

Notes for XXX. THE WOOD HAS RUN OUT

1)Acala:
An incarnation of Mahavairocana. Since he took a vow to destroy all evils in the world, he looks very fierce, holding a sword in his right hand, a lasso in his left hand. Behind him rises a mass of burning flames.

2) April 21:
March 21 (the anniversary of Kūkai's death) in the lunar calendar roughly falls on April 21 in the Gregorian Calendar.

3) the Seven-Day Prayer for the New Year:
Until 1867 it had been performed at Shingon-in in the Imperial Court. Since 1868, it has been done at Tō-ji.

4) Esoteric Buddhism *is* within exoteric Buddhism, too,:
According to Kūkai, the historical Buddha (Sakyamuni) was, after all, but one manifestation of Mahavairocana. It was only natural then that the Esoteric Buddhist doctrine preached by the historical Buddha should contain Esoteric Buddhist elements, no matter how imperfect they might be and no matter how they might be disguised. Specifically Kūkai regarded two elements as Esoteric: passages in Exoteric texts to the effect that the Dharmakaya Buddha preached or expressed himself; and the appearance in Exoteric texts of mantra and dharani (comparatively longer mantra). YOSHITO S. HAKEDA, *Kukai: Major Works.*

5) his Shingon religion *can be* the synthesis of all other religions and teachings:
Kūkai's final view point was that the other varieties of Buddhism were as steps ascending toward the final, exalted level of Shingon. Anyone who practiced any form of exoteric Buddhism should necessarily, as his religious mind developed, come to Shingon itself. By 822 Kūkai was well prepared to attempt a grand synthesis of "the sea of Dharma (Truth)," as well as of existing non-Buddhist religion and philosophy, in the light of Shingon Buddhism. It was in 830, that Kūkai produced his most ambitious work, *The Ten Stages of the Development of Human Mind*, perhaps the most comprehensive religious work that has come down to us in Japan. These ten categories are the ten levels of mind from the lowest to the highest:

The First Stage: The Mind of Lowly Man, Goatish in Its Desires....
The Second Stage: The Mind That Is Ignorant and Childlike, Yet Abstemious....
The Third Stage: The Mind That Is Infantlike and Fearless....
The Fourth Stage: The Mind That Recognizes the Existence of Psychophysical Constituents Only, Not That of a Permanent Ego....
The Fifth Stage: The Mind Freed from the Seed of the Cause of Karma....
The Sixth Stage: The Mahayana Mind with Sympathetic Concern for Others....
The Seventh Stage: The Mind That Realizes that the Mind Is Unborn....
The Eighth Stage: The Mind That Is Truly in Harmony with the One Way....
The Ninth Stage: The Profoundest Exoteric Buddhist Mind That Is Aware of Its Nonimmutable Nature....
The Tenth Stage: The Glorious Mind, the Most Secret and Sacred....

In the *Ten Stages* Kūkai begins his presentation of this mind with the following definition: "The glorious mind, the most secret and sacred is, ultimately, to realize one's own mind in its fountainhead and to have insight into the nature of one's own existence." He conceives man as "body-mind," not as mind or body, nor body and mind, and holds that this "body-mind" is grounded in the "Body-Mind," the secret and sacred living Body-Mind of all, the Dharmakaya Mahavairocana. His premise is that our mind in its essence is united with the Mind of Mahavairocana and that our body, so long as it is in the universe, is part of the Body of Mahavairocana; all men as well as all other sentient beings are particular "body-mind" beings participating in the "Body-Mind." It is this "Body-Mind" that is represented in the Shingon mandalas, which describe various aspects of Mahavairocana. YOSHITO S. HAKEDA, *Kukai: Major Works.*

☆ What led to the completion of *The Ten Stages of the Development of Human Mind* (10 volumes) and its sister version, *The Precious Key to the Secret Treasury* (3 volumes), was the Tennō Junna's order issued in 830: that each of the Buddhist religions should present a treatise on its own gist.

The other treatises presented on that occasion were: *Daijō Hossō Kenshin-shō* (5 volumes) from the *Hossō* school, *Kegon-shū Ichijō Kaishin-ron* (6 volumes) from the Kegon school, *Tendai Hokke Shūgi-shū* (1 volume) from the Tendai religion, *Daijō Sanron Taigi-shō* (4 volumes) from the Sanron school, and *Kairitsu Denrai-ki* (3 volumes) from the Ritsu school.

6) he was no longer able to go on seeking the way to realize this conviction:

Though Kūkai's wish to realize his thought in some form or other remains unfulfilled, the Shikoku Pilgrimage seems to have achieved something in this line: it is nonsectarian; not all the eighty-eight temples are of the Shingon religion: four are of Tendai religion, three are of Zen school, and one is of Ji or a sect of Jōdo pietism; pilgrims from all over the country and nowadays even from abroad seem to have forgotten their religions or sects while walking around the huge mandala laid out on the Shikoku Island (see Note 10 for V).

7) *Dentō Dai-Hōshi*:

In Kūkai's days this was a title awarded by the Court to Buddhist priests who had well upheld their *Dentō* (the Light of their Religion).

8) a Pali word:

Pali is a classical language in which the Buddhist scriptures were written in Sri Lanka, Myanmar, Thailand and some other Southeast Asian countries. It belongs to the same language family as Sanskrit.

9) Jichie took great pains in sending a letter to Qinglong-si temple:

In the year that followed Kūkai's death (836), Shinzei and Shinzen (Kūkai's nephew) left for China together with the embassy, only to return soon because of a terrible wreck they suffered. Almost the same thing happened in the following year, too, but the embassy, which was to be the last one, was sent again the next year (838), accompanied by some Buddhist priests including a Tendai priest Ennin (see Note 4 for XI) and a Shingon priest Engyō. By the latter Jichie was able to send a letter before another year came.

10) their revered priest:

Enchin reports: While he was studying in Tang China in 850's, about twenty years after Kūkai's death, he met several Chinese priests, including Huigun, Yixin and Yizhou (direct disciples of Huiguo), who still talked affectionately about Kūkai whom they had met and parted from about fifty years before. Even today "Konghai (Kūkai)" seems to be a familiar name to the Chinese, just as the name of the Chinese priest "Jianzhen (Ganjin in Japanese)" is an unforgettable name to the Japanese.

① Dewa Province ▲Mt. Haguro, ▲Mt. Yudono
② Mutsu Province ⚓the fortress of Izawa
③ Echigo Province
④ Kamitsukeno Province
⑤ Shimotsuke Province Yakushi-ji
⑥ Ettchu Province ▲Mt. Tateyama
⑦ Mino Province
⑧ Tōtōmi Province
⑨ Izu Province
⑩ Ise Province Ise Jingū Shrine
⑪ Kii Province ▲Mt. Kōya & Kōya-san, Cape Shio-no-misaki
⑫ Yamato Province* the Nara Capital, ▲Mt. Katsuragi, ▲Mt. Kimpusen
⑬ Yamashiro Province* the Nagaoka Capital, the Heian Capital, ▲Mt. Takao
⑭ Ōmi Province ▲Mt. Hiei & Hiei-zan, Lake Biwa
⑮ Tamba Province ▲Tamba Heights
⑯ Settsu Province* Naniwa-zu
⑰ Kawachi Province*
⑱ Izumi Province* ▲Mt. Makino'o & Makino'o-san-ji, Koki-ji
⑲ Harima Province
⑳ Tajima Province
㉑ Awaji Island
㉒ Sanuki Province Zentsū-ji, Mannō-ike reservoir
㉓ Awa Province ▲Mt. Ōtaki, Yakuō-ji
㉔ Tosa Province
㉕ Cape Muroto
㉖ Iyo Province ▲Mt. Ishizuchi
㉗ Aki Province
㉘ Izumo Province
㉙ Oki Island
㉚ Hibiki-nada
㉛ Kammon Channel
㉜ Tsushima Islands
㉝ Iki Island
㉞ Genkai-nada
㉟ Chikuzen Province the Dazai-fu capital,
　(Tsukushi) Kanzeon-ji, Hakata Bay
㊱ Gotō Islands

*　The province with an asterisk are among
　　the central province.

the Japan Sea

Hokkaidō

Shikoku

the Pacific Ocean

Kyūshū

the East
China Sea

JAPAN

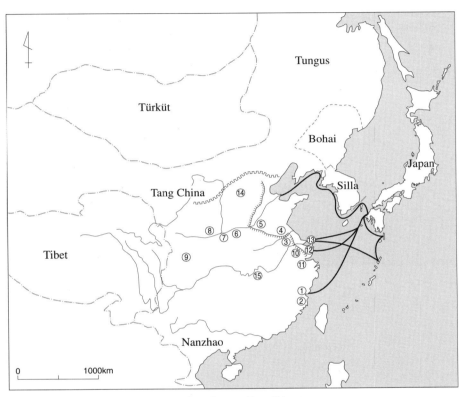

——— northern route & southern routes from Japan to Tang China

① Chi'an Town ② Fuzhou ③ Hangzhou ④ Yangzhou ⑤ Bianzhou ⑥ Luoyang ⑦ Hanguguan
⑧ Chang'an ⑨ the Land of Shu/Yizhou ⑩ Yuezhou (Mt. Guiji) ⑪ Taizhou (Mt. Tiantai) ⑫ Mingzhou
⑬ the mouth of the Yangzi River ⑭ Mt. Wutai ⑮ Lake Dongting

①—⑧ Kūkai's route to Chang'an
⊓⊓⊓⊓⊓ the Great Canal
⊔⊔⊔⊓ the Great Wall

Tang China & Neighboring Countries

① – ⑧⑧ the Eighty-Eight Temples on the Shikoku Pilgrimage Route

⑫ Shōzan-ji ㉑ Mt. Ōtaki & Tairyū-ji ㉓ Yakuō-ji
㉔ Hotsumisaki-ji ㉗⑤ Zentsū-ji (the Birthplace Temple)
⑦⑥ Konzō-ji

a Muya b Tsubaki Village c Mugi d Sabase
e Yasaka Yahama f No'ne g Cape Muroto
h Mt.Ishizuchi i Mannō-ike reservoir j Kaigan-ji

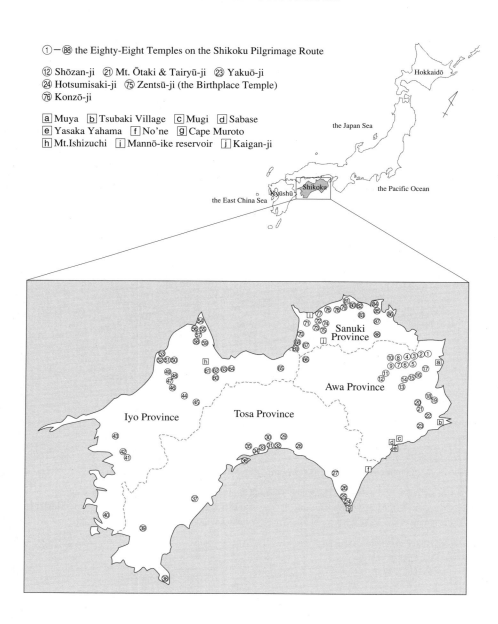

the Shikoku Pilgrimage

338

SELECTED BIBLIOGRAPHY
for Translation

Kūkai

Takagi Shingen, *Kūkai: Shōgai to Sono Shūhen*『空海：生涯とその周辺』(Tōkyō: Yoshikawa Kōbun-kan, 1997)

Takagi Shingen, *Kūkai to Saichō no Tegami*『空海と最澄の手紙』(Tōkyō: Hōzō-kan, 1999)

Yoshito S. Hakeda, *Kūkai*: Major Works (New York, Columbia University Press, 1971)

Miyasaka Yūshō & Umehara Takeshi, *Bukkyō no Shisō Vol. 9: Seimei no Umi: Kūkai*『仏教の思想 第 9 巻、生命の海：空海』(Tōkyō, Kadokawa Shoten, 1976)

Yoritomi Motohiro, *Kūkai*『空海』(Tōkyō, Chikuma Shobō, 1988)

Hasuo Zenryū & Mizobuchi Kazuyuki, *Kōbō Daishi to Shikoku Reijō*『弘法大師と四国霊場』(Takamatsu, Bikō-sha, 1976)

Hasuo Zenryū, *Ningen Kōbō Daishi*『人間弘法大師』(Zentsūji, Zentsū-ji Temple, 1984)

Hasuo Zenryū, *O-Daishi-san no Oshie to Goshōgai*『お大師さんの教えと御生涯』(Zentsūji, Zentsū-ji temple, 1995)

Katō Seiichi, *Kōbō Daishi-Den*『弘法大師伝』(Tōkyō: Shingon-shū Buzan-ha Shūmu-sho, 1983)

Miyasaka Yūshō, Miyazaki Ninshō & Muraoka Kū, *Kūkai Mikkyō no Subete*『空海密教のすべて』(Tōkyō, Toki-Shobō, 1983)

Yamamoto Chikyō & fourteen others, *Kōbō Daishi no Subete*『弘法大師のすべて』(Tōkyō, Daihōrin-kaku, 1999)

Matsunaga Yūkei, *Dai-Uchū ni Ikiru—KŪKAI*『大宇宙に生きる—空海』(Tōkyō, Chūō Kōron Shinsha, 1999)

Chin Shunshin, *Mandara no Hito: Kūkai Guhō-den*『曼荼羅の人—空海求法伝』(Tōkyō, Tokuma Shoten, 1990)

Akita Shoten (ed.), "A Special Number to Memorialize the 1150th Anniversary of Kūkai's Nyūjō", *Rekishi to Tabi*, June 1984「弘法大師御入定千百五十年御遠忌記念大特集」『歴史と旅』昭和59年 6 月号 (Tōkyō, Akita Shoten, 1984)

Dai Hōrin-kaku (ed.), "A Special Number Featuring Kūkai, Mikkyō & Shikoku Henro", *Dai Hōrin*, February 2000「特集：空海・密教・四国遍路」『大法輪』平成12年 2 月号 (Tōkyō, Dai Hōrin-kaku, 2000)

Matsuoka Seigō, *Kūkai no Yume*『空海の夢』(Tōkyō, Shunjū-sha, 1995)

Religion

Masaharu Anesaki, *History of Japanese Religion* (Rutland & Tōkyō: Charles E. Tuttle Company, 1963)

Chikyō Yamamoto, *History of Mantrayana in Japan* (New Delhi: Aditya Prakashan, 1987)

Taiko Yamasaki, *Shingon: Japanese Esoteric Buddhism*, trans. and adapt. Richard and Cynthia Peterson, ed. Yasuyoshi Morimoto and David Kidd (Boston & London: Shambhala, 1988)

Kalpakam Sankarnarayan, Motohiro Yoritomi and Shubhada A. Joshi (ed.), *Buddhism in India and Abroad* (Mumbai & New Delhi: Somaiya Publications Pvt. Ltd., 1996)

Oliver Statler, *Japanese Pilgrimage* (London: Pan Books, 1984)

Yuki Hideo, Ōgida Mikio & Sekioka Kazushige, *Shūkyō no Rekishi* 『宗教の歴史：仏教・キリスト教・イスラム教・神道』 (Ōsaka: Sōgen-sha, 1990)

Nishimura Kōchō, *Mikkyō Nyūmon* 『密教入門』 (Tōkyō: Shinchō-sha, 1996)

Matsunaga Yūkei, *Mikkyō* 『密教』 (Tōkyō: Iwanami-shoten, 1991)

Yoritomi Motohiro, *Mikkyō—Satori to Hotoke e no Michi* 『悟りとほとけへの道』 (Tōkyō: Kōdan-sha, 1988)

Sawa Ryūken, *Nihon Mikkyō—Sono Tenkai to Bijutsu*, 『日本密教―その展開と美術』 (Tōkyō: NHK Publishing, 1990)

Ishida Hisatoyo, *Mandara no Mikata* 『曼荼羅のみかた』 (Tōkyō: Iwanami Shoten)

Yoritomi Motohiro, *Mandara Kōwa* 『まんだら講話』 (Ōsaka: Toki Shobō, 1996)

Yoritomi Motohiro & Akao Eikei, *Shakyō no Kanshō Kiso Chishiki* 『写経の鑑賞基礎知識』 (Tōkyō: Shibun-dō, 1994)

Tachikawa Musashi & Yoritomi Motohiro (ed.), *Nihon Mikkyō* 『日本密教』 (Tōkyō: Shunjū-sha, 2000)

History

Joseph M.Goedertier, *A Dictionary of Japanese History* (New York & Tōkyō: Walker/Weatherhill, 1968)

Ōno Susumu, *Nihongo no Kigen—Shimpan* 『日本語の起源―新版』 (Tōkyō: Iwanami Shoten, 1994)

Project Team of Zentsūji City (ed.), *Zentsūji Shi-shi* 『善通寺市史』 (Zentsūji: Zentsūji City, 1977)

Yamamoto Takeshi & Tanaka Toshio, *Shikoku no Fūdo to Rekishi* 『四国の風土と歴史』 (Tōkyō: Yamakawa Shuppan-sha, 1977)

Hasuo Zenryū, *Rekishi Yowa* 『歴史余話』 (Zentsūji: Zentsū-ji temple, 1995)

Geishin-sha (ed.), *Chronological Chart of World Cultural History* 『世界文化史年表』 (Tōkyō: Geishin-sha, 1990)

Tang China

Ishida Mikinosuke, *Chōan no Haru* 『長安の春』 (Tōkyō: Kōdan-sha, 1979)

Art Publishing Company of People's Republic of China (ed.), *Seian no Tabi* 『西安の旅』 (Kyōto: Bi-no-Bi Ltd., 1981)

Suzuki Torao, *Toho Zen-Shishū* 『杜甫全詩集』 (Tōkyō: Nihon Tosho, 1978-79)

Kubo Tenzui, *Rihaku Zen-Shishū* 『李白全詩集』 (Tōkyō: Nihon Tosho, 1978)

Saku Takashi, *Hakurakuten Zen-Shishū* 『白楽天全詩集』 (Tōkyō: Nihon Tosho, 1978)

Maeno Naoaki, *Tōdai Shishū* 『唐代詩集』 (Tōkyō: Nihon Tosho)

Kawaguchi Hisao (ed.), *Chōgonka Emaki* 『長恨歌絵巻』 (Tōkyō: Taishūkan Shoten, 1982)

Mukōjima Shigeyoshi, *Kanshi no Kotoba* 『漢詩のことば』 (Tōkyō: Taishūkan Shoten, 1998)

Calligraphy

John Stevens, *Sacred Calligraphy of the East* (Boulder & London: Shambhala, 1981)

Tō-ji Hōmotsu-kan (ed.), *Kōbō Daishi no Sho to Sono Shūhen* 『弘法大師の書とその周辺』 (Kyōto: Tō-ji temple, 1987)

Exhibitions & Their Related Publications

Kyōto National Museum, Tōkyō National Museum, Society of the Head Temples of the Shingon Religion & Asahi Shimbun (ed.), *Kōbō Daishi & the Art of Esoteric Buddhism* 『弘法大師と密教

美術』(Ōsaka: Asahi Shimbun, 1983)

Nara National Museum (ed.), *Special Exhibition: Applied Art of Japanese Esoteric Buddhism* 『特別展覧：密教工芸—神秘のかたち』(Nara: Nara National Museum, 1992)

Kyōto Cultural Museum (ed.), *Special Exhibition of Chang'an, The Capital of Tang Dynasty—In Commemoration of the 1200th Anniversary of the Founding of Kyoto as The Heian Capital & The 10th Anniversary of Friendship Agreement between Kyoto Prefecture and Shaanxi Province* 『大唐長安展』(Kyōto, Kyōto Cultural Museum, 1994)

Kyōto National Museum, Tō-ji as Shingon-shū Head Temple & Asahi Shimbun (ed.), *Treasures from the Tō-ji Temple* 『東寺国宝展』(Ōsaka: Asahi Shimbun, 1995)

Nara National Museum (ed.), *Masterpieces of Japanese Buddhist Art* 『日本仏教美術名宝展』(Nara: Nara National Museum, 1995)

Project Team for the Exhibition (Kagawa Prefecture) (ed.), *Exhibition of the Great Tang's Civilization—In Celebration of Friendship Agreement between Kagawa Prefecture and Shaanxi Province* 『大唐文明展』(Takamatsu: Project Team for the Exhibition, 1998)

Project Team for the Exhibition (NHK, Ehime Shimbun, Shikoku Shimbun, Kōchi Shimbun, Tokushima Shimbun & NHK Kinki Media Plan) (ed.), *Special Exhibition: Kōbō Diashi and National Treasures* 『国宝：弘法大師空海展』(Takamatsu: Project Team for the Exhibition, 1999)

TEMPLES

Shiba Ryōtarō & Washio Ryūki, *Koji Junrei: Kyōto—Tō-ji* 『古寺巡礼：京都・東寺』(Kyōto: Tankō-sha, 1976)

Hayashiya Tatsusaburō & Taniuchi Kengaku, *Koji Junrei: Kyōtō—Jingo-ji* 『古寺巡礼：京都・神護寺』(Kyōto: Tankō-sha, 1976)

Zentsū-ji (ed.), *The History of Zentsū-ji* 『善通寺』(Zentsūji: Zentsū-ji temple, 1972)

Inui Sentarō, *Kōbō Daishi Tanjō-chi no Kenkyū* 『弘法大師誕生地の研究』(Zentsūji: Zentsū-ji temple, reprinted in 1991)

Shinchō-sha (ed.), "A Special Number Featuring Tō-ji", *Geijutsu Shinchō*, July 1997 『芸術新潮 7月号：特集・東寺よ開け』(Tōkyō: shinchō-sha, 1997)

Morimoto Kōsei, *Tōdai-ji* 『東大寺』(Nara: Tōdai-ji temple, 1993)

Hōryū-ji (ed.), *Hōryū-ji to Shiruku Rōdo Bukkyō Bunka* 『法隆寺とシルクロード仏教文化』(Nara: Hōryū-ji temple, 1988)

Saba Daishi Honbō (ed.), *Shikoku Reijō—Saba Daishi Honbō* 『四国霊場・鯖大師本坊』(Kaifu: Saba Daishi Honbō, 1995)

Nishiyama Atsushi, *Nara no Tera-dera: Kanshō no Tebiki* 『奈良の寺寺：鑑賞の手引き』(Nara: Fujita Ltd.)

Encyclopedia & Dictionaries

Heibon-sha (ed.), *Heibon-sha's World Encyclopedia*『世界大百科事典』(Tōkyō: Heibon-sha, 1986)

Sansei-dō (ed.), *A Concise International Biographical Dictionary*『外国人名事典』(Tōkyō: Sansei-dō Press, 1985)

Sansei-dō (ed.), *A Concise International Geographical Dictionary*『外国地名事典』(Tōkyō: Sansei-dō Press, 1985)

Takeda Yūkichi & Hisamatsu Sen'ichi (ed.), *Kogo Jiten*『古語辞典』(Tōkyō: Kadokawa Shoten, 1971)

Daitō Shuppan-sha (ed.), *Japanese-English Buddhist Dictionary*『日英仏教辞典』(Tōkyō: Daitō Shuppan-sha, 1991)

BIBLIOGRAPHICAL INDEX

Bibliographical Index

CHARACTER INDEX

Shiba Ryotaro (1923–1996) was born and raised in Ōsaka, Japan, and studied three languages—Mongol, Chinese and Russian—at Ōsaka University of Foreign Languages. In his third year there (1943), he was called up for military service, only to be involved in the prevalent absurdities of the Imperial Japanese Army until Japan was defeated in 1945. This unforgettable experience kept him wondering what caused such irrationalities in Japan, gripping her for as long as twenty years since the beginning of the Showa Era (1925), thus inflicting a great deal of misery to many other countries, too. In his effort to find the answer to this undying question, Mr.Shiba traced back Japan's history. There he was to meet not a few interesting persons, known and unknown, who had bravery tried to improve their situations. They did so in their own inimitable way, feeding the spirit of their own times, which, unlike "that anomalous period of Japan," as he later called, were generally respectable ones, to his great relief.

In his thirties, Mr. Shiba began to write about them one by one as if trying to share his pleasure of knowing them with the growing numbers of his enthusiastic readers. By 1988 when he finished his last novel, he had written 57 novels. The great deal of field work he did in writing these novels was to yield a huge by-product—forty-one volumes of travel books, *Kaidō wo Yuku* (*Traveling along the Ancient Thoroughfares*) that coverd not only the breadth and length of the Japanese Islands but also the Korean Peninsula, the ancient islands lying between Korea and Japan, Taiwan, Mongolia, Russia, China, Vietnam, Western Pyrenees, Spain, Portugal, Ireland, England, Holland, France and the United States. He failed, however, to write a novel set in "that anomalous period of Japan," even if he had collected a great amount of material for it. Instead, he had written a long series of essays for a national monthly magazine, which was later published as *Kono Kuni no Katachi* (*What Shaped This Country*: five volumes). Until the very end of his life, he never missed an opportunity to deliver his anxieties about contemporary Japan and Japanese. His meritorious efforts as a writer and critic were rewarded with many prizes, including the Naoki Prize for one of his earliest novels (1960), the Imperial Award of the Japan Academy for *Kūkai no Fūkei* (*Kūkai, the Universal: Scenes from His Life*) and other historical novels (1976), and the Order of Culture for his work as a whole (1993).